JOHN AND JUDAISM

RESOURCES FOR BIBLICAL STUDY

Editor
Tom Thatcher, New Testament

Number 87

JOHN AND JUDAISM

A Contested Relationship in Context

Edited by

R. Alan Culpepper and Paul N. Anderson

Atlanta

Library of Congress Cataloging-in-Publication Data

Names: Culpepper, R. Alan, editor. | Anderson, Paul N., 1956- editor.
Title: John and Judaism : a contested relationship in context / edited by R. Alan Culpepper and Paul N. Anderson.
Description: Atlanta : SBL Press, [2017] | Series: Resources for biblical study ; number 87 | Includes bibliographical references and index.
Identifiers: LCCN 2017021414 (print) | LCCN 2017022026 (ebook) | ISBN 9780884142416 (ebook) | ISBN 9781628371864 (pbk. : alk. paper) | ISBN 9780884142423 (hardcover : alk. paper)
Subjects: LCSH: Judaism—Relations—Christianity. | Christianity—Relations—Judaism. | Bible. N.T. John—Criticism, interpretation, etc. | Judaism—History—Post-exilic period, 586 B.C.–210 A.D..
Classification: LCC BM535 (ebook) | LCC BM535 .J576 2017 (print) | DDC 226.5/06—dc23
LC record available at https://lccn.loc.gov/2017021414

Printed on acid-free paper.

Contents

Abbreviations

Primary Sources

1 Apol.	Justin Martyr, *First Apology*
1 En.	1 Enoch
1 Esd	1 Esdras
11Q18	New Jerusalem
11QT	Temple Scroll
1QIsa[a]	Isaiah[a]
1QM	War Scroll
1QS	Rule of the Community
2 Bar.	2 Baruch
2 Macc	2 Maccabees
3 En.	3 Enoch
3Q15	Copper Scroll
4 Macc	4 Maccabees
4Q174	Florilegium, also Midrash on Eschatology[a]
4Q339	List of False Prophets ar
4Q385	psEzek[c]
Aen.	Vergil, *Aeneid*
Ag. Ap.	Josephus, *Against Apion*
Agriculture	Philo, *On Agriculture*
Alleg. Interp.	Philo, *Allegorical Interpretation*
Ant.	Josephus, *Jewish Antiquites*
Apoc. Mos.	Apocalypse of Moses
Arakh.	Arakhin
Arch.	Vitruvius Pollio, *On Architecture*
Avot R. Nat.	Avot de Rabbi Nathan
b.	Babylonian
Bar	Baruch
Bar.	Barnabas

Ber.	Berakhot
CD	Cairo Genizah copy of the Damascus Document
Cherubim	Philo, *On the Cherubim*
Dial.	Justin Martyr, *Dialogue with Trypho*
Dreams	Philo, *On Dreams*
Embassy	Philo, *On the Embassy to Gaius*
Ep.	*Epistula*
Eph.	Ignatius, *To the Ephesians*
Exod. Rab.	Exodus Rabbah
Fin.	Cicero, *De finibus*
Flaccus	Philo, *Against Flaccus*
Gen. Rab.	Genesis Rabbah
Geogr.	Strabo, *Geography*
Hom.	Pseudo-Clementine, *Homilies*
Ign.	Polycarp, *To the Philippians*
J.W.	Josephus, *Jewish War*
Jos. Asen.	Joseph and Aseneth
Jub.	Jubilees
LAE	Life of Adam and Eve
Life	Josephus, *The Life*
LXX	Septuagint
m.	Mishnah
Magn.	Ignatius, *To the Magnesians*
Mek.	Mekilta
Moses	Philo, *On the Life of Moses*
MT	Masoretic Text
Names	Philo, *On the Change of Names*
Ned.	Nedarim
Odes. Sol.	Odes of Solomon
Or.	Aelius Aristides, *Orations*
Phld.	Ignatius, *To the Philadelphians*
Pol.	Aristotle, *Politics*
Posterity	Philo, *On the Posterity of Cain*
Pss. Sol.	Psalms of Solomon
Q	Qur'an
Rab.	Rabbah
Rec.	Pseudo-Clementine, *Recognitions*
Resp.	Plato, *Republic*
Rom.	Ignatius, *To the Romans*

Sacrifices	Philo, *On the Sacrifices of Cain and Abel*
Sanh.	Sanhedrin
Shabb.	Shabbat
Spec. Laws	Philo, *On the Special Laws*
t.	Tosefta
T. Benj.	Testament of Benjamin
T. Iss.	Testament of Issachar
T. Job	Testament of Job
T. Levi	Testament of Levi
T. Reu.	Testament of Reuben
Ta'an.	Ta'anit
Ter.	Terumot
Tg.	Targum
Tg. Neof.	Targum Neofiti
Tg. Onq.	Targum Onqelos
Wis	Wisdom of Solomon
y.	Jerusalem

Secondary Sources

AB	Anchor Bible
ABRL	Anchor Bible Reference Library
ACNT	Augsburg Commentary on the New Testament
AcT	*Acta Theologica*
AGJU	Arbeiten zur Geschichte des antiken Judentums des Urchristentums
AJEC	Ancient Judaism and Early Christianity
ALGHJ	Arbeiten zur Literatur und Geschichte des hellenistischen Judentums
AnBib	Analecta Biblica
ANTC	Abingdon New Testament Commentaries
APF	*Archiv für Papyrusforschung*
AThR	*Anglican Theological Review*
BAR	*Biblical Archaeology Review*
BBB	Bonner biblische Beiträge
BBR	*Bulletin for Biblical Research*
BCR	Biblioteca di cultura religiosa

BDAG	Danker, Frederick W., Walter Bauer, William F. Arndt, and F. Wilbur Gingrich, *Greek-English Lexicon of the New Testament and Other Early Christian Literature*. 3rd ed. Chicago: University of Chicago Press, 2000 (Danker-Bauer-Arndt-Gingrich)
BETL	Bibliotheca Ephemeridum Theologicarum Lovaniensium
BEvT	Beiträge zur evangelischen Theologie
Bib	*Biblica*
BibInt	*Biblical Interpretation*
BibInt	Biblical Interpretation Series
Bijdr	*Bijdragen: Tijdschrift voor filosofie en theologie*
BJS	Brown Judaic Studies
BLS	Bible and Literature Series
BNTC	Black's New Testament Commentaries
BT	*The Bible Translator*
BTS	Biblical Tools and Studies
BTZ	*Berliner Theologische Zeitschrift*
BZ	*Biblische Zeitschrift*
BZAW	Beihefte zur Zeitschrift für die alttestamentliche Wissenschaft
BZNW	Beihefte zur Zeitschrift für die neutestamentliche Wissenschaft
CBET	Contributions to Biblical Exegesis and Theology
CBQ	*Catholic Biblical Quarterly*
CNT	Commentaire du Nouveau Testament
CSHJ	Chicago Studies in the History of Judaism
CurBR	*Currents in Biblical Research*
ECC	Eerdmans Critical Commentary
ECL	Early Christianity and Its Literature
EKKNT	Evangelisch-Katholischer Kommentar zum Neuen Testament
EncJud	*Encyclopedia Judaica*. Edited by Fred Skolnik and Michael Berenbaum. 2nd ed. 22 vols. Detroit: Macmillan Reference USA, 2007
ETL	*Ephemerides Theologicae Lovaniensis*
EvQ	*Evangelical Quarterly*
EvT	*Evangelische Theologie*
ExpTim	*Expository Times*

FAT	Forschungen zum Alten Testament
FB	Forschung zur Bibel
FRLANT	Forschungen zur Literatur des Alten und Neuen Testaments
HNT	Handbuch zum Neuen Testament
HThkNT	Herders Theological Commentary on the New Testament
HTR	*Harvard Theological Review*
HTS	*Hervormde Teologiese Studies*
HUCA	*Hebrew Union College Annual*
HvTSt	*HTS Teologiese Studies/Theological Studies*
ICC	International Critical Commentary
Int	*Interpretation*
JANT	*Jewish Annotated New Testament*
JBL	*Journal of Biblical Literature*
JCH	Jewish Christian Heritage
JCP	Jewish and Christian Perspectives
JES	*Journal of Ecumenical Studies*
JJS	*Journal of Jewish Studies*
JQR	*Jewish Quarterly Review*
JSHJ	*Journal for the Study of the Historical Jesus*
JSNT	*Journal for the Study of the New Testament*
JSNTSup	Journal for the Study of the New Testament Supplement Series
JSOTSup	Journal for the Study of the Old Testament Supplement Series
JTS	*Journal of Theological Studies*
KD	*Kerygma und Dogma*
KEK	Kritisch-Exegetischer Kommentar über das Neue Testament (Meyer-Kommentar)
LCL	Loeb Classical Library
LHBOTS	Library of Hebrew Bible/Old Testament Studies
LNTS	The Library of New Testament Studies
MS(S)	manuscript(s)
MTSR	*Method and Theory in the Study of Religion*
NCB	New Century Bible
NedTT	*Nederlands theologisch tijdschrift*
Neot	*Neotestamentica*
NGTT	*Nederduitse gereformeerde teologiese tydskrif*

NIDB	*New Interpreter's Dictionary of the Bible*
NIGTC	New International Greek Testament Commentary
NovT	*Novum Testamentum*
NovTSup	Supplements to Novum Testamentum
NTAbh	Neutestamentliche Abhandlungen
NTG	New Testament Guides
NTL	New Testament Library
NTS	*New Testament Studies*
OBT	Overtures to Biblical Theology
OiC	*One in Christ*
ÖTK	Ökumenischer Taschenbuch-Kommentar
OTP	Charlesworth, James H., ed. *Old Testament Pseudepigrapha*. 2 vols. New York: Doubleday, 1983–1985.
PIBA	*Proceedings of the Irish Biblical Association*
PTMS	Pittsburgh Theological Monograph Series
RB	*Revue biblique*
RBL	*Review of Biblical Literature*
RBS	Resources for Biblical Study
REJ	*Revue des études juives*
RelSRev	*Religious Studies Review*
RevExp	*Review and Expositor*
RevQ	*Revue de Qumran*
RivB	*Rivista Biblica*
RNT	Regensburger Neues Testament
SANT	Studien zum Alten und Neuen Testaments
SBLDS	Society of Biblical Literature Dissertation Series
SBLSBS	Society of Biblical Literature Sources for Biblical Study
SBLTT	Society of Biblical Literature Texts and Translations
SBS	Stuttgarter Bibelstudien
SBT	Studies in Biblical Theology
ScEs	*Science et esprit*
SEÅ	*Svensk exegetisk årsbok*
SemeiaSt	Semeia Studies
SFSHJ	South Florida Studies in the History of Judaism
Sir	Sirach/Ecclesiasticus
SJHC	Studies in Jewish History and Culture
SJLA	Studies in Judaism in Late Antiquity
SNTSMS	Society for New Testament Studies Monograph Series

SNTSU	*Studien zum Neuen Testament und seiner Umwelt*
SNTW	Studies in the New Testament and Its World
SP	Sacra Pagina
SPhiloA	*Studia Philonica Annual*
STDJ	Studies on the Texts of the Desert of Judah
STR	Studies in Theology and Religion
SubBi	Subsidia Biblica
SymS	Symposium Series
TB	Theologische Bücheriei: Neudrucke und Berichte aus dem 20. Jahrhundert
TDNT	*Theological Dictionary of the New Testament*. Edited by Gerhard Kittel and Gerhard Friedrich. Translated by Geoffrey W. Bromiley. 10 vols. Grand Rapids: Eerdmans, 1964–1976
TDOT	*Theological Dictionary of the Old Testament*. Edited by G. Johannes Botterweck and Helmer Ringgren. Translated by John T. Willis et al. 8 vols. Grand Rapids: Eerdmans, 1974–2006
TENTS	Texts and Editions for New Testament Study
TGl	*Theologie und Glaube*
Them	*Themelios*
THKNT	Theologischer Handkommentar zum Neuen Testament
TLZ	*Theologische Literaturzeitung*
TRE	*Theologische Realenzyklopädie*. Edited by Gerhard Krause and Gerhard Müller. Berlin: de Gruyter, 1977–
TRev	*Theologische Revue*
TSAJ	Texte und Studien zum antiken Judentum
TThSt	Trierer Theologische Studien
TU	Texte und Untersuchungen
TvT	*Tijdschrift voor Theologie*
TynBul	*Tyndale Bulletin*
Types & Shadows	*Types & Shadows: Journal of the Fellowship of Quakers in the Arts*
VC	*Vigiliae Christianae*
VCSup	Vigliae Christianae Supplements
VT	*Vetus Testamentum*
VTSup	Supplements to Vetus Testamentum

WBC	Word Biblical Commentary
WMANT	Wissenschaftliche Monographien zum Alten und Neuen Testament
WTJ	*Westminster Theological Journal*
WUNT	Wissenschaftliche Untersuchungen zum Neuen Testament
ZAC	*Zeitschrift für antikes Christentum/Journal of Early Christianity*
ZBK	Zürcher Bibelkommentare
ZNW	*Zeitschrift für die neutestamentliche Wissenschaft und die Kunde der älteren Kirche*

Preface

R. Alan Culpepper and Paul N. Anderson

The title of this volume, *John and Judaism*, can be understood in two ways. In the narrower sense, it is a shorthand way of specifying the study of how Judaism is characterized in the Gospel of John, a ferociously difficult subject. For example, scholars do not even agree on what the term Ἰουδαῖοι means in John, although it occurs some seventy-two times in the gospel. Is it best understood and translated as "Jews," "Judeans," "religious authorities," or even "religious authorities in Jerusalem"? Some of the references are neutral; others are hostile. Also debated is the question of what kind of Judaism is reflected in or influenced the gospel: the Judaism of Jesus's time or of the time in which the gospel was composed, Judaism in Judea or diaspora Judaism? In the early part of the twentieth century, the gospel was interpreted primarily against the background of Hellenistic, Greco-Roman, gnostic, and hermetic literature and thought. Following the discovery of the Dead Sea Scrolls and renewed attention to Jewish wisdom literature, the Gospel of John began to be set in a Jewish context. Scholars saw the influence of diaspora Judaism, the Essenes, Philo, the wisdom tradition, and synagogal homilies.

Focusing on John's Jewish context raised further questions. What we know about Judaism in the first century is an amalgam of information drawn from later rabbinic sources (the Mishnah, Talmud, Tosefta, and Midrashim), sectarian writings found at Qumran and elsewhere, Philo's interpretation of Judaism for a literate readership of gentile (and Jewish) scholars in Alexandria and elsewhere, and archaeological finds in Judea, Galilee, and other places where Jewish communities left evidence of their way of life. Scholars have also proposed divergent views regarding whether John's characterization of Judaism is consistent throughout or provides evidence of sources with different views and terminology or different stages in the composition of the gospel. Are the neutral and hostile references to the Ἰουδαῖοι to be assigned to different sources, hands, or editions of the gospel? Some "solutions" look like diagrams of plays for an American football team—with lots of motion in the backfield!

In the broader sense, *John and Judaism* evokes the subject of how the gospel and its author(s) and their community were related to Judaism, and more broadly still its legacy of influence on the relationship between Christians and Jews over the past two millennia. The issues here can be treated chronologically, taking two terms from German scholarship as rubrics: the gospel's *Stiz im Leben* and its *Nachleben*, the context in which it was written and its function in that setting, and its later influence and history of interpretation, respectively. The key point in the former is the interpretation of the three references in John to being separated from the synagogue (9:22; 12:42; 16:2), and especially the theory that the gospel reflects a setting in which the Johannine believers were being put out of the synagogue. What did this "parting of the ways" look like? How and when did it occur, and is it best understood as an intra-Jewish phenomenon (like the withdrawal of the Essenes to Qumran) or as a defining step in the separation of Christians from Jews? Both views are defended in this volume.

Whatever the original context and intent of the gospel, it has had a profound effect on Christian readers through the centuries. Johannine theology shaped the articulations of Christian Christology and theology by the early church councils. In the process, its hostile references to Jews and the supersessionist overtones of its theme of the fulfillment/replacement of Jewish scriptures, Jewish festivals, and the Jewish temple fueled anti-Jewish and often anti-Semitic attitudes, hostility, and violence. In the past seventy years, since the Holocaust, the founding of the state of Israel, and Vatican II (especially the publication of *Nostra Aetate*), the church has undergone a dramatic reversal in its relationship with its parent faith. In the process, Christians have had to reexamine the gospel, recognize its tragic role in Christian and Jewish history, and ask how John (with its hostile references to Jews) should be read, taught, and preached today. As a step in the process of addressing "the Gospel of John and anti-Judaism," this volume raises afresh the array of issues related to "John and Judaism."

The essays contained in this volume offer variously sweeping surveys of the field and detailed analyses, reviews of the history of scholarship, critiques of earlier theories, and new proposals. The hope is that this exercise in biblical and historical scholarship will not only lead to clearer understandings of the Gospel of John and its historical context but to better informed and more nuanced ways of reading and characterizing the gospel and its relationship to Judaism in the broader sense.

The volume is divided into four parts: (1) an introduction to recent research, reflections on the Jewish nature of the gospel, and questions for future research; (2) John as a source for understanding Judaism—a twist on the more prevalent approach of studying Judaism for the purpose of understanding John; (3) reappraisals of John's relationship to Judaism and Jewish Christianity; and (4) reading John as Jews and Christians.

Most of these essays were presented at a conference on John and Judaism hosted by the James and Carolyn McAfee School of Theology at Mercer University in November 2015. This conference was supported by funds for a lectureship in New Testament studies provided by Peter Rhea and Ellen Jones. It was the second conference at Mercer supported by this lectureship. Papers from the first conference, in November 2010, on the Johannine Epistles, were subsequently published by SBL Press in the Early Christianity and Its Literature series under the title *Communities in Dispute: Current Scholarship on the Johannine Epistles* (2014). Both conferences were planned and organized with the support of the steering committee of the John, Jesus, and History Group (JJH) as extensions of its reassessment of the Gospel of John as a historical source. This volume, therefore, has been made possible by the investment of time, financial resources, and the commitment to teaching and learning, scholarship, and service from an exceptional constellation of partners: James and Carolyn McAfee; Peter Rhea and Ellen Jones; the faculty, staff, and administration of Mercer University and the McAfee School of Theology; the steering committee of JJH; presenters and participants at the conference at Mercer and the authors of supplementary essays; the Society of Biblical Literature and SBL Press; and especially our editors, Bob Buller, editorial director of SBL Press, and Tom Thatcher, New Testament editor of the Resources for Biblical Study series.

May the contributions of all who have had a part in producing this volume and the scholarship it represents move us, however incrementally, toward the greater goals of knowledge and truth in the service of wholeness of life, religious devotion, and reconciliation and common purpose between Christians and Jews.

Part 1
Introduction

John and the Jews: Recent Research and Future Questions

Tom Thatcher

The meaning of the word Ἰουδαῖοι in John's Gospel has long been a puzzle.
—Malcolm Lowe, "Who Are the Ἰουδαῖοι?"

On October 28, 1965, Pope Paul VI and the Second Vatican Council issued a "Declaration on the Relation of the Church to Non-Christian Religions." Appropriately catalogued under the title *Nostra Aetate* ("In our times…"), the declaration addresses relationships between Christians and members of other world religions and specifically encourages positive dialogue on critical questions of the universal human experience (sec. 1). Section 4 of the document, which discusses Jewish-Christian relations specifically, emphasizes the spiritual and historical bonds that tie "the people of the New Covenant to Abraham's stock" (4). Spiritually, both faiths began "among the Patriarchs, Moses and the prophets" and are grounded in the call of Abraham; historically, Jesus and "most of the early disciples who proclaimed Christ's Gospel to the world" (4) were themselves Jewish. Of course, the majority of Jews in Jesus's time did not accept the gospel, and some opposed it, yet this historical reality certainly does not make "the Jews of today" responsible for his death. Indeed, the church believes, and has always believed, that Christ "underwent His passion and death freely, because of the sins of men and out of infinite love" (4)—in other words, sinners, not Jews, are to blame for the pain of the cross. In view of these considerations, the church condemns "hatred, persecutions, [or] displays of anti-Semitism, directed against Jews at any time by anyone" (4). Viewed in its historical context, it seems clear that *Nostra Aetate* very much breathed the spirit of its age. Although the document insists that its rulings were "moved not by political reasons but by the Gospel's spiritual love" (4), one can scarcely overlook that it was produced in Europe only two decades after the Holocaust and, further, at a time when the Roman Catholic Church was substantially reflecting on its methods of interpreting and applying the biblical texts.

For purposes of the present discussion—the current state of research on John and Judaism—it is notable that *Nostra Aetate* explicitly refers to the Johannine literature three times.[1] Two of these citations—the only direct quotations of the New Testament in the main body of the document—are used to encourage Catholics to adopt a more open posture toward interfaith dialogue. Thus, Christians should appreciate the philosophical and moral truths advocated by Buddhists and Hindus because Jesus is "the way, the truth, and the life" (John 14:6)—Christ, in other words, is the ultimate source of any "truth" that may be found in any faith system (*Nostra Aetate* 2). Further, and more significantly, those who "refuse to treat any man in a brotherly way" should not expect to receive God's love themselves, for "the one who does not love does not know God" (5; see 1 John 4:8). In these cases, the Vatican Council found in the Johannine literature resources for the promotion of a new spirit of openness and unity in a post-Shoah world.

Yet when viewed in terms of the larger history of Christian interpretation, the citations of the Johannine literature in *Nostra Aetate* are overshadowed by another passage that is noted but not directly quoted in the declaration: "Then when the chief priests and the guards saw him, they cried out saying, 'Crucify, crucify!'" (John 19:6; all translations mine except as noted). "True," the authors of the declaration observe, in John's view "the Jewish authorities and those who followed their lead pressed for the death of Christ" (*Nostra Aetate* 4; see also "Notes" 4.2). True also is that this element of John's presentation, rather than his noble teachings on truth and love, has dominated the landscape of Jewish-Christian relations for almost two millennia.[2] Regardless of the evangelist's intentions,

1. A fourth Johannine passage, though not explicitly cited in the declaration, appears to underlie the statement "Christ underwent his passion and death freely" (*Nostra Aetate* 4). This theme is stressed emphatically in the "Good Shepherd" discourse in John 10:11–18, particularly in Jesus's insistence that "no one takes [my life] from me, but rather I myself lay it down on my own" (10:18).

2. A somewhat more realistic, if less hopeful, evaluation of the Johannine perspective appears in a subsequent report by the Commission for Religious Relations with the Jews (1985). The Commission cites John 10:6; 14:6; 17:23 to clarify that a willingness to participate in interfaith dialogue does *not* mean affirming Judaism as a means of salvation, since eternal life comes only through belief in Christ. Indeed, the "Church and Judaism cannot then be seen as parallel ways of salvation and the Church

the history of biblical interpretation is scarred with readings of the Fourth Gospel that have motivated, or at least justified, egregious acts of violence against Jewish people.

The particular attention given to the Johannine literature in the Roman Church's guiding documents on Jewish-Christian relations reflects the larger recent history of biblical scholarship. One may safely say that the question of "John and the Judaism"—the question of the relationship between first-century Judaism and the evangelist "John," the Johannine churches, and the Fourth Gospel—has been one of the most significant research problems in New Testament studies since the Second World War. In their excellent introduction to the collected papers from a 2000 Leuven colloquium on "Anti-Judaism and the Fourth Gospel," Reimund Bieringer, Didier Pollefeyt, and Frederique Vandecasteele-Vanneuville (2001c, 5) note that five interrelated questions have driven discussions of this topic:

- Is John's Gospel anti-Jewish?
- Who are οἱ Ἰουδαῖοι in the Gospel of John?
- How does one understand the nature of the presumed conflict between John and the Jews?
- Is John supersessionist?
- What implications does all this have for hermeneutics, particularly for the interpretation and application of the Fourth Gospel as a document of faith?[3]

The present discussion will focus particularly on the second and third of these questions—Who are οἱ Ἰουδαῖοι? What was the nature of John's conflict with them?—in an attempt to survey the range of current views on the interplay between the Gospel of John and the historical context in which it was produced. This essay, then, will seek to frame the remainder of this volume by answering the question: how has recent research on the Fourth Gospel attempted to explain the origin of John's distinctive, and often hostile, presentation of those characters in his story whom he calls Ἰουδαῖοι?

must witness to Christ as the Redeemer for all" ("Notes on the Correct Way to Present Jews and Judaism in Preaching and Catechesis in the Roman Catholic Church," 7).

3. Their first question—Is the Gospel of John anti-Jewish?—seeks to differentiate varying views on whether anti-Semitic readings reflect the actual beliefs of the evangelist and the data from the text or simply the prejudices of later interpreters (see Bieringer, Pollefeyt, and Vandecasteele-Vanneuville 2001c, 5–17).

As will be seen, attempts to develop a comprehensive theory on John's posture toward Judaism are immediately confronted with a paradox: the Fourth Gospel seems to be at once both *the most Jewish* and *the most anti-Jewish* of the gospels, deeply embedded in the thought world of the Judaism of its day but also giving the strongest sense of a "parting of the ways" between Christians and Jews. John's Gospel is most Jewish in the sense that it uses the Scriptures and symbols of Judaism more systematically than any other gospel in developing the key points of its Christology and also in the sense that the structural framework of Johannine thought is clearly indebted to strains of Jewish apocalyptic dualism—hence its oft-noted connections to the Dead Sea Scrolls and other artifacts of ancient "heterodox" Jewish thought. At the same time, however, John also gives the strongest sense that Jews and Christians are different, indicating in various ways that he and the members of his churches are not Jews, or at least are no longer Jews. Attempts to explain John's relationship to ancient Judaism must somehow reconcile these conflicting points of view, and the inherent difficulty of this task explains the large number and wide range of proposals current today. Simply put, one may safely say that the Gospel of John is ambivalent in its posture toward Jews and Judaism, or at least that the textual data appears to point to this conclusion within the current frameworks for discussing the issue. Perhaps more accurately, recent research has suggested that John's view of Judaism must be distinguished from his view of Jews: he seems to associate himself closely with Judaism as a faith system while distancing himself from its practitioners.

The remainder of this paper will review research pertaining to both sides of the paradox noted above. I will first survey significant approaches that illustrate John's indebtedness to the Judaism of his day, then summarize various theories on the evangelist's hostile posture toward characters in his story who are labeled Ἰουδαῖοι/Jews. On the former topic, the Fourth Gospel's positive relationship with Judaism is particularly evident in John's appropriation of Jewish Scriptures and theological themes. On the latter, theories on the evangelist's hostile posture toward Jews attempt to reconstruct credible historical scenarios that might explain who these people were—who is John talking about when he refers to οἱ Ἰουδαῖοι?—and why he had come to feel this way toward them. Following this overview, I will close by noting key questions that must be answered before a new, and more comprehensive, consensus position can emerge, then situate the remaining essays in the volume in reference to these questions.

The Gospel of John and First-Century Judaism

It has been widely observed and is now largely taken as an established fact that the Gospel of John is deeply embedded in first-century Judaism. The Johannine Jesus himself admits that "salvation is from the Jews" (John 4:22), a statement that would be true for John not only in the obvious sense that Christ, who gives eternal life and salvation, was Jewish by race and religion but also and more deeply in the sense that the significance of Jesus's deeds, words, and identity can only be understood against the backdrop of Jewish Scriptures, symbols, and institutions. John's positive engagement with and indebtedness to Jewish thought may be conveniently illustrated by a brief review of his use of the Hebrew Bible and his appropriation of Jewish theological themes. Convenient illustrations of the latter that have been frequently discussed in recent scholarship include the distinctive Johannine "I am" sayings and John's christological appropriation of images surrounding the Jerusalem temple and its cult.

Jesus as the Fulfillment of Israel's Scriptures

Even a casual reader will quickly observe that the Gospel of John portrays Jesus as the "fulfillment" of the Jewish Scriptures. Most obviously, John, like the Synoptics, frequently connects things that Jesus did or said with passages from the Old Testament. As a notable example, in the important transition at the end of chapter 12 between the Book of Signs (Jesus's public ministry) and the Farewell Address (the upper-room discourse), John quotes Isa 53:1 and 6:10 to summarize the entire story up to this point: Jesus revealed himself, but οἱ Ἰουδαῖοι could not see or understand him because "their eyes were blinded" (John 12:38–41). Mark, following a similar logic, cites these same passages to explain why people cannot understand Jesus's parables (4:10–12); John intensifies the "fulfillment" theme by saying that Isaiah in fact "said these things because he saw his [Christ's] glory and spoke about him" (12:41), and also by applying the Isaianic motif of misunderstanding to all aspects of Jesus's teaching, not just the parabolic elements.

Further, as a point of narrative style, John normally uses explicit, and in many cases syntactically heavy-handed, citation formulae to draw the reader's attention to the fact that he is quoting the Old Testament, apparently in an effort to ensure that his audience will not miss the connection between Jesus's life and Jewish Scriptures. This trend is particularly noticeable when John's story of Jesus's death is compared to Mark's account. Obviously, both Mark and John have been influenced by Ps 22, which opens with the infamous line "My God, why have you forsaken me?" As has often been noted, one may fairly say that Mark 15 *is* Ps 22: not only does the dying Jesus quote the psalm directly (15:34), but everything that happens in Mark's story finds a direct parallel in themes from the psalm. Yet Mark never explicitly states that he is quoting, or even alluding to, any text from the Old Testament; the reader is left to perceive, or to miss, the connection. By contrast, John goes out of his way to draw the reader's attention to every Scripture he cites in the Calvary story, noting several times that certain things happened "so that the Scripture would be finished" (19:24, 28, 36, 37). Even the most biblically illiterate reader of the Fourth Gospel could not fail to miss the point that many events from Jesus's life were fulfillments of Old Testament texts.

John's portrayal of Christ as the fulfillment of the sacred Scriptures of Judaism is perhaps most obvious in those cases where it is not immediately clear what Scriptures he is talking about. For example, when the dying Jesus says from the cross, "I am thirsty" (John 19:28), John indicates that this happened "so that Scripture would be completed," yet it is impossible to determine with certainty what passage he might be thinking of, and a number of possibilities have been suggested.[4] The same is true of Jesus's promise that he will give "living water" to those who come to him and "drink"—John explains that Jesus was thus referring obliquely to the Holy Spirit (7:37–39) yet fails to clarify exactly which Scripture Jesus is citing in support of this promise, and no known verse from the Hebrew Bible or LXX corresponds to his words.[5] Vague references to Scripture are common in the Fourth Gospel (see also 17:12; 19:36; 20:9), suggesting that John saw Jesus's ministry as a fulfillment and "completion" of the entire revelation of God that began with the Old Testament, not just of specific biblical passages drawn from here and there. Building on these observations, Francis Moloney (2005, 456) has argued that, "For the Fourth Evangelist … the

4. Proposals include Pss 22:15; 42:2; 63:1; 69:3, all of which mention "thirst" in a context of suffering.

5. Craig Keener (2003, 1:728), after an exhaustive discussion of the various possibilities and the historical background of Jewish "water" symbolism, concludes that "John elsewhere midrashically blends various texts and … he is following that practice here"—in other words, John appears to be citing a general theme in the Hebrew Bible rather than any specific passage.

Gospel [of John] brings *the biblical narrative* to an end." John's use of the word *Scripture* (ἡ γραφή) shows that he viewed his written account of Jesus's career both as the fulfillment of the Old Testament and as its logical conclusion, meaning that John regarded his gospel as one more book in the sacred library of Judaism (Moloney 2005, 456–66). In Moloney's view, then, John not only believed that Jesus was the fulfillment of the Scriptures but also that he himself was writing the last chapter in the Jewish Bible.

The "I Am" Sayings

As noted earlier, John views Christ not only as the completion of the Hebrew Bible but also as the supreme expression of key Jewish theological themes. As a result, John's Christology is characterized by numerous comparisons between Jesus and institutes of ancient Judaism, normally in a matrix that asserts the superiority of Christ's revelation of God. This theme is particularly evident in the various "I am" sayings in the Gospel of John, which have long been viewed as keys to Johannine Christology. Johannine scholars generally divide the "I am" sayings of the Fourth Gospel into two broad categories: absolute/unpredicated and metaphorical/predicated. The former category includes those instances where Jesus simply says ἐγώ εἰμι without specifying exactly what he "is" (see 6:20; 8:58; 13:19; 18:5–6), while the latter include well-known metaphors such as "I am the bread of life" (6:35) and "I am the light of the world" (8:12). While many of the "I am" sayings have become foundational elements of Western Christian imagination—innumerable stained-glass windows and Sunday school visual aids have represented Jesus as the good shepherd and the vine—they in fact draw their energy and significance from the symbolic universe of ancient Judaism.

In an extensive study of biblical and rabbinic parallels to the absolute ἐγώ εἰμι sayings, Catrin Williams shows that John has clearly drawn on and developed the "I am" terminology in Deutero-Isaiah (see, e.g., Isa 41:4; 43:10; 46:4). Williams (2000, 299–303) stresses that John not only has borrowed Isaiah's language but also, and more significantly, has appropriated the theological significance that Isaiah attributes to this title. For example, Jesus's pronouncement of ἐγώ εἰμι during the sea crossing after the feeding of five thousand (John 6:16–21) "evokes the image of God creating a way across the waters" (302) from Isa 43:2 and 51:10. As another example, Williams associates the oft-noted trial motifs in John 8 with the "Deutero-Isaianic trial speeches," with Jesus serving both as a witness to the truth that he himself proclaims and also as the divine judge, condemning those who reject but offering life to those who repent and accept (301). John also borrows and plays on the call story in Isa 6 to portray the prophet as a witness to Christ's divine glory (see John 12:37–41), making Isaiah's words a testimony "that Jesus is the eschatological revelation of God" (301). Williams concludes that "several traditions from the book of Isaiah, including their interpretation in the Septuagint and certain early Jewish texts, were a major factor in the development and presentation of Johannine Christology" (301).

Turning to the predicated "I am" sayings, it has often been noted that statements such as "I am the light of the world" and "I am the vine" generally function in their respective contexts to compare Jesus to Jewish theological themes and institutions. To take but one notable example, Gale Yee (1988, 70–82) and others have noted that John situates Jesus's self-acclamation as "the light of the world" in the temple courts during the Feast of Booths (John 7:2; 8:20). According to Josephus, Philo, the Mishnah, and the Tosefta, the Feast of Booths was notable for the public pageantry surrounding its commemorative rituals. Aside from the obvious symbolism of living in tents, festivities included daily parades of worshipers waving a *lulab* and *etrog* (the former a bundle of palm shoots tied together with myrtle twigs and willow branches, following the prescription of Lev 23:40; the latter a thick-skinned species of citron) while singing selections from the Hallel psalms (Pss 113–118; see Josephus, *Ant* 3.245; 13.372; m. Sukkah 3:9–12; 4:1). According to the Mishnah, the temple courts in Jerusalem were illuminated late into the night by giant golden lamps, providing a venue for singing, dancing, and general revelry (m. Sukkah 5:2–4). John 8:12–20 seems to allude to the torchlight ceremony in the temple complex during the feast, especially in view of the note that Jesus called himself "the light of the world" "in the treasury" (8:20), which was adjacent to the Court of Women, the site of the nocturnal festivities. Here, Christ claims to be the highest expression of the symbolic values associated with Tabernacles: divine redemption and provision, revelation of God's law, source of eschatological abundance. In this case as in others, John's distinctive "I am" sayings draw on symbolic resources that were well established in ancient Judaism.

Jesus and the Jerusalem Cult

The "light of the world" saying is only one of many instances in which John borrows from the bank of theological themes associated with the

Jerusalem temple and its cult. This element of John's presentation has been highlighted in a series of books and articles by Mary Coloe. Coloe's research attempts to take seriously that the destruction of the Jerusalem temple was a catastrophic event with profound implications for Jewish and Jewish-Christian understandings of God. "For the people of Israel, the Jerusalem Temple had been the focal point of their faith that God dwelt in their midst, enabling them to be a holy people through the Temple's ongoing sacrificial cult" (Coloe 2001, 1; see also Coloe 2006; Kerr 2002). Following the catastrophe of 70 CE, rabbinic Jews sought to replace the temple with a heightened obedience to torah. The Johannine Christians, by contrast, shifted the significance of the temple as a symbol of God's presence and atonement to Christ himself and then, subsequently, to their own community. Jesus's resurrected body thus became the new center of divine presence and revelation, a presence that continued after his departure through the indwelling of the Spirit within the church, God's "household with many rooms" (John 14). This portrayal of the church, and of the Christ whom the church worships, allowed Jewish-Christian readers of the Fourth Gospel to understand themselves as "the real inheritors of all that Judaism promised" (Coloe 2001, 214). In Coloe's view, then, John's understandings of both Christ and the church drew heavily on concepts that were central to ancient Jewish thought.

In these and many other ways that will be explored by the papers in the present volume, it seems clear that the Gospel of John is thoroughly at home in the world of first-century Judaism. The gospel draws on a wide range of Jewish Scriptures, themes, and theological conceptions to explain Jesus's significance to its readers. In this respect, one may say that John's is the "most Jewish" gospel.

The Gospel of John and the Jews

In view of the Fourth Gospel's many and deep connections to its Jewish matrix, it is somewhat surprising to discover that John, while clearly at home in the thought world of ancient Judaism, does not seem to think of either Jesus or himself as Jews. Put another way, John talks about Jesus, the disciples, and some other characters in his story in ways that clearly distinguish them from those characters whom he calls Jews/Ἰουδαῖοι. Thus, for example, at John 5:17 the lame man at Bethesda "told *the Jews* that it was Jesus who made him well," despite the fact that both the lame man himself and Jesus are also Jewish. Similarly, at 13:3 Jesus says to the disciples,

"As I told *the Jews*, I now tell you: Where I am going you cannot come." This would seem to suggest that the disciples are not Jews, although they are obviously Jewish by both race and religion. Apparently following this same logic, John sees no inconsistency in the fact that Jesus several times reminds the Jews about things written in "your law" (8:17; 10:34), even though Jesus himself is Jewish, is regarded as a rabbi/prophet (1:38, 49; 3:2; 4:31; 6:25; 9:2; 11:8, 28; 13:13–14; 20:16), and is, as the Word and Wisdom of God incarnate (1:14), presumably the author of the Hebrew Scriptures.

While John's suggestion that certain Jewish characters in his story are not Ἰουδαῖοι is itself remarkable, the significance of this element of his presentation is enhanced by the fact that he clearly views the characters whom he calls Jews as qualitatively different from, and ontologically inferior to, Jesus and his disciples. Specifically, οἱ Ἰουδαῖοι are different from Jesus and his followers because they are members of "the world," which John portrays as given over to evil and hateful toward God. Thus, Nicodemus, a "leader of οἱ Ἰουδαῖοι," is told that he has not believed in Jesus because he "loves darkness," since his "deeds are evil" (3:19–20). In chapter 8, in the context of the "light of the world" discourse, Jesus tells οἱ Ἰουδαῖοι two times that they will "die in their sins" because they are "of this world" (8:21–24) and then punctuates the point by proceeding to tell them that their "father" is not the righteous Abraham, as they claim, but rather "the devil" (8:38–44). Further, because the devil is a liar and murderer (8:44; 1 John 3:8–12), οἱ Ἰουδαῖοι constantly do the devil's work of persecuting those who follow Jesus (John 9:22; 19:38–39). The moral inferiority of οἱ Ἰουδαῖοι is stressed in a summary statement at the end of Jesus's public ministry (12:37–43). Here John explains that οἱ Ἰουδαῖοι were not able to believe Jesus's many signs because, as Isaiah predicted, God had blinded them and hardened their hearts. Further, and perhaps much worse, even some Ἰουδαῖοι who were able to see willfully chose to reject the truth of Jesus's message because they feared persecution from the Pharisees. John has no sympathy for these people, because clearly "they loved the glory of men more than the glory of God" (12:43). Simply put, in the words of the Johannine Jesus, "whoever is from God hears the words of God. You [Ἰουδαῖοι] do not listen to me because you are not from God" (8:47).

Attempts to explain John's unusual characterization of Ἰουδαῖοι as a group separate from and morally inferior to himself and other Christians have focused on two broad questions that each combine historical and literary concerns. First, who are οἱ Ἰουδαῖοι to whom John refers? What is the referent of this term? Three basic answers to this question are typically offered: (1) John uses the term οἱ Ἰουδαῖοι in what would appear to be the "normal" sense, referring to those individuals who adhere to the religious precepts of Judaism (i.e., to the members of a faith system); (2) John uses the term οἱ Ἰουδαῖοι more narrowly in reference to a specific subgroup within the total Jewish population of his day; and (3) John does not use the term οἱ Ἰουδαῖοι in reference to Jewish people at all but rather as a way of characterizing other Christians who do not accept his theological position. The second question is closely related to the first: what circumstances or experiences have led John to characterize this group of people (οἱ Ἰουδαῖοι) in the way that he does? Answers to this question fall into two major categories, depending on how one understands the historical relationship between the Johannine Christians and οἱ Ἰουδαῖοι at the time the Fourth Gospel was written: (1) Christian Jews have been forced to leave the Jewish community, whether because of their belief in Christ or for some other reason; (2) Christian Jews have chosen to leave the Jewish community but remain in dialogue with members of the parent synagogue. Almost all recent approaches to the relationship between John and Judaism may be categorized on the basis of their answers to these two questions.

Οἱ Ἰουδαῖοι = All Jewish People

Many Johannine scholars take the word Ἰουδαῖοι in the Fourth Gospel in what might be called the "normal" sense of that term: as a broad reference to all people in John's day who subscribed to the traditional faith of Israel and whose religious imagination was animated by the sacred texts, traditions, and institutions of Judaism. Since the majority of scholars today also adhere to the traditional view that the Fourth Gospel was composed in the late first or early second century CE, these sacred texts, traditions, and institutions focused primarily on adherence to the Jewish Scriptures, particularly the Law, and to participation in a community life that was increasingly centered in the synagogue in the aftermath of the destruction of the Jerusalem temple in 70 CE.

But while these scholars agree that John uses the term Jews/Ἰουδαῖοι in a broad way to refer to all Jewish people, they differ sharply in their answers to the second question above: Why does John characterize Jewish people in the way that he does? The following survey will outline the spectrum of concerns and conclusions represented by this approach by highlighting the work of J. Louis Martyn, Raymond Brown, Adele Reinhartz, and Raimo Hakola.

Today any attempt to answer the question of the relationship between John and οἱ Ἰουδαῖοι must begin with the groundbreaking research of Martyn (1968). Martyn's theory focuses on the three occurrences of the word ἀποσυνάγωγος ("[to be] put out of the synagogue") in the Gospel of John (9:22; 12:42; 16:2). The first occurrence of this term, in the story of the healing of an anonymous blind man at the Pool of Siloam, is particularly significant. After the man receives his sight, the Pharisees question him about Jesus's healing techniques because the miracle was performed on a Sabbath (9:13). Unsatisfied with the man's answers, οἱ Ἰουδαῖοι (perhaps specifically the Pharisees; 9:13, 15, 16) call for his parents to ascertain whether he was truly blind; his parents, however, refuse to comment because "the Jews had already agreed that anyone who confessed Jesus to be the Messiah would be put out of the synagogue [ἀποσυνάγωγος]" (9:22). Martyn argues that this passage can be read at two levels: as an episode from the life of Jesus and as a reflection of the later experiences of the Johannine community. Read on the level of Jesus's life, the story is not historically credible, since there is no clear evidence that discipleship was somehow seen as antithetical to participation in the synagogue during Jesus's lifetime. Yet John 9 is "easily understood under circumstances in which the synagogue has begun to view the rival Christian movement as an essential … rival" (Martyn 2003, 47), suggesting that the story may actually be an allegory for the later experiences of Johannine Christians (46–49).

After exploring a number of historical possibilities that might support his reading, Martyn concludes that John 9:22 must refer to the Birkat Haminim, or "Benediction against Heretics," a prayer added to the synagogue liturgy by the Jamnia rabbinic academy in the mid-80s CE. In reciting this prayer, Christian Jews would be forced to condemn themselves as heretics because of their faith in Christ. Eventually the social pressures associated with this weekly ritual led to the Johannine community's excommunication from the synagogue. These Johannine Christians, symbolized by the blind man in John 9, continued to proclaim Christ to their Jewish friends and relatives, provoking the Jewish authorities to take the more drastic steps hinted at in Jesus's prophecy at John 16:2 (Martyn 2003, 83). According to Martyn, then, John's portrait of the Jews as both distinct from and hostile to Jesus and his followers is a reflection of the Johannine community's real-world experiences of persecution and excommunication.

While Martyn's theory remains influential, certain details of his historical reconstruction have generated substantial controversy. Most notably, many scholars have insisted that his portrait of early post-70 CE Judaism is inadequate, thus calling his entire theory into question. Steven Katz (1984, 71–74) and Reuven Kimelman (1981, 226–44, 391–403), for example, insist that "Martyn's argument is unacceptable" (Katz 1984, 71) because the evidence does not suggest that the Birkat Haminim was aimed at Jewish Christians. In fact, "no official anti-Christian policy" (76) existed in late first-century Judaism and, even if such a policy were in force, Martyn's theory "turns on a voluntary exile from the synagogue on the part of the *min* ["heretic"].... As long as a person did not consider himself a *min* the benediction would be irrelevant and his participation in synagogue life would continue" (74). John, in other words, would feel pressured to leave the synagogue only if he believed himself to be a heretic, an unlikely proposal.

Against these criticisms, however, Martyn's two-level approach was significantly bolstered by the work of Brown, certainly the most significant Johannine scholar in the English-speaking world in the latter half of the twentieth century. Brown avoids many of the criticisms leveled against Martyn by offering a reconstruction of the history of the Johannine community that was both more comprehensive and also less dependent on the specific details of late first-century Jewish history. Brown's model is more comprehensive in the sense that it attempted to trace the history of Johannine Christianity from pre-70 CE Palestine to the emergence of the "great church" in the second century, using data from both the Gospel of John and the Johannine epistles. In the most recent version of his model, Brown argues that the Johannine community was originally composed of heterodox Jewish followers of Jesus, including former disciples of John the Baptist, Samaritans, and others who held antitemple views. The mixed nature of this group and its high Christology, based largely on Jewish wisdom traditions, eventually led to its expulsion from the synagogue (Brown 2003, 68, 74–78). This experience, in Brown's view, affected the presentation of Jesus in the Fourth Gospel in a number of ways and, most significantly here, led the members of the Johannine churches "no longer to think of themselves as 'Jews'" (Brown 2003, 69). The various forensic motifs in the Fourth Gospel—testimony, witness, marshaling proofs, answering charges, "confessing"—likely also emerged from this conflict, as the Johannine Christians imagined Jesus and his earliest followers (and John the Baptist) experiencing interrogations similar to their own trials at the hands of the synagogue authorities (69). Yet, despite these similarities to Martyn's approach, Brown's model is less dependent on the specific details of late first-century Jewish history in the sense that Brown does not tie John's personal experiences to any single historical event. Rather, "it is increasingly accepted that there is no need to invoke the *Birkat ha-minim*.... The idea that it was a universal Jewish decree against Christians is almost certainly wrong and the dating of that blessing to A.D. 85 is dubious" (68 n. 65). Following Brown's precedent, most current proponents of the Martyn hypothesis interpret John's references to "excommunication" as a local and temporary rather than global and permanent measure against confessing Christian Jews (see, for example, Culpepper 1992, 21–43; D. M. Smith 2008, 3–56).

At the present time, the Martyn-Brown hypothesis and its numerous variants remain perhaps the most influential model for understanding the relationship between the Gospel of John and late first-century Judaism. This has been the case simply because this approach readily explains the paradox noted earlier: John's indebtedness to Jewish themes and Scriptures in explaining Jesus (that John's is the most Jewish gospel), and John's evident sense of alienation from the Jewish community (that John's is also the most anti-Jewish gospel). Following the Martyn-Brown theory, John, as a Jew himself and possibly even from Palestine, would naturally think of Jesus in Jewish terms, connecting Christ's life and teachings to the Old Testament and talking about him in ways that would be consistent with the theological language of other Jews, such as the group that produced and preserved the Dead Sea Scrolls. But this theory also readily explains why John, as a Christian Jew, would feel alienated from other Jews after being expelled from the synagogue. The explanatory power of this model perhaps explains the fact that forty years of critique and criticism did not lead Martyn to change his mind. In his last article on the topic, a reflective essay in the volume *What We Have Heard from the Beginning*, Martyn (2007) insists that debates over the historical details of the Birkat Haminim and the political atmosphere of first-century Judaism cannot change the basic facts. "The word *aposynagogos* ... is there in the text, and it was not coined in an individual's private fit of paranoia: the occurrences of this term are communal references to a communal experience" (2007, 187).[6]

The Martyn-Brown hypothesis, then, explains John's tortured relationship with Judaism by arguing that John, as a Jew, built his Christology and

---

6. Martyn also suggests that attempts to reduce the apparent tensions between John and the synagogue may reflect the ecumenical spirit of today's post-Shoah world more accurately than they reflect the actual data from the Fourth Gospel (2007).

then his story of Jesus on a Jewish framework and was eventually expelled from the synagogue for this very reason—the Johannine Christians were excommunicated because their views were considered blasphemous. In recent years, however, some scholars who affirm a break between John and the synagogue have offered alternate explanations for the textual data. These scholars contend that the Johannine Christians had *not* been "put out of the synagogue" but rather had chosen to leave the Jewish fold and were perhaps seeking to encourage other Jews to join them.

The leading proponent of this approach, Reinhartz, has critiqued the Martyn-Brown theory on several grounds in a series of papers and publications. Reinhartz (2001b, 342, 346–49, 354–56) agrees with Martyn that the term οἱ Ἰουδαῖοι is used in the Fourth Gospel in a global way, in reference to all Jewish people (including diaspora Jews) in the real world of John's own experience.[7] But Martyn's interpretation of the relationship between John and the Jews is weakened by inherent limitations in his two-level reading of the narrative. First, "there is no internal evidence that the gospel [of John] was intended to encode the story of a community [as Martyn and Brown suggested]. Rather, there are explicit indications … that it was meant to be read precisely as a story of Jesus" (Reinhartz 2005a, 113; see also Reinhartz 1998, 131–33), whether or not verses such as 9:22 and 12:42 are historically reliable.[8] Second, and more substantially, a broader application of Martyn's own two-level reading strategy produces a much more complex portrait of the historical situation behind the Johannine literature.[9] While Martyn focused primarily on John 9, Reinhartz (2001b, 351–53; 1998, 121–30) points to two verses that received little attention in

7. "The Fourth Evangelist is not operating with a narrow and limited definition of Ἰουδαῖοι. While some cases may permit a narrower translation according to the context, the sense in all cases is best met by the direct translation of Ἰουδαῖος as 'Jew,' with all of its connotations of a national but not a geographically limited religious, political and cultural identity" (Reinhartz 2001b, 348).

8. Reinhartz agrees with Martyn that John's references to an expulsion from the synagogue during Jesus's lifetime are anachronistic; indeed, John 9:22 is "unthinkable in the time of Jesus" (1998, 112; see Martyn 2003, 47–48).

9. Reinhartz's critique here is predicated on the theorem that a "two-level reading" should provide consistent results when applied not only to John 9 (the primary focus of Martyn's discussion) but also to the entire gospel narrative. "If application of the two-level reading strategy yields … a conflicting set of images, however, then the expulsion theory itself, as well as its historical-critical and homiletical ramifications, are called into question" (1998, 118).

Martyn's and Brown's analyses: John 11:19 and 12:11. The former indicates that a large number of Jews had come to comfort Mary and Martha, who are clearly presented as faithful followers of Christ, after Lazarus's death, a compassionate gesture that scarcely suggests any tension between the disciples and the Jews.[10] Similarly, John 12:11 says that the chief priests wished to kill the resurrected Lazarus because many Jews were "deserting" (ὑπῆγον) and believing in Jesus because of him—clearly here, the choice to join Jesus's movement is voluntary, not the result of a policy of expulsion.[11] Building on these observations, Reinhartz has tended to stress the possibility that the Johannine Christians had voluntarily withdrawn from the synagogue because they no longer found its liturgy and community life sufficient to nourish their emerging faith, and that John raises the threat of possible expulsion (9:22; 16:2) to discourage them from returning. Following this reading, John 16:2 is a warning to Jewish-Christian readers of what *might* happen *if* they decide to go back to the synagogue rather than a description of an actual past experience (Reinhartz 2007, 193; see also 1998, 121–24, 136–37; and her entry in the present volume). The question, in other words, is whether the Gospel of John is *the product* of a formal separation between church and synagogue or *an attempt to effect* a formal separation between church and synagogue.

Extending this line of reasoning, Hakola has attempted to identify the precise reasons why the Johannine Christians may have chosen to leave the Jewish community. Hakola agrees with Martyn that John portrays Christians as distinct from Jews because he himself is no longer a member of the synagogue. The Jews, however, were not responsible for this separation; rather, the Johannine Christians chose to leave because they no longer found meaning in the Jewish religion. "What John says of the Jews and Jewishness is not a response to hostile actions of a Jewish establishment....

10. "In a two-level reading of the Gospel, these sisters [Mary and Martha of Bethany] would represent Johannine Christians. If, as the consensus view asserts, such Christians had already been excluded from the synagogue and hence from the Jewish community as a whole, how is it that they are surrounded by Jewish mourners?" (Reinhartz 1998, 121).

11. Reinhartz concludes from these observations that "the [Fourth] Gospel implies at least three different models of the historical relationship between the Johannine community and the Jewish community": Christians were excluded from the synagogue for their confession of Jesus (John 9); Christians were comforted in times of mourning by fellow Jews who did not share their faith (John 11); Jewish Christians voluntarily left the synagogue to join Johannine churches (1998, 121–22).

The Johannine Christians themselves interpreted their faith in Jesus in such a way that it led them on a collision course with basic matters of Jewishness" (Hakola 2005b, 215–16). These "basic matters of Jewishness" included many of the key expressions of Jewish identity. Several aspects of John's presentation show that he had come to view Christian faith as superior to Jewish belief: Christian worship "in spirit" is far better than Jewish worship in Jerusalem or Samaritan worship on Mount Gerizim; Jesus has replaced the law of Moses with a better revelation of God's grace and truth (see esp. 109–13 [on temple worship], 170–76 [on the law]). In Hakola's view, these new beliefs had led the Johannine Christians to abandon basic Jewish religious practices such as Sabbath observance and circumcision, making it effectively impossible for them to remain active in the synagogue (126–45, 234–36). Following this logic, Hakola agrees with Reinhartz that "John's sharp dualism may be taken as both a result of the growing alienation of the Johannine group from its surrounding [Jewish] society and as an attempt to intensify this alienation" (218). In other words, the Jews did not give up on John; John gave up on the Jews.

In summary, then, scholars such as Reinhartz and Hakola agree with Martyn and Brown that John uses the term οἱ Ἰουδαῖοι to refer to members of the post-70 CE synagogue. They disagree with Martyn on the reasons why John does this. While Martyn and Brown say that John is angry because he was excommunicated from the synagogue because of his belief in Jesus, Reinhartz and Hakola say that John left the synagogue by his own choice and that he talks about Jews as a separate group because he does not want the Jewish members of his churches to think of themselves as Jews any longer.

Οἱ Ἰουδαῖοι = "Only Some Jewish People"

As noted above, theories on the historical relationship between John and οἱ Ἰουδαῖοι may be categorized on the basis of their answers to two questions: Who are οἱ Ἰουδαῖοι to whom John refers? And why does he talk about this group of people the way he does? The current consensus tends to answer the former question by suggesting that John uses the term οἱ Ἰουδαῖοι as a generalization for all people of Jewish faith and/or ethnicity. Most scholars who take this position then answer the second question by suggesting that the Johannine Christians had left or were forced to leave the synagogue, either because their Christology was deemed incompatible with Jewish sensitivities, because they had ceased to observe certain key religious practices that defined Jewish identity, or because they simply did not feel that the synagogue and its liturgy could adequately nourish their new faith.

Another group of scholars, however, has offered a different solution to the first question, arguing that John uses the term Jews/Ἰουδαῖοι in a narrower and more limited sense. Two of the more influential proposals in this category will be noted here: the view that John uses the term οἱ Ἰουδαῖοι *geographically*, to distinguish Jewish people who lived in a particular region from Jews who lived in other areas; and the view that John uses the term οἱ Ἰουδαῖοι *socially*, to distinguish a particular class of Jewish people from Jews of other social classes.

First, some scholars have argued that John uses the term Ἰουδαῖοι in a *geographical* rather than ethnic or religious sense. This approach is reflected in the Jesus Seminar's Scholars Version, which generally translates the word Ἰουδαῖοι as "Judeans," residents of Jerusalem and/or the Roman province of Judea.[12] Thus, for example, when Jesus asks the Samaritan woman at the well for a drink of water, she replies, "You are a Judean [σὺ Ἰουδαῖος ὢν]; how can you ask a Samaritan woman for a drink?" John then explains that she said this because "Judeans [Ἰουδαῖοι] don't associate with Samaritans" (John 4:9 Scholars Version). The geographical approach was promoted by a number of important studies in the 1970s and 1980s, including significant articles in *Novum Testamentum* by Malcolm Lowe (1976) and John Ashton (1985).

Lowe's study represents perhaps the most thorough application of the principle that the Ἰουδαῖοι in the Fourth Gospel are residents of the Roman province of Judea. John clearly uses the term *Judea* to refer to a distinct geographical region, noting, for example, that Jesus had to pass through Samaria in order to go from Judea to Galilee (John 4:3–4; Lowe 1976, 112).[13] Logically, then, John would use the term Judeans to refer to residents of this region, and Lowe finds no real exceptions to this rule, over against the strong evidence that passages such as John 7:1; 10:19–33; 11:7–8, 19–45 refer specifically to people who live in Judea/Jerusalem

---

12. In some instances, the Scholars Version understands Ἰουδαῖοι to refer more generally to all practitioners of the Jewish faith. Thus, for example, the SV translates τὸ πάσχα, ἡ ἑορτὴ τῶν Ἰουδαίων (lit. "the Passover, the feast of the Judeans") at John 6:4 as "the Jewish celebration of Passover."

13. Lowe (114–15) concludes that this is the primary referent of the term "Judea" in all four canonical gospels, except where the context specifically indicates a broader referent.

as opposed to Galileans or Jews from the diaspora. Following this logic, Lowe (1976, 115–24, 117–18 n. 54, 128–29) argues that John's references to various "feasts of τῶν Ἰουδαίων" (123; see John 2:13; 5:1; 6:4; 7:1; 11:55) simply reflect that these pilgrimage festivals were celebrated in Jerusalem/Judea; that the jars of water that Jesus turns to wine in John 2 were used for the customary "purification rites of the Judeans" (123; κατὰ τὸν καθαρισμὸν τῶν Ἰουδαίων; John 2:6); that the titulus on Jesus's cross, ὁ βασιλεὺς τῶν Ἰουδαίων, should be translated "King of Judea" (123; see John 19:19–21); and, that the "nine or ten clear" instances where John uses the term Ἰουδαῖοι in reference to the Sanhedrin or other religious authority figures reflects the fact that the Jewish religious leadership was centered in Judea ("the Judean authorities"; 123). Of course, John 4 is something of an exception: Jesus, a Galilean (see 4:43–45; 6:42; 19:19), is called an Ἰουδαῖος ("Judean") by the Samaritan woman (4:9). This chapter, however, "gives us *Samaritan* usage of the [term in that] period" and thus does not reflect John's own understanding of the word Ἰουδαῖοι. Further, even here the woman seems to use the term in reference to devotees of "the aberrant [in her view] Judean version of the true faith of Israel" (Lowe 1976, 125)—in other words, she classifies Jesus as a Judean because she assumes that he, though a Galilean, worships at the Jerusalem temple rather than at Mount Gerizim (126). In Lowe's view, then, the Fourth Gospel says almost nothing about Jews generally and reserves its more hostile comments for residents of ancient Judea specifically.

A second group of scholars who limit the scope of the term Ἰουδαῖοι suggests that John uses the word Jews to identify *a particular social class* among the larger Jewish population: the religious authorities. This approach builds on passages in the Fourth Gospel where the term Ἰουδαῖοι seems to refer obviously to the Pharisees, chief priests, and other Jewish leaders, all of whom are consistently presented as hostile to Jesus and his followers. Thus, in John 5, the Jews seek to kill Jesus because he healed a lame man on the Sabbath and claimed that he was only doing his Father's work (5:10–18)—logically, the religious leaders of the day would be concerned about Sabbath violations and would want to limit Jesus's influence. Similarly, when Pilate tells the Jews that they should crucify Jesus themselves and they respond that Jesus must die because he claimed to be Son of God, it seems clear that the Jews in question are the members of the Sanhedrin who had earlier brought Jesus to trial and who would presumably be most concerned about his theological irregularities and political aspirations (18:24, 28–30; 19:6–7).

Building on these more obvious instances, Urban von Wahlde (1979, 233–42; 1989, 31–35, 40 n. 34, 63; 2010a, 1:27–30, 59, 63–68, 91–93) has argued that John almost always uses the term Ἰουδαῖοι to refer to the Jewish religious leaders, not to all Jews everywhere.[14] In von Wahlde's view, John's source documents referred to these individuals as "Pharisees," "chief priests," "rulers," or some combination of these terms; when John incorporated these sources into his own account, he himself used the more general term οἱ Ἰουδαῖοι for this group. For this reason, the Gospel of John sometimes calls the authorities "Jews," sometimes calls them "rulers," sometimes calls them "chief priests," and sometimes calls them "Pharisees." John himself referred to the authorities as Jews because, in his view, the Jewish population at large had allowed their leaders to expel him and other Christians from the synagogue. The Ἰουδαῖοι, then, are simply the Jewish authorities, not all Jewish people, and John's anger is directed only to this ruling elite and not to all of his Jewish kinsfolk.

In summary, then, some scholars answer the question "Who are the Ἰουδαῖοι?" by arguing that John does not use the word Ἰουδαῖοι to refer to all Jewish people. The Ἰουδαῖοι may be people who live in Judea, the Jewish religious leadership, or some other group within the larger Jewish population, but the term Ἰουδαῖοι does not refer to all Jews everywhere. At the same time, these scholars generally agree with Martyn, Brown, and others that John is hostile toward the Jews because he has had some kind of bad experience with them—the Judeans or Pharisees have persecuted John, and this has led him to think that they are allies of the world and the devil.

Οἱ Ἰουδαῖοι = John's Christian Opponents

As the above survey has shown, most scholars today conclude that John uses the word Ἰουδαῖοι as a label for devotees of Judaism, the only question

14. Of course, many lay members of the synagogue may have held the same opinion of Jesus and Christians as their leaders. "Undoubtedly many of the [Jewish] populace held views similar to those of the religious authorities, but the views expressed by 'the Jews' in the Gospel of John seem to represent the official religious opposition to Jesus" (von Wahlde 2007, 350). This same approach is reflected in the "Guidelines and Suggestions for Implementing the Conciliar Declaration *Nostra Aetate*" (1974) issued by the Commission for Religious Relations with the Jews. The "Guidelines" suggest that translations of the Fourth Gospel should render the word Ἰουδαῖοι in ways that will indicate that John is referring to "the leaders of the Jews" or "the adversaries of Jesus" rather than to all Jewish people (footnote to sec. 2).

being whether the Ἰουδαῖοι mentioned in the Fourth Gospel include all Jews everywhere or only a smaller group within the total Jewish population. Scholars who take this approach generally argue that John's hostile posture toward Jews is a result of his own experiences of persecution and excommunication, although some argue that the Johannine Christians had left the Jewish fold voluntarily. A radically different thesis, however, has been advanced by Henk Jan de Jonge, who builds on the work of his former doctoral student at the University of Leiden B. W. J. de Ruyter. While de Jonge (2001, 237–38) and de Ruyter (1998) agree that John has had hostile experiences with those people whom he labels Jews, they contend that this term does not refer to adherents of Judaism but rather to Christians from trajectories within the primitive church that did not accept elements of Johannine Christology, specifically John's belief that Jesus was one with the Father.

This approach may be conveniently illustrated by comparing de Jonge's reading of John 9, the story of the healing and excommunication of the man born blind, with that of Martyn outlined above. Like Martyn, de Jonge argues that this narrative can be read at two levels: as an account of an event involving Jesus, a blind man, and the Pharisees; and, at the same time, as the story of John's own experiences of conflict over the precise identity of Christ.[15] Unlike Martyn, however, de Jonge (2001) suggests that the Jews in the second level of the story do not represent Jewish people in the sphere of John's own experience. A careful reading of John 9:16 reveals that the Pharisees respond to the healing of the blind man in two different ways. Some affirm the reality of the miracle but conclude that Jesus is a sinner; clearly, these people do not believe that Jesus holds the divine authority to override commandments regulating work on Sabbath. The same verdict is reached by οἱ Ἰουδαῖοι, who suddenly appear in the story at 9:18. A second group of Pharisees, however, contests this objection by insisting that Jesus's ability to perform signs proves that he has not sinned; rather, Jesus "works the work of the Father." Both groups, then, accept Jesus's divine power, yet some question whether this display of power establishes "the functional unity of Jesus and God." De Jonge concludes that the Jews and those Pharisees who accept Jesus's power but label him a "sinner" represent non-Johannine Christians, while those who argue in

15. De Jonge stresses that, at the level of the narrative of the Fourth Gospel, the term *Pharisees* "undoubtedly" refers to "nothing other than genuine Pharisees, contemporaries of Jesus" (2001, 251–52 for what follows, here 251).

Jesus's favor represent the Fourth Evangelist and his allies. Both groups, as believers, affirm Christ, yet John's opponents deny that "Jesus is one with God" and thus display an inadequate Christology.

De Jonge, then, agrees with Martyn that the Fourth Gospel evidences a polemical tone toward Jews but concludes that the object of John's attack was "contemporary Christians who refused to accept the particular christological understanding of the Johannine group" (239). These other Christians are labeled Jews in the Fourth Gospel simply because this was the only way they could be identified in a story about Jesus. Since the historical Jesus interacted with Jews and not heretical Christians, John could only discuss the theological conflicts of his own time by associating the beliefs of his own Christian opponents with the Jews whom Jesus encountered—obviously, John could not refer to these people as "Christians" simply because there were no Christians during Jesus's lifetime (240).

Open Questions and Future Directions

Clearly, then, the Gospel of John is a paradox. On one hand, John's presentation of Jesus is deeply colored by and largely dependent on themes and ideas drawn from first-century Judaism and its sacred literature. On the other hand, John regularly speaks about Jesus and his followers in a way that distinguishes them from the Jews and in a way that portrays Jews as morally inferior to Christians and as members of the world. The question, then, is not whether the Gospel of John is Jewish but how one can explain its separatist outlook.

Methodologically, and despite the specific conclusions reached by different scholars, discussions of John's relationship to Judaism are concerned with two types of questions. The first type concerns *the historical past*: How has John drawn on the Scriptures and symbols of Judaism in his own understanding and presentation of Christ? Who are the people whom he calls Jews, and what kinds of experiences led John to talk about these people in the way that he does? To what extent, if any, does John's presentation of Jewish characters align with realities from the context and career of the historical Jesus? The second type concerns *hermeneutical problems* emerging from the canonical status of the Fourth Gospel: How should John's difficult statements about Jews be presented to modern Christian audiences who view his narrative as sacred Scripture? What role, if any, can John's Gospel play in interfaith dialogue? Both sets of questions are important, and both will continue to generate discussion. This essay will close by noting six specific questions that seem particularly significant to future conversations on John and Judaism, and then locating the remaining essays in the volume in reference to these concerns.

First, in what ways was the Gospel of John positively connected to first-century Jewish thought and life? Put another way: how has John appropriated Jewish Scriptures, institutions (e.g., the temple), language, and themes in his presentation of Jesus? Future answers to this question must proceed from the growing awareness that first-century Judaism was not a single fixed entity but rather a broad spectrum of theological, political, and social beliefs that varied across time, geographical regions, and social classes. The Johannine tradition originated in Palestine at a time when the temple was still the symbolic center of Jewish religious life; John's Gospel was written at a time when Jews were rebuilding their religious identity around heightened obedience to torah and the community of the synagogue. Further, most scholars still believe that John's Gospel was written in the diaspora, most likely in Asia Minor, and many believe that foundational figures in the Johannine community may have subscribed to heterodox forms of Jewish thought. Thus, future consideration of John's appropriation of Jewish Scriptures, institutions, and themes must be based on more precise reconstructions of the varying values that these Scriptures, institutions, and themes would have carried for which Jews in what part of the world in what time period.

Second, who are οἱ Ἰουδαῖοι who appear in John's Gospel? What does the word Ἰουδαῖοι mean? As noted above, current scholarship is divided, and Johannes Beutler may be correct to conclude that there is no single way to answer this question simply because John uses the term with a number of different shades of meaning.[16] It seems clear that John sometimes uses the word Ἰουδαῖοι to refer to people who live in Judea; in other cases, Ἰουδαῖοι clearly refers to the Jewish religious authorities; often it seems to describe all Jewish people; sometimes it refers to Jewish people who are disciples of Jesus for a time but then leave him (John 8:31). Beutler (2001, 230–31)

16. In view of this problem, Beutler (2001, 229–38) has suggested that translations of difficult passages such as John 8:31–58 might put the term Jews in quotation marks to alert modern readers that John is using the term in a nuanced way. Of course, "one problem would remain, i.e. the question how to pronounce quotations [sic] marks, but this could be met with the procedure that either the reader speaks of 'so called Jews', or the preacher immediately before or after the reading explains the particular meaning of 'the Jews' in John to the audience" (237–38).

suggests that John's original readers would understand that the word could have multiple meanings in different contexts; others argue that the different usages reflect differing sources of material or layers of editorial revision. In any case, it seems clear that any discussion of John's relationship to Judaism will be grounded in an answer to the question "Who are the Ἰουδαῖοι?"

The second question above leads to two others that are closely related: How is John's use of the term οἱ Ἰουδαῖοι related to the experiences of the Johannine community? How is his use of this term related to events from the life of the historical Jesus? All scholars today would agree that John's presentation of the Jews has been colored by his own experiences, and most would also argue that John's presentation does *not* reflect the ministry of the historical Jesus. The latter conclusion, however, is significant, for if John is simply describing what he believes to be facts about the career of Jesus, his remarks about Jews may not reflect his personal experiences and as a result would not necessarily speak to relations between the Johannine Christians and the Jews of their time. For example, if John 9 is simply a (more or less accurate) story about Jesus's life—or if John at least believes that it is—with no connection to the experiences of the Johannine community, then this chapter provides little information that would help us understand the relationship between church and synagogue in the late first century. In terms of exegesis, this means asking whether and to what extent the Fourth Gospel can be read at two levels, and which level will best explain why John talks about the Jews in the way that he does.

Fifth, how does John's presentation of the Jews fit with other presentations of Jews and Judaism in the New Testament and other early Christian documents? Obviously this question has both historical and hermeneutical implications. From a historical point of view, the question concerns how John's presentation relates to Paul's thinking on Jews, Mark's thinking on Jews, Luke's thinking on Jews, Justin Martyr's thinking on Jews, and so on. Such comparative research will reveal the extent to which John's perspective was the same as that of other Christians (to the extent that Christians can be distinguished from Jews in the time period under consideration) and the ways in which it was distinct. Presumably, these distinctions would reflect unique experiences with Jewish people that may have affected John's presentation, thus leading to a fuller picture of the history of Johannine Christianity. From a hermeneutical point of view, John's thinking on this issue must be considered within the larger biblical perspective on the relationship between Christianity and Judaism. Obviously John 8:44, which refers to Jews as "children of the devil," should not be viewed in isolation from Paul's more positive statements in Rom 9 and 11. A holistic approach that seeks to understand John's perspective within the larger canonical witness will help to clarify the Gospel of John's appropriate place in contemporary Christian thought.

Sixth and finally, after the historical and theological questions have been answered, how do we present the Gospel of John in a way that is relevant and meaningful to contemporary Christian faith and to dialogue with other faiths? Should difficult verses such as John 8:44 be left untranslated so that most people cannot read them (see Pippin 1996)? Or should scholars and preachers simply ignore them and hope that Christian laypeople do not notice them? The latter approach is reflected in the post-Vatican II lectionary, which excludes John 8:43–50; notably, John 8:46–59 was included in the pre-Vatican II *missal*, being read alongside Heb 9:11–15 on the First Passion Sunday. Those biblical scholars who wish to claim immunity from these questions under the guise of historical objectivity must also acknowledge that the Holocaust is an event of recent history, not the distant past.

The remaining essays in this volume interact with one or, normally, several of the six questions above and reflect a wide range of methodologies and perspectives on these issues. Jan G. van der Watt's entry extends his previous research on the Johannine symbolic universe to examine John's presentation of Jesus as King of Israel/the Jews. Van der Watt's approach squarely addresses the central concerns of the second and third questions above, regarding the meaning of the term οἱ Ἰουδαῖοι in John and ways in which the value of that term, and of John's larger presentation of Jesus, were influenced by John's experiences with the Jews of his own day. Van der Watt's analysis proceeds from the important observation that John's Gospel operates on two narrative levels that are intertwined in its presentation: on the cosmic, "heavenly" level God sends his Son into the world to reveal himself in a unique way that will bring life and salvation; this mission is played out on the physical, "earthly" level at which the historical Jesus engages other real-world characters in otherwise mundane situations. For John, the earthly narrative of the historical Jesus can only be correctly understood against the backdrop of the heavenly story of salvation; at the same time, the Jewish characters who inhabit John's Gospel, lacking this perspective, engage Jesus in terms of their own existing conceptions of salvation history and its related hopes. This narrative tension answers, for van der Watt, the first question noted above: the events of John's Gospel are played out on a stage that is "nearly exclusively Jewish";

to the extent that Christ's story can be acclimated to that setting, his (and John's) dialogue with Judaism is positive, but to the extent that it cannot Jesus comes into radical conflict with Jewish characters. As a case in point, the Fourth Gospel's claims that Jesus is Christ and King of Israel, while reflecting certain theological realities in the heavenly realm, are delivered "in a politically sensitive environment" in the earthly realm in which Jesus encounters Jewish people. Unlike these characters, and also unlike Jews of their own time, the Johannine Christians viewed that all hopes associated with these titles had already been somehow fulfilled in Jesus. But while these differing perspectives on kingship created conflict between John and other Jews, they in fact emerged just because John and other Jews shared certain common theological understandings and expectations. The vilification of Jesus's opponents in the gospel thus should be viewed as a stylized narrative exposition of "an inner-Jewish situation" of conflict.

The three essays in part 2 of the volume reverse conventional approaches to the question of John's relationship to Judaism, which have focused heavily on ways that Jewish Scriptures, beliefs, and institutions frame the presentation of Jesus in the Fourth Gospel, by asking how the Gospel of John might in turn serve as a source text for understanding first-century Judaism. Craig R. Koester notes that John's christological claims are situated in a story about the life of a remarkable first-century rabbi, a story whose settings include many details that are not directly tied to the gospel's distinctive theological perspective. Methodologically, Koester creates a dialogue between the Fourth Gospel and later rabbinic materials, with a view to identifying parallels between them in the areas of temple practice, use of the title Rabbi, synagogue liturgy (particularly the nature and role of preaching), and popular folk beliefs in pre-70 Judea and Galilee. Inasmuch as John's presentation of these issues and themes predates the rabbinic sources by at least century, his gospel can serve as a potential reference point for measuring the historical value of the presentations in those texts, and Koester finds that John indeed sheds important light on topics that are otherwise "not clearly attested in Jewish texts from the first century or earlier." Koester thus touches on the first question above, John's positive interactions with Jewish beliefs and institutions, while being careful to consider the third question regarding ways that John's experiences may have colored his presentation of those institutions.

Also directly addressing the first question above, Catrin H. Williams's entry proceeds from the observation that the Fourth Gospel's indebtedness to and embeddedness within the larger universe of first-century Judaism is particularly evident in John's appropriation of Israel's Scriptures to characterize Christ. Williams considers ways that John's use of Scripture might serve as a source for understanding Jewish hermeneutics and exegesis in the first century rather than vice versa. This methodology allows for an analysis of the gospel that does not view other Jewish texts as "background" to John's presentation but that instead understands John's contribution "as part of a broader Jewish religious and cultural environment." As a case study, Williams considers ways that John and other Jewish sources (including both later rabbinic sources and also contemporary documents) utilize the interpretive device *gezerah shavah*, a technique that connects scriptural texts on the basis of shared words or phrases and then reads them in parallel with a view to limiting or expanding the meaning of one or the other (or both). Like other ancient Jewish texts, the Fourth Gospel utilizes serial quotations of passages from the Hebrew Bible and creates composite/conflated citations on the basis of common terms. While the conclusions John derives from these texts in support of his christological agenda obviously differ radically from those of other Jewish documents of the period, the "mutual exegetical interest in catchword combinations helps to position John's Gospel as a significant participant in and valuable witness to the range of interpretative possibilities within Jewish exegetical activity during the first century CE." Here again, the Fourth Gospel is shown to be profoundly connected to its Jewish roots even at points where it differs most significantly from mainstream Jewish understandings.

Finally in this section, Harold W. Attridge's entry skillfully combines the concerns of the second and third questions above—the identity of the Jews in John and how their characterization in the gospel might relate to John's own real-world experiences with members of this group—to explore how the Fourth Gospel might enhance our understanding of first-century ethical discourse. As Attridge notes, the role of the Ἰουδαῖοι shifts through the course of John's narrative, distinctly in such a way that positive reactions to Jesus on the part of this group completely disappear after the end of Jesus's public ministry in chapter 12. While through much of the Book of Signs Jewish responses to Jesus are mixed, the comments of the high priest Caiaphas following the resurrection of Lazarus mark a turning point: it is better for Jesus to die than for the nation to be destroyed (11:49–50). Viewed through the lens of ancient philosophical discourse on ethics, Caiaphas's determination and the resolution of the Jews as a group to destroy Jesus following its pronouncement would reflect a line of argument based on the "beneficial" rather than "the good": while it would be politically expedient for the rulers to sacrifice Jesus, most Greco-Roman moralists and ancient rabbis would not have judged it good to act from this motive rather than on the basis of principle. Specifically, while ancient ethics may have viewed it as a noble deed for Jesus to sacrifice himself on behalf of the nation, Caiaphas's notion that it would be right for others to do this to him for sake of expedience would be widely rejected. In this respect, the Fourth Gospel's presentation of the morality of the ruling Jews' rejection of Jesus both reflects and illustrates a common ethical norm: right action proceeds from right reasoning; since Caiaphas's reasoning is unethical (expedience over principle), his actions must be also. John's emphasis that such reasoning was that of the ruling class doubtless reflects his own experiences with the Jewish community of his own day, whose leaders have also used flawed reasoning to wrongfully discourage their compatriots from accepting Jesus.

The eight essays in part 3 of the volume, constituting the bulk of the discussion, touch in a variety of ways on all six questions above while proceeding from the third: What was John's relationship to the Jews of his own day, and how has that experience colored the presentation of the Ἰουδαῖοι in the Fourth Gospel? Adele Reinhartz's entry continues her research program on this question by critically engaging Martyn's two-level reading of the Fourth Gospel as an allegory for hostilities between the Johannine community and the synagogue. While Martyn discredited the historical validity of the gospel's suggestion that those who confessed Christ were already being put out of the synagogue during Jesus's lifetime, he emphatically asserted this historical reality in John's own post-70 context. In Reinhartz's view, the enduring popularity of Martyn's proposal has less to do with its historical claims, which have been widely challenged, than with its mode of argumentation: the theory's success was less a function of its intrinsic value than of the elegance of Martyn's presentation. A more adequate approach, Reinhartz argues, would focus on the interaction between the third and second questions above: how was the identity of the Jews being defined, and perhaps redefined, in John's own context? Viewed from this angle, it becomes clear that John's implied audience is not an excommunicated Jew who no longer has access to the synagogue but rather a participant in the synagogue who does not see belief in Jesus as incompatible with Jewish identity. Put another way, "rather than reflecting a parting of the ways that had already happened—traumatically through expulsion—the gospel hopes to create a parting of the ways between its hearers and the Jews among whom they may have lived." John, in other words, is not suffering a loss of Jewish identity but is rather attempting to redefine it. Returning to the sixth question above, Reinhartz's model opens space for contemporary readings of the Gospel of John that do not inadvertently normalize the notion that early Christians were victims of Jewish hostility, or that Judaism and Christianity are inherently in tension.

Jonathan Bernier's entry, a concise summary of his earlier monograph on the subject (2013), approaches the Fourth Gospel's presentation of the Jews in direct dialogue with the concerns of the fourth question above: how might John's characterization reflect historical realities in the relationship between Jesus himself and his Jewish contemporaries? Building on recent research into the synagogue as a social institution in the late Second Temple period, Bernier contends that the much-discussed references to believers in Jesus being "put out of the synagogue" (becoming *ἀποσυνάγωγος*) "should be understood to suppose institutional realities that were altogether plausible in the pre-70 period"—that is, during the lifetime of Jesus as well as John. In Bernier's view, much of the confusion over this issue has resulted from a misunderstanding of what John seeks to portray. While supporters of the Martyn hypothesis have tended to understand explusion in the technical sense of formal excommunication from a religious community, John 9:22; 12:42; and 16:2 seem to allude not to formal heresy trials but rather to informal acts of mob aggression inspired by the Pharisees, who viewed Jesus as heretical. Such actions would not reflect established judicial processes tied to fixed rabbinic rulings but rather spontaneous populist attempts to protect Jewish identity in the face of an apparent threat to its hegemony. For Bernier, then, John's portrayal of the Jews, and particularly the Pharisees, as hostile to Jesus's followers and prone to informal acts of aggression toward them fits well with the sociological dimensions of the pre-70 synagogue and should therefore be located primarily in the historical relationship between Jesus and the Jews rather than in the later relationship between Judaism and the Johannine community.

Craig A. Evans's entry takes the arguments of both Martyn and Bernier as a starting point to address a key concern tied to the third question above, the extent to which the presentation of the Jews may reflect John's own experiences. In terms of scope, Evans expands the discussion in an attempt to locate not only the Fourth Gospel but also the Johannine Epistles against a historical backdrop that might assist our understandings of the contexts and the dates of all four documents. Proceeding from a close review of Reinhartz's research, Evans concludes that some aspects of the

Johannine affirmation of believers in the face of Jewish hostility seem most likely to reflect the language of, or at least the social setting envisioned by, the twelfth "benediction against heretics" of the later synagogue liturgy. Similarly, Evans reads the descriptions of the antichrists mentioned in 1–3 John against a late first-century Jewish context and concludes that these individuals, who deny Jesus's identity as Messiah, are most likely once-Christian Jews who have abandoned the Johannine community and returned to the synagogue. Similarly, the letters to the seven churches in Rev 2–3, a book Evans judges "Johannine" in some sense, depend heavily on Jewish concepts and include a number of polemical statements against the Jews/synagogue. These observations suggest that 1–3 John and Revelation were written in an environment where opposition from the synagogue and/or individuals within the synagogue was perceived as normal by Johannine Christians. Such a situation, also envisioned within the presentation of the Jews in the Fourth Gospel, would tend to locate all five of these Johannine books in the late first century and would also suggest that John's presentation of the Ἰουδαῖοι has been heavily colored by the realities of that setting.

Joel Marcus's entry begins with a reaffirmation of the consensus view on the third question above, that John's presentation is heavily colored by negative experiences with Jews of his own time. Marcus proceeds to emphasize an overlooked factor relating to the second question, the identity of those characters whom John calls Jews, by noting that the Jews in the Fourth Gospel (and John's own situation) would include not only the larger Jewish populace and the Pharisees but also John the Baptist and his followers. The Fourth Gospel consistently presents the Baptist as self-admittedly inferior to Jesus, and this has often been explained as John the Evangelist's own attempt to persuade followers of the Baptist in his own day of Christ's superiority. Marcus notes, however, that John's presentation of the Baptist's relationship to Jesus never rises to the level of hostility evident in the Fourth Gospel's portrait of the Pharisees, whom Martyn had identified as John's primary antagonists in his own late first-century context. This suggests that, while Johannine Christians and followers of the Baptist may have competed for converts, the former likely outnumbered the latter and viewed them as potential believers rather than a source of threat. Perhaps both groups had been marginalized in the emerging debate over Jewish identity and experienced similar pressures from the Pharisees to abandon their respective heterodox beliefs in new revelatory figures (Jesus and the Baptist). In this respect, whether or not John's Gospel accurately portrays the relationship between the historical Jesus and his antagonists, it opens a window onto the emerging complexity of Jewish identity in the decades following the Jewish War.

Lori Baron's entry combines the concerns of the first and third questions above, ways in which the Fourth Gospel appropriates Jewish themes and symbols and also ways in which John's own experience has colored both this appropriation and his portrayal of Jewish characters, in a case study focused on John's use of a central element of Jewish piety, the Shema confession/prayer derived from Deut 6:4–5. On the one hand, John's appropriation and development of this passage is thoroughly Jewish, reflecting an eschatological reading of the Shema derived from the canonical prophets (particularly Ezekiel) that emphasizes national unity and restoration; on the other hand, John applies this theme specifically to Christ and the Christian community in a way that likely reflects the emerging tensions between the church and the synagogue in the late first century. In Baron's view, this reading is consistent with the realities of John's experiences of the trauma of 70 CE and subsequent expulsion from the synagogue, a situation similar in many ways to that of Ezekiel and one that also required Jewish individuals such as John to forge a new identity based on hope in an eschatological future. For John, this hope was based on an understanding of Christ's role as the founder of a new eschatological community of the exiled that, ironically, excluded many of Jewish heritage. Baron thus concludes that both the famous discourse of the Johannine Jesus on the good shepherd (John 10) and his final prayer (John 17) speak directly to John's own post-70 situation.

William R. G. Loader's entry expands the first and fifth questions above, John's appropriation of Jewish theological themes and the relationship between his presentation and those of other early Christian texts, by considering the soteriologies of both the Fourth Gospel and the Gospel of Matthew. As scholars have often noted, while Matthew and John both emphasize the atoning significance of Jesus's death, both also include prepassion scenes and sayings that would imply that Jesus offered forgiveness and salvation in various ways throughout his ministry. How can this tension be explained? While many scholars have attempted to address this problem by minimizing textual evidence that works against their own conclusions and highlighting evidence that supports them, Loader seeks an answer in "the strongly Jewish background of both documents [Matthew and John]." In reference to the third and fourth questions above, Loader finds a solution not in the life and message of the historical Jesus but rather in the interplay between Matthew and John and the respective

Jewish communities with which they were in dialogue. Specifically, while both Matthew and John attribute saving value to Jesus's death, they do not do so to the exclusion of other means of receiving forgiveness; further, John's soteriology, typical of Jewish thought of that time, remains profoundly theocentric, the main difference being that John depicts faithfulness to God as a function of belief in Christ rather than obedience to torah. Loader's conclusions also point to the sixth question above, ways that John's perspective might participate in contemporary interfaith dialogue, by suggesting that both Matthew and John open space for a broader conception of sin and salvation.

R. Alan Culpepper's entry, like Loader's, provides a focused comparison between the Johannine and Matthean presentations of Jews and Judaism, both produced in the "period following the destruction of Jerusalem and the temple in 70 CE when what it meant to be Jewish was being redefined both among the postwar Pharisees and Jewish Christians." In reference to the first question above, Culpepper observes that both Matthew and John appear to be addressing Christian Jews "near the point of their separation from the synagogue"; not surprisingly, then, both searched for resources for the establishment of a new identity within Jewish scriptural and theological themes. Systematically addressing the concerns of the fifth question above, ways that John's presentation of the Jews and Judaism compares to other ancient witnesses, Culpepper proceeds to compare the Johannine and Matthean presentations of seven key themes, including analogies between Jesus and Moses; Christ's relationship to the Jewish Scriptures; key institutions of ancient Judaism (law, Sabbath, purity, and synagogue); and the posture and role of the Pharisees. Overall, and addressing the concerns of the third question above regarding the impact of John's own experiences on his presentation, Culpepper concludes that the Gospel of John reflects a situation in which believers are no longer "organically related to the synagogue"—in fact, at almost every point, John appears to be further than Matthew along the trajectory of separation from the Jewish origins of the emerging Christian faith. While Matthew appears to be reinterpreting his Jewish heritage in a way that would make it possible for Christian Jews to maintain their religious identity, John's reinterpretation is aimed at a group engaged "in a polemical hermeneutic" that seeks to justify what appears to be a past break with the synagogue with a view to forging a new religious heritage. Thus, Matthew and John both color Jesus, his world, and his opponents in ways that significantly reflect their own social locations.

Finally in this section, Jörg Frey's entry addresses the third question above, the relationship between John's presentation and his own context, through an ingeniously localized reading of the Fourth Gospel in the context of late first-century Ephesus, traditionally (and still by the majority of scholars) viewed as the location in which the Johannine books were composed. Like Koester and Williams, Frey proposes to use the Johannine writings as a data point in considerations of the much-debated "parting of the ways" between ancient Judaism and early Christianity: What can we learn from John about whether, when, or how Christians began to distinguish themselves from Jews and/or vice versa? Frey concludes that the available data do not allow one to answer this question in a global or linear way but instead suggest that the separation happened in different ways and at different moments in time in different geographical contexts. His analysis explores the fifth question above, John's relationship to other early Christian witnesses, by comparing the Johannine presentation to other documents connected to and/or interested in Ephesus, including Acts, Revelation, and the letters of Paul and Ignatius. The evidence suggests that Ephesus was a microcosm of the state of early Christianity, with diverse Christian communities existing side by side with one another, a vibrant Jewish community centered in the synagogue, and the larger world. In respect to the third and fourth questions above, Frey contends that John's suggestion that Jesus followers might be expelled from synagogues cannot represent Jesus's historical context but must be understood as a retrojection of realities from John's own time and own relationship with the synagogue and its leaders. Through reasoned analysis of the other documents under consideration and the strains of early Christianity that they represent, Frey sees the Johannine departure from the synagogue as a complex phenomenon resulting from the development of a high view of Jesus that other Jews could not accept combined with the challenges to social identity raised by the Roman imposition of the *fiscus Iudaicus* tax on individuals classified by the state as Jewish after the Jewish War. Overall, the Johannine evidence represents one particular and unique point on the total spectrum of emerging Jewish-Christian relations, a point characterized particularly by a sudden and traumatic departure of the distinct Christian group.

The four essays in part 4 of the volume focus primarily on the sixth question above, significantly addressing the hermeneutical implications of reading John's presentation of the Jews in a modern context. Each author explores this issue in dialogue with aspects of the other questions to provide an exegetically balanced perspective. Thus, Reimund Bieringer's entry provides a helpful review of research on John and Judaism at the fifteenth anniversary of the historic Leuven colloquium on that topic, which produced the milestone volume *Anti-Judaism and the Fourth Gospel* (2001). As Bieringer notes, this collection and the larger international research project that produced it in many ways signaled a shift away from considerations of John's anti-Semitism toward ways that the Fourth Gospel may be read as positively engaging its Jewish heritage and context. This more hopeful approach, as Bieringer also observes, has generally been framed by question one above (John's positive appropriation of Jewish themes and concepts) and thus is driven by a historical-critical impetus that seeks to redefine the gospel's relationship to the Judaism from which it emerged, particularly in regard to reconsiderations of the Martyn-Brown hypothesis, rather than by hermeneutical or theological considerations of the contemporary impact of certain readings of the text. While affirming the achievements of such research, Bieringer reasserts his earlier warning that exegetes must take seriously "a dangerous potential in the theology of the Gospel of John that goes beyond the first-century conflict and inner-Jewish dispute" and into contemporary interfaith relations. Part 2 of Bieringer's paper provides a convenient summary of research on John and Judaism since 2001, with particular focus on several significant projects conducted at KU Leuven. Touching on the concerns of question two above (Who are the Jews in John?), Bieringer suggests that the term Ἰουδαῖοι may best be understood as a reference to Jewish individuals who do not accept John's own perspective on Jesus, a reading that shifts the conversation from a consideration of the ethnic identity of the Jews toward the religious orientation of Johannine characters who bear this label. Bieringer closes with a renewal of his earlier call to take seriously the anti-Jewish potential of the Fourth Gospel while also affirming its inclusive vision toward an eschatological horizon in which the love of God predominates.

Paul N. Anderson's entry explicitly frames the hermeneutical ramifications of John's presentation (question six) within a thorough reassessment of issues relating to questions one (the gospel's embeddedness in its Jewish context), three (the relationship between the gospel's presentation of Jews and the evangelist's own experiences with Jewish individuals), and four (the extent to which John's presentation reflects the circumstances of Jesus's career). After helpfully reviewing six major approaches to the meaning of the term Ἰουδαῖοι in John (question two above), Anderson concludes that all may be correct to some degree, inasmuch as the meaning of this word seems to shift from context to context within the gospel, perhaps as a reflection of the text's layered composition history. In fact, while the Fourth Gospel has obviously been used to justify anti-Semitism, Anderson proposes that John has been as much a victim as a source of these flawed readings of his text. The gospel itself is thoroughly Semitic in its worldview, orientation, and presentation of Christ and his world; anti-Semitic readings have therefore reflected more the spirits of their own ages and the widening parting of the ways between Christianity and Judaism in the second century and beyond than anything truly native to the gospel. In Anderson's view, the evangelist does not present Judaism negatively but rather reflects in his gospel his own evolving conflict with the Jewish religious authorities of his own time. Further, and reflecting the concerns of question four above, one must seriously consider the extent to which John's presentation may simply represent historical memory of events from Jesus's career rather than the evangelist's own theological perspective.

Ruth Sheridan's entry addresses the concerns of question six, how John's presentation of Jews and Judaism could and should be read today, through a critical review of analyses of John 8:31–34 in commentaries produced over the past century. Sheridan's target passage is notorious for its concentration of statements that have historically fueled and validated Christian anti-Semitism, particularly the notions that Jews need to accept "the truth" of Christ so that they can be freed from their slavery to sin and that Jewish claims to be the seed of Abraham are misguided, especially in view of the fact that Jesus proceeds to label them children of the devil (8:39–44). Sheridan's case study is particularly significant because it tends to expose ways that biblical scholars can and have implicitly affirmed the anti-Semitic potential of the Fourth Gospel even when they do not intend to do so. As she demonstrates, many commentators have interpreted the Jews' claim that Abraham is their father (8:33) not as a commonsense rejoinder to what appears to be an ambiguous statement by Jesus ("the truth will set you free," v. 32) but rather as an expression of nationalistic pridefulness and spiritual entitlement. The significance of these conclusions is magnified by the fact that commentaries as a genre operate under a mantel of assumed objectivity that has tended to exempt them from responsibility for the promotion and popularization of biases and stereotypes, in this case particularly stereotypes about the identity and character of Jews. Methodologically, those commentators who have avoided reproducing or magnifying the potential anti-Semitism of the passage have done so by returning to the first question above, exploring how John's presentation of the Jews in this passage aligns with other texts from antiquity, including Jewish texts that explore the question of Jewish identity from a positive, in-group perspective. In this important case, commitment to a neutral or positive posture regarding the Fourth Gospel's engagement with the Judaism of its day tends to empower readings that avoid patronizing presentations of John's Jewish characters.

The question of John's place in contemporary Christian thought and dialogue is also prominent throughout Noam E. Maran's entry, which significantly expands the above discussion of the document *Nostra Aetate* in reflection on its fiftieth anniversary in 2015. Maran characterizes the declaration as an unprecedented call for positive dialogue between Jews and Catholics on the basis of a renewed understanding of the Scriptures, including particularly the Gospel of John. At the same time, Maran notes, the question of how the gospel might be interpreted today is ultimately intertwined with the first and fourth questions above: whether or how this text might reflect events from the life of the historical Jesus, and whether or to what extent our understanding of that reflection accounts for the fact that John himself was a Jew. In Maran's view, the historical and hermeneutical challenges of the Fourth Gospel are best addressed through a foundationalist approach, one that acknowledges historical realities in Jesus's and John's respective relationships to the Jews of their own times but also "take[s] up the whole text and discredit[s] that which offends, and … emphasize[s] the overriding messages of love, hope, and redemption that characterize the foundation of sacred religious texts."

Overall, the present volume, collectively and in its individual entries, reorients discussion of the nature, historical origins, and hermeneutical implications of John's presentation of the Ἰουδαῖοι. The discussion is timely, not only on the advent of the fiftieth anniversary of Martyn's milestone *History and Theology in the Fourth Gospel* (1968) but also at the beginning of a new millennium of religious discourse and dialogue.

"Is Jesus the King of Israel?": Reflections on the Jewish Nature of the Gospel of John

Jan G. van der Watt

The diversity of views and opinions as well as the complexity of the issue of the Jews in the Gospel of John (hereafter John) can be overwhelming (see Bieringer et al. 2001a). Reasons for this are also multiple and challenging and are in a certain sense a classical illustration of the difficulties of reading and applying ancient texts today.

These differences of opinion are wide ranging, dealing with a variety of issues, such as struggling to solve the tensions created by the intensity of the negative language toward οἱ Ἰουδαῖοι in John, asking whether John is anti-Jewish,[1] reconstructing a possible historical scenario to explain

1. The tension between the positive and negative remarks related to the use of the Ἰουδαῖοι in John remains a contentious issue in Johannine scholarship. Schnelle (1999), for instance, estimates that about two-thirds of the references to the Jews in John are positive, while Petersen (2008, 33) opines that of the seventy-one occurrences of the word Ἰουδαῖος in John most of them are used negatively, not denying the significant number that are positive. This illustrates the difficulty in determining the ambiguous use of this term in John. It is not used with a single meaning, which complicates the analysis. Zimmermann (2013) gives a very good description of the variety of ways in which this term is used in John. Some feel that the Gospel of John is not anti-Jewish in its intention, and a variety of arguments are used to motivate this position, including that it is an inner-Jewish debate, that the Jews in the gospel are only a narrative construct, and that it reflects Christian identity replacing Jewish identity among Johannine believers. At the other end of the spectrum are those who declare the gospel as clearly anti-Jewish because of sections such as 8:44 (branding) or 14:6 (Christology). To deal with the situation, approaches such as censorship of the text of John or simple acceptance of the fact of the matter are suggested. In between a large variety of views carrying different emphases are found, either playing down one side or the other, or proposing an interpretation of the different views to reach a tempered view of both sides. Beutler (2001, 230) makes an interesting remark, namely, that the

the diverse activities of Jews in John (see Tomson 2001, 305; Dunn 2001, 62–64), dealing with the *Wirkungsgeschichte* especially after the Holocaust that led to diverse presuppositions related to current sociocultural pressures (see van Belle 2013, 119–50, esp. 150; Carson 2007, 143–44; Broer 1991, 326; Reinhartz 2001b, 355–56), and the ethics of reading (canonical) texts in light of current-day interreligious debates (see Culpepper 2001a; Söding 2001; de Jonge 2001)[2] that challenge hermeneutical applications of the material today (see Frey 2004, 33–35; Petersen 2008, 49–53; Reinhartz 2004, 415). The remark that the debate reached an impasse is not uncommon, and judging by the bulk of literature teeming with diverging opinions, this view might not be far off the mark.[3]

An overview of this debate will not be given here, since it is widely available (see Bieringer 2001a). Although the same points are consistently debated over and over again, in my opinion there are some areas that could still benefit from further consideration. These are, for instance, the at times confusing use of terminology such as *Jews* in John or *anti-Judaism* and also aspects of hermeneutics, the ethics of reading canonical texts, and the implications for the canon and Christianity as religion in light of the different positions taken in current-day interreligious debates.

variety of uses of the term Ἰουδαῖος implies that the readers of the gospel would be able to differentiate between the uses. This of course fits more a situation from the inside than from the outside. In the latter case one would expect the opponents to see their opposition as a more unified entity.

2. Wengst (2000, 20) correctly notes, "Dieselben Aussagen, in veränderter Situation wiederholt, bleiben nicht dieselbe Aussagen."

3. The identity of οἱ Ἰουδαῖοι in the gospel is a widely discussed topic in recent literature. Keener (2003, 171–232) gives a detailed overview over the Jewish context of the gospel. The term *Jews* should not be identified with modern Jews, neither with all genealogical Jews in ancient times. Jesus and his disciples were also Jews. See de Jonge 2001; Schnelle 1999; von Wahlde 2000; Lieu 2001, 126–43, here 135–39. De Boer (2001) argues that the Jews indicated in the gospel are a socioreligious category of people who identify themselves as "disciples of Moses" (9:28). See Schnackenburg 1968, 287; Brown 1970, lxx–lxxv; Ashton 1994, 44–49; 1985; Köstenberger 2004, 231; Motyer 1997; Hakola 2005b. Barrett (1978, 314) sees Jews as a technical term for John. No effort to identify the Jews as such will be made here. The Jews will be described according to the material given in the gospel itself, and it can at least be argued that the Jews exist in this narrative as a fictive group with these qualities. I would not like to go further than that here. See also the balanced discussion of Jesus and Judaism in Smith 1999, 34–38, 45; Petersen 2008, 49–53; van Belle 2013, 119–50.

In this essay two issues that still need such further consideration will receive attention,[4] namely, (1) What is the significance of Jesus being called Messiah, King of the Jews/Israel for understanding the position of the Jews in John in relation to the Johannine group? What do we learn from this for our understanding of the Johannine group's perception of their own identity in relation to their Jewish heritage? (2) Claims that the Johannine group made about Jesus, not the least that he is King of the Jews, of course, led to conflict between the protagonists and antagonists in the narrative. Within this context strong rhetorical remarks (vilification) are found aimed at the Jewish opponents not having God or even being children of the devil, and, on the other hand, the Jewish opponents calling Jesus a Samaritan or having a demon. The question now is: what can we learn from the rhetoric of these oral conflicts in John? These two issues might shed additional light on our efforts to understand οἱ Ἰουδαῖοι in John.

1. John as Transcendental Narrative

Before dealing with these two issues, the complex nature of space in the plot of John must first be noted. Two clear spaces, each with its own narrative, are presented, namely, the above and the below, heaven and earth.

The above represents the divine, transcendental space of the unseen God, the Creator and King. John narrates certain events taking place in this transcendental space, forming its own transcendental narrative. In this transcendental narrative the reader learns about what happened in heaven, about the Father having a Son, the preexistent Logos, who is in a communicative and loving relationship in the bosom of the Father, knowing him intimately. Out of love the Father equipped his Son for his mission and sent him into the world to bring eternal life to his people and thus to gather God's family, a family that will share the Spirit of truth on earth and for whom there is a place in the house of the Father where they will spend eternal life. This transcendental narrative eludes historical verification, since it unfolds in the transcendental reality of God.

Likewise a narrative unfolds within the physical world, the *κόσμος*. This is the narrative of people such as John (the Baptist), Jesus and his

4. For instance, neither of these themes was addressed in the comprehensive volume on anti-Judaism by Bieringer et al. 2001a.

disciples, people getting married, a woman at a well, Jews in Jerusalem, and so on.

Through the incarnation of Jesus, God's divine reality is introduced into this world, and the realities described by the two narratives start to interrelate. Once this transcendental reality became incarnated through Jesus into the earthly historical reality, interaction started to take place, and the presence of the transcendental reality gradually unfolds within the events, actions, and lives of people on earth. This is what incarnation is all about. The transcendental narrative of the Son of God then heuristically serves to enlighten what is happening on earth among the Jews. Human events become understandable in light of the transcendental narrative. Through the incarnation of Jesus, coming to his own, the transcendental reality, expressed in his transcendental narrative, is introduced in and integrated with the earthly reality, impacting directly on the understanding of the existing earthly narrative, like a light shining into the darkness (8:12). To understand earthly events, for instance, what happens when Jesus acts or speaks, how the behavior of the Jewish opponents toward Jesus should be understood, and so on, this transcendental narrative provides the perspective within which these physical events should be interpreted and explained. For example, Jesus's death on the cross is an event in physical history, but its real meaning is explained in the light of God's transcendental narrative: he sent his Son to lay down his life on behalf of others and take it up again (10:17–18). In light of the transcendental narrative, earthly actions and events are interpreted to make sense.

Obviously the Jews, including Jesus and his disciples, also had their traditional transcendental narrative, explaining why they go to the temple or feasts (2:11–25), why they read the Scriptures (5:39), or why wash themselves in purification (2:1–11). This narrative was inspired by God, but with a prophetic open-endedness—the hour will come, the Messiah-King will arrive. They were waiting for these expectations to be fulfilled as part of their narrative. They were therefore constantly looking out for possibilities in this direction (see, for instance, 1:19–28; 10:24; see also 4:25–30) on the level of expectations of the prophets and Messiah, the presence of the kingdom of God, Scriptures being fulfilled, or the power of God being illustrated anew. This "openness" of their narrative, expecting fulfillment, serves as a point of connection between the Jews' traditional narrative and the further revelation of God as it is presented in the transcendental narrative of John, where Jesus is the incarnated Word who makes the Father known.

With the engagement of Jesus with the Jews, Jesus directly and powerfully engages the expectations that were part of the Jews' traditional narrative. As these antennas of expectations of the Jewish tradition are touched by Jesus's incarnational presence, they are interpreted in light of the transcendental reality Jesus represents and are thus seen as fulfilled. This integration and interaction of these two narratives through the fulfillment of the traditional expectations "refreshes" and "adjusts" and even reorganizes the existing Jewish narrative related to the presence of God among his people. John argues that with the coming of the Son, who incarnates God's transcendental reality in the midst of his own people, God is now present through Jesus even when thinking in terms of temple, Scripture, festivals, and the like.

By accepting this Johannine transcendental narrative and allowing it to become the dominant and interpretative narrative in relation to the traditional Jewish narrative, the Jewish identity and life are redefined, leading to a new evaluation of especially their religious reality. The Jewish reality now has a new look that includes the Father and his house with many rooms, the Son with his self-sacrificing love, representing the temple, light, and truth. According to John, God's people, Israel, do not cease to exist but now exist as people who have eternal life, as people whose king is crucified as "King of the Jews." Likewise, John opines that those who do not acknowledge the incarnational reality of Jesus will not see it this way and thus will not be able to associate with this new reality.

Those who accept the incarnated reality with its enlightening narrative will now answer the question "Where can one find the God of Israel?" differently, since the transcendental narrative of Jesus connects with the Jewish tradition and its expectations and develops it further in light of the new eternal future. In this way the transcendental narrative becomes the heuristic and interpretative principle for existing Jewish, and eventually broader earthly, religious perspectives. This is, according to John, the major difference between the Jewish opponents and the Johannine believers: they shared the same traditional Jewish narrative but differed in the way they saw the impact of the incarnated transcendental narrative of Jesus on their shared traditional narrative.

The Jewish opponents did not accept this, and that caused considerable discussion and conflict not only among themselves but also with the believers. Jesus's Jewish opponents still held with zeal to their understanding of their traditional narrative of the transcendental reality as expressed in the temple, cultic rituals, Scripture, and the like, while the transcendental narrative as it is revealed by the Son formed the existential narrative of the disciples of Jesus. Thus the agenda for separation was set.

It should be noted that what is "on stage," that is, the narrative setting or space, is nearly exclusively Jewish.[5] The setting unfolds within the physical (Jewish), cultural, and religious confines (holy books, holy places, holy times, etc., were shared) of the Jews. It was a truly Jewish affair appealing to the Jewish God, Jewish Scriptures, Jewish prophecies, and Jewish religious language (the others, the Greeks—or Greek-speaking Jews—and Romans only play a peripheral role). The narratological differentiations developed through the unfolding of the plot are also inner-Jewish. It was not a matter of a foreign group overwhelming the Jews, destroying their holy place and replacing their traditions. It was their own who responded in a specific way to their own Scriptures, prophecies, and ultimately their own God, the Creator God of Israel (Wengst 2000, 40–43). Obviously, the different responses to Jesus caused conflict and indeed separation among the Jews (see John 7) that had consequences of their own for the self-identity of the Jews. Time will not allow us to explore this further, but it is nevertheless important to note for the further argument.

2. Behold, Your King Is Coming

In light of the above, we will now consider our first question, namely, what is the significance of the Jesus being called Messiah, King of the Jews/Israel for understanding the position of the Jews in John in relation to the Johannine group? The expression "kingdom of God" lacks the frequency and apparent prominence in John that it has in the Synoptic Gospels. Although there is a mosaic of perspectives[6] in John that enlightens the issue of God's presence among his people—such as the issues of new birth and life in the family of God, a form of predestination, or selfish love—recent research into the imagery of kingship in John has shown that it should be regarded as one of the major metaphorical networks in John (Busse 2006, 279–317). Kingship is first mentioned in 3:3, 5, but then John prefers to describe and unfold the identity of believers in terms of the concept of a family that shares eternal life (3:16 and further; see van der Watt 2000, 161–393).

5. It is debated to what measure John is a Jewish document (see Petersen 2008, 35, 44–45), but the setting is Jewish. See Wengst 2000, 282.

6. In reference to Zimmermann (2004), who illustrated the metaphorical dynamics of the gospel in terms of a mosaic. See also van der Watt 2000.

Ulrich Busse (2006, 303) has shown that conceptually the elements of the kingdom of God are present throughout the gospel in the form of typical royal actions such as judgment, protection, salvation, perhaps friendship, not to mention the sporadic direct references to kingship in 1:50; 3:3, 5; 6:15; and 12:13, 15, with the climax in chapters 18–20. Jesus is called Messiah, "King of Israel" by his disciples (Nathanael, 1:49), the "King of the Jews" according to Pilate (19:19–22), and "king of the daughter of Zion" (12:15), as Scripture says (Zech 9:9), drawing witnesses for his kingship from different perspectives and people. John Robinson (1970, 198) even goes so far as to claim that Messiah "is the category which controls Christology in the body of the Gospel." This remark might be a little exaggerated, especially in light of the prominence of the Son and his mission in John, but it nevertheless notes the importance of the concept of messiahship.

In the Johannine narrative the politically loaded remarks that Jesus is the Messiah, the Christ, King of Israel/Jews are made in a politically sensitive environment. These terms refer to political concepts that reflect the historical expectations and political aspirations of the Jews, based on their history and prophetic past.[7] A brief bird's-eye view on a rather high level of abstraction gives some perspective on these expectations.[8] In the sixth century BCE the Judeans lost their temple and their political autonomy and were exiled.[9] In their dire situation of being dispersed among other nations, they measured their experience in exile against what once was, namely, the kingdoms of David and Solomon. They, inter alia, understood their current situation as the result of their ancestors' disobedience toward God. However, since they regarded themselves as the elect people of God, their hope was focused on the liberating actions of God, which were expected according to the message of some of their prophets. In spite

7. Kaiser (2014, 67), remarks, "Mithin bezeichnet das Wort den Gesalbten und meint damit im vorliegenden Zusammenhang den König der Heilszeit aus Davids Geschlecht." See Isa 2:1–5; 9:6; 11:1–5; Mic 4:1–5. The Jews are aware that their prophecies are about to be fulfilled. They send a delegation to John to ask whether he is the one, which he denies, pointing to Jesus (1:19–34); the Jews who became Jesus's disciples link Jesus to the political expectations of the Jews (1:41–52); the crowds sense that Jesus could be their Messiah (7:26, 31; 10:24), and Pilate concludes that (19:19).

8. Obviously the history is much more complex than the description given here, but since the interest of this essay is in the broad lines that explain the situation at the time of Jesus, a broad description suffices.

9. The following paragraph follows the line of argument presented by Kaiser (2014, specifically 64).

of a variety of views,[10] one conviction was that the Messiah would come to restore the kingdom of God and would then rule in righteousness over his freed people and country, as well as over the kings and their nations, which will be subjected to him. This seems to form the broad master narrative for the expectations regarding the Messiah, to which John's narrative links. Daniel Boyarin (2014, 62) argues that the concept of messiahship was so well developed by the time of Jesus that "Alle Vorstellungen über Christus sind altvertraut; [das (der) Neue ist Jesus.] Es gibt nichts in der Lehre des Christus was neu ist, außer der Ausrufung *dieses* Menschen als Menschensohn."

Norman Gottwald gives another perspective on the history, which is also relevant to our discussion. In the history of Israel he identifies "a trajectory through three political horizons":

1. The *first horizon* includes the beginnings of Israel, when it practiced a form of decentralized politics embedded and diffused throughout its social institutions (approximately 1250–1000 BCE).
2. The *second horizon* refers to the "midlife" of Israel, when it adopted centralized autonomous politics in a double sense: specialized state institutions were developed with a monopoly of domestic power that was also autonomous over against other states (approximately 1000–586 BCE).
3. The *third horizon* represents the reconstituted life of Israel after the loss of statehood.[11] "They were forcibly subjected to a colonial form of centralized politics dictated by foreign sovereignties with which a native Israelite/Judahite hierarchy was empowered to act in local matters subject to the limits imposed by imperial powers" (Gottwald 2001, 15).

The situation of the Jewish people during the time of Jesus fell within the *third horizon*. In the Johannine narrative the Jews are embedded in Roman

10. Boyarin (2014) and J. J. Collins (2014), for instance, give overviews of the varying expectations in ancient Judaism. The expectation of a Messiah was strong but not the only expectation that existed. The Messiah was also seen in different ways, for instance, especially as a military messiah who will restore the kingdom of Israel, but there were also descriptions of a prophetic or priestly messiah.

11. The Hasmonean period, of course, represented a period of independence.

rule; they accept and confess that they are inherently part of the Roman Empire (11:48), at the end also claiming that Caesar is their king (19:15). They were allowed a measure of political autonomy by the Romans, which was administratively possible within the Roman Empire, but in essence their state and freedom were under Roman control (Gottwald 2001). They were, however, allowed to govern their cultural and religious matters, which were regarded as lover-level political matters by the Romans, and could even organize themselves in a council for this purpose (Gottwald 2001, 9). This was clearly reason enough for the Jews, also as portrayed in John, to passionately await the expected Messiah, the King of Israel, as the First Testament promised (12:12–19). The coming of the Messiah would mean freedom and new life.

This brings us to the perceptions of the Johannine group within such a political situation where the political reality consistently stood in the shade of Jewish eschatological expectations. The Johannine believers shared the same expectations as their fellow Jews, but with a difference: for them these promises of the coming kingdom were fulfilled in Jesus. This conviction formed and determined the self-understanding and identity of these believers. That is why they could see themselves as members of the true, prophesied kingdom of the God of Israel that was now powerfully and victoriously present in this world. They have a King, the Messiah, King of the Jews, through whom the kingdom of God became a reality, and they were part of it. They did not perceive their situation as a break from the history and promises of the God of Israel and the Scriptures, but as the legitimate and authentic progression of the fulfillment of what was promised. This was who they perceived themselves to be.

Substantiating the above view, Busse (2006, 303–17) aptly describes the centrality of the kingship and kingdom metaphor in John, identifying the Johannine group as part of the kingdom with Jesus as the Messiah, King of Israel/Jews.[12] As Messiah, Jesus displays the qualities of a true king in the gospel: all power is given to him (3:35; 5:20) to fulfill the tasks of an ideal (vassal) king, such as caring (chap. 6), shepherding and protecting his own (10:28–30), giving and interpreting the law (van der Watt 2016), as well as judging the world (5:19–24, 30; see also 8:16; 9:31–34; 10:17–18), ensuring the presence of God, the King, inter alia by being the symbolic

---

12. He shows that not only the terms *king/kingdom* are of importance, but also the "damaligen Mentalität" about king and kingdom, which is evident throughout the gospel.

temple (2:18–21). Otto Kaiser's (2014, 107) analysis of concept of Messiah in the First Testament convinces him that the Messiah-King, who was the mediator between God and his people (69), was expected to do four things, namely, to serve as cultic mediator between God and his people, sacrificing for their sin and praying for them in times of need (72–73); to be a just regent who protects righteousness, inter alia by looking after the poor and powerless (Ps 72; 1 Kgs 3:5–9; see Kaiser 2014, 73); to be a wise teacher of his people since through the Spirit of God he possesses knowledge of God that empowers him to rule with insight and resolve (75, 80–81); and to defend his country (77–80).[13] As such, the Messiah will be the universal "Prince of peace."[14] These qualities are all integrated in the Johannine description of Jesus that conceptually confirms but also enhances his role as Messiah.

The above information illustrates aptly that the Johannine group faithfully saw Jesus as the expected Jewish Messiah who inaugurated the promised kingdom of which they were part. The Johannine group did not experience themselves as standing apart from the Jewish expectations and traditions. Instead they saw themselves as being solidly part of the messianic expectations of the Jewish people. Boyarin (2014, esp. 63) points out that the teachings about Jesus basically added nothing to the Jewish expectations, except identifying Jesus as the Messiah. It is therefore not a matter that the concept of messiahship was adapted to "fit" Jesus. The followers of Jesus were convinced that Jesus fit the profile of the Messiah that was expected. They clearly committed themselves to the God of that particular history (the God that is worshiped in the temple in Jerusalem, 2:13; 4:20; see Lindars 1972, 98; Köstenberger 2004, 47; Keener 2003, 422). The God to whose kingdom they belong is the Creator God of Israel (1:1–5), who now shows even more grace through Jesus than through the Baptist or Moses (1:15–17). That is most probably also the reason there is such a positive attitude in John toward the religious and cultural goods of the Jews (see van der Watt 2005, 105–6) and even toward many of the activities of the Jewish opponents. In and through their shared Jewish tradition they make sense of what is happening to them by interpreting it in light

13. By linking Ps 72 and Isa 11:1–5, Kaiser (p. 76) also shows that the preexilic ideas were linked to the ideas of the rulership at the end of times (see Pss. Sol. 17:32–43).

14. Kaiser (2014, 81) remarks, "der Sohn (Gottes) aus Davids Geschlecht (wird) als wahrer Friedenfürst herrschen."

of what they experience in and through the presence of Jesus.[15] Anybody who accepts that Jesus was sent by the Father will share in the salvation that comes from the Jews.

In political terms this represents the Johannine group's "national identity" as the people of God's kingdom, who find themselves in line with Moses and Abraham and can call Jesus their Messiah, King of Israel. This national identity of the members of the kingdom is linked to the national history of Israel (John 5 and 8) requiring absolute loyalty and obedience toward the God of Israel, through faith, trust in, and acceptance of the Messiah-King (6:28). The promised kingdom is now present as eschatological reality among the Jews and the rest of the world.

This eschatological coming and presence of the kingdom does not happen next to or outside the ordinary Jewish narrative. It takes place as an inherent part of what is expected within the Jewish narrative as continuation of God's eschatological presence among his people. It is not a new story but the continuation of the old story, although it is new.[16] There is an organic and logical growth in the existential religious reality of the Jews.

We must now remind ourselves of the plot of the gospel, as R. Alan Culpepper (1980; 1983) identified it (1:11–13): his own did not want to receive him (1:9–11); however, those who received him were granted the right to be children of God (1:12–13). In John the promised Messiah-King (1:41, 45) confronts the Jews as well as the wider world with the reality of the incarnated eschatological kingdom of God, of which he is the king. He challenges his Jewish opponents, who are convinced that they are the authoritative and legal representatives of God's people, with the message of the arrival of God's eschatological kingdom among them. He invites these fellow Jews to be part of the coming of God's promised kingdom that may be entered by acceptance of the Messiah and spiritual birth (1:12–13; 3:1–8). This is based on the transcendental narrative that came into effect with the incarnation of Jesus. From John's perspective the question is whether the Jews, his own (1:11), are going to accept their own king or acknowledge Caesar as king. For understanding the Jewish or anti-Jewish nature of the gospel, this seems to be a crucial point.

---

15. Van Belle (2013, 147) emphasizes that Jesus is presented as strongly associating himself with the Jewish beliefs (4:22) and messiahship (4:25–26).

16. This is in reference to the remark that the law is old but also new (1 John 2:7–8).

What we see in the Johannine narrative is a description of the return of the Jewish people from the *third horizon* to the *second horizon* (see Gottwald above), that is, from being dominated by an external power to belonging to the independent and victorious kingdom of God, where love and peace reign. Even the "prince of this world" is thrown out (12:31; 14:30), claiming cosmic victory. The Johannine narrative presents believers as the existential and real expression of the prophetically announced *second horizon* that was expected by the Jews. The expected kingdom with its King is here, although not in the form the Jews expected (6:15). Associated with this horizon is absolute power and rulership. The victorious Messiah-King arrived, establishing supreme power through victory over the composite enemy, including the "prince of this world."

This makes Israel what it is supposed to be—the victorious kingdom of God. It is envisioned as it is portrayed in the First Testament as the primary and only true kingdom and thus a political entity that is greater than the world has to offer. God and the King of Israel again form the focal points in the cosmos that invite everybody to enter the light of this kingdom.[17] This is in no way anti-Jewish but profoundly Jewish.[18] The highest expectations of the Jews are fulfilled: their king is here. To interpret this

---

17. On the split between the Jews and Christians, Hiemstra (2009, 193) notes that "Jewish Christians started to think of themselves as the 'real Israel' in contrast to those Jews who did not recognize Jesus as the Messiah, sent by God. In this context the position of the mainstream Judaism to exclude Jewish Christians from their theological system is the other side of the coin." He sees this gradual process as moving to a decisive point of separation at the turn of the first century, when Nerva in 96 CE turned against Christians. He adds, further, that at the end of the first century the Christians were so well identified that Jewish Christians were treated as Christians and not Jews (p. 198). Bultmann (1941, 87) also notes that once such a clear and decisive split occurs between two groups, the description of the groups becomes less detailed. The tendency will then rather be to deal with the Jews as a unified group.

18. See also the views of Rensberger (1999, 138) and Vouga (1993, 88). De Boer (2001, 261–62) also opines that one should not read texts out of context, especially the ones with anti-Jewish tendencies. The narrative contexts of these sayings are part of an inner-Jewish debate, people who are all Jews. For instance, in John 8 the Jewishness of all parties involved who share in the Jewish traditions is continuously stated (see 8:12–14, 20, 33, 39–41, 52–58). Reinhartz (2004, 342) goes against this line of interpretation by claiming that the gospel is inherently anti-Jewish, and it is not the perspective of the reader that results in such a reading. See also Casey (2010, 511–12); Culpepper (2001b, 90–91), who also acknowledges the anti-Judaistic nature of John, taking a nuanced view; and Tomson (2001, 340).

as anti-Jewish per se would not make sense in this Johannine context. What is at stake is whether the reader accepts this point of view, but that is another issue.

This view was, of course, controversial within the confines of the variety of other views within a not-so-homogeneous Judaism during the first century. The claim that the kingdom of God is here through the person of Jesus caused conflict with the Jewish opponents since they did not want to progress on the road to the Father (14:6). They remained loyal to their own views regarding themselves as the authoritative and legal representatives of the Jewish people. E. P. Sanders (1985, 280–81) formulated this aptly: "If we give full weight to Jesus' extraordinary statements about the kingdom and about the role of his disciples—and thus, by implication, about himself—we have no trouble seeing that his claims were truly offensive.... There were *specific* issues at stake between Jesus and the Jewish hierarchy, and ... the specific issues revolved around a *basic question:* who spoke for God?" This is the existential question put by John.[19] The position offered by John is that the Jesus-events should be interpreted solidly within the Jewish tradition, announcing the coming of the King of the Jews, but they should also, as transcendental narrative, heuristically determine the understanding of the earthly events.

3. Vilification as Genre?

If the argument is correct that John is not aiming at being anti-Jewish, why is the rhetoric against Jesus's Jewish opponents in places so sharp? By asking this question the difficult area of the vilifying language of John is entered. In ancient times, the rhetorical technique of vilification was widely used in especially argumentative communication to discredit opponents and develop disassociation with the opponents (see L. T. Johnson 1989). Strong words and expressions were therefore part of the rhetorical strategy used in speech conflicts (*Streitgesprächen*; see de Boer 2001, 264–65). Vilification as rhetorical device aims at stereotyping[20] or labeling people negatively (Malina and Rohrbaugh 1998, 33), thus negotiating identity.

19. Due to space the question cannot be treated in detail whether rejecting Jesus as Messiah and therefore not being regarded as part of this eschatological kingdom is anti-Jewish or not.

20. On stereotyping see Aristotle, *Pol.* 7.6.1–2; Josephus, *Life* 352; Strabo, *Geogr.* 16.2.23; Vergil, *Aen.* 2.65. See also Malina and Neyrey (1996, 169–74); du Toit (1994).

Through the use of vilification a reality is rhetorically created in which the opponents are negatively presented, mostly with overemphasis, to gain ground in the argument.[21] The dualistic nature of Johannine rhetoric also contributes to the absoluteness of the presentation of the different contrasting elements in the Gospel of John (van Belle 2013, 137).

Here it is important to be aware of "referential fallacy," whereby the image created by the use of vilification is not to be equated with the actual or complete image of the persons vilified (see du Toit 1994, 404). When vilifying or stereotyping a person, simple descriptions or accurate portrayals are not the aim. In this regard Knust indicates that accusations leveled by some Roman authors against early Christians "may be understood as entirely believable to his audience—not because the accusation was thought to be 'true' but because it efficiently expressed a collective distaste for the characteristic Christian refusal to participate in the common culture of city and empire" (2006, 7). To read or interpret vilification as precise factual expression of reality is to commit a genre error.

Vilification is present throughout the Gospel of John and is to be found on the lips of people on all sides of the conflict (see van der Watt and Kok 2012 for a more detailed discussion). Jesus, for instance, calls his opponents children of the devil, while the opponents call Jesus a Samaritan (Jesus is not literally a Samaritan, but they vilify him through stereotyping), a blasphemer and evildoer, and even as having a demon. He is thus vilified as somebody with no social standing with the Jewish community. So, he is denied his Jewishness by his Jewish opponents, who (wrongly) call him a Samaritan. In this process it should be noted that both sides vilify the other by grouping their opponents with evil or the devil, just to underscore the point that vilification is grounded in stereotyping and overemphasis.

A detailed analysis of the phenomenon of vilification in John cannot be offered here. One point to be noted is that there is an essential difference in John between the vilification by the opponents and that by Jesus. The respective aims of their vilification differ (see van der Watt and Kok 2012, 175–84). In the case of the opponents of Jesus, their vilification seems to be rooted in what John calls "hate" and results in murder. Different is the aim of vilification in the case of Jesus. His use of vilification

21. Luke Timothy Johnson (1989) notes that vilification was common in polemics in New Testament times, and it would not be out of the ordinary for John to present his polemics in this way also.

is motivated by love, against the background of his mission, and in the end aims at the opponents realizing their position, coming to faith, and receiving life.[22] Martinus C. de Boer (2001, 263) aptly remarks that there are sounds of irritation, or even sadness, in John, but not hate or open enmity.[23] Wherever Jesus uses vilifying language it is always within the context or rhetorical atmosphere of his offer of eternal life, indicating to the addressees their problem that prevents them from sharing in the promised kingdom of God.

There is no indication that Jesus hates or wants to destroy his opponents, to the contrary. This becomes most evident in the context where Peter violently draws his sword and cuts off the ear of Malchus, to which Jesus immediately reprimands him and restores the damage done by Peter's violent act (18:10–11). There is no hermeneutic analogy in John that can be used to motivate the argument that the followers of Jesus would have used physical violence if they were, for example, in the majority position. Violence in John, on the part of the followers of Jesus, is tempered by the love of the Father for the world, which also should find expression through the message of his children as they share it with the world.[24] Vilification always has the aim of convincing people that Jesus is the light of the world, the bread of life (6:35), and to offer them an opportunity to experience this truth so that they might receive eternal life (3:16). This is even the case with the notorious 8:44, in which context Jesus questions the unbelief of the Jews, asking in 8:46, "Which of you convicts Me of sin? And if I tell the truth, *why do you not believe Me*?" (NKJV). This is not language spurred on by hatred but speaks of an invitation to join the family of God.[25]

In short, the followers of Jesus understood their own identity and their actions against the background of God's mission, which was inherently

22. For a more detailed discussion with proper examples and motivation, see van der Watt and Kok 2012.

23. It would therefore be incorrect to see all the negative remarks in John as anti-Jewish.

24. In contrast to what Attridge (2010b, 17) wants to maintain, namely, that the "harsh words against enemies (John 8:44) … perhaps mirror the hatred of an inimical 'world.' "

25. This point cannot be developed further here, but see van der Watt and Kok 2012; Dunn (2001, 57) also notes that it is "hard not to hear the gospel as John's attempt to state his case, to preach his good news, within the context of a late first century Judaism uncertain of what God's will was for them and uncertain as to who could speak authoritatively for God."

motivated by love. Vilification, and the use thereof, was in no way seen as being outside that particular framework. The purpose of vilification was essentially seen as a way to convince people that Jesus is the light of the world, the bread of life (6:35), and to offer them an opportunity to experience this truth so that they might receive eternal life (3:16). They should gain insight into their own position of rejecting the Son of God.

Vilification in John fits into what was suggested with the kingdom theme, namely, that the response, even through vilification, toward the opponents was in love, not hate, with an open invitation to accept and believe the King and thus become part of the kingdom of God. From the perspective of the Johannine believers, the borders remained open, or at least porous; the opponents were constantly invited to accept Jesus as the Messiah.

4. A Few Concluding Considerations

By making two cross-cuts through John on issues that directly relate to Judaism in the gospel, the results suggest that an inner-Jewish debate is indeed part of the picture in the Johannine narrative. Care should be taken, however, not to focus only on certain aspects of the issue, as if that were the whole story. What was offered here is only a partial view of one aspect that forms part of the comprehensive picture. I am convinced that it would be a major flaw for any scenario not to cover all the perspectives present in the Johannine narrative, also satisfactorily explaining their interrelatedness. A comprehensive and balanced scenario is crucial, especially with a complex and multilayered situation such as the one John describes.[26] The perspective of the inner-Jewish understanding of Jesus as the King of Israel is not the only part but nevertheless an important part of the picture as a whole.

On this basis any scenario that does not explain the presence of the inner-Jewish debate within the Johannine understanding of Judaism

---

26. Obviously, issues such as the remarks about the break between Christianity and the Jews as expressed by *ἀποσυνάγωγος* and the description of the Jews as being of another family, etc., should be taken into account. Reinhartz (2001a, 201) remarks that the term *ἀποσυνάγωγος* does not point to the exclusion from the synagogue but simply implies formal distance also on a juridical level between the two groups. De Boer (2001, 279) states that the Jewishness of the followers of Jesus is thus denied; it is a matter of difference of identity.

should be questioned. Attention should be given to this aspect.[27] For instance, if the argument is correct that John's transcendental narrative actually links up with and takes the expectations of the Jewish narrative further, as the prophets promised would happen, the idea of continuation within the confines of Judaism should be taken seriously. Not only fulfillment plays a role but also continuation of the presence of God with his people. In this particular case terms such as *supersession* would not be ideal.[28] Supersession would normally require two separated religions in which one supersedes the other, which is not yet the case in an inner-Jewish situation.[29]

Why is it so important to emphasize that the picture presented above is only part of the whole? In light of the current research it cannot be denied that the description of the Jews in John is varied and complex and cannot be confined to single aspect or perspective only.[30] For instance, Ruben Zimmermann (2013) indicates that John offers an unstable description of the Jews as character on purpose, meaning that no precise, clear-cut description is possible but that a variety of perspectives simultaneously determine the flow of the narrative. If this is indeed the case, it implies that in a scenario of the Jews in John multiple aspects, even contrasting aspects,

27. Considering the situation within Judaism, it should be noted that criticizing and negatively confronting different groups within Judaism as part of an inner-Jewish debate were in no way foreign to Judaism during the relevant period. When the prophets such as Jeremiah or Amos call their people to convert, they do not do this in antagonistic opposition and conflict but as part of the loving message from the inside. They try to conserve and protect the people of God. The motifs of this pattern did not change with, for instance, John the Baptist and the Qumran community, or for that matter Jesus (Petersen 2008, 39). In none of these cases should the critical stance be seen as anti-Judaism. This would be anachronistic, according to Petersen (2008, 39). The criticism comes from within and aims at preserving the identity of the community on the basis of what that particular faction of Judaism believes to be true.

28. Lieu (2001, 140–41) comments on how foundational Christian convictions play a role in the problem of how to interpret the Fourth Gospel.

29. The question of what this view of John on the inner-Jewish debate and split implies for current-day interreligious and specifically Jewish-Christian debates cannot be addressed here but lies at the heart of the debate. See Petersen 2008, 30–31. She remarks, "Es gibt keine Übereinstimmung in der Sekundärliteratur, ob und inwiefern das Johannesevangelium antijudaistisch ist" (34).

30. Van Belle (2013, 124–25) lists at least eight types of uses for the word Ἰουδαῖος in John, which underlines the variety when it comes to the Jews in John. See also Bennema 2009.

should be allowed for in formulating any acceptable scenario. We have Jews who accept Jesus and Jews who reject him; we have Jews who accept and then reject; we have Jews who wonder about him and others who have already made up their minds—all in the same narrative.[31] The impression created in the narrative is that there is not a single Jewish group with a single response to Jesus but a varied picture of some rejecting Jesus but others still prepared to listen, still asking, still being interested, and having some contact with the Johannine group. This is also positively supported by the multiple invitations of Jesus for them to believe. Rather than two separate poles, it seems to be an open continuum between two poles. The discussion is still inner-Jewish (so Dunn 2001, 59), although direct signs of a break are already evident.

This does not seem to represent the picture of a few decades later, when second-century Christians such as Barnabas or Ignatius seem to accept a more decisive split between Christians and Jews and dealt with the Jews as an opposing group in their writings.[32] This is evident in second-century Christian documents such as the Letter of Ignatius (*Magn.* 8.1; 10.1–3), the Letter of Barnabas (14.1–5), or the Passover homily of Melito of Sardis (§96–97), which display open enmity toward the Jews, apparently as a different religion. This is not John's picture. John seems to cover the middle ground between (1) the inner-Jewish style of discussions that is evident in the First Testament prophets when they address their fellow Jews in a rather harsh way and (2) the critical views of the second-century Christians, who seem to distance the Christian religion from the Jewish religion.[33] What we have in John still seems to be a complex picture of an unfinished but unpreventable process of separation, a process in which people within the Jewish tradition had to answer the question "Who is Jesus?" and indeed still responded to it in different ways. Like any debate, there were those who were still thinking and arguing, but also those who had already made up their minds. The situation was still fluid; the split was inevitable, but not yet complete.

31. See Petersen 2008, 46–48; van Belle 2013, 127. See also Dunn (2001, 47–53) on the diversity of Judaism in the first century.

32. Theißen (2007, 184) remarks, "Aus einer innerjüdischen Umkehrbewegung wurde zunächst eine missionierende Sekte, dann ein endgültiges Schisma."

33. Petersen (2008, 40) remarks, "Die streckenweise antijüdische Rhetorik des Johannesevangeliums setzt nicht notwendigerweise voraus, dass dieses Evangelium von einer Position *außerhalb* des Judentums aus spricht."

Part 2
John as a Source for Understanding Judaism

The Gospel of John as a Source for First-Century Judaism

Craig R. Koester

The value of John's Gospel as a source for first-century Judaism is a topic that is both intriguing and challenging. The question of the gospel's relationship to Judaism has usually been framed in other ways. In the 1950s and 1960s it was common to consider forms of Judaism as *background* for the Fourth Gospel. Scholars in that period would look at various thought forms in rabbinic texts and Hellenistic Jewish writings such as those of Philo, and they would ask about the extent to which the Fourth Evangelist worked within the same thought world (Dodd 1953, 54–96). After the discovery of the Dead Sea Scrolls, those too were considered as a possible background for Johannine thought. Of special interest was the pronounced dualism of light and darkness in some of the scrolls. The dualism helped make the case that interpreters did not need to seek the background of John's imagery in gnostic texts from later centuries. It was already there in Judaism before the beginning of the first century (Brown 1966, lii–lxvi; Schnackenburg 1968, 125–35; Barrett 1978, 31–34).

Later the manner of framing the question shifted. Instead of focusing on backgrounds and thought worlds, the discussion turned to contexts and social worlds. It became more common to ask how the Fourth Gospel reflected the emerging conflict between the followers of Jesus and the wider Jewish community in the late first century. Interpreters asked how Jews who believed that Jesus was the Messiah came to have a distinctive identity within the synagogue. There were efforts to discern how tensions arose with Jews who did not share their beliefs and how the disputes in that first-century social setting contributed to shaping of the gospel (Brown 1966, lxx–lxxv; 1979; Martyn 1979).

But looking at John as a *source* for our understanding of first-century Judaism invites a different way of reading the gospel. One reason for approaching the gospel in this way is that John includes scenes from first-century Jewish life. Settings range from households to the temple in Jerusalem and to a synagogue in Galilee. The people who play key roles in the narrative include groups of Jews and Pharisees, and the gospel includes conversations and debates about Jewish practice and the Jewish Scriptures. Yet reframing the question to ask what the gospel might contribute to our understanding of Judaism focuses more on points of commonality than on points of difference between the writer and the wider Jewish community of his time. It invites appreciative inquiry into aspects of the gospel that both Jewish and Christian scholars might find helpful contributions to our sense of what first-century Jewish life was like.

Methodological Considerations

Here I want to consider John's Gospel, which was composed in the late first century, alongside rabbinic texts, which in their present form date from 200 CE and later. The reason is that New Testament scholars often turn to rabbinic writings when reconstructing first-century Jewish life, yet they face the challenge of discerning how closely those later texts preserve older material.[1] The rabbinic collections weave together oral traditions stemming back multiple generations, and they both preserve and reshape the material in the process. Jewish scholars have called for greater awareness of the dynamic quality of rabbinic tradition, which developed over time, and they point out how difficult it can be to determine which traditions can firmly be dated to the early first century.[2] Accordingly, John's Gospel may provide glimpses of Jewish life that predate the written form of rabbinic materials by a century and more.

At the same time, we will keep in mind that John's Gospel is not primarily an account of first-century Jewish life. The gospel was written in order that people might believe that Jesus is the Messiah and Son of God

---

1. For several generations interpreters have used the commentary by Strack and Billerbeck (1922–1961), which collects various rabbinic materials for each part of the New Testament. Although the commentary notes the dates for the rabbis cited, it is easy to get the impression that the rabbinic sources can be used directly as evidence of Jewish perspectives in the first century without adequately accounting for the developments that took place in the second and third centuries and later.

2. See Strack and Stemberger (1992, 35–61). Visotzky (1995) notes that rabbinic texts from the second to fifth centuries CE can better be compared to patristic texts from that same period.

(20:31), and Jewish life is portrayed as it related to that central concern. We will also be attuned to the polemical aspects of the gospel, especially as they relate to the depiction of Jews and Pharisees who do not believe in Jesus. We cannot construe the negative elements in the gospel's portrayal of Jesus's opponents as representative of Judaism generally. Finally, we will reckon with the fact that the gospel preserves traditions from the early first century, but it shapes them in light of developments in the later first century. Perhaps the best-known example is the way the gospel sometimes equates Jews and Pharisees. In the early first century that would be more difficult to do, because there were various Jewish groups on the scene—Sadducees, Essenes, Zealots, and others—as is clear from Josephus and the Synoptic Gospels. But in the later first century, after the temple's destruction, the Pharisees came to have greater prominence in the shaping of Jewish life (Levine 1990, 23–24). With that in mind we can explore several areas in which John might serve as a source for first-century Judaism.

Temple Practice

The most extensive rabbinic description of the Jerusalem temple is found in the Mishnah's tractate Middot. The tractate is written as historical reminiscence and presumably conveys some reliable information about the pre-70 temple. At the same time, the tractate often supports its descriptions by appealing to biblical warrants, which include the accounts of Solomon's temple and Ezekiel's idealized description of the temple of the future—a temple that never existed in the form Ezekiel envisioned. In Middot, historical memory is being reshaped by Scripture, which gives an imaginative element to the portrayal, and many aspects of the temple in the tractate could never have been built as described (Kraemer 2016, 24–44). At some points, the Mishnah's depiction of the temple can be correlated with that of Josephus's earlier descriptions, but at other points the two sources are difficult to reconcile (Schwartz and Peleg 2007). The point is that it is not always easy to determine the extent to which the Mishnah preserves memories of the temple and the extent to which it reshapes them.

With that in mind we turn to a passage from the Mishnah that has been of special interest to interpreters of John's Gospel: the description of temple practices during the festival of Sukkot. In its present form, the Mishnaic tractate offers an account of rituals that were practiced in the temple before 70 CE, but in its present form the text itself dates from about 200 CE—that is, more than 130 years later (m. Sukkah 4:1–5:4). The Mishnah describes the crowds of worshipers gathering in the temple with the *lulavs*, or ceremonial branches, in their hands. It pictures a priest going to the Pool of Siloam with a golden pitcher to draw water, which he would pour out on the altar. It also says that the procession was made around the altar once each day and then seven times on the final day of the festival. There is also a description of the huge menorahs that were lighted in the temple courts each evening, and there was music and dancing to the Songs of Ascents in the lamplight throughout the night.

The description is vivid and written as historical memory, like the tractate Middot. Yet the temple rituals described in tractate Sukkot are not clearly attested in earlier Jewish sources. Josephus does mention an incident in which a priest was sacrificing during Sukkot and offended the crowd, and this passage could be correlated with the Mishnah's comment about a priest inappropriately pouring water over his feet at the festival (*Ant.* 13.372; m. Sukkah 4:9), but Josephus does not actually describe the water-drawing ceremony. Philo mentions the theme of light in connection with Sukkot, but he links it to the solar equinox rather than the menorahs that illuminated the nocturnal ceremonies in the temple (*Spec. Laws* 2.210).

Here the Fourth Gospel might provide at least some first-century corroboration for the rabbinic tradition about the light and water-drawing rituals in the temple. The description in tractate Sukkot has often been read as background for John 7–10, which is set during the festival, because Jesus invokes the themes of water and light when speaking of his identity and work. But the reverse might also be true: John might offer some first-century corroboration for the rituals that are more fully described later in the Mishnah.[3]

When considering this possibility it is important to recognize that the primary associations of the water and light imagery in John 7–10 are from the Old Testament. The setting in 7:37–39 is the temple on the last day of

3. In addition to the commentaries on John, specialized studies of the gospel have explored the connections between the light and water images used for Jesus in John 7–10 (Yee 1988, 70–82; Koester 2003, 152–60, 192–200; Coloe 2001, 115–44). Gerry Wheaton (2015, 127–58) focuses only on the water imagery. Using biblical and rabbinic sources, he argues that Jesus identifies himself not only with the temple but with the altar in relation to the water-drawing ceremony. Given the evocative character of the imagery, however, it seems unlikely that readers could be expected to make such a specific correlation. The work of Michael Daise (2007) devotes more attention to the chronology of the festivals in John than to the imagery involved.

Sukkot, and Jesus invites those who thirst to come and drink of the living water that he provides. It is clear that on a primary level the imagery is biblical. Jesus refers to the Scripture that says, "Out of his heart shall flow rivers of living water," though it is not clear which biblical text is being cited. It seems likely that it recalls the promise in Zechariah about living water flowing from Jerusalem—a text that also mentions Sukkot (Zech 14:8, 18; see 13:1)—although the imagery also evokes associations from other texts.[4] Later Jesus says, "I am the light of the world" (John 8:12), which seems to recall biblical passages about God's servant bringing light to the nations (Isa 42:6; 49:9), along with other texts.[5]

But on a secondary level it seems likely that the gospel's imagery recalls traditions about the water and light rituals in the temple (Brown 1966, 327, 344; Barrett 1978, 327, 335). For example, the invitation to drink of the living water is given on the last day of Sukkot, which is called "the great day," when the water-drawing ritual reached its climax (John 7:37). Moreover, the scene in the temple is followed by Jesus sending a blind man to the Pool of Siloam, which was the place from which the water used for the temple ritual was drawn (9:7). Finally, Jesus's claim to be the light of the world is made in the temple treasury, which was apparently near the place where the light ceremony was held during Sukkot (8:12, 20; Barrett 1978, 340; Moloney 1998, 269). The interplay of the water and light themes, along with the references to the last day of Sukkot and locations in the temple and Pool of Siloam, suggest that the gospel presupposes traditions about temple rituals like those described in the Mishnah. The gospel does not provide enough to corroborate most of the details in the Mishnah's description, but it may supply some first-century evidence for the tradition that the Mishnah would later develop.

---

4. The flowing water might also recall Moses bringing water from the rock in the desert (Exod 17:1–6; Num 20:2–13), which would lead the crowds to think that Jesus was a prophet (John 7:40). It is also reminiscent of God himself providing streams of water in the desert (Ps 78:16; Isa 41:18; 43:20; 48:21; 49:10) and inviting the thirsty to drink (Isa 55:1), since God is the fountain of living waters (Jer 2:13; 17:13). Water flows from the temple in the vision in Ezek 47:1 (Koester 2003, 192–200).

5. Light imagery that uses language similar to that in John's Gospel can also be found in Isa 9:1–7, which relates to the coming of a Davidic king. Light was a common image for God, who led Israel by a pillar of fire in the desert (Exod 12:37; 13:20–22) and whose light gave guidance and salvation (Pss 27:1; 36:9; Isa 2:5; 60:1–2, 19–20; Koester 2003, 152–60).

Use of the Title *Rabbi*

The title commonly given to the sages in the Mishnah and other rabbinic sources is *rabbi*. In a basic sense *rab* (רב) means "master" as opposed to a slave: "Be not like slaves that minister to the master [רב] for the sake of receiving a bounty, but be like slaves that minister to the master not for the sake of receiving bounty; and let the fear of Heaven be upon you" (m. Avot 1:3, trans. Danby 1933). With the added suffix, *rabbi* (רבי) means "my master," which is a respectful form of address. The related term *rabboun* (רבון) is also means "master" or "lord" in both Hebrew and Aramaic. It is used in the Mishnah for God (m. Ta'an. 3:8) and in other sources for God (b. Yoma 87b) and for human masters (Tg. Neof. Exod 21:4; Tg. Ps 12:5).[6]

In the Mishnah the term rabbi comes to have more specific connotations of someone recognized for their learning and ability to instruct others in the tradition. Notable figures from the late first and early second centuries CE include Eliezer ben Hyrcanus, Akiva ben Joseph, and Joshua ben Hananiah, all of whom are called rabbi and are depicted as engaged in discussion about the interpretation of the Torah. This way of using rabbi for Torah scholars continued in the generations that followed. What is significant, however, is that Jewish sources do not suggest that rabbi came into use as a title for a sage until the very end of the first century CE. The term is not used by Philo, Josephus, or in other Jewish texts from this period. In the rabbinic sources themselves, the title is not used for sages such as Hillel and Shammai, who were contemporaries of Jesus. The related title *rabban* (רבן) was used for leaders of the Sanhedrin in the mid- to late first century, including Gamaliel the Elder, Gamaliel II, Simeon ben Gamaliel, and Yohanan ben Zakkai, who established a Jewish academy at Yavneh after the fall of Jerusalem. So according to these sources, it was within the circle of Jewish learning that developed after 70 CE that rabbi came to be used as title for recognized sages (Shanks 1963; 1968; Schürer 1979, 325–26; Overman 1990, 44–48).

6. In the Aramaic targums *rabboun* (רבון) is a translation for *ʾadōn* (אדון, Tg. Neof. Exod 21:6). It is used in both Hebrew and Aramaic forms for God as Master of the universe (רבון העלמים, b. Yoma 87b; רבונו של עולם, b. Ber. 9b; רבון כל עלמיא, Tg. Neof. Exod 34:23). God is the *rabboun* who is superior to the human beings who claim that status. He is "Lord of lords" (רבון על כל רבוניא, Tg. Neof. Exod 18:11).

Jewish inscriptions show that in the second and third century CE forms of the word rabbi were used to indicate respect.[7] Those who were given the title had some status within the community, and many were well-to-do. One inscription from the late second century CE refers to "the school" (בית מדרשו) of Rabbi Eliezer Hakappar, which indicates that he was a teacher (Visotzsky 2009). But in most cases the inscriptions only allow us to conclude that the title had an honorific quality, since they do not make any clear connection to giving instruction. In the diaspora, the title was not widely used. Although hundreds of Jewish inscriptions have been found outside Israel, only a handful refer to someone as rabbi. Of the more than five hundred Jewish inscriptions from Rome, none refers to a rabbi. More common designations for leaders within the Jewish community are "head of the synagogue" (ἀρχισυνάγωγος), "head of the elders" (γερουσιάρχης), and "official' (ἄρχων; Cohen 1981, 15). In sum, inscriptions suggest that in the second and third centuries CE, Jewish communities in Israel could use the term rabbi for a teacher or other respected member of the community, while in the diaspora the term remained rare. Rabbinic sources show that the more specific use of the term to indicate a sage emerged in the late first to early second century.

The earliest extant occurrences of *rabbi* and *rabbouni* as forms of address are in the New Testament. The gospels provide valuable evidence for the use of these terms in sources composed in the last three decades of the first century. In the Synoptics, the term rabbi could be used as mainly an expression of respect. For example, Mark 9:5 uses rabbi for Jesus, while the parallel passage in Matthew replaces it with κύριος or "lord" (Matt 17:4) and Luke with ἐπιστάτης or "master" (Luke 9:33). Similarly, Mark 10:51 uses *rabbouni*, while the parallels in Matt 20:33 and Luke 18:41 replace it with κύριος or "lord." At the same time, Matthew seems to show the transition in the use of the term from one of respect to one that includes teaching. Jesus refers to those who want to be honored at banquets and in the marketplace especially being called rabbi (Matt 23:6–7). Then he adds that his followers should not be called rabbi because they have one teacher and are all students (23:8).

What is disputed is whether the gospels provide reliable evidence that Jesus was actually called rabbi during his ministry in the early first

7. Cohen (1981, 7–8) notes that in the inscriptions rabbi is spelled in different ways, including *rebbi*, *rabbē*, *ribbi*, and *rabban*.

century or whether he was given this title anachronistically by the gospel writers, since the title was becoming more common at the time they wrote in the later first century (Shanks 1963; 1968; Zeitlin 1963; 1968). Reasons to think that the gospels do preserve early tradition are that the term could broadly indicate respect and did not need to have all the connotations it acquired in the circles that later produced the Mishnah. Moreover, the term is used in Mark's version of the Jesus story, which was probably composed around 70, whereas Matthew and Luke show a tendency to replace the Hebrew title with Greek equivalents, even though they were both written after 70, when the use of rabbi as a title was becoming more common. At the same time, the critique of the Pharisees' use of the title in Matt 23:7–8 seems to reflect social patterns at the time the gospel was written (Overman 1990, 44–48).

John's Gospel uses *rabbi* and *rabbouni* more than the other gospels combined, and it may provide glimpses into Jewish practice in the late first century, at the time the gospel was composed. The narrative reflects a shift from the more general use of the term toward the sense of a rabbi as a teacher. In the opening chapter, John the Baptist identifies Jesus as the Lamb of God, and two of his disciples follow Jesus. They address Jesus as rabbi, which could initially be construed as the equivalent of κύριος or "sir" (John 1:38). The gospel, however, focuses the meaning by defining the title as "teacher." Something similar occurs at the end of the gospel, when Mary Magdalene initially thinks the risen Jesus is a gardener and addresses him as "sir" (κύριος), but after recognizing him, she calls him *rabbouni*, which is said to mean "teacher" (20:15–16). The main reason for defining the term is presumably that the writer assumes that readers do not know Hebrew. If the Fourth Gospel was put into final form outside Judea or Galilee, the need for translation also fits what emerged from the inscriptions: they not suggest that rabbi was a familiar a title outside Israel, even in Jewish circles. Finally, even where the term was known, it was only gradually coming into use as a specific term for a teacher, so that sense had to be made explicit, since it could not be assumed.[8]

The Fourth Gospel is distinctive in that it shows both Jesus (1:38, 49; 4:31; 9:2; 11:8) and John the Baptist (3:26) being called rabbi by their

8. People outside Jesus's inner circle sometimes address him in ways that reflect this general pattern. When Nicodemus greets Jesus as Rabbi, he goes on to focus on Jesus's role as a teacher (John 3:2), and the crowd that greets Jesus as Rabbi in Galilee does so as he teaches in a synagogue (6:25, 59).

respective groups of disciples. The narrative assumes that Jesus and John each play unique roles, but it also includes features that readers might assume give credence to calling each figure a rabbi who teaches. Both Jesus and John the Baptist have an ability to work with Scripture: John quotes Isa 40:3 (John 1:23), and Jesus makes frequent references to biblical texts. Forms of ritual washing were practiced by both groups of disciples (3:22–23), and both discussed questions of belief and practice: John's followers debate purification with another Jewish person before bringing the issue to their rabbi (3:25–26), whereas Jesus's followers ask him as their rabbi to explain the relationship of sin to congenital blindness (9:2). Both groups of disciples also seem protective of their rabbis: John's disciples are concerned about the way Jesus's popularity is drawing people away from their own circle (3:26), while Jesus's disciples are concerned that their rabbi eats properly and remains safe (4:31; 11:8). Similar dynamics characterize relationships between the sages and their disciples according to later rabbinic sources (Levine 1990, 59–61).

Yet John's narrative also assumes that as rabbis, neither Jesus nor John derived their authority from a recognized chain of earlier Torah scholars. In the rabbinic sources, locating oneself in an ongoing sequence of recognized teachers was important because continuity was essential in maintaining the integrity of the Oral Torah. The Mishnah tractate Avot begins by tracing the transmission of the Oral Torah through generations of teachers. The idea is that Moses put some of the torah in writing and transmitted other parts orally. The Oral Torah was handed down from teacher to disciple, so it relied on maintaining the chain of tradition from one generation to the next (Neusner 2002, 103–17).

Although John the Baptist is called rabbi by a circle of followers (3:26), he does not locate himself within a chain of recognized teachers. When a delegation from the Pharisees ask him about his identity and reasons for baptizing, he cites Isa 40:3 as descriptive of his work and claims direct authorization from God (1:19–28). Later, some Jewish listeners in the temple wonder about Jesus's teaching authority: "How does he have learning when he never studied?" (7:15). The assumption seems to be that credibility is linked to having studied under a recognized teacher and passing on the tradition with integrity (Brown 1966, 316). So Jesus accepts this basic premise by saying that his teaching is not his own, since he has received it from a recognized master. The twist is that the master teacher is God himself (7:16–17).

It is clear that neither Jesus nor John the Baptist can be considered conventional rabbis. But the way each of them is called rabbi shows the growing tendency to identify the title with teaching, and especially with teachers who had groups of disciples that engaged in discussion over belief and practice. Moreover, it suggests that in the late first century there were various ways in which someone might come to be called rabbi. Later Jewish tradition assumed that the title rabbi came into vogue in the circle of sages that produced the Mishnah and that it was associated with the laying on of hands by Johanan ben Zakkai and his successors (Shanks 1963, 338; Schürer 1979, 325–26). But the picture that emerges from John's Gospel correlates better with the point made by Shaye Cohen in his study of Jewish inscriptions. He notes that in the second and third centuries there "was no central registry of Rabbis, no central office which had exclusive rights to bestow Rabbinic ordination" (1981, 12). The Fourth Gospel suggests that in the first century the title rabbi could be used in various Jewish groups, whose reasons for using the title might differ.

Synagogue Sermons

Reading and interpreting Scripture was a feature of synagogue life in the first century. Philo says that the practice was to assemble on the seventh day of the week and "hear the laws read so that none should be ignorant of them"; a "priest who is present or one of the elders reads the holy laws to them and expounds them point by point till about the late afternoon, when they depart" (*Hypothetica* 7.12–13, trans. Colson 1954; see Philo, *Embassy* 156; *Dreams* 3.127; *Moses* 2.215–16; *Spec. Laws* 2.62–64). Josephus spoke of the Jewish practice of hearing and learning the law each week (*Ag. Ap.* 2.175). The New Testament includes synagogue scenes in which the Scriptures are read and expounded (Luke 4:16–22; Acts 13:14–15; 15:21). In later periods, both rabbinic sources and studies of ancient synagogue architecture point to the importance of reading and interpreting the Torah (Levine 2005, 145–57). What is more difficult to know is how the interpretation of Scripture was done in first-century synagogues and whether it took the form of a sermon.

Studies of rabbinic texts give some idea of what homiletical patterns might have been like in the third, fourth, and fifth centuries CE (Heinemann 2007). The targums show how texts could be paraphrased in the process of translating from Hebrew to Aramaic, and the paraphrases are an important form of interpretation. Another device was the proem or *petichtah*, which preceded the reading from the Torah. The *petichtah* engaged the listeners' attention by beginning with a verse from one of the

Writings, which seemed to have nothing to do with the Torah reading for the day. It was the task of the speaker to move from that disconnected verse through an artful interweaving of ideas to conclude with the Torah passage that was about to be read. This device may have come into use in the second century CE (Shinan 1987). Later sources such as the Pesiqta Rabati give evidence of more complex forms that include the *petichtah*, a middle section that expounds a section of text, and a closing that is usually paraenetical (Ulmer 2013; see Stegner 1988). Whether these more complex forms were actually preached or were literary creations is unclear.

For first-century evidence about biblical exposition in synagogues, scholars have turned to the New Testament (Levine 2005, 157–58). One example is Jesus's preaching in the synagogue at Nazareth in Luke 4:16–30. There Jesus reads from the scroll of Isaiah and then sits down and begins to speak. The most distinctive element is that Jesus says that the prophetic passage is being fulfilled in his own ministry. That approach was presumably not typical of Jewish biblical exposition more widely. But another feature is that the message is not a sustained discussion of the text from Isaiah that was read; rather, it turns to other biblical passages about Elijah and Elisha. It suggests a form of synagogue preaching that was not closely tied to a particular text but might range more widely to other topics. Finally, the people in the synagogue interact with the speaker. They do not sit in silence while the speaker finishes but voice approval and disapproval toward what is said.

A second example is Paul's sermon in the synagogue at Antioch in Pisidia in Acts 13:13–43. There it says that someone else read from both the Law and the Prophets, although specific texts are not given. Afterward Paul was invited to give a "word of exhortation."[9] The pattern differs to some extent from that in Luke. Here Paul speaks while standing instead of sitting, as Jesus did, and here the sermon is a sustained address that includes no interaction with the listeners until the end. But like the sermon in Luke, Paul's message is not a sustained exposition of a specific text. Instead, it surveys Israel's history from the ancestral period to King

9. For studies of this homiletical form see Lawrence Wills (1984) and C. Clifton Black (1988). The conclusion of the book of Hebrews calls it a "word of exhortation" (Heb 13:22), the same expression used for Paul's sermon in Acts 13:15. Hebrews does have the quality of a homily, and its structure follows patterns of Greco-Roman rhetoric, but it is not clear how closely it reflects patterns current in first-century synagogues synagogue preaching (Koester 2001, 80–82).

David, then it shifts to the story of Jesus, which is interpreted through citations from the Psalms, and a hortatory conclusion that quotes Hab 1:5. The sermon differs in form and content from the speech Paul gives in Athens, which is addressed to non-Jewish listeners (Acts 17:22–31), but it resembles the speech of Stephen, which set in a hearing before the Jewish council in Jerusalem rather than in a synagogue. The author seems to differentiate speeches given to Jewish and Greek audiences, but without distinguishing a typical synagogue form from one that would be used in a more judicial setting.

Here John's Gospel may provide additional perspectives on possible forms of synagogue preaching in the first century. The bread of life discourse in John 6:25–59 is set in a synagogue in Capernaum. It does not include a formal reading of a biblical text, as was the case in Luke and Acts. Instead, the crowd engages Jesus in discussion in the synagogue at Capernaum, and in the process they paraphrase Scripture. They say, "Our ancestors ate manna in the wilderness. As it is written, 'He gave them bread from heaven to eat'" (6:31). The language is drawn from the manna story in Exod 16, and Jesus responds with a sustained exposition of the text, which may reflect Jewish homiletical patterns of the period. The pioneering study was that of Peder Borgen (1965, 28–58), who showed how Jesus's message successively expounds each section of the text that was cited. Part one deals with the words "He gave them," part two with "bread from heaven," and part three with what it means "to eat."

In part one (6:32–34) the exposition begins with a clarification of how the text should be read. The crowd apparently assumes that the words "he gave them" refer to what Moses did in the past, when he gave manna to Israel. Jesus counters by using a pattern in which the basic sense of the reading is altered. In rabbinic sources the debates were done on the basis of the Hebrew text. In the biblical passage paraphrased by the group in the Capernaum synagogue, the unpointed Hebrew verb נתן could be read as the *qal* perfect *nāthan* ("he gave") or as a participle *nōthēn* ("he gives"). Although John's Gospel is written in Greek, the same pattern is apparent. Jesus insists that the subject of the verb is God, not Moses, that the tense of the verb is present, not past, and the recipients are not limited to Israel but include the world. He says, "It was not Moses who gave you the bread from heaven [past tense]. My Father gives you the true bread from heaven [present tense], and by doing so he gives life to the world" (Borgen 1965, 62–69).

In part two (6:35–48) the exposition continues by saying that "bread from heaven" refers to Jesus himself. The section is neatly framed by the statement "I am the bread of life." In between, Jesus explains that he has come down from heaven to do the will of the one who sent him, which is to bring eternal life and resurrection on the last day. At one point Jesus bolsters his exposition of the Torah passage by weaving in a quotation from the Prophets. He cites Isa 54:13: "They shall all be taught by God" (John 6:45). Weaving a secondary text into the primary exposition may also be a part of the homiletical form (Borgen 1965, 38–43). Finally, in part three (6:49–58) Jesus explains what it means "to eat." If God is the giver and Jesus is the bread, then people "eat" of Jesus by believing in him. The passage is framed by references to Israel's ancestors eating manna or bread in the wilderness and dying (6:49, 58), which establishes the contrast with the eternal life that Jesus offers.

Now the content of this exposition is Johannine Christology, and the perspective would not have been shared by most first-century Jews. But our interest here is in the pattern of exposition, where the speaker comments successively on each main element in the biblical passage and relates the passage to the contemporary situation. Borgen rightly notes that in this discourse key words are repeated, and there is overlap between the various parts. But despite the repetitions, there is a progression of thought that uses framing techniques to mark transitions, as well as a summary of the key points at the end. Borgen strengthens his case that John 6 uses a homiletical pattern by noting places where Philo and rabbinic sources use similar techniques. Others have discerned similar homiletical patterns in the Tanchuma literature (Stegner 1988).

I would like to add a different kind of support for the idea that John 6 might contribute to our understanding of Jewish homiletical practices in the first century. It is significant that the bread of life discourse is set in a synagogue and unfolds through biblical exposition; the form corresponds to the setting. In the previous chapter there is also a discourse, but there the setting is different and so is the form. The idea is that readers should see that in each case the kind of discourse given is appropriate for the context.

In John 5:1–16 Jesus heals a lame man on the Sabbath, and the authorities persecute him for that action. The context is one of accusation and defense, and Jesus responds with a speech that uses patterns of judicial rhetoric (5:17–47; Koester 2003, 91–94). A central task of a judicial speech was to identify the crux or stasis of an issue. The parties in the case might disagree on the facts of the case, on the kind of action that was performed, on justification for the act, or on matters of jurisdiction over the case.

Then, having identified the stasis, the speaker would formulate a thesis, support it with arguments and witnesses, and refute the opponents' case.

Jesus makes sustained use of this judicial approach by shifting the stasis from the issue of Sabbath violation to the question of whether he was working in unity with God or in opposition to God (5:17–18). Then he defends his claim by developing arguments that his actions reflect God's own activity on the Sabbath, which include giving life-making judgments (5:19–30). Then he invokes the witnesses needed to support his claims, including John the Baptist, the Scriptures, and the inherent life-giving quality of the healing itself, all of which point to divine authorization (5:31–40). Finally, the concluding section discredits the opposition by turning the charge of disregard for the law against them. They are faulting Jesus for violating the Sabbath command, whereas Jesus faults them for refusing to believe Moses's witness about the one who was coming (5:41–47).

The point is that the speech given in a judicial setting follows patterns of judicial rhetoric, while the speech given in the synagogue follows a form of biblical exposition. Given the correlation of form and setting, John 6 could reflect patterns that were familiar in Judaism in the late first century. The bread of life discourse also suggests that communication had an interactive quality in first-century synagogues. This differs from the impression we have through Paul's "word of exhortation" in Acts 13, which does unfold as a sustained speech without interruption. In contrast, the discourse in John 6 includes points at which the listeners respond positively or negatively to Jesus and even talk among themselves. The more dialogical quality of this preaching style is also evident in Luke 4, where the listeners give assent or voice opposition to what is being said. Together, the synagogue scenes in John 6 and Luke 4 suggest that in synagogues of this period, the lines between preaching and discussion were not firmly fixed. Someone might take the lead in explicating a biblical text, but others would interact with the speaker and one another in the process.

עם הארץ and Jewish Folk Belief

In this final section we move aspects of Judaism that were on the boundaries or outside torah observance. One aspect was associated with the עם הארץ or "people of the land." The expression recalls the contrast between the observant Jews, who returned from Babylonia in the period of Ezra and Nehemiah, and the many unobservant people who had remained in Judea, marrying non-Jews and adopting non-Jewish beliefs and practices (Ezra

4:4; 9:1–2). In rabbinic literature, the expression can designate the uneducated rural population, as well as any Jewish person who remains ignorant of the torah. It can also be used for those who are lax in their practices, especially around questions of purity (Oppenheimer 1977; Levine 1990, 112–27). A related aspect concerns Jews whose beliefs show an unacceptable blend of traditions from other religious traditions, including practices that might be deemed superstitious.

John's Gospel shows familiarity with the group that became known as the עם הארץ when the Pharisees disparage "this crowd which does not know the law—they are accursed" (John 7:49). In the portrayal of the invalid at Bethesda, the gospel provides perspectives on this kind of Judaism. The episode is found in John 5:1–16. The setting is in Jerusalem, at a place near the Sheep Gate where there was a pool that was called Bethesda or perhaps Bethzatha. It was said to have five porticoes. The location has been identified by correlating references in Josephus (*J.W.* 2.328) and the Dead Sea Copper Scroll (3Q15 11 XII–XIII) with archaeological excavation of the site.

Recent studies of the evidence make a good case that the Pool of Bethesda was a large *mikveh* or ritual bath (von Wahlde 2009; 2011). The pool was divided into two parts, separated by a wall. The southern part was the bathing pool. It had steps that ran across its entire width, like terraces. The steps enabled large numbers of people to go down into the pool to bathe. Some of the steps were wider than others, and they apparently served as landings, where people could stand while doing the ritual bath. The other half of the pool was a reservoir, which held water that could be let into the bathing pool as needed by means of a shaft with a doorway that could be opened and closed. The occasional infusion of fresh water from the reservoir would purify and replenish the water in the bathing pool.

If this interpretation is correct, then historically we would picture the Pool of Bethesda as a large public *mikveh*. It was located north of the temple, which would be convenient for people seeking access to the temple. It also has a design similar to that of the smaller *mikveh* that was located south of the temple, and well as to the Pool of Siloam, which could also have been a *mikveh* (von Wahlde 2009; 2011). Given that reconstruction, we would assume that people would go to the pool of Bethesda to purify themselves according to the rules outlined in the Torah, and some would presumably go to the temple.

Yet John 5 gives a surprisingly different picture. Here the crowd consists of people with health problems. They are the blind, the lame, and the paralyzed. What at least one of these invalids is looking for is not purity but healing. The man says he is waiting for the water to be stirred up, because when it was stirred up, the person who entered the pool would be healed. His frustration is that he has no one to help him make that well-timed entry into the water, and inevitably someone else gets into the pool ahead of him.

This picture of a place where the sick gather around a pool looking for healing has little to do with Jewish tradition. There is nothing like it in the Old Testament or in other Jewish sources from the period. But sanctuaries where invalids would gather and seek healing were common elsewhere in the Greco-Roman world. The sanctuaries of Asclepius, the god of healing, were located by springs of water, because it was understood that water could help cure people. Vitruvius Pollio, a leading builder of the Augustan age, said that the "most healthy sites with suitable springs" were chosen for all temples and especially those of Asclepius and other gods of healing, because when the sick are "moved to a healthy place and the water supply is from wholesome fountains they will more quickly recover" (*Arch.* 1.2.7, trans. Granger 1931). The orator Aelius Aristides said that at the sanctuary of Asclepius at Pergamum, the blind and the lame would bathe in the water and would be cured of their illnesses (*Or.* 39.15).[10]

It is striking that the invalid in John 5 seemed to think that the troubled water itself had healing properties. It is a perspective that can be described as quasi-magical. Although the category of magic is notoriously difficult to define, David Aune (2006, 376) has proposed two criteria that are helpful here. First, magic is "that form of religious deviance whereby individual or social goals are sought by means alternate to those normally sanctioned by the dominant religious institution." John makes clear that the invalid is Jewish. After all, when Jesus heals him, other Jews fault him for carrying

10. On other waters purported to heal see Pausanias, *Description of Greece* 4.31.4; 5.5.11; 6.22.7; 8.19.2. Urban von Wahlde (2009, 131) gives references to hot springs in and around Israel that were said to have healing properties. But since Bethesda did not involve hot springs, the connections are closer to other sites where water was connected to healing in popular belief. Connections between the Pool of Bethesda and the Greco-Roman healing cults were proposed by A. Duprez (1970). He notes that when Jerusalem became the Roman city of Aelia Capitolina after 135 CE, there is evidence of worship of Asclepius or Serapis at Bethesda. He suggests that some form of healing cult existed there in the first century CE as well. Von Wahlde (2009, 128–29) offers a nuanced critique of many aspects of Duprez's work, while agreeing that the invalid at Bethesda voices a kind of heterodox belief.

his mat on the Sabbath, and eventually the man goes to the temple, where Jesus meets him again. But the man does not seem to be engaged in prayer, and he makes no mention of the God of Israel. Later additions to the story try to explain that it was actually "an angel of the Lord" who stirred up the water, so that the first person into the pool would be healed of their disease (John 5:4). That detail brings the agency of God into the picture, but the best manuscripts of the gospel lack that verse and make no reference to an angel. They simply depict a man who thought the mysterious troubling of the water had healing power.

Second, Aune (2006, 376) proposes that magic involves "the management of supernatural powers in such a way that results are virtually guaranteed." Although certain forms of ancient magic involved incantations and rituals, Aune's definition more broadly refers to "management" of supernatural powers to guarantee results. In the case of the invalid, the management involved waiting for the water to be troubled, and he seems to assume that with a well-timed entry into the pool, healing was virtually guaranteed.[11] It is noteworthy that in the narrative, Jesus makes no use of the water of Bethesda, so it is clear that his approach does not follow the invalid's expectations. Jesus simply speaks and the man is healed (5:9), and in the discourse that follows he presents his action as an extension of God's power to give life (5:21). Later, Jesus will use water from the Pool of Siloam to heal a blind man (9:7), but in that case the man who was cured seemed to have no sense that the water itself had any special powers.

John's characterization of the invalid at Bethesda is a valuable reminder that not all Judaism was Pharisaic Judaism and the boundaries of Jewish practice were not always well defined.[12] It seems likely that the pool was designed as a *mikveh*, which was located near the temple and was to be used for purification. But the invalid—and presumably the other blind, lame, and paralyzed people who gathered there (5:2)—had other reasons for visiting the pool. To some extent, his views might reflect Greco-Roman practices, like those associated with Asclepius, although nothing is said

11. Similar beliefs are evident in New Testament scenes where people have the idea that healing can come by touching the fringe of Jesus's garment (Luke 8:44), Peter's shadow (Acts 5:15), or Paul's handkerchief (19:12).

12. Studies of ancient Jewish magical practices note that in rabbinic tradition the emphasis was on prayer. But other evidence also shows people bringing amulets associated with healing and protection into synagogues (Bohak 2008, 314–18, 403). Popular beliefs did not always correspond to those of the sages.

about him seeking divine aid through incubation or utilizing other forms of treatment, which were common at the shrines of Asclepius. But more important is the quasi-magical perspective on the curative power of the water, which moved outside the more torah-centered forms of Judaism.

Conclusion

When taken together, the examples considered here suggest that John's Gospel can contribute to our understanding of first-century Judaism. Our focus has been on aspects of Judaism that appear in later rabbinic literature but are not clearly attested in Jewish texts from the first century or earlier. First, the gospel can provide some limited corroboration for what we see in later texts, as in the depiction of the pre-70 Sukkot rituals in the temple. Second, the gospel helps nuance our understanding of the use of the term *rabbi* for teachers in the late first century. It shows how the title functioned in groups other than those whose sages later produced the Mishnah. Third, the gospel provides a glimpse of biblical exposition in synagogues that predates and differs from later rabbinic forms. The evidence in John suggests that sermons in first-century synagogues combined biblical exposition by the main speaker with interaction among the listeners. The lines between preaching and discussion were not firmly fixed. Finally, the gospel enhances what we know about the kinds of folk belief that were part of Jewish life, especially among those whom the rabbis called the עם הארץ. It shows ways in which aspects of Greco-Roman belief and quasi-magical ideas circulated in some Jewish circles around questions of healing.

The descriptions of Jewish life and practice that we find in John's Gospel are shaped by the writer's own understanding of Jesus. But his perspectives are also shaped by the social world around him, and it is helpful to see that the gospel is not dismissive of Jewish tradition but deeply engaged with it. To read John's portrayal of Jewish life with care is to be taken more deeply into a context that was dynamic, not static; one that was varied, not uniform. If the gospel challenges us to see the world of first-century Judaism in a more multiform and complex way, that would be a valuable contribution to our work.

John, Judaism, and "Searching the Scriptures"

Catrin H. Williams

There is an increasing awareness in Johannine studies that the widespread, often creative use of scriptural citations, themes, and motifs in the Gospel of John is to be situated within the broader context of Jewish exegetical activity during the late Second Temple period. The Fourth Evangelist did not approach the Jewish Scriptures in a vacuum; his understanding of them was indelibly shaped by a rich legacy of Jewish interpretation. Placing John's Gospel within this context can illuminate several aspects of its engagement with the Jewish Scriptures, including its preference for certain scriptural texts and its use of well-documented Jewish exegetical methods and devices, as well as the author's close familiarity with the ways in which the original biblical texts were being received and interpreted in Jewish circles many centuries after their composition.

Such considerations are, of course, part and parcel of what is involved in exploring the "Jewishness" of John's Gospel. Investigating John's distinctive engagement with Scripture belongs to the wider task of establishing the gospel's origins through comparisons with Jewish customs, beliefs, and practices (Hengel 1999; Frey 2012a, 175–80). It can also shed light on the ways in which Johannine Christians made use of their Jewish heritage to shape their self-understanding as a group. Yet, while many attempts have been made in Johannine scholarship to illustrate how knowledge of the extant Jewish sources can inform discussion of John's appropriation of Scripture, only on a few rare occasions has the issue been turned on its head and the question asked: how can the Jewishness of John's Gospel help us understand the character of Jewish scriptural interpretation during and beyond the late Second Temple period? In other words: is John's reception of the authoritative writings of Judaism, and his use of Jewish hermeneutical operations and practices, an important source of information about first-century Jewish exegetical activity?

In many respects it is understandable why scholars are reluctant to probe John's Gospel as a source for understanding Judaism. Given its strong christological orientation, with all key matters subsumed under the issue of belief in Jesus as "the Christ and Son of God," is it conceivable that Jewish elements of interpretation are recoverable from John's thoroughly Christocentric understanding of the Scriptures as witnesses finding their fulfillment in Jesus? To pose the question in this way assumes, of course, that the task involves nothing more than sifting through and separating Jewish hermeneutical methods and traditions from their remodeled Johannine counterparts. It is also a task that becomes fraught with difficulties when examining scripturally based arguments designed as rhetorical expressions of self-definition, that is, for the purpose of setting up boundaries between those on the Jewish and Johannine sides of the fence (Williams 2011). The process of recovering markedly Jewish elements is achievable to some degree, particularly if exegetical material in John can be matched, through comparative study, to existing—and in some cases later—Jewish sources. It does, however, leave open to discussion whether distinctive and otherwise unparalleled interpretative features in John's Gospel must be excluded from any such handling of the text as a potential source for understanding Judaism. What is the relationship between the "inherited" and "innovative" features of John's scriptural interpretation (see Ruzer 2007, 5–6)? Is it only the former that warrants the description of *Jewish* exegesis? Consequently, if the use of the term *Judaism* requires clarification in a venture of this kind, the same applies to the word *Johannine* when seeking to determine the contours and characteristics of Johannine exegetical traditions. As with all such projects, each potentially fruitful avenue must be explored carefully, with all possible Jewish/Johannine analogues scrutinized on a case-by-case basis.

Interpreting John's use of Scripture against a broad Jewish exegetical canvas can open up new questions and generate new interpretative possibilities, not only in relation to the Johannine text but also with a view to the rich diversity in evidence within first-century Judaism. When examined as part of a larger whole, John's Gospel has the potential to serve as a valuable witness to aspects of Jewish scriptural interpretation during the late Second Temple period (Vermes 1980, 13–14; 1985, 157: "all-inclusive approach"). Rather than being quarried for possible parallels (Vermes 1980, 13; Brooke 2005a, 69),[1] Jewish sources shed light on the wider

1. Vermes (1982, 374) offers the following assessment of the tendency among

Jewish matrix from which John's Gospel emerged (see especially Vermes 1982, 375; Brooke 2005b, xxii, 69; Ruzer 2007, 4–6). In other words, analyzing John not so much against the *background* of Jewish exegetical trends but as part of a broader Jewish religious and cultural environment can lead to what George Brooke repeatedly describes as an opportunity for "mutual illumination."[2]

This can be pursued along a number of different trajectories. First, it can involve *placing* John's Gospel within late Second Temple Jewish interpretation in a variety of settings and contexts, thereby mapping out and drawing comparisons between its engagement with Scripture and the various techniques and traditions attested in Jewish sources such as the Dead Sea Scrolls, the Apocrypha, and the Pseudepigrapha, as well as Josephus and the writings of Philo. This kind of exercise does not necessarily involve the search for genealogical, historical relationships—something that has been overdone in some circles with reference to possible links between John and the Dead Sea Scrolls (as noted especially by Frey 2010, 536–38; also Aune 2003, 281–303; Frey 2004, 117–203; 2009b). The aim rather is to assess John's Gospel within a larger body of Jewish material, taking account of their shared and distinctive features when it comes to using, interpreting, and applying the Jewish Scriptures.

Second, there may be some Jewish interpretative devices and patterns for which John's Gospel provides the earliest attestation and which are otherwise only found in much later (rabbinic or targumic) sources. The methodological problems associated with the use of rabbinic texts for the study of the New Testament are well documented and need not be rehearsed in this essay (see especially Alexander 1983; Holtz 2009, 173–86; and, with reference to John's Gospel, Williams 2013, 114–23). What can be noted is that comparisons with John may assist in the earlier dating of what are otherwise *rabbinic* strains, but rabbinic traditions do not automatically illuminate specific Johannine traditions other than perhaps to affirm their Jewish roots (see Segal 1994, 1–2). It is when a certain tradition or

New Testament scholars to treat Jewish sources as no more than background material for New Testament exegesis: "The New Testament is the mistress, and Jewish documents, especially of the post-biblical variety, mere ancillaries at best." See also Schäfer (1986, 140) on what he describes as "the exploitative-apologetic" approach to Jewish rabbinic sources.

2. See the title of Brooke's 2005 collection of essays: *The Dead Sea Scrolls and the New Testament: Essays in Mutual Illumination*.

method is paralleled in first-century (or earlier) Jewish sources that more diachronically extended traditions can be brought into play (this has been affirmed with reference to John's Gospel by Visotzky 2005, 96; Reinhartz 2005a, 109).

However, as I aim to demonstrate in the second part of this essay, there is also need for greater clarity as to what is meant by *parallel*, whether with reference to Second Temple sources or later rabbinic and targumic developments. One cannot simply assert that because a midrashic technique or interpretation bears some resemblance to a pattern attested in the Dead Sea Scrolls that they must accordingly share a common exegetical pattern or tradition. Once again, a rigorous methodological approach is required when evaluating John's Gospel against the backdrop of contemporary (and later) Jewish interpreters; every possible connection must be examined individually, and the differences as well as the similarities are to be openly acknowledged,[3] not only between John and the Jewish sources but also among the Jewish texts themselves.

Mapping Out Shared Exegetical Methods: The Case of Catchword Links

The task of setting John's Gospel within a wider Jewish matrix will now be explored with reference to some shared exegetical principles and devices. I will focus more on interpretative techniques than traditions, for the reason that the former allows comparisons to be drawn with a broader range of Jewish sources, which, in turn, can lead to a preliminary mapping out of specific exegetical trends. A profiling of this kind, one that inevitably involves a fairly wide casting of the net, can provide a helpful framework for assessing certain exegetical practices attested in both Jewish and Johannine material. The aim is to determine how their hermeneutical assumptions and strategies can offer illumination not only in one but in both directions.

The exegetical device selected for closer scrutiny is one that is frequently cited in discussions of possible links between John's Gospel and Jewish scriptural exegesis, namely, the technique whereby analogous scriptural passages sharing the same words or phrases are interpreted in relation to each other. This involves "searching the Scriptures" for lexical

3. See the insightful comments on "comparison" ("a mixture of identity and difference") by Doering (2006, 20–22), drawing on J. Z. Smith 1990.

links or overlaps between what are often "distant" texts and then combining them for the purpose of "keying."[4] The technique can be labeled in a variety of ways—catchword assimilation, associative/analogical exegesis, lexematic association. However, given that it is more commonly known by the term *gezerah shavah* (inference by analogy, or, literally, "equal ordinance"), some comments are necessary about its status as a technical rabbinic term.

The Matter of *Gezerah Shavah*

This exegetical device is mentioned in all three rabbinic lists of *middot* (or hermeneutical rules): it is the second interpretative technique to be included in the lists attributed to Rabbi Hillel (t. Sanh. 7:11), Rabbi Ishmael (prologue of Sifra Wayyiqra), and then, from a much later period, Rabbi Eliezer ben Yose ha-Gelili (Mishnah of Rabbi Eliezer 1–2). The links that David Daube, Saul Lieberman, and others have recognized, albeit focusing more on terminology than on any shared substance,[5] between some of the *middot* and Greco-Roman rhetorical techniques do not in any way lessen the value of these hermeneutical methods as a source for understanding Judaism. Possible cross-fertilization between classical and rabbinic exegetical techniques attests rather to the character of Judaism during this period

4. *Keying* is the term favored by Samely (2002, 214): "The meaning of the term in one co-text is being 'keyed' (or: unlocked) according to the other co-text, in a manner of speaking."

5. See David Daube (1949, esp. 241 n. 7, 251, 259), where he argues that Hillel's hermeneutical method of *gezerah shavah* was derived from Hellenistic rhetorical techniques. Saul Lieberman (1950, 59–60) proposes that the Greek rhetorical equivalent, indeed the likely origin, of the strange term *gezerah shavah* was σύγκρισις πρὸς ἴσον ("a comparison with what is equal")—a "favorite tool" in the *progymnasmata* (62; but see Alexander 1984, 113)—although he notes that in Hillel's hermeneutical rules the analogy is based on identical words not (more general) content (Lieberman 1950, 61). Lieberman therefore offers a more cautious assessment than Daube, in that he emphasizes the difference between the definition of the method (that is, the terminology that the rabbis may have borrowed from Hellenistic rhetoric) and the content of the method itself (logical and verbal analogy, as applied in halakic contexts). See now Myers (2012a, esp. 12, 14–16), whose own analysis of the ancient rhetorical technique of σύγκρισις with reference to John's Gospel focuses on comparisons/exemplars for the purpose of characterization rather than on verbal analogies between scriptural texts.

as functioning actively in relation to its wider Greco-Roman environment (Alexander 1990, 117).

In the rabbinic sources *gezerah shavah* functions more often than not as an important exegetical device in legal or halakic interpretation: the juxtaposition of lexically overlapping scriptural passages allows certain details absent from one biblical injunction to be supplied from another. This "analogical transfer" (Samely 2002, 214–15) is underpinned by the principle that both scriptural texts are concerned with the same legal matters but that one text provides the framework for the other (see further Mielziner 1925, 142–52; Instone-Brewer 1992, 17–18). Lexical analogues thus provide the scriptural warrant for texts to be read in a way that brings new meaning to them. One such example is the halakic discussion on divorce and witnesses in m. Sotah 6:3:

> There is an inference to be drawn from the less to the more stringent concerning the first testimony from this very fact [that only one witness is necessary]: Just as the last testimony which renders her forbidden for ever, behold, is established by one witness [only], should not the first testimony which does not render her forbidden for ever also be capable of being established by one witness [only]? In this regard it is instructive that Scripture says: "For he has found in her the indecency of a *matter* [דבר] [and he writes for her a bill of divorce]" [Deut 24:1], and above it says, "According to two witnesses [or according to three witnesses] shall the *matter* [דבר] be established" [Deut 19:15]. Just as the "matter" enunciated above is [established] according to two witnessees, so the "matter" enunciated here is according to two witnesses also.[6]

The second half of this discussion presents an analogy arguing that more than one witness is required in the case of a wife suspected of adultery (see Num 5). The ambiguous phrase "indecency of a matter" (Deut 24:1) is interpreted here to include adultery, whereas Deut 19:15 stipulates that two or three witnesses are necessary for the purpose of prosecution. The connecting link between the two scriptural passages is the word "matter" (דבר), which becomes the lexical lever to enable the transference of the reference to two/three witnesses from Deut 19:15 to 24:1. As there are no further links in terms of subject matter between these two passages, it appears that the presence of the word דבר in Deut 24:1 is interpreted as somehow being

6. For the translation and analysis that follows I am indebted to Samely 2002, 215–17.

able to appropriate the specific function of its occurrence in the other scriptural citation (19:15, i.e., a matter proven by two witnesses).

The phrase *gezerah shavah* does not occur in this mishnaic unit; indeed it is only found once in the Mishnah (m. Arakh. 4:4). Nevertheless, the exegetical illustrations tied directly to the *middot* of Hillel and Ishmael similarly juxtapose two scriptural texts whose combination leads to the required clarification, for halakic purposes, of the implicit (hidden) meaning of one of the two cited passages. In other words, this process of semantic "gap filling" represents a very specific application of associative/analogical exegesis as tied to the term *gezerah shavah*—one that certainly does not characterize all cases of lexical association in (later) midrashic exegesis.[7] Furthermore, given the problems associated with the lists of *middot*—the uncertain dating of the lists, their incompleteness, and lack of clear definition as to what these principles encompass (especially Alexander 1984, 99–115; see Alexander 1983, 242–43; Samely 2002, 12, 26–27, 220–21; Porton 2004)—it cannot be assumed, as is often done in New Testament scholarship, that they represent a comprehensive, indeed the definitive, template of rabbinic exegetical principles and techniques.

Some Johannine scholars continue to use—indeed give prominence to—the term *gezerah shavah* in their analyses of John's exegetical practices, most recently Richard Bauckham in his 2015 book *Gospel of Glory: Major Themes in Johannine Theology*.[8] However, the late but also highly precise applica-

7. See also Chernick (1990), who argues that postmishnaic (Amoraic) *gezerah shavah* interpretations in the halakic midrashim "place strict formulary requirements on the verses which they will accept as their sources" (255–56), whereas these restrictions do not necessarily apply to word-comparison interpretations that lack the *gezerah shavah* designation. The application of the exegetical technique of *gezerah shavah* must, as a result, conform to the following requirements: (1) "simple" cases of *gezerah shavah* are limited to comparisons of words, phrases, or formulas that appear only twice in the Pentateuch; (2) *gezerah shavah mufnah* ("free") compares only "extraneous" terms to similar ones in the same pentateuchal passage or in a different pentateuchal text that shares a similar legal rubric. See further Mielziner 1925, 150–52; Avemarie 2009, 83 n. 2.

8. See, e.g., the repeated references to examples of *gezerah shavah* in John's Gospel noted by Bauckham (2015, 96 n. 81, 154 ["the Jewish exegetical principle that the rabbis later called *gezerah shavah*"], 156, 158, 167, 168 n. 90). Note also Menken (1996, 52): "[the technique] is very similar to the later rabbinic hermeneutical rule of *gezerah shavah*." Although displaying clear awareness of the dating issues, Menken does not consider the specificity of the use and application of the term *gezerah shavah* in the rabbinic sources. See also Manns 1991, 314–15.

tion of this term in rabbinic sources suggests that, unless it is used with greater specificity, it should—like the term *pesher* (Witmer 2006; see Myers 2015, 10–11)—be abandoned in Johannine studies in favor of a designation that more aptly and comprehensively captures the range of lexical associative techniques that are found in much earlier sources (see Avemarie 2009, 83–86), including John's Gospel. As a result, due weight must be given to the broad similarities but also to the striking differences between the application of *gezerah shavah* in rabbinic sources and the more widely established use of catchword links in a variety of patterns, and for diverse exegetical purposes, in the New Testament, the Dead Sea Scrolls, and other postbiblical writings.

For that reason, Johannine exegetical techniques will now be examined against a broad canvas of analogical exegesis or catchword association in late Second Temple Judaism, that is, outside—and prior to—the rabbinic sources.[9] A rich diversity of such interpretative practices—albeit without the later terminological categorization—is widely attested before and during the first century CE (see Brooke 1985, 8–44), early traces of which, as Michael Fishbane has convincingly demonstrated, are already visible in the Hebrew Bible itself.[10] Of particular significance is the comparative material provided by the Dead Sea Scrolls, the writings of Philo, and some of the texts in the Apocrypha and Pseudepigrapha. As will now be shown, all related techniques follow the overarching principle that (new) meaning is produced when texts are brought into exegetical conversation with others; the use of analogy in such conversations has the ability to restrict, expand, and, above all else, to explain the meaning of sacred texts.

The practice of searching the Scriptures for analogies—that is, for catchword links—has the capacity to be a valuable candidate for the

9. It is interesting to note in this respect that Samely (2002, 11–12) opts for the term "resources of interpretation" rather than "techniques" or "methods" to denote rabbinic hermeneutics, because "resource" suggests something that is available but in an undefined form or can appear in many forms. He notes: "The nature of reading itself mitigates against any purely instrumental or mechanical application of hermeneutic rules to textual phenomena" (12).

10. See Fishbane (1985, 155–57, 247–50), who proposes that analogy by extension in innerbiblical exegesis can involve the specification of certain characteristics that are ambiguous or potentially problematic in nature, or an extension by examples in order to make the original rule more comprehensive or explicit; expansion by a new topic to bring about a shift of legal categories or principles; and transformation of meaning and intent to the original rule (see further 1985, 99, 160–62, 183, 210–11, 218–20, 298, 313, 525).

description, investigation, and even classification of certain Jewish exegetical techniques and devices. For that purpose, the following preliminary attempt at categorizing broadly contemporaneous methods of scriptural interpretation seeks to draw together Johannine and Jewish examples of link-word combinations under two main headings: serial quotations and composite quotations. As we shall see, these two categories have the capacity to capture several cases of associative scriptural exegesis in Jewish and early Christian sources, and the second category in particular (composite citations) is now becoming the subject of detailed scrutiny (Adams and Ehorn 2016b). The content of Jewish and Johannine serial/composite scriptural quotations may be very different from each other, with several distinctive characteristics coming to light in individual texts, but the techniques undergirding the use of analogy or association through catchword for exegetical purposes often share a number of striking features. It must nevertheless be acknowledged that focusing on serial/composite *quotations* does not exhaust the range of catchword combination techniques attested in ancient Judaism and the New Testament writings (including John's Gospel), and, where significant for this study, attention will also be drawn to other exegetical practices such as the importance of catchword links for interpretative purposes in translations of the Hebrew Scriptures.

Serial Quotations

Associative exegesis through catchword links can take numerous forms, the most recognizable of which—as the earlier example from the Mishnah has demonstrated—is the deliberate juxtaposition of two or more scriptural passages that have at least one common word through their explicit citation in serial fashion (to form what can be termed "serial quotations"). While the scriptural passages in question may also have similar content, this is not always the case, and the connection between them may or may not be accompanied by an explanatory comment. Delineating the various forms of and the strategies underpinning this method of scriptural juxtaposition is greatly assisted by the fact that numerous examples of this hermeneutical procedure can be found in the Dead Sea Scrolls.[11]

11. See esp. 4Q174 1 I, 1–3; 1 I, 10–13, 14–16; 1 II, 1–4; 1QM X, 6–8; 1QS II, 2–4; CD VII, 15–19. See further Slomovic (1969, 5–10); Brooke (1985, 166, 294–95, 297–98, 306–7); and, with reference to legal material (e.g., 11QT XVII, 6–8; LI, 11–18), see Bernstein (2013, 471–73).

In 4Q Florilegium (4Q174 1 I, 10–13) one such example involves the juxtaposition of 2 Sam 7:11c–14a and Amos 9:11 because of the presence in both texts of the phrase "and I will raise up" (והקימותי), which leads to the following interpretation:

> (10) "And the Lord de[clares] to you that he will build you a house. I will raise up [והקימותי] your seed after you and establish the throne of his kingdom (11) [for ev]er. I will be as a father to him, and he will be as a son to me" [2 Sam 7:11c, 12b, 13b–14a]: This [refers to the] branch of David, who will arise with the Interpreter of the Law, who (12) [will rise up] in Z[ion in] the last days, as it is written, "I will raise up [והקימותי] the booth of David which has fallen" [Amos 9:11]: This [refers to] the booth [or, branch] of (13) David which was fallen, who will arise to save Israel.[12]

The quotation from 2 Sam 7:11c–14a has been significantly edited, with only key components being cited in order to align it more closely with the explanation that follows; this, in turn, is supported by the quotation from Amos 9:11 (see Brooke 1985, 111–12, 138–39). In this respect, the shared catchword found in the prophetic excerpt not only triggers an intertextual link in the form of a lexical match[13] but also offers "added value" by clarifying that the promise in 2 Sam 7 will be fulfilled despite the possibility of adverse circumstances: that is, even if the "throne of his kingdom" that was established for ever has fallen, God—through the messianic booth/branch of David—will raise it up in order to save Israel (see Avemarie 2009, 89). A similar example of catchword association follows immediately, in a new section, in 4QFlor 1 I, 14–16:

> (14) Midrash of "Blessed the man who does not walk in the counsel of the wicked" [Ps 1:1a]. The interpretation of this sa[ying: they are those who turn] aside from the path [דרך] of [the wicked,] (15) as it is written in the book of Isaiah, the prophet, for the last days, "And it happened that with a strong [hand he turned me aside from walking on the path [דרך] of] (16) this people" [Isa 8:11]. This [refers to] those about whom

12. This translation is a slightly modified version of García Martínez 1994, 136.

13. The presence of the verbal form והקימותי in Amos 9:11 is possibly as a result of scribal assimilation with 2 Sam 7:12 (since MT Amos 9:11 reads אקים), although it also occurs in the quotation of the same verse from Amos in CD VII, 16 (see Avemarie 2009, 88–89).

> it is written in the book of Ezekiel the prophet that "[they should] not [defile themselves any more with all] (17) of their idols" [Ezek 37:23]. This [refers to] the sons of Zadok and to the men of his council, those who seek jus[tice] eagerly, who will come after them to the council of the community.[14]

Once again, a second—prophetic—citation (Isa 8:11) provides the "missing" explanatory component of the base text's declaration about not walking in "the counsel of the wicked" (Ps 1:1a), although in this particular case, as indeed in others,[15] the link-word (דרך) is assumed rather than cited in the psalm text. This is confirmed by its occurrence in the immediately subsequent "interpretation of this saying." This variation of the analogical-associative technique demonstrates that such exegetical combinations can be based on elements that are close to the quotation without themselves being actually cited.

The notion of one scriptural passage providing information that is missing from another (analogous) text is not, however, a fixed feature of catchword exegesis, particularly in Jewish sources outside the Dead Sea Scrolls. Thus, in *On Agriculture* (72–84, especially 78–82), Philo quotes two passages that feature the phrase "horse and rider" (ἵππον καὶ ἀναβάτην; Deut 20:1 and Exod 15:2), although the one passage is not intended to clarify the other; indeed, their function is to provide verbal cues that will enable Philo to proceed, in chain-like fashion, to the next stage of his allegorical argument by providing additional, illustrative scriptural support in relation to the central topic.[16] Philo, particularly in his allegorical treatises, makes frequent use of the analogical technique of "verbal mode of transition" to link together scriptural quotations drawn from the Pentateuch (Runia 1984, 239; 2010, 95), and it thus represents one particular

---

14. Again, this is a slightly modified version of the translation in García Martínez 1994, 136.

15. E.g., in CD-A VII, 14–19, Amos 5:26–27 and Num 24:17 are combined because of the presence of the word "star" in both passages (= the Interpreter of the Law), even though this term is only explicitly quoted in the second scriptural citation.

16. See esp. Hamerton-Kelly 1976, 55–56. See Brooke (1985, 22–24), where attention is also drawn to the similar function of catchword association in *Sacrifices* 1–10, and, more recently, Runia 1984, 239–45; 1987, 119–20, 130–31; 2010, 92–93, 95–96, 100–104.

model of how catchword combinations were put into practice in late Second Temple Judaism.[17]

Various features of catchword-based serial quotations in Jewish sources relate, in this respect, to cases of double scriptural citations in the Gospel of John. The two quotations cited and enacted in the account of Jesus's entry into Jerusalem (12:13–15) are bound together by their shared use of the verb ἔρχομαι, which is now interpreted with reference to Jesus: "the one who comes [ὁ ἐρχόμενος] in the name of the Lord" (Ps 117[118]:26 LXX), "the king who comes [ἔρχεται] sitting on a donkey's colt" (Zech 9:9). The inclusion of the additional words ὁ βασιλεὺς τοῦ Ἰσραήλ at the end of the psalm citation (see Isa 44:2; Zeph 3:15 LXX) heightens the lexical match between the two scriptural references, so that Jesus's act of sitting on a donkey to manifest his kingly identity (Zech 9:9) serves as a corrective interpretation of his acclamation as "king of Israel" by the crowd (Manns 1991, 314; Daly-Denton 2000, 178–79).

Yet another passage in John's Gospel whose combination of scriptural citations is widely regarded as derived from similar exegetical principles is the juxtaposition of Isa 53:1 and 6:10 in the summary reflections on Jesus's public ministry in John 12:37–40(41), even though their analogous features are not to be found in the quotations themselves. The bringing together of these two Isaianic passages in John 12 has prompted the identification of several distinctive verbal and thematic links between their wider contexts, both in the opening verses of Isaiah's temple vision (6:1–13) and in the introduction to the fourth Servant Song (52:13–53:12; see esp. Evans 1987, 230–32; Bauckham 1998a, 49–51; Frey 2008, 385–86; Lett 2016, 169–72). These catchword links have the capacity to activate a profound intratextual connection that, in turn, shapes and directs John's understanding of both passages.

With regard to the Hebrew text, the most remarkable verbal connection between the two passages is the use of the distinctive phrase "high and lifted up" to describe the divine throne in the temple (Isa 6:1: רם ונשא) as well as the future exaltation and lifting up of the Servant (52:13: ירום ונשא). In addition, according to the Septuagint, Isaiah sees the glory (δόξα) that fills the temple (6:1 LXX) and distinctively speaks of the glorification (δοξασθήσεται) of the Servant (52:13 LXX; see Chibici-Revneanu 2007,

17. Runia (2010, 96): "It is this feature of his [Philo's] exegesis that recalls the use of the method of *gezerah shawa* by the scribes and rabbis, though I would maintain that what Philo does cannot be reduced to that method" (see Runia 1987, 119, 120).

196–98). Both Isaianic passages also contain strong visual emphasis, and one of their most striking connections is the link between Isaiah "seeing" the Lord (6:1, 5 LXX: εἶδον; see 6:9–10 LXX) and the "seeing" of the glorification of the Servant (52:13 LXX: ἰδοὺ; see 52:15 LXX: many nations and kings will see [ὄψονται] the Servant). With regard to the quotation of these passages in John 12, there are significant clues within, and in the lead-up to, this unit (12:37–41) that they are not simply linked together by their focus on obduracy and unbelief. Rather, if John 12:41, as seems likely, acts as a commentary on both Isaiah quotations—"Isaiah said these things [ταῦτα][18] because he saw his glory and spoke about him"—two Isaianic "events" or "acts" of seeing are mutually clarified and linked together in the closest possible terms by being subsumed under the single reference to glory: the Fourth Evangelist interprets Isaiah's call-vision in terms of him seeing Jesus as the glorious figure in the temple but also as the occasion for the prophet having seen, ahead of time, the glory manifested by Jesus during his earthly life, and whose rejection ultimately leads to his enthronement ("lifting up"; see John 12:32–33) and glorification (12:23) on the cross (see Frey 2008, 386).

Despite significant differences in terms of content and aims when compared to other examples in the Jewish sources, several features of John 12:37–41 support its inclusion in the broad Jewish exegetical category of "catchword links" within serial quotations. While this particular Johannine case of scriptural combination does not involve a close lexical match between the two explicit quotations from Isaiah, the textual form and sequence of the two citations in John 12 strongly indicate that the relationship between them, on a verbal level, is one of implied or inferential clarification rather than the accumulation of shared motifs: the first scriptural text expresses the reality of unbelief (Isa 53:1), and the second outlines the reasons for it (6:10). The lexical parallels between the two passages are to be identified in their wider literary context, with the result that John's accompanying explanatory remarks (John 12:41) indicate that the hidden implications of the one passage also apply to the other in a process of dynamic interaction through the analogical transfer of meaning. The other factor to be taken into consideration in this particular case is that John is building on a long history of associative

18. Although ταῦτα can be used in John's Gospel to refer to an earlier single statement (e.g., 9:22, 40), it is more commonly used to denote a series of preceding statements (e.g., 6:59; 8:30; 12:16; 13:21; 14:25).

exegesis with reference to Isa 6 and 52–53: connections between them are already established at a compositional level in the Hebrew text (Gosse 1991; Sommer 1998, 93–96), and, as recent studies have shown (Ekblad 1999, 179; see Koenig 1982, 47–52; Frey 2008, 385 n. 53), these intratextual links are developed further in the Septuagint of Isaiah to strengthen the mutually interpretative relationship of these two scriptural passages. Regardless, therefore, of John's christological interpretation of the Isaiah texts, his exegetical strategy in John 12:37–41 is not an innovation but an elaboration of what was already at his disposal in the Hebrew and Greek versions of this prophetic text.

Composite Quotations

I now move on to consider another category of scriptural citations that displays signs of operating according to the exegetical procedure of catchword links, but a category where the juxtaposition of texts is far less overt than in the case of serial quotations. Instead of stringing together two or more citations but separating them from each other with brief comments (such as a connective καὶ or πάλιν), in this particular category of explicit quotations "an author, although apparently only citing one text, is actually drawing one or more source texts together into a single, composite citation" (Adams and Ehorn 2016a, 1).[19] This can be a creative and highly complex exegetical process, frequently trigged by lexical parallels in different scriptural passages, but a process in which it is often difficult to pin down the "new element" to a single scriptural source.

The presence of composite citations in New Testament writings has long been acknowledged,[20] particularly in Hebrews and the letters of Paul, and this textual feature has figured prominently in source- and redaction-critical investigations of some of the explicit quotations in John's Gospel (Schuchard 1992; Menken 1996). What has not so far been undertaken is a comparative analysis of composite citations in the Jewish sources of

19. The following working definition is offered by Adams and Ehorn (2016a, 4): "A text may be considered a composite citation when literary borrowing occurs in a manner that includes two or more passages (from the same or different authors) fused together and conveyed as though they are only one."

20. Building on Stanley (1992), the two-volume project led by Adams and Ehorn (2016b; 2017) seeks to situate this citation technique within the broader Jewish, Greco-Roman and early Christian contexts.

the late Second Temple period with those in John's Gospel that are best described as the amalgamation of multiple texts in a single citation to produce *one* scriptural witness. To demonstrate that John's practice of this hermeneutical procedure fits comfortably within ancient Jewish exegetical activity, some examples from the relevant Jewish sources will now be examined. The examples in question are drawn from two different types of composite citations as identified by Christopher Stanley (1992, 258–59, 342; 2016, 204–5), namely, combined quotations and conflated quotations.

1. Combined Citations

In the case of combined quotations, excerpts from two or more separate scriptural passages are joined back-to-back under a single citation formula (or other explicit marker); while an uninformed audience could easily regard the citation as drawn from a single source, its textual form evinces two components that are, to some degree, "separable" from each other. Several examples of combined citations can be identified in Jewish exegetical literature (e.g., 4 Macc 18:18–19; 1 Esd 1:55),[21] including the following case attested in the Damascus Document (CD-A VIII, 14–15) where two excerpts from the book of Deuteronomy are combined in reverse sequence (9:5a; 7:8a) under a single citation ("and Moses said"): "And Moses said, 'It is not because of your righteousness or the uprightness of your heart that you are going to possess these nations [Deut 9:5a], but [it is] because [כי] of his love for your ancestors that he is keeping the oath' [7:8a]."[22]

In the wider context of both of these scriptural passages Moses addresses Israel and outlines God's grace toward his people since the exodus and before their entry into the land: faithfulness to God and his commandments will lead to prosperity. Here, in the Damascus Document, the combined quotation is applied to the Qumran sect: they are the heirs to the true covenant because of God's love for "the ancestors" and his faithfulness to his promises (Campbell 1995, 148; Norton 2016, 108–9). The linking together of the two excerpts is brought about by the connecting word "because" (כי), a term that they both share, as well as a number of

21. See Adams and Ehorn 2016b, 119–30: 4 Macc 18:18–19 combines Deut 32:39c LXX and Deut 30:20c LXX in this sequence with reference to death followed by life (see deSilva 2006, 264–65); 1 Esd 1:55 combines elements from Lev 26:34–35 and Jer 25:11–12.

22. The translation is a modification of Norton 2016, 108.

other phrases and concepts ("oath to the ancestors" in the uncited part of Deut 9:5 as well as in the cited part of Deut 7:8; "it is not because of ... but because of...");[23] the citations are also condensed to remove references to the wickedness of the nations (Deut 9:5) and to Israel's election and the exodus (7:8; see Dimant 2014, 108). The shift to Deut 7:8 takes place, nevertheless, in order to include an explicit reference to God's love toward the ancestors, a motif that is absent from the other Deuteronomic passage but, by extension, is then applied to members of the Qumran sect (CD-A VIII, 18: "the Penitents of Israel").

A similar procedure, but one that draws from more distant scriptural texts, is adopted by Philo in *Sacrifices* 87:

> Yet even if we are slow to do this, he [God] himself is not slow to take to himself those who are fit for his service. "I will take you," he says, "to be my people [Exod 6:7] *and I will be your God* [καὶ ἔσομαι ὑμῶν θεός Exod 6:7/Lev 26:12–13], and you shall be to me a people. I am the Lord" [Lev 26:12–13]. (Colson 1954, slightly modified)

As in the combined quotation noted in the Damascus Document, Philo here quotes two scriptural passages that share a common phrase (καὶ ἔσομαι ὑμῶν θεός) to form a single citation that runs seamlessly from one excerpt to the other. Indeed, since the shared words "I will be your God" occur at the end of the excerpt from Exod 6:7 but also at the beginning of the quotation from Lev 26:12(–13), it could be drawn from either text but in all probability acts as a catchword phrase linking the two together to form a composite quotation. Philo's reason for quoting both excerpts is that each one offers scriptural support for different aspects of Philo's argument (Royse 2016, 83): the first emphasizes God's initiative ("I will take you to be my people"), while the second highlights the close reciprocity between God and his people.

In both these cases of (combined) composite citations, sound exegetical reasons can be forwarded to support the view that the textual form of the quotation is not because of a lapse of memory on the part of the author but as a result of the skillful weaving together of distinct scriptural components whose fusion can be legitimated on the basis of their

23. "Verbal commonalities" between three scriptural passages (Ezek 44:7, 13, 15) also characterize the other example of a composite quotation in CD-A (III, 21) examined in Norton 2016, 103–7.

analogous, here complementary-expansive, features. These components were not randomly selected but betray the interpreters' awareness of and respect for the literary context from which these quotations were taken.

2. Conflated Quotations

There are fewer identifiable cases in Jewish sources of what can be described as "conflated quotations," that is, scriptural citations where one text is dominant but a word or phrase from another scriptural passage has deliberately, albeit without explicit signaling, been inserted into the quotation. Thus, in *Names* 187, and with reference to Jacob's wrestling, Philo provides a conflated citation in which one word from Gen 32:32 LXX (ἐπέσκαζεν), set in place with the aid of a connecting phrase (ᾧ καὶ), is included at the end of the quotation from Gen 32:25 LXX to explain the consequence of touching Jacob's thigh: "And [it] became numb," it is said, "[that is], the flat part of his thigh upon which he was limping" (τὸ πλάτος τοῦ μηροῦ, ᾧ καὶ ἐπέσκαζεν). Once again, this exegetical maneuver can be justified on the grounds that the word "thigh" (μηρός) occurs in both verses drawn from Gen 32 LXX, although in this particular case the positioning of the "foreign" word at the end of the quotation points to the fluidity of the given categorizations, in that it could be defined both as a conflated and combined composite citation.

In contrast to this short and relatively straightforward example from the writings of Philo, other extant cases of conflated quotations are often highly intricate (e.g., Bar 2:28–35; 2 Macc 2:11; Jub. 2:26–27),[24] in which the additional (or replacement) scriptural excerpt functions more like an allusion than a clearly identifiable citation. They can occur in exegetical texts of various genres, but conflated interpretations—rather than "citations" in the technical sense—are particularly prevalent in various LXX translations, thus highlighting the status of the Septuagint as a rich deposit of Jewish scriptural interpretation during the late Second Temple period. One frequently cited example is the Septuagint's rendering of Exod 15:3, where the anthropomorphic connotations of the designation of God as "man of war" (15:3) in the Hebrew text (יהוה איש מלחמה) are toned down in the Greek translation: "The Lord, the one who shat-

24. The difficulty of determining precise scriptural references in passages such as 2 Macc 2:11 (and hence their *composite* character) is highlighted in Adams and Ehorn 2016b, 130–34, 135–39; Allen 2016, 145–49.

ters wars, the Lord is his name" (κύριος συντρίβων πολέμους κύριος ὄνομα αὐτῷ). This substitution occurs, in all likelihood, under the influence of the Hebrew text of Ps 76:4 and Hos 2:20, where God is said to have shattered (or will shatter) war (שבר מלחמה),[25] and for which the same Greek verb as in Exod 15:3 LXX (συντρίβειν) is used to describe God as the one who "shatters war." As a result, the catchword shared by all three passages, מלחמה ("war"), acts as an interpretative bridge that generates the innovative translation encountered in Exod 15:3.

Similarly, the most plausible explanation of the curious rendering "just like in your promise" (ὡς καὶ ἐν τῇ ἐπαγγελίᾳ σου) for the Hebrew words "is it not in your ledger?" (הלא בספרתך) in Ps 55[56]:9c LXX is as follows: the Greek translator is alluding to Isa 25:8 LXX, a passage that—like Ps 55[56]:9b LXX—describes how God takes pity on his people and their tears:

> Isa 25:8 LXX: God has again wiped away every tear (πᾶν δάκρυον) from every face.

> Ps 55:9bc LXX: You have put my tears (τὰ δάκρυά μου) before yourself, *just like in your promise.*

In this particular case, the catchword link ("tear[s]") between these two scriptural passages does not bring about the lexical transfer of an identical word from the prophetic passage to the psalm text but rather triggers a deliberate allusion, in the final clause of Ps 55:9, to God's "earlier" promise (Isa 25:8) of eschatological intervention on behalf of his people and which involves him displaying pity on their tears (Schaper 1995, 63–64; see Aitken 2015, 325–26). It therefore represents yet another instance of the wide range of exegetical maneuvers underpinned by catchword assimilation that can be identified in late Second Temple Jewish texts, including the various Septuagint translations.[26]

---

25. Koenig 1982, 59–63; Menken 1996, 52–53. See also Isa 42:13 LXX, where the description of God "like a man of wars" (כאיש מלחמות) becomes "and he shall shatter war" (καὶ συντρίψει πόλεμον), probably under the influence of Exod 15:3 LXX and possibly Ps 75(76):4 LXX and Hos 2:20(18) LXX (see Baer 2001, 88–95).

26. For analyses of other examples of catchword/associative exegesis in LXX translations, see Joosten 2003, 359–63; 2012, 153–54; Theocharous 2012, 107–48. On the use of this exegetical technique in 1QIsa[a] (noting the influence of Isa 59:3 on the rendering of Isa 1:15), see Mackie 2015, 60–61.

3. Composite Citations in John's Gospel

The principle, then, behind all of these examples of composite quotations drawn from Jewish sources is that when two or more scriptural passages are fused to form a composite text (either combined or conflated) they enter into a mutually interpretative relationship. In this respect they supply significant comparative material for the explicit quotations in John's Gospel, many of which can also most plausibly be viewed as composite citations drawn from more than one scriptural source.[27] In comparison with other Jewish analogues, the Johannine composite quotations are, more often than not, to be categorized as belonging to the *conflated type*, in which short excerpts from analogous scriptural resources are inserted, through a process of expansion (additional element) or contraction (replacement element), to the primary source text. Admittedly, every individual citation must be analyzed on a case-by-case basis, but, as Maarten Menken (1996, 14, 206–9) has repeatedly emphasized, arguments about textual pluriformity and fluidity during the Second Temple period must only be drawn on when it is not possible to build a strong case for identifying exegetical motives behind the form of John's explicit quotations, that is, the identification of textual features that can be legitimated on the grounds of what is consistent with Jewish biblical exegesis.

The evidence so far surveyed does, however, offer a firm foothold for pursuing links between Jewish and Johannine hermeneutical methods, not only for the purpose of clarifying John's techniques but also for expanding our understanding of Jewish scriptural interpretation. The identification of catchword combinations behind some of John's explicit quotations provides a viable explanation of their textual form, and it also affords valuable exemplars of the ways in which this exegetical technique could be put into practice.

A few examples can be adduced to illustrate this point. In the Johannine account of Jesus's entry into Jerusalem, the second scriptural quotation, "Do not fear, daughter of Zion; behold, your king is coming, sitting on a donkey's colt" (12:15)—though clearly identifiable as a condensed cita-

---

27. For a detailed examination of all the composite citations in John's Gospel, see Williams forthcoming. See esp. John 6:31 (Exod 16:4, 15; Ps 78:24); John 7:38 (Ps 77:16, 20 LXX; Zech 14:8; Ps 114:8); John 12:15 (Zech 9:9; Isa 40:9; Zeph 3:16); John 13:18 (Ps 41:10; 2 Sam 18:28); John 19:36 (Ps 34:21; Exod 12:10 [LXX], 46; Num 9:12).

tion of Zech 9:9[28]—also includes elements that cannot be traced to this prophetic text.[29] The seemingly curious replacement of the words "rejoice greatly" with "do not fear" (μὴ φοβοῦ) is undoubtedly striking, and, for readers/hearers who would be able to identify the phrase as a deviation from Zech 9:9, it marks itself out as an intentional allusion to a different scriptural passage with the aim of bringing the meaning of both texts together to describe the arrival of Jesus as king (see Mackie 2015, 66–67, on the function and effect of "intentional allusions"). As far as its new Johannine context is concerned, the christological motivation for this change to "do not fear" may lie in the evangelist's attempt to align this scriptural quotation more closely with the fact that Jesus will ultimately manifest his kingship by means of his death, with which an exhortation to rejoice would appear incompatible (Bynum 2015, 59). Of particular significance, moreover, is the long scriptural—particularly Isaianic (35:4; 41:10, 13, 14; 43:1, 5; 44:2; 51:7; 54:4; see Zeph 3:15–16)—heritage of associating the phrase "do not fear" with the assurance of God's eschatological coming and presence and the proclamation of his salvation, now actualized through Jesus's entry into Jerusalem (Obermann 1996, 208–9; Brunson 2003, 236–39). These proposals provide more satisfactory explanations of the motive behind the modification to this quotation, particularly in view of its function as a retrospective reflection, than that it serves to allay the fear of the crowd, which, after the Lazarus miracle (see 12:18), misinterprets Jesus as a national king whose divine power is "frightening" (Menken 1996, 85–88).

The phrase "do not fear" is, of course, attested in a large number of texts in the Jewish Scriptures, including as an address to Israel in the already-noted passages from the prophecies of Isaiah, but its inclusion in the quotation of John 12:15 has not been randomly selected from any such source but is drawn specifically—in all probability—from another prophetic passage whose mutually interpretative relationship with the Zechariah text is supported by striking contextual similarities, including shared verbal and thematic patterns. Both Zeph 3:16 and Isa 40:9, which proclaim the eschatological coming of God or the messianic king, are pos-

28. The following elements in Zech 9:9 that are missing from John 12:15 are noted by Menken (1996, 79): (1) the second half of the appeal to rejoice as addressed to "daughter Jerusalem"; (2) the words "to you" in the next line, which describes the coming of the king; and (3) references to the king as "righteous and triumphant" and "humble."

29. In addition to the replacement of "rejoice greatly" with "do not fear," the king is said to be "sitting" (rather than "riding") on the donkey's colt.

sible contenders because of the decisive keywords that they share with Zech 9:9 in their wider context. Some of these link-words, in the Hebrew and/ or the Greek text, are found in Zeph 3:14–17 ("daughter Zion," "rejoice," "king [of Israel]"), others in Isa 40:9–10 ("behold," "Zion," "come"), whereas the phrase "do not fear" occurs in the plural form in Isa 40:9 LXX (μὴ φοβεῖσθε) and in the singular in the Hebrew text of Zeph 3:16 (אל תיראי; LXX: θάρσει). Indeed, it may not be necessary to decide between Zeph 3:16 and Isa 40:9 as the relevant lexical resources, since—both individually and collectively—they are closely aligned with the primary text (Zech 9:9). The exegetical trigger, in this respect, should be described as one of mutual activation: the textual change to the quotation is *motivated* by the need to identify a scriptural phrase ("do not fear") that fits its new Johannine context, but it is *legitimated* by the fact that the fusion of two or more scriptural texts that share common catchwords would be permissible within a Jewish exegetical milieu. It also points, as with the Isaianic quotations in chapter 12,[30] to John's sensitivity to the immediate and sometimes wider literary context of the primary and secondary scriptural sources of the citation.

Similar conclusions can be drawn about other quotations in John's Gospel, including the scriptural words cited after Jesus's death: "Not one of his bones shall be broken" (19:36: ὀστοῦν οὐ συντριβήσεται αὐτου). Whereas the primary text in this case is a pentateuchal regulation about eating the Passover lamb (Exod 12:46: "and you shall not break [LXX: συντρίψετε] a bone of it"; see Exod 12:10 LXX; Num 9:12), the future passive verbal form (συντριβήσεται) can once again, despite the different contexts, be legitimately viewed—on the basis of lexical association—as drawn from Ps 33(34):21 LXX: "he [the Lord] guards all his bones; not one of them shall be broken." Here, as a result, catchword assimilation enables John to present a deliberately composite portrayal of Jesus: he is not only the righteous sufferer of the Psalms who is protected and vindicated by God,[31] but, at the

30. Frey (2009a, 490): John demonstrates knowledge of the whole manna episode, and although only Isa 53:1 is explicitly quoted, the immediate setting of the fourth Servant Song, and indeed other Servant sayings, is evoked in Jesus's speech about his exaltation and glorification (see Isa 52:13 LXX) and as light of the world (see Isa 42:6; 49:6).

31. On other traces of the influence of "righteous sufferer" motifs on the Johannine presentation of Jesus, see, e.g., John 2:17 (Ps 69:10); 13:18 (Ps 41:10); 15:25 (Ps 35:19); 19:24 (Ps 22:19).

same time, he is the Passover lamb whose bones will not be broken upon his death (see John 1:29, 36; 18:28; 19:14, 28).[32]

Another potentially fruitful avenue, which must nevertheless be pursued in a separate study, is the possibility that the models of associative or analogical exegesis surveyed in this essay can assist in assessing composite allusions in the Gospel of John.[33] The exegetical maneuvers identifiable in the composite citations can serve as a helpful hermeneutical guide for mapping out the mechanics of but also some of the restrictions demanded by the technique of catchword association. As commentators repeatedly note, it is often difficult to pin down John's rich deposit of scriptural allusions to individual references and single meanings. Some motifs bear traces of several scriptural sources, recalling not one but a configuration of passages from the Jewish Scriptures (see Lincoln 2005, 79–80). However, in many such cases, it may not be necessary to trace the motif to a single source, as association through catchwords may deliver the necessary exegetical lever to enable allusions to function as metonymic scriptural markers that have the capacity to fulfill an innovative—even kaleidoscopic—function within the new text. Metaphorical images such as shepherd (John 10:1–18) and the vine (15:1–10) gather in themselves not one but a variety of mutually interpretative passages,[34] and the exegetical procedure of catchword assimilation can provide the necessary legitimating interpretative key. This kind of process is certainly not unique to John's Gospel; one need only consider the clustering of metaphorical images from a variety of scriptural sources attested, for example, in the Qumran Hodayot (Hughes 2006, 150–73; see

32. Cf. especially Schuchard 1992, 136–40; Menken 1996, 166; Bauckham 2015, 154 n. 61. The fusion of Passover and righteous sufferer traditions also has Jewish analogues (e.g., Jub. 49:13), as noted by Lincoln 2005, 481.

33. See also John 7:38, which uses an introductory citation formula, although what follows cannot be linked to one clear, primary scriptural source. It appears to bring together the water from the rock struck by Moses (Exod 17:6; Ps 78:16, 20; Isa 48:21 LXX), the water in the time of future salvation (Isa 43:20; 44:3), the water flowing from the temple (Ezek 47:1–12; Zech 14:7–8), and *living* water (Song 4:15; Zech 14:8; Jer 2:13). The phenomenon of "composite allusions" is acknowledged but not investigated by Adams and Ehorn (2016a, 2).

34. For scriptural analogues to the image of the shepherd in John 10:1–18, see, e.g., Num 27:12–23; 2 Sam 7:7–8; Pss 23:1; 78:70–71; Isa 40:11; Ezek 34:1–31; 37:24; Mic 5:2–4; Zech 11:3–17; and for the image of the vine (John 15:1–17), see, e.g., Ps 80:8–19; Isa 5:1–7; 27:2–6; Jer 2:21; 6:9; Ezek 15:1–8; 17:1–10; 19:10–14; Hos 10:1.

Manning 2004, 52–59) to be able to claim that this feature again places John's engagement with Scripture firmly within a Jewish environment.

An examination of John's composite quotations also reveals that shared catchwords do not necessarily have to be derived from the same text-type but can be drawn from the Hebrew text and the Septuagint translation. For this reason, it may not be necessary to pin down a metaphorical image such as "lamb of God" to an individual scriptural source or indeed to a single text-type (e.g., Nielsen 2006, 226–56; Bauckham 2015, 154–57). Thus, when John the Baptist sees Jesus coming toward him and declares, "Behold the Lamb of God who takes away the sin of the world" (1:29; see 1:36), the most likely interpretation is that Passover lamb imagery, which is later unfolded to play a significant role in the passion narrative (see 19:14, 29, 36), has been combined—through a lexical match—with echoes of the description of the Servant of God in the Septuagint version of Isa 53. The Servant, "like a lamb [ὡς ἀμνὸς] before the shearer" (53:7), is one who "bears [φέρει] our sins" (53:4) and "bore the sins of many" (53:12; Hebrew text: singular, "sin"), although, for the purpose of this composite allusion in its new Johannine context, the verb "to bear" (ἀναφέρειν) is replaced by the verb "to take away" (αἴρειν), whose scope is expanded to include "the sin of the world." Once again, a metaphorical description—like a composite citation—can act as the "carrier" of several scriptural sources at the same time, with clues supplied in the immediate context as to the particular contribution of each source through their innovative transfer to Jesus.

Concluding Comments

The aim of this essay has been to bring together the terms *John* and *Judaism* by focusing on some shared hermeneutical principles and methods. More specifically, I have attempted to demonstrate that a mutual exegetical interest in catchword combinations helps to position John's Gospel as a significant participant in and valuable witness to the range of interpretative possibilities within Jewish exegetical activity during the first century CE. It inevitably follows, from John's christological hermeneutic, that his interpretative aims are radically different from those of his Jewish contemporaries, but the methods whereby his conclusions are reached are the product of his rootedness in a rich tradition of Jewish scriptural interpretation. Some specific aspects of his hermeneutical methods may be unique to the Fourth Gospel, such as some of the interpretative maneuvers behind his composite quotations, but they may also be regarded as an elaboration or variation of existing patterns and trends that are sometimes more obliquely attested in the Jewish sources. A comparative analysis of the relevant Jewish and Johannine evidence certainly suggests that the exegetical procedures followed by John, if not the motives and results, would be deemed acceptable and hermeneutically valid in a wider Jewish context.

It has also been proposed that associative exegesis—or analogy through the use of link-words—was more widespread and varied in first-century Judaism than is generally thought. It certainly finds its most detailed—but highly specific—articulation in later rabbinic traditions, but it is also found in a variety of forms in much earlier texts. It is important, therefore, to recognize that, traditionally, a wide range of exegetical operations has been subsumed under the term *gezerah shavah*, whereas the evidence surveyed in this study—both from the Jewish sources and from John's Gospel—has demonstrated the need to look beyond surface resemblances in order to acquire a better understanding of the similarities *and* differences between early Jewish hermeneutical trends and later rabbinic practices. What John's Gospel brings to the table is a rich selection of hermeneutical "catchword" patterns that can sharpen our awareness and deepen our understanding of Jewish scriptural interpretation during the first century CE and beyond.

John, the Jews, and Philosophy

Harold W. Attridge

The vast literature on the *Jews* in the Fourth Gospel is well known and does not need extensive review here. In brief, use of the term in the gospel is not consistent; it displays a range of meanings and may have developed with the gospel's growth. Some of its sixty-six occurrences, for example, 2:30; 3:35, can be understood as simply or primarily geographical in character, referring to inhabitants of Judea. Yet it comes to function as a comprehensive term for those who represented loyalty to the traditions of Israel, led by the high priests and prominently involving the Pharisees. Several scholars have recently provided helpful surveys of recent treatments. Ruben Zimmermann (2013, 73) correctly notes that the term displays a "multifaceted semantic." Cornelis Bennema (2013b, 88–89) offers another useful summary. For him the Jews are "a particular religious group of Torah- and temple-loyalists found especially, but not exclusively, in Judaea." They are also "a composite group with the chief priests or temple authorities as the core or in leadership and the Pharisees as the influential laity."[1] As portrayed in the gospel, some people in this large group reacted positively to Jesus; others, including the leadership, rejected him. Yet, as Bennema also insists, many of these people "believe" in Jesus (8:31; 10:42; 11:45; see 2:23), and we shall explore that phenomenon in due course. It may be significant that the references to believing Ἰουδαῖοι are a phenomenon of the first half of the gospel. Although Nicodemus, because of his participation in the burial of Jesus, might be reckoned as some kind of believer, the believing Ἰουδαῖοι are said to have been silenced "on account of the Pharisees" at 12:42 and thereafter are absent from the narrative.

A challenging question about this set of characters within the gospel is whether they have some referential relationship to the world of the evan-

1. Bennema builds on his earlier work, 2009, 2013. See recently Porter 2015.

gelist and his readers. The Ἰουδαῖοι who opposed Jesus in the gospel's story world probably stand in some relationship with those who have been or threaten to be involved in the expulsion of Jesus's disciples from synagogues. The scenario of communal strife and, finally of a sectarian Johannine group, developed by J. Louis Martyn (1979), Raymond Brown (1979), and others has been influential but also subject to significant criticism, by, for example, Raimo Hakola (2005a) and, most recently, by David Lamb (2014). Whatever its audience, a small group or, as Richard Bauckham (1998b), suggests, "all Christians," there probably were extratextual referents that readers of the gospel identified as successors to the characters in the text. This paper will explore the possibility that something more than ethnic or social identity is involved in the extratextual reference and that the symbolic value of Ἰουδαῖοι has something to do with the fact that believing members of that group are not much in evidence in the second half of the gospel.

One intriguing feature of the gospel is the way in which interwoven in its highly dramatic narrative and glittering arabesque of evocative symbols is an attempt to address certain fundamental philosophical or conceptual issues arising from belief in Christ. Contemporary philosophers debated these issues, including the relationship between divine sovereignty and human responsibility (Attridge 2014), or the possibility of knowing or naming a divine being who is, by definition, unnamable and unknowable (Attridge 2016).

The treatment of ethics is another of the gospel's conceptual riddles. Recent discussion of the Johannine ethics has reacted against the judgment that the gospel is unconcerned with ethics apart from the "love command." Scholars have raised the possibility that the gospel contains some form of "implicit ethics" (Kanagaraj 2001 and other essays in van der Watt and Zimmermann 2012), perhaps in the form of an embedded community "ethos" (van der Watt 2006a; 2006b), fostering solidarity, a sense of mission (Kok 2010), and a commitment to loving service. Jesus displayed that kind of ethos in the foot washing, and his approach may have evinced a marked contrast to the ethics of the Roman Empire (Carter 2008). There may also be some explicit practical ethics in the epistles (van der Merwe 2006; Frey 2013f, 174–85), but their concerns do not necessarily explain the gospel's focus.

The gospel's concern with ethics is akin to its engagement with philosophical issues. It focuses on a fundamental principle and does not provide detailed advice about how to behave. Contemporary Stoics and other philosophers asked the question: How does one know what is the right thing to do? The gospel's answer is formally close to that of the Stoics: one knows what is right by understanding a basic truth and acting on it (Engberg-Pedersen 2000). This is not the only similarity to the Stoic tradition in the gospel, as I have argued elsewhere (Attridge 2010a). The gospel finds the locus of the truth that illuminates ethics in a place that might surprise Stoics, in the example of self-giving love presented by the death of Jesus and interpreted by his farewell discourse.

This sketch of what is going on in John is by way of background. What does it have to do with the Jews? Here we turn to focus on a crucial passage, the reactions to the raising of Lazarus in Jerusalem. One of the remarkable things about those reactions is, according to 11:45–46, that "many of the Ἰουδαῖοι who had come to Mary and who had seen what he [Jesus] had done believed [ἐπίστευσεν] in him." This is not the first report that many Ἰουδαῖοι believe in Jesus. Some murmur about his remarkable claims (6:41, 52; 7:11–12), think he has a demon (7:20), are out to kill him (5:18; 7:1, 30). Nonetheless, many outside the circle of Pharisees and high priests believe in him (7:31), even if they are baffled by some of his teaching (7:35). These believers include Nicodemus, who comes to his defense in 7:45–52. The inhabitants of Jerusalem at the feast of Sukkot ask stupid questions, but many still believe in him (8:31). Some of those believers mock his claims in the heated dialogue of chapter 8 (8:48, 52, 57) and seek to stone him (8:59). Yet the crowd of Ἰουδαῖοι is fickle, and here they are again in chapter 11, after seeing the shrouded Lazarus emerge from the tomb, believing in Jesus.

One could explain all this variation on the basis of the evangelist's use of sources or redactional layers, but whatever the sources, the resulting picture has two prominent dimensions. Opinions about Jesus are generally divided up through chapter 11. If we did not know the ending of the gospel, we might suspect at the end of chapter 11 that the plot was hanging in the balance. Which way would the Ἰουδαῖοι finally move, in support of Jesus or off to the roadside to pick up stones?

The high priests and the Pharisees determine the course of events. When some of the Ἰουδαῖοι report to them the marvelous deed that Jesus has done, they call an assembly, asking what to do since Jesus is doing so many "signs." The scene is drenched with irony. The "signs," understood as "wonders," are a cause for concern. "If we let him continue," the leaders say, "the signs will have the effect just manifested among the Ἰουδαῖοι. People will believe" (What? That Jesus is the King of the Jews? Perhaps, but the content of belief remains unspecified). "Moreover," the leaders say, "the Romans will come and they will obliterate our 'place.'" As it turns out, the authorities will see that Jesus is put to death, people will believe, the Romans will come, and the "place" of the Ἰουδαῖοι will be obliterated. The formula has a deeply ironic twist: From the point of view of the evangelist, all of this happened *not* because people believed in Jesus but because they did *not* do so.

What interests us is the next stage of the dialogue, the intervention by Caiaphas, who famously declares: "You know nothing at all! You do not understand that it is better for you to have one man die for the people than to have the whole nation destroyed" (11:49–50). So the NRSV. To be a bit more precise, Caiaphas should say, "You don't reckon [λογίζεσθε] that it is beneficial for you that one man die for the people and that the whole nation not perish." We shall return to that language.

The narrator then helpfully interprets the remarks of Caiaphas, "He did not say this on his own, but being high priest that year he prophesied that Jesus was about to die for the nation, and not for the nation only, but to gather into one the dispersed children of God." The narrator also notes the effects of Caiaphas's declaration, "So from that day on they planned to put him to death."

The narrator's comments call attention to the speech of Caiaphas and signal its importance for the plot. The narrator's recollection of the speech at 18:14 confirms its significance. Although some opponents among the Ἰουδαῖοι have been working to eliminate Jesus before chapter 11 (5:18; 7:1, 19, 25, 30; 8:37, 40; see Matt 12:14), the effort is now sanctioned by the highest authority, and believing Ἰουδαῖοι begin to fall silent.

But what is it that silences belief, however unstable that belief might have been? The narrator's comment on the statement of Caiaphas highlights the irony that the high priest unknowingly articulates what the gospel advances as a profound theological truth, that the death of Jesus was indeed a benefit not only for his own people but for all God's children. This claim is grounded in traditional affirmations by followers of Jesus that his divinely ordained death had salvific import for humankind. The evangelist does not simply repeat those claims; he also explores how the salvific effect is produced, not by magic but by a revelation of a liberating truth. The narrator's comment at 11:51–52, noting the irony of Caiaphas's remark, gestures toward this major theoretical strand of the gospel's conceptual tapestry, but, as usual, there is more to the passage than what the narrator explicitly says. That more is bound up with the narrator's final comment on the episode in verse 53: "from that day they plotted to kill him."

The Ἰουδαῖοι, now resolute and united in their opposition to Jesus, are persuaded by Caiaphas, not by the ironic truth that he unwittingly articulates but by the logic of his literal argument. Caiaphas is no fool. The case he presents is a perfectly rational one. He might even be thought to echo the opinion of Cicero in *Fin.* 3.64:

> From this [that the world is governed by divine will] it is a natural consequence that we prefer the common advantage to our own.... This explains the fact that someone who dies for the state is praiseworthy, because our country should be dearer to us than ourselves. (Long and Sedley 1987)

Cicero seems to be talking about an act of self-sacrifice, which both Greek and Roman traditions would have viewed favorably, but what of the judgment that it is "beneficial" to sacrifice *someone else* for the good of the whole? How would such an argument from expediency, an argument that the end justifies the means, be viewed in the first century?

The general answer is "unfavorably," and that obtains both in the Greek and Jewish traditions. The antithesis of "beneficial" and "good" is a famous Socratic trope, in which the sophist argues only for the "beneficial," neglecting what is truly good. The contrast is enshrined in the dialogue *Alcibiades*, in which Socrates confronts the young politician and tries to convert him from a devotion to expediency to a dedication to justice. Although the authenticity of the dialogue has been challenged, it was considered in antiquity an excellent introduction to Platonism.

The contrast between making moral judgments on the basis of principle, not expediency, is assumed in later philosophers, as commentators on John such as Craig Keener (2003, 854–57, especially 856 n. 189) have noted. Stoics, for example, praise "the good" as being all the things that are desirable for humankind. This praise is not a way of prioritizing the "beneficial" in making moral judgments. That claim is, like the famous Stoic paradoxes, an affirmation that only the morally good can be truly beneficial. So, from the philosophical point of view, someone who argues, as does Caiaphas, that the end justifies the means, that what is "beneficial" is what is right, would be judged morally defective, an ethical cripple.

What of Jewish judgments on the topic? Commentators sometimes suggest that the position of Caiaphas is indeed represented in some sources. However, a close examination of those sources suggests a more complex situation.

The recommendation of Caiaphas that it is beneficial for one to die for the collective good finds parallels in stories where a similar judgment seems to be made. The prime example is the account of the death of Shebah the son of Bichri, a rebel against King David, slain by the inhabitants of Abel of Bethmaacah when the town was besieged by Joab (2 Sam 20:14–22). This story, of which Roger Aus (1992) has argued that the Johannine account is a midrash, is cited frequently in rabbinic sources. Another clear case is that of Jonah, thrown into the sea to save his shipmates (Jonah 1:11–16). Yet one important element is regularly lacking in these cases. The people in the stories act instinctively. They are not called to make a "reckoning" of what is to their benefit.

Rabbinic reflections on the topic are intriguing. An attempt to address the ethical issue, to make some "reckoning" of the principles involved, appears in m. Ter. 8:11, which is based on Exod 29:27 and Num 15:18–19. The Mishnah chapter deals with the issue of the purity of the *terumot*, under what circumstances the offering might be rendered unclean and under what circumstances it might be consumed. The Mishnah presents an interesting hypothetical over which Rabbi Eliezer and Rabbi Joshua (famous first-generation Tannaim) disagreed:

> If a man was passing from one place to another with heave-offering loaves in his hand and a gentile said to him, "Give me one them and I will defile it, and if not I will defile them all." R. Eliezer says: "Let him defile them all but do not give him one in order that he may defile it." R. Joshua says: "He should leave one of them on a stone before him." (trans. Danby 1933, 62)

Rabbi Eliezer will have no part of an end-justifies-means calculus. One should not participate in creating impurity. Rabbi Joshua is a bit more flexible: yes, it may be acceptable to allow the desecration of a portion of something that is pure, but one should not do so *actively*.

The case of a bit of consecrated bread may seem trivial, but the following Mishnah (m. Ter. 8:12) ups the ante, with a gendered twist. If gentiles demand of a group of Jewish women that they give one over to be raped or the gentiles will rape the lot, the Mishnah says, "Let them make all of them unclean, but they should not hand over a single Israelite."

Tosefta Terumot 7:20 presents a slightly different and equally disturbing scenario. A group of Jews encounters a group of gentiles who demand that they turn over one of their number to be killed or else all the Jews will be slain. Like m. Ter. 8:12, the first opinion of the Tosefta rejects the possibility that the one should be handed over. A conflicting opinion is that if the gentiles do not specify a particular individual, the rest of the group cannot turn one over, but if the gentiles do specify someone, as Joab's forces specified Sheba son of Bichri, that individual may be turned over.

The opinion allowing the sacrifice of one for many does not end the analysis. Rabbi Judah asks under what circumstances the second opinion might apply. The response is that when both the individual and the rest of the Jews are "inside," presumably inside a besieged town, and all would die in any case, it would be legitimate to turn the man over. In support of his opinion, the actions of the woman of 2 Sam 20:22 are cited, with the additional information that she told her fellow citizens that precisely the situation just described by the Tosefta applies: "Since he is going to be killed, and you are going to be killed, give him to them that you all may not be killed." So far, then, the Tosefta argues that, *in extremis*, the expedient logic of "one instead of many" applies.

Yet the Tosefta is not finished with the issue. The final opinion is that of Rabbi Simeon, who continues to put words into the mouth of the woman: "Thus she said to them, 'Anyone who rebels against the kingship of the House of David is [in any case] liable to execution'" (trans. Avery-Peck 2002, 184). In the paradigm case, Sheba son of Bichri was in fact guilty of a capital offense, revolt against the king. He therefore deserved to die. In handing him over, the townspeople were doing their duty. An argument on principle trumps an argument from expediency.

The Jerusalem Talmud (y. Ter. 46b)—the Bavli has no Gemara on this tractate—and Genesis Rabbah (94:9) continue the discussion about when "one for many" is a legitimate move. Yerushalmi first tackles the case of the women threatened by rape and argues that it might be possible to give one for many under very restricted circumstances, if the woman has already been rendered unclean. The issue is framed not as one of life and death but of purity, the main subject of the tractate of the Mishnah. Yerushalmi then tackles the issue of the man to be handed over.

Before considering Yerushalmi further, it is useful to compare how Genesis Rabbah handles the topic. The midrash starts with the story of Sheba ben Bichri and picks up more or less where the Tosefta leaves off. After discussing the situation with Joab, the woman declares, "He who is insolent toward the royal house of David will be decapitated by divine decree" (trans. Freedman and Simon 1983, 2:877). As the Midrash Rabbah tells the tale, the woman then goes to Joab and, like Abraham bargaining with Yahweh over Sodom and Gomorrah, she haggles with David's general. He begins by demanding a thousand souls; she finally argues him down to one. And sure enough, the one is a "lodger" there, Sheba son of Bichri, who immediately loses his head, but, as we have already learned, he deserved it!

Yerushalmi invokes the same principles but stages a debate between Rabbi Simeon b. Laqish and Rabbi Yochanan, who defends the position that Sheba son of Bichri was *not* subject to capital punishment but could nonetheless have been given over (Avery-Peck 1982, 417–22).

Both the Yerushalmi and Genesis Rabbah continue their reflection with a story that is even closer to the case before Caiaphas. The story tells of one Ulla bar Koshev, who has been condemned to death by the Romans. Ulla seeks protection in the home of Rabbi Joshua ben Levi. According to the Yerushalmi, Rabbi Joshua convinces Ulla to turn himself in. Genesis Rabbah adds another note and depicts Rabbi Joshua offering, in effect, the reasoning of Caiaphas: "It is better that you should die than that the community should be punished because of you."[2] The rabbi hands Ulla over. Rabbi Joshua would seem, therefore, to side with Caiaphas and with those in the tradition of this continuing debate who take the side of expedience.

Yet the story continues, and Yerushalmi and Genesis Rabbah report that the prophet Elijah, who has been prone to visit Rabbi Joshua, ceases doing so for some time, displeased with the way the rabbi has behaved. When he finally does reappear, he listens to Rabbi Joshua's defense of his action. Then the prophet rebukes the rabbi, saying, "Am I then the companion of informers?" Rabbi Joshua defends himself to the prophet by saying he was simply abiding by the letter of the mishnaic law allowing defilement of *terumot* under threat. Elijah responds with a pointed question: "Is this indeed the law for pious ones?"[3] Elijah, at least, does not totally approve of Rabbi Judah's reasoning, and nor do the rabbinic authors. As the story in the Yerushalmi and Genesis Rabbah already showed, the case of Sheba son of Bikri was not a good precedent for a lifeboat ethic that sacrifices one for many, since Sheba was clearly guilty of a capital crime.

---

2. מוטב דלקטיל ההוא גברא ולא ליענשי ציבורא על ידיה, trans. Freedman and Simon 1983, 2:879.

3. For Yerushalmi, Avery-Peck 1982, 419; for Genesis Rabbah, Freedman and Simon 1983, 2:879. Another treatment of the passage appears in Falk (1985, 130–47), who discusses it in the context of his dubious theory that Jesus was part of an effort on the part of some Pharisees to create a religion for the gentiles.

That the Jewish tradition of Mishnah, Tosefta, Talmud Yerushalmi, and Midrash Rabbah reflects in some way or other the story in John 11, or the history behind it, is hardly likely. The tradition shows at the very least that there were Jewish sages who wrestled with the issue of whether "one for many" was morally justifiable and who rejected the kind of reasoning attributed to Caiaphas in John 11. That reasoning may have involved the sort of political realism that Josephus attributes to Agrippa II, who, on the verge of the great revolt, warned the inhabitants of Jerusalem that if they did rebel the Romans "would make you an example to the rest of the nations, they will burn the holy city to the ground and exterminate your race" (*J.W.* 2.397, Thackeray 1927–1928). But is expediency, based on a realistic assessment of political risk, a proper way to "reason" toward a decision about an ethical matter? One of the things that the story of Caiaphas in the Fourth Gospel does, like Plato's *Alcibiades*, and like the story of Rabbi Joshua in Genesis Rabbah, is to answer definitely, "No!"

How then does this little tale help our efforts to understand John and the Jews?

1. It reminds us that there is a conceptual point being made in the gospel: the key to right action is right reasoning. Caiaphas challenges the members of the Sanhedrin to do some "reckoning," and the gospel challenges its readers to do so too. With that part of the gospel's position many, both Jew and Greek, would agree. The gospel also claims that the ground for right reasoning about ethical matters is to be found in the revelation of the principle of divine life encountered on the cross (John 15:13). That claim will probably win more limited acceptance.

2. In the person of Caiaphas the gospel also addresses some of the social difficulties that its addressees face: many, but not all of their Jewish friends and neighbors, or at least quondam friends and distant neighbors, do not accept their claims about Jesus. Behind that rejection resides not some inimical supernatural power (John 8:44) but a flawed reason, not on the part of all members of the community but on the part of its leaders. The evangelist's effort here is not unlike that of Paul in Rom 9–11, where he tries to read the minds of his Jewish critics and point to the ways in which they fail to understand the logic of their own tradition. The evangelist finds the critical failure in another location than does Paul, but his result is similar, a blinding of hearts and minds to the truth of which he is convinced.

3. In sum, what the evangelist does through Caiaphas and his appeal to reason is to set up a model that teaches a lesson and perhaps helps to explain an inimical social reality. In doing so, he also creates a stereotype

that has played its own deleterious role in the history of Jewish-Christian relations. Understanding what he was up to, and even agreeing with him, as do many of the voices in the Jewish halakic tradition noted here, does not take away the sting of how the passage has been used.

Part 3
Reappraising John's Relationship to Judaism and Jewish Christianity

Story and History: John, Judaism, and the Historical Imagination

Adele Reinhartz

A "tipping point," says Malcolm Gladwell, is "that magic moment when an idea, trend, or social behavior crosses a threshold, tips, and spreads like wildfire."[1] Gladwell's examples come from the headlines, or widespread social phenomena such as big-city crime rates and Hush Puppies shoes. But tipping points happen also in the small and more specialized areas that we inhabit as scholars.

In the Johannine corner of New Testament studies, one such tipping point occurred with the publication of J. Louis Martyn's book *History and Theology in the Fourth Gospel* (1968). When the book was first published, I was still in high school and had barely heard of the Gospel of John, let alone read it. But by the time the second edition came out in 1979, I was already in graduate school and contemplating a dissertation on the Fourth Gospel.[2] This book hit me like a thunderbolt, and frequent rereadings have not substantially lessened its impact. Into the rarefied—and often sleep-inducing—atmosphere of mid-twentieth-century Johannine scholarship, Martyn's book injected a refreshing reminder that John's Gospel was not only a puzzle for theological inquiry, source analysis, and *Religionswissenschaft* but also, potentially, a clue to the actual lives of long-ago individuals and groups.

---

* This essay is dedicated to the memory of J. Louis Martyn, who died on June 4, 2015.

1. "The Tipping Point: Reading Guide Introduction," Malcolm Gladwell, http://tinyurl.com/SBL0398a. See Gladwell 2000.

2. A third edition appeared in 2003, with a new preface, a few minor revisions, some additional notes, and a helpful introduction by D. Moody Smith (Martyn 2003).

Martyn urges his readers to think concretely about the Johannine community—the group within which and for which, he argues, the gospel was written. His questions are compelling and down to earth: "How are we to picture daily life in John's church? Have elements of its peculiar experience left their stamp on the Gospel penned by one of its members?" In order to grasp anything at all about these early Christ confessors, Martyn (2003, 29) insists,

> It becomes imperative that we make every effort to take up temporary residence in the Johannine community. We must see with the eyes and hear with the ears of that community. We must sense at least some of the crises that helped to shape the lives of its members. And we must listen carefully to the kind of conversations in which all of its members found themselves engaged. Only in the midst of this endeavor will we be able to hear the Fourth Evangelist speak *in his own terms*, rather than in words which we moderns merely want to hear from his mouth. (emphasis original)

This description of the task of the interpreter captured my imagination, and I could resist it no more successfully than Odysseus the call of the sirens. Martyn put into words the inchoate impulse that had drawn me to the study of the past: the desire to imagine myself back into an ancient world populated by personalities and shaped by events whose profound impact is still felt today.

I was not the only one. By the time I read Martyn's book, other scholars, including Wayne Meeks (1972) and Raymond E. Brown (1979), had published important studies based on his work, and before long, Martyn's account of the Johannine community and its dramatic falling-out with the Jewish community was repeated as fact in many specialized studies of John and in New Testament introductions alike. Bart Ehrman's (2004, 172) *The New Testament: A Historical Introduction to the Early Christian Writings*, for example, states that

> the story of Jesus healing the blind man reflects the experience of the later community that stood behind the Fourth Gospel. These believers in Jesus had been expelled from the Jewish community.... This expulsion from their synagogue had serious implications for the Christian community's social life and for the way it began to understand its world and its stories about its messiah, Jesus.

Martyn's book has had its fair share of critics, myself among them, who have argued (convincingly, in my view) that neither his approach nor his narrative stands up to close scrutiny. Yet his work still has a powerful hold on the Johannine corner of New Testament studies and on me as well. I do not normally spend much time pondering, say, the Johannine signs source, possible Mandaean influences on Johannine symbolism, or the conundrum of realized versus future eschatology, all hot topics in the late 1970s and early 1980s when I did my doctoral work. But Martyn's hypothesis still teases at me not only because of its enduring popularity but because of my own enduring interests.

The Narrative

In Martyn's view, the Gospel of John was written for an existing community that had already formed around the particular Christology and worldview that later reached its final expression in the gospel. The community was composed primarily of ethnically Jewish believers in Christ who had continued to participate in Jewish community life, including the synagogue. After a time, the Jewish community became uncomfortable with the presence of Christ confessors among them and took measures to exclude them from the synagogue, which in effect meant expelling them from the Jewish community as such. This traumatic event marked the separation of this Jewish-Christian community from the Jewish mainstream and provides the background for the gospel's often antagonistic language about the Jews.

The Approach

The starting point for Martyn's narrative is the gospel's references to the *ἀποσυνάγωγος*. The term, in singular or plural, appears in three passages. In 9:21–22, the parents of a blind man whose sight had been restored by Jesus deny knowledge of his healing "because they were afraid of the Jews; for the Jews had already agreed that anyone who confessed Jesus to be the Messiah would be put out of the synagogue."[3] In 12:42–43, the gospel narrator states that "many, even of the authorities, believed in him. But because of the Pharisees they did not confess it, for fear that they would be put out of the synagogue; for they loved human glory more than the glory that comes from God." Finally, in 16:2, Jesus warns his disciples that "they

3. Unless otherwise noted, Bible translations conform to the NRSV.

will put you out of the synagogues. Indeed, an hour is coming when those who kill you will think that by doing so they are offering worship to God."

Martyn argues that it was anachronistic to imagine that Jesus's followers would have been excluded from the synagogue during his lifetime.[4] Instead, these three passages must refer indirectly to a situation closer to the time that the gospel itself was written. This observation suggests to him that the gospel was intended to be read on two levels: the *einmalig* level, which is the story of Jesus in the first third of the first century CE, and a second level, which is the story of the Johannine community in the last decade of the first century.

Form of Presentation

Martyn presents his narrative not in the turgid academic prose that was de rigueur in the latter half of the last century but in ordinary language and in dramatic form. Out of the text of John 9, Martyn (2003, 30–36) creates a play, divided into scenes, complete with dramatis personae and dialogue.

> Scene 1: A street in Jerusalem near the temple (in the Jewish quarter of John's City?), verses 1–7. Jesus (a Christian preacher) heals a blind beggar.
>
> Scene 2: Near the man's home (the Jewish quarter?), verses 8–12. The amazed neighbors discuss the event.
>
> Scene 3: The Sanhedrin of Jerusalem (a meeting of the Gerousia in John's city?), verses 13–17. The Jewish authorities interrogate the healed man.
>
> Scene 4: The same courtroom: verses 18–23. The Jewish authorities interrogate his parents.
>
> Scene 5: The same courtroom: verses 24–34. The Jewish authorities recall the beggar for further questioning.
>
> Scene 6: A street (near the meeting place of the Gerousia?), verses 35–38. The preacher hears that the beggar has been expelled from the fellow-

4. This view has been critiqued extensively but in my view unconvincingly by Jonathan Bernier (2013), who wishes to argue that exclusion from the synagogue could indeed have taken place during Jesus's own lifetime.

> ship of the synagogue, finds the man, and "puts to him the decision of faith" (p. 35).
>
> Scene 7: The same street, verses 39–41. The preacher accuses the Jews of blindness and introduces the sermon of the shepherd and the sheep (John 10). (Martyn 2003, 40–45)

The key scene for our purposes is scene 4. When interrogated by the Jewish authorities, the blind man's parents hesitate: "We do not know how it is that now he sees, nor do we know who opened his eyes. Ask him; he is of age. He will speak for himself" (9:21). The scene continues:

> From offstage a voice informs the audience that the parents did indeed know who had healed their son. And it is frightening to possess this particular knowledge, as they stand before the Jewish court. For they know two things: that the healer is Jesus, whom the Christians confess as Messiah, and that the Jews have already agreed that if any of their number confesses this Jesus to be Messiah, he will be put out of the synagogue. This is why they are frightened, the voice repeats, and the audience can readily understand. (Martyn 2003, 43)

In scene 6, the Christian preacher—Jesus's analogue in the second-level narrative—

> hears that the man has been expelled from the fellowship of the synagogue. It is not an uncommon event in the experience of this preacher. He knows that even among the synagogue authorities themselves are some who believe the Christians' Jesus to be Messiah (12:42). To be sure, many of these are afraid to confess their faith just as this man's parents were afraid earlier today. All of them know of the dreaded agreement. (Martyn 2003, 45)

Despite the dramatic form, Martyn insists that this is not a fiction but a historical occurrence:

> At some time prior to John's writing, an authoritative body within Judaism reached a formal decision regarding messianic faith in Jesus. Henceforth, whoever confesses such faith is to be separated from the synagogue.… Indeed, John's church has a number of members who have personally experienced the operation of the awesome agreement. They are Jewish excommunicates (ἀποσυνάγωγοι). (Martyn 2003, 49)

Martyn's narrative is constructed entirely from the gospel itself. But crucial to his case is the claim that in about 85 CE the central Jewish authority, established at Jamnia or Yavneh, promulgated a decree that forbade Jewish believers in Jesus from participating in synagogue services. This authoritative body inserted a curse—euphemistically called the blessing on or of the heretics (Birkat Haminim) into the daily liturgy in order to flush out Christ confessors.

למשומדים אל תהי תקוה
ומלכות זדון מהרה תעקר בימינו
והנצרים והמינים כרגע יאבדו
ימחו מספר החיים
ועם צדיקים אל יכתבו
ברוך אתה יי
מכניע זדים

For those doomed to destruction may there be no hope
and may the dominion of arrogance be quickly uprooted in our days
and may the Nazarenes and the heretics be destroyed in a moment
and may they be blotted out of the book of life
and may they not be inscribed with the righteous.
Blessed are you, O Lord,
who subdues the arrogant. (trans. Marcus 2009, 524)

The expulsion mechanism required that suspected Christ confessors would be asked to lead the services and would then find themselves unable to recite this passage of the liturgy. For Martyn, the rabbinic legends that credit a late first-century sage with the formulation of this curse support his hypothesis that the Gospel of John narrates the traumatic expulsion of Johannine Christians from the synagogue.[5] Although Martyn himself

5. The relevant passage is Ber. 28b–29a: ת"ר שמעון הפקולי הסדיר י"ח ברכות לפני רבן גמליאל על הסדר ביבנה אמר להם ר"ג לחכמים כלום יש אדם שיודע לתקן ברכת הצדוקים עמד שמואל הקטן ותקנה לשנה אחרת שכחה והשקיף בה שתים ושלש שעות ולא העלוהו אמאי לא העלוהו והאמר רב יהודה אמר רב טעה בכל הברכות כלן אין מעלין אותו בברכת הצדוקים מעלין אותו חיישינן שמא מין הוא שאני שמואל הקטן דאיהו תקנה. "Our rabbis taught: Simeon ha-Paquli organized the Eighteen Benedictions in order before Rabban Gamaliel in Yavneh. Rabban Gamaliel said to the sages: 'Isn't there anyone who knows how to fix the Benediction of the Heretics?' Samuel the Small stood up and fixed it, but another year he forgot it. And he thought about it for two or three hours, [and he did not recall it], but they did not remove him. Why then did they not remove him? Did not R. Judah say that Rav said: 'If someone makes a

was concerned primarily with the experience of the Johannine community, the hypothesis has broader significance for the issue of the separation between Judaism and Christianity, often called "the parting of the ways." If the Jewish authorities excluded or expelled Christ believers from the synagogue, then it is the Jews who bear responsibility for initiating the process of separation.

Critique

Most scholars now concede that Birkat Haminim probably was not yet in wide circulation, or perhaps even not formulated, in the late first century, and even if it were it could not have been used to exclude Christ confessors from the synagogue.[6] This point was made as early as Reuven Kimelman's 1981 article, "Birkat Ha-Minim and the Lack of Evidence for an Anti-Christian Jewish Prayer in Late Antiquity," and was clinched in Ruth Langer's exhaustive 2011 study *Cursing the Christians?* Some scholars who acknowledge this point nevertheless abide by the expulsion hypothesis but suggest that it was a local edict and not mandated by a central Jewish authoritative body (Rensberger 1988, 24).

Many have pointed out the methodological flaws with the two-level reading strategy, which amounts to an allegorical reading of the gospel that is tautological and unverifiable (Hägerland 2003). Others have considered the phenomenon of exclusion in the broader context of Greco-Roman voluntary associations and suggested that being excluded from the synagogue would not necessarily have been tantamount to expulsion from the Jewish community (Kloppenborg 2011).

More disturbing, however, is the way in which Martyn's hypothesis has been used by others to justify the harsh things that the gospel's Jesus says about and to the Jews. Cynthia Kittredge describes this view—without

---

mistake in any of the benedictions, they don't remove him, but if [he makes a mistake] in the Benediction of the Heretics, they do remove him, since they suspect that perhaps he is a heretic'? Samuel the Small is different, because he formulated it" (Epstein 1935, 2:107–8

6. A notable exception is Marcus 2009. Through the 1970s it was generally thought that Yavneh was the central authority of post-70 Judaism and that it was preoccupied with self-definition and therefore excluding those who did not conform to proto-rabbinic Judaism. See, for example, Berger 1998, 42. This view has been challenged, in my view successfully, by numerous scholars. See, for example, Cohen 1984 and Boyarin 2000.

explicitly endorsing it—in her 2007 book, *Conversations with Scripture: The Gospel of John*, in which she writes that "the language of enmity against 'the Jews' in the gospel reflects the intense feelings of loss and hurt of those who had become socially separated from their kinspeople" (53). This perspective, however nicely it is phrased, lets the gospel off the hook for its anti-Jewish expressions. Here, then, is another possible reason for the allegiance to Martyn's hypothesis: it keeps the gospel free of the taint of anti-Judaism and therefore lessens the tensions that some liberal Christian theologians feel between the canonical status of John's Gospel and their own discomfort with and condemnation of anti-Judaism and its close cousin, anti-Semitism.

Martyn fully believed in the accuracy of his historical reconstruction, but he knew that the evidence was both slim and problematic. He presented his work with appropriate cautions about its speculative nature. His followers, however, exercised no such caution. In their hands Martyn's imaginative description of the Johannine community and its struggles became gospel truth. In the words of Robert Kysar, these scholars built "a skyscraper on top of a toothpick."[7] Kysar (2006, 238–39) notes that Martyn's

> proposal swept through Johannine studies and took deep and healthy roots that grew until it was regarded almost as a given fact. By the 1990s in many circles, it was often a foregone assumption that this was the setting for the writing of the Gospel of John. Like other hypotheses, this model was so widely embraced that at times many of us may have forgotten that it was only a hypothesis. Indeed, along with the speculative Q document, the theory has now become one of the best examples of how scholarship tends to transform hypotheses into truth. The tale of this theory demonstrates the necessity to keep reminding ourselves of the difference between truth and hypothesis, as well as the fact that we never really prove much of anything.

Yet despite its many critics, the paradigm persists. Why? It is always possible, of course, that we critics are simply wrong and that Martyn was right. In the absence of any real evidence, however, I am inclined to look in a different direction and that is to the sheer persuasiveness—the rhetorical

---

7. In his essay "What's the Meaning of This?," Kysar (2006, 173) contrasts the ease with which he personally dismissed Q due to the historical fragility of the hypothesis with the momentousness of his turn from the Martyn expulsion theory, which had been a cornerstone of his own understanding of the Fourth Gospel for decades.

finesse—of Martyn's book itself. Three elements of this rhetoric seem to me to be the most important: writing style, dramatic mode of presentation, and explanatory power.

Style

For those of us who were in New Testament doctoral programs in the late 1970s and early 1980s, Martyn's book, so clear, so easy to understand, and yet so engaging, was a breath of fresh air. We admired his audacity in departing from the usual thick prose of the era. Here, for example, is Werner Kümmel (1975, 232) on the purpose of John's Gospel, from his *Introduction to the New Testament* (and here I take a deep breath):

> If J[oh]n is not an expansion of, nor an improvement of, nor a substitute for the Synoptics, which it knows and can presuppose that its readers know, the only remaining possibility is that it presupposes (without directly saying so) knowledge of the existing Gospels and on that basis gives its own representation of Jesus, which seeks to reveal in a complete way that Jesus is the Anointed One, the Son of God (20:31).

Compare now Martyn (2003, 30):

> One thing, at least, is shared by all New Testament authors in this regard: none of them merely repeats the tradition. Everyone hears it in his own present and that means in his own way; everyone shapes it, bends it, makes selections from among its riches, even adds to it. Put in other terms, everyone reverences the tradition enough to make it his own.

Kümmel and Martyn are making the same point; Martyn's, however, is far more accessible, and more persuasive for that very reason.

Mode of Presentation

Martyn's use of the dramatic form also set him apart from other scholars of his time and ours. The use of drama underscores the striking similarities between historiography and historical fiction, whether in the form of novels, drama, or film. Whereas we generally presume an opposition between history and fiction, philosophers of history have pointed out the degree to which historiography itself is an imaginative exercise not unlike that involved in writing historical fiction.

In his classic book *The Idea of History*, R. G. Collingwood (1946, 233) notes that historical thought, by definition, is always about absence: "events which have finished happening, and conditions no longer in existence." Historical thinking, therefore, is "that activity of the imagination by which we endeavor to provide 'the idea of the past' with detailed content" (247). The historical imagination entails reenactment, that is, a "perpetuation of past acts in the present" (218). The historian, concludes Collingwood (288; see Dray 1995), reenacts the past in his or her own mind. The imagination plays a major role in such reenactment, and for that reason, the narratives constructed by historians have much in common with the narratives constructed by playwrights, novelists, and filmmakers.[8]

Martyn does not acknowledge the affinity between historiography and historical fiction, and indeed the mere suggestion might be seen as wrongheaded by the scholars who have accepted his hypothesis. Nevertheless, his use of the dramatic form gestures toward the role of the imagination in the very attempt to take up residence in the Johannine community, a point that must be acknowledged even by those who view his hypothesis as historical fact.

Detail

Martyn's book is persuasive not only because of the clear language and dramatic form but because his imaginative reconstruction—or reenactment—of the historical situation of the Johannine community satisfies our own deep-seated desire to live in the past. He singlehandedly creates the community, builds its church, peoples it with preachers and parishioners, and shapes a dramatic narrative of conflict, ostracism, and resolution. In doing so, he satisfies the craving for detail that the gospel itself denies us, and, like a good novelist, allows us to inhabit this world while providing our scholarly selves with the reassurance that in fact it could have happened this way. Martyn's book not only urges us to "take up temporary residence in the Johannine community" but becomes the means through which we can do so.

Even the most eloquent text or speaker will not succeed in persuading its audience of anything unless it in some way fulfills or satisfies the

8. My own detailed study comparing life of Jesus research and Jesus novels provides ample support for Collingwood's position. See Reinhartz 2011.

desires, overt or implicit, of that audience. Martyn's work satisfies not only the desire to absolve the Gospel of John of charges of anti-Judaism but also, more subtly, the desire of scholars to imagine ourselves back into an ancient community, in much the same way as visiting ancient sites such as Ephesus or Beit Shean can do.

My Approach

Having engaged in detailed critique of the expulsion hypothesis (Reinhartz 1998), I could have gone the route that Kysar took, which was to leave aside historical questions altogether. Kysar (2006, 218) comments that

> most historical reconstructions done for the sake of interpreting the Fourth Gospel are excessively speculative and beyond provability.... This suspicion of historical reconstruction resulted in my abandonment of the theory of the expulsion of the Johannine Christians from the synagogue ... and the effort to reconstruct the Christian community related to the Fourth Gospel.

But I cannot take that step. Skeptical and cautious as I am, I nevertheless long "to take up temporary residence in the Johannine community ... [and to] see with the eyes and hear with the ears of that community." The challenge is to imagine a way of taking up such residence without falling into the very same methodological and historical pits that attend Martyn's own attempt. My starting point in addressing this challenge is nevertheless inspired by Martyn's work: to think concretely about the gospel's first audience, yet without assuming, as he did, that this first audience was a formally constituted community or well-defined group.

In this task I owe much to the work of Carol Harrison, especially her recent book, *The Art of Listening in the Early Church*. Carol Harrison (2013, 2) comments that

> in reading an early Christian text we are in fact eavesdropping on a conversation: we are overhearing words which are being spoken to someone else. What we are trying to establish, from what we *can* hear, is just what, precisely, is going on; who is saying what, to whom, and why? Above all, who is the silent interlocutor, how do they affect and influence the speaker, how do they hear and receive what is said, what is their response, how does it affect them? If we ignore the listener then we also close our ears to the real resonances of what is being said.

Harrison has persuaded me that, contrary to usual practice, we must think not so much about first readers of the gospel but about first hearers. We cannot see through their eyes, but we can try to hear the gospel through their ears. This requires paying attention to the rhetorical dimension of the gospel, the means by which the gospel aims to capture and hold the attention of its hearers, and, most important, to persuade them to listen, absorb, and act according to the perspective and convictions that it expresses. If the power of Martyn's book stems from its rhetorical—its persuasive—power, the same and more can be said of the Gospel of John. This suggests, furthermore, that, pace Martyn, we should not approach the gospel as a window to the past experiences of its first hearers. Rather, I suggest, we should think about how that gospel might shape, or wish to shape, the future of those same audiences.

The gospel speaks directly and explicitly to these first hearers, and to us, near the end of its story. In John 20:30–31, the narrator declares that while

> Jesus did many other signs in the presence of his disciples, which are not written in this book … these are written so that *you* [may come to] believe that Jesus is the Messiah, the Son of God, and that through believing *you* may have life in his name. (emphases added)[9]

The gospel in which these signs are written does not merely look back on the life of Jesus. It also looks forward, with an explicit persuasive, indeed, transformative intention: to shape the very lives—present and future—of its audience. The gospel calls on "you" (second-person plural) to believe and thereby have "life in his name."

How would the first hearers have heard, understood, and responded to the gospel's rallying cry? Most important for the question of the parting of the ways, how would their reading of the gospel affect the ways in which they viewed their relationship to the Jews and the Jewish institu-

9. Some manuscripts (Ì[66vid] ℵ* B Θ 0250 *pc*) read the present subjunctive πιστεύητε after ἵνα ("that you may continue to believe"), while others (ℵ[2] A C D L W Ψ Ë[1,13] 33 Ï) read the aorist subjunctive πιστεύσητε after ἵνα ("that you may come to believe"). The present tense therefore implies that the gospel was addressed to believers and encouraged them to maintain their faith; the aorist suggests that the gospel was speaking to potential believers and encouraged them to adopt this faith. The present subjunctive has slightly greater textual support and is considered by many scholars to be more consistent with the overall tone of the gospel. For detailed discussion, see Brown 1970, 1056–61.

tions around them, which by and large did not accept Jesus as the Messiah and Son of God?

Just as Martyn's book taps into the desire of scholars to reenact, recreate, or inhabit the past, so too does the Fourth Gospel tap into the desires of its presumed hearers: the desire for eternal life. Just as Martyn proposed the two-level reading strategy as the path to fulfilling that desire, so does the gospel propose faith in Jesus as the Messiah and Son of God as the "way and the truth and the life" (14:6). The gospel, like Martyn, provides a broad range of arguments to support that proposition. Martyn's argumentation follows the norms of historical-critical New Testament scholarship, that is, exegesis of the gospel and recourse to external sources. John's argument uses the methods of classical rhetoric, including external proofs (invention, appealing to a series of witnesses, to Scripture, and to Jesus's signs), internal proofs (logical argument), ethos (the identity and therefore credibility of the speaker), and pathos (play on the emotions; Kennedy 1984, 7).

The basic message about the necessity of faith in Jesus as the Christ and Son of God is not much different from that of other books of the New Testament. What is interesting about the Fourth Gospel is the final step in the rhetorical argument: that while every individual must come to faith, the full expression of that faith, and the attainment of "life in his name," can take place only in community. It is in this sense that the Fourth Gospel in effect creates, or strives to create, a Johannine community composed of like-minded believers who have heard and internalized its imperatives.

The communal element is expressed in several ways, including the frequent use of first- and second-person plural verbs and collective metaphors such as the vine and the sheepfold. Most powerful, however, is the language of affiliation and disaffiliation: believers must affiliate with one another and disaffiliate from those who do not believe, especially the Ἰουδαῖοι.

It is the language of disaffiliation that in my view relates directly to the question of the parting of the ways. According to the expulsion hypothesis, the language of disaffiliation is a consequence and expression of the trauma that the community experienced when they were excluded from the synagogue. But the rhetorical thrust of the gospel suggests another possibility: that the gospel was pushing its hearers to separate themselves from the Ἰουδαῖοι. In other words, the gospel was not reacting to a forcible parting but rather attempting to produce one. If so, the Fourth Gospel does not reflect the Jews' expulsion of Johannine believers from the synagogue but in fact meant to dissuade Johannine believers from participating in synagogue worship or otherwise associating or identifying with Jews. Rather than reflecting a parting of the ways that had already happened—traumatically through expulsion—the gospel hopes to create a parting of the ways between its hearers and the Jews among whom they may have lived.

Social-identity theory emphasizes the importance of boundary formation and the push/pull of internal and external factors: the need to create connection with some and distance from others (Jenkins 2008; Nagel 1994). This perspective, which, as far as I can see, is rather uncontroversial, meshes well with the focus on affiliation and disaffiliation that I believe is key to understanding the Gospel of John. The question then becomes, what concrete circumstances would have necessitated such a thoroughgoing attempt at boundary creation? Martyn, of course, identified one possible set of circumstances: the expulsion of Johannine Christ confessors from the synagogue. Disaffiliation would have been a natural response to such an experience. But this is not the only possibility. My own work on the Fourth Gospel over many years has suggested that the gospel is addressing an audience that is mixed with respect to ethnic identity, consisting not only of Jews but also of pagans, and perhaps, as Raymond E. Brown (1979) suggests, also Samaritans. At the same time, the conceptual framework within which the gospel is working, while amenable to both pagan and Samaritan ideas, is fundamentally Jewish, involving an exclusive covenantal relationship with the one God of Israel and a privileging of the Jewish Scriptures as a source of prophecy about Jesus. The rhetoric of affiliation and disaffiliation may reflect the tension inherent in this situation.

It may be too much to expect that this rhetorical perspective on the Gospel of John and the parting of the ways will become a tipping point in Johannine studies. In the years since Martyn's work, particularly since the turn of the millennium, even this small corner has become increasingly diffuse and fractured. It is hard to imagine a consensus forming around any constructed narrative, even the most compelling. I do not at all lament this development, nor do I look back with nostalgia to the days when clarity and drama could light a fire under a normally staid community of scholars. I do, however, regret the recent passing of Martyn. While we disagreed on many things, in print and in public, I respected him tremendously, and, I am proud to say, we enjoyed a warm collegial relationship over a long period of time. I am truly grateful for his work, which I have found so stimulating and productive for my own.

Jesus, Ἀποσυνάγωγος, and Modes of Religiosity

Jonathan Bernier

The last quarter-century has seen the advent of what we might call a "New Perspective on the Second Temple Synagogue" (see Binder 1999; Levine 2005, 21–173; 2014; Runesson 2001; Runesson, Binder, and Olsson, 2008). Our understanding of this ancient institution has been thoroughly revised, and with such revision we must consider the implications for the broader study of the Second Temple and early posttemple periods. This paper, which summarizes the argument put forth in Jonathan Bernier (2013), will consider the implications for our understanding of one particular set of texts, namely, the Johannine ἀποσυνάγωγος passages (John 9:22; 12:42; 16:2), designated as such because of their unique use of this somewhat enigmatic Greek term. My work has sought to demonstrate that, given the current knowledge of the contemporary state of synagogue studies, these passages should be understood to suppose institutional realities that were altogether plausible in the pre-70 period.

Such an argument defies conventional wisdom in Johannine studies, which, due to the influence of J. Louis Martyn (2003), has long supposed as received wisdom that the institutional realities envisioned by these passages could not have existed prior to 70. Unfortunately, Martyn's argument on this matter is strikingly weak, resting on argument from silence, namely, that we do not have corroborating evidence that the pre-70 synagogue had the formal capacity to expel members, and therefore it did not. Not only is this an argument from silence, but it is also an answer to a question *mal posée*, as it is actually not clear from any of the ἀποσυνάγωγος passages that John understands this to have been any sort of formal expulsion. These logical and empirical difficulties notwithstanding, Martyn proceeds to argue that there was corroborating evidence for synagogue expulsion post-70 setting, namely, the Jewish prayer known as the Birkat Haminim and the rabbinic material that discusses its origin and purpose.

Empirically this vaunted corroboration was questionable from the beginning. By circa 1980 a consensus had emerged among rabbinic scholars, namely, that Martyn's interpretation was historically untenable, for at least three reasons (Finkel 1981; Katz 1984; Kimelman 1981; Langer 2011, 26–39; Urbach 1981; Visotzky 2005). One, it is possible if not probable that the Birkat Haminim postdates John's Gospel. Two, it is not clear that in its earliest form it was a specifically anti-Christian prayer, as Martyn wants to argue. Three, even if the Birkat Haminim predates John's Gospel and was a specifically anti-Christian prayer, it is not clear that it was ever used to expel anyone in the way that Martyn envisions. I would like to pick up on that third objection, as I think it to be the strongest.

The reality is that the Birkat Haminim and the rabbinic material that discusses its origin and purpose were always an odd set of texts to partner with the ἀποσυνάγωγος passages. Babylonian Talmud Berakhot 28b–29a states that if a reader falters on the Birkat Haminim he will be removed *from the position of reader*. It is not even clear whether that removal is permanent or just for the duration of the current liturgy. As such, in the rabbinic material the Birkat Haminim is presented as a prayer that does not lead to expulsion, whereas in the Johannine material the ἀποσυνάγωγος passages envision expulsion that does not involve prayer. As a general rule of thumb, when one thing consists of A but not B and the other B but not A, we are probably not looking at the same sort of things. As such, it is highly unlikely that the rabbinic materials relevant to the Birkat Haminim are describing the same institutional realities as the ἀποσυνάγωγος passages, which makes using the former to substantiate and explicate the latter a highly dubious procedure. Add in that these institutional realities might well be decades if not centuries removed from each other, that in its earliest form the Birkat Haminim might very well not be referring to Christians at all, and, as recently emphasized by John Kloppenborg (2011, 1), that 9:22 presupposes a temple context (exactly what is lacking in the post-70 scenario envisioned by Martyn), and there are some insuperable difficulties in thinking the Birkat Haminim is at all relevant to Johannine studies.

These insuperable difficulties have led some scholars to conclude rightly that the Birkat Haminim does not refer to the same institutional reality as do the ἀποσυνάγωγος passages. This either has led (1) to the search for alternative realities in the post-70 period, so as to sustain in however modified a form the Martynian two-level reading (Kloppenborg 2011); or (2) to treat the institutional realities envisioned by the ἀποσυνάγωγος passages as little more than fiction. The altogether logical possibility, namely, that the ἀποσυνάγωγος passages might in fact be describing institutional realities of the pre-70 period, has, until Bernier (2013), lacked extended investigation. This altogether logical possibility seems to have been closed off due to a series of untenable suppositions, of which I will discuss three below: one having to do with the nature of historical argument, one having to do with the current state of synagogue studies, and a third having to do with exegetical error.

A first untenable supposition regards the nature of historical argument. Implicit in Martyn's work is the supposition that the ἀποσυνάγωγος passages can be taken as evidence for actual institutional realities only if corroborated by another source. His insistence on and search for such corroborating evidence is unintelligible absent such a supposition. Yet such a supposition is untenable on logical grounds and unfortunately seems to have been taken up by those who would conclude that the ἀποσυνάγωγος passages describe institutional realities of neither the pre- nor post-70 period. Consider. If source A can be taken as evidence for actual institutional realities only if corroborated by source B, then we must ask: what corroborates source B? If one answers "source A," then we are compelled to ask what corroborates source A, to which the answer, given the argument in question, must be "source B." This is nothing more than a circular argument in which A corroborates B corroborates A corroborates B. If to the question "What corroborates source B?" the answer is "source C," then the question becomes "What corroborates source C?" We are now in exactly the same situation and must either resort to circularity or to an infinite regress in which nothing ever is corroborated.

Consequent to the above logical reality, Martyn must suppose that the material surrounding the Birkat Haminim provides evidence for post-70 institutional realities *independent* of the ἀποσυνάγωγος passages or any other corroborating material, and even if he provided corroborating material for the Birkat Haminim it would not suffice, for his insistence on corroboration for the ἀποσυνάγωγος passages would require him to corroborate that material in turn, and then that further material, ad infinitum. Yet that is precisely what he does not do, and this because it is in fact impossible. The material surrounding the Birkat Haminim stands on its own, as must any other material used to corroborate the ἀποσυνάγωγος passages (as in Kloppenborg 2011), and if that is permissible, then there is no reason in principle that the ἀποσυνάγωγος passages cannot stand on their own as well. While Martyn might avoid circularity or infinite regress in demanding corroboration for the ἀποσυνάγωγος passages but not the Birkat Haminim, Martyn has committed the sin of special pleading.

A second untenable supposition that has stood as a barrier to considering the ἀποσυνάγωγος passages as evidence for pre-70 institutional realities has to do with an acute lack of familiarity with contemporary synagogue studies among New Testament scholars. Into the new millennium there were still scholars who argued that there were no such things as synagogue buildings in the land during the Second Temple period (Claußen 2003; Horsley 1996, 222–37; Kee 1999). Such arguments had to dispense with the fact that our best sources for Jewish life in the first century prior to 70—namely, Josephus (*Ant.* 14. 259–261, 19.300–305; *J.W.* 2.289) and Philo (*Flaccus* 48), the gospels (passim), and the Acts of the Apostles (passim)—are all quite aware of such buildings. Today to this cloud of witnesses for the pre-70 synagogue building in the land we might add archaeological finds at Magdala and Gamla (Levine 2014). Given the current state of synagogue studies, appeals to the nonexistence of synagogue buildings in the land must be rejected out of hand. This reality does not yet seem to have fully penetrated the disciplinary consciousness of New Testament studies and perhaps accounts in part for the reluctance to consider more closely matters related to the synagogue in Jesus's ministry.

A third supposition has to do with an exegetical error, namely, the continuing acceptance of Martyn's supposition that the institutional realities envisioned by the ἀποσυνάγωγος passages must entail a formal expulsion. As already noted, there is nothing in the passages that requires this to be the case. Yes, 9:22 informs the reader that the Ἰουδαῖοι had agreed (συνετέθειντο) that anyone who confessed Jesus as the Messiah would be made ἀποσυνάγωγος, but neither the verb συντίθεμαι nor the context of this or the other two passages requires a formal mechanism of expulsion. Moreover, a careful examination of 12:42 and 16:2 in fact gives us reason to think that the ἀποσυνάγωγος passages envision something informal. Beginning with 12:42, we note that some among the rulers feared being made ἀποσυνάγωγος by the Pharisees. The import is clear: it is not the rulers who make people ἀποσυνάγωγος but rather the Pharisees. It is quite questionable whether John would envision a scenario in which the rulers are *formally* subject to the Pharisees. As such, one has an initial reason to suspect that in fact we may be dealing with some sort of less formal situation.

Such suspicion is deepened when one reads 16:2: ἀποσυναγώγους ποιήσουσιν ὑμᾶς· ἀλλ' ἔρχεται ὥρα ἵνα πᾶς ὁ ἀποκτείνας ὑμᾶς δόξῃ λατρείαν προσφέρειν τῷ θεῷ. It is of interest that when any of the ἀποσυνάγωγος passages describe concrete operations, the operations that are described consist of murder. This literary association between a statement about being made ἀποσυνάγωγος and a statement about murder is of greater interest when considered alongside other material, as the fact that in Luke-Acts the characters of Jesus and Stephen are both dragged from synagogues and then subjected to violence: the former surviving and the latter not (see Luke 4:28–30; Acts 6:8–7:60). Interestingly enough, these accounts do not suggest that any sort of formal mechanism was operative but rather narrate Jesus and Stephen being taken out of the synagogue extrajudicially (see also John 9:34, which gives no hint that the formerly blind man whose healing provoked the conflict of chapter 9 was driven out *formally*). This broader literary pattern, and I would suggest also John 16:2 and by extension 9:22 and 12:42, seems to envision something closer to lynching than to formal proceeding.

What we find then is a retroactive awareness among emergent Christians that circa 30, in the land of Israel, Jewish persons could be driven out of the synagogue informally and with violence. Given that, as mentioned, the gospels and Acts constitute some of our best sources for Jewish life in the land toward the end of the Second Temple period, we should demand powerful countervailing evidence or arguments if we are to avoid the conclusion that they do in fact suppose institutional realities of that time. I know of no such evidence or arguments. Indeed, if there is one thing that we have learned from the "New Perspective on the Synagogue" it is that the synagogue constituted an institutional space central to Second Temple Jewish life, both in the land and in the diaspora, and whenever something is central to collective life it will tend to arouse strong emotions. We do not require a particularly sophisticated social theory to recognize that violations of (often unstated) rules will tend to lead to (often informal) censure of various sorts, and that such censure might very well involve expulsion and violence. If such occurrences were not reported in our sources, then we should nonetheless suspect that they occurred. Since they are reported, we have all the more reason to do so.

Although one does not need a particularly sophisticated social theory to recognize the plausibility of such censure, let us put on our social-theorist hats. Jewish religion is an epitome of a tradition that tends to operate in what Harvey Whitehouse (1995; 2000; 2004) describes as "doctrinal" (as opposed to "imagistic") mode of religiosity. Such religiosity is marked by high-frequency but low-arousal rituals by which the tradition is codified and transmitted. Central to Whitehouse's thesis is that both high-frequency, high-arousal rituals and low-frequency, low-arousal rituals will tend in the long run to give way to either high-frequency, low-arousal rituals or low-frequency, high-arousal rituals. The reasoning has to do with the distinction between semantic and episodic memory: high-frequency rituals aim to generate semantic memories that abstract general principles garnered initially through episodic memories, while high-arousal rituals aim to resist such abstraction by ensuring that each instance of the ritual is remembered as an event unique in itself. As such, high frequency and high arousal work at cross purposes, and if the ritual is to survive in the long run, one will give way to the other, while a combination of low frequency and low arousal would fail to adequately activate either semantic or episodic memory.

Now, as forms of high-frequency but low-arousal rituals, synagogue practices, including but not limited to liturgy, aim to inculcate in Jewish persons the semantic memories that stand at the core of the tradition. What do we believe? How do we live? In what ways are we distinct from the gentiles? The answers to these questions are all repeated regularly in synagogue. Put otherwise, the synagogue was the primary (although of course not only) space in which specifically Jewish identity was created and maintained. In order to satisfy this role, the synagogue relied on repetition, relying on carefully defined scripts, precisely because the role of the synagogue was to teach those scripts.

What happens, then, when a man or a movement comes along that fails to follow the scripts? Why, such a person or group will be seen as an existential threat, for if the script is not followed, then the appropriate operations are not carried out, and the semantic memories essential to maintaining Jewish identity are not generated and reinforced. Indeed, as an exceptional instance a disruption cannot be abstracted, thus remaining on the level of episodic memory: the habituating function of the synagogue has been endangered. What one has, in that particular instance, is a high-arousal event. The only options before the group are to integrate it into the high-frequency rituals, thus decreasing its arousal over time but fundamentally transforming the semantic memories to be generated and reinforced, or to ensure that the high-arousal event does not recur. I would suggest that the violence recalled in the *ἀποσυνάγωγος* and cognate passages represented exactly this latter response: an extreme but socially explicable response to an existential threat.

We then might conclude the following. (1) The Birkat Haminim is of very questionable relevance to the study of the *ἀποσυνάγωγος* passages. (2) There is nothing in our evidence that would preclude the possibility that the *ἀποσυνάγωγος* passages describe institutional realities circa 30 CE in the land. (3) Such realities were more likely informal than formal and are also attested in Luke-Acts. (4) These realities make sociological sense. (5) There is nothing in our evidence that would preclude the possibility that Jesus and his followers were subjected to such institutional realities, both during and in the period immediately following his life. The cases for relating the *ἀποσυνάγωγος* passages to the Birkat Haminim or treating them as little more than fiction begin to look quite weak compared to the case for relating them to events of Jesus's life and the lives of his followers.

Evidence of Conflict with the Synagogue in the Johannine Writings

Craig A. Evans

A number of objections have been raised against Louis Martyn's (1968; 2003) classic interpretation of the Fourth Gospel against the backdrop of a Jewish-rabbinic council at Yavneh toward the end of the first century. In this scenario the threat of being thrust out of the synagogue (seen at John 9:22; 12:42; 16:2) is associated with the modification of the twelfth benediction of the Amidah, which apparently occurred sometime toward the end of the first century.[1] Recently Jonathan Bernier has made a surprisingly strong case for understanding John's ἀποσυνάγωγος passages (9:22; 12:42; 16:2) as reflecting the *Sitz im Leben Jesu* in and around Jerusalem.[2] His thesis is intriguing, and we shall return to it later in this paper.

Whether we follow Martyn or Bernier (or neither), significant evidence remains for understanding the entire Johannine corpus (i.e., the gospel, the epistles, and the Apocalypse) against the backdrop of conflict

1. "Rabban Gamaliel said to the Sages: 'Is there one among you who can word a benediction relating to the *Minim* [heretics]?' Samuel the Small arose and composed it.... If a reader [of the Amidah] made a mistake in any of the other [seventeen] benedictions, they do not remove him, but if in the benediction of the *Minim*, he is removed, because we suspect him of being a *Min*" (b. Ber. 28b–29a). The original form of the twelfth benediction apparently read something like this: "For apostates let there be no hope, and the dominion of arrogance [= Roman Empire] do speedily root out. Blessed are you, O Lord, who humble the arrogant!" The revised form of the benediction reads: "For apostates let there be no hope, and the dominion of arrogance do speedily root out. Let the Nazarenes and Minim be destroyed in a moment, and let them be blotted out of the book of life and not be inscribed with the righteous. Blessed are you, O Lord, who humble the arrogant!"

2. Bernier (2013) offers a detailed critique of Martyn's semiallegorical reading of the Fourth Gospel.

with or within the synagogue at the end of the first century or, perhaps, in the first decades of the second century. The present paper will explore some of this evidence. My guiding question asks whether we can find a coherent *Sitz im Leben* for all five of the Johannine writings. I will also address the question of the date of the Gospel of John, which in a few recent studies has been pushed into the middle of the second century, or even later.

As a point of departure, I shall engage the commentary on the Johannine writings that we find in the *Jewish Annotated New Testament* (*JANT*), edited by Amy-Jill Levine and Marc Brettler (2011). This landmark work provides me with an interesting opportunity to test, as it were, the hypothesis of my paper, at least from a Jewish perspective. The whole point of *JANT* is to probe the Jewish character of New Testament literature.

The Gospel of John from a Jewish Perspective

Adele Reinhartz (2011b) wrote the introduction and the annotations for the Gospel of John in *JANT*. She is eminently qualified for this assignment, having published a number of important studies on the Gospel of John, usually from the perspective of the evangelist's relationship to Judaism (Reinhartz 1992; 2001a; 2001b; 2004; 2009b). She rightly recognizes the Judaic character of the Fourth Gospel, saying that it

> makes abundant use of the Hebrew Bible, through direct quotations and allusions, as well as, more subtly, through its appropriation of some of its characters, motifs and stories.... The Gospel also has numerous parallels to other Jewish sources, from the second temple and rabbinic periods, as well as references to Jewish practices.[3] (Reinhartz 2011b, 152)

Reinhartz (154) adds that the Fourth Gospel "reflects deep and broad knowledge of Jerusalem, Jewish practices, and methods of biblical interpretation." She is quite correct on all of these points.

Reinhartz dates the Gospel of John to circa 85–95 CE. She recognizes that the gospel likely had a long history of composition and editing and that the author probably made use of sources, such as the much-discussed signs source. Reinhartz rightly doubts the tradition of John son of Zebedee as author, primarily because the Fourth Gospel reflects Judea, not

3. I assess many of these parallels in Evans 1993, 77–145.

Galilee. She further doubts that the author was an original follower of Jesus (153–54).

Reinhartz (154–56) provides a brief but nuanced discussion of the negative role played by the Jews in the Fourth Gospel. She recognizes that often οἱ Ἰουδαῖοι is in reference to the Jews of Judea and Jerusalem, in contrast to the Galileans, Samaritans, and Hellenists. But she also observes that in some places the epithet οἱ Ἰουδαῖοι seems to refer to the Jewish people as a whole and not simply to Judeans or to Jewish religious leaders. Reinhartz does not regard this as anti-Semitism but, rather, as a form of anti-Judaism, in that it is an explicit rejection and criticism of Judaism as a religion, a religion that has not recognized Jesus as Israel's Messiah and as God's Son.[4]

Reinhartz's annotations throughout call attention to the Judaic perspective of the Gospel of John. I begin with some of her comments on key passages in the prologue (John 1:1–18). With respect to the prologue as a whole, Reinhartz (2011b, 157) appeals to Gen 1, clearly echoed in verse 1 ("In the beginning was the Word"), wisdom terminology (such as Ps 33:6; Prov 8:7–10; Wis 9:1, 9; Sir 24:9), the work of Philo of Alexandria (*Alleg. Interp.* 3.175, in reference to the Logos), and later rabbinic and targumic traditions. With regard to the light-darkness dualism, she rightly calls attention to the dualism in 1QS III, 13–IV, 26. In almost every verse of the prologue she finds significant parallels with Jewish wisdom (2011b, 157–58).

Perhaps her most interesting comments concern verse 14, the well-known confession that "the Word became flesh and dwelt among us." Reinhartz draws attention to the contrast between flesh and word in Old Testament tradition. She cites Isa 40:6–8 ("All flesh is grass.... The grass withers ... but the word of our God will stand for ever"). One also thinks of Zech 4:6 ("Not by might, nor by power, but by my Spirit, says the LORD of hosts"). The contrast between flesh and spirit notwithstanding, Reinhartz (2011b, 158) notes, "Jews in the Second Temple period believed in the existence of supernatural beings, such as angels, who could at times take human form.... The boundaries between human and divine were understood in a more porous and less absolute way at this time."

4. For a similar assessment, see Kysar 1993. One will also want to consult Donaldson 2010, 81–108. Reinhartz (2011b, 156) suggests that John's anti-Jewish rhetoric "can be understood as part of the author's process of self-definition, of distinguishing the followers of Jesus from the synagogue and so from Jews and Judaism."

The claim that the Logos "dwelt" or "tabernacled among us" alludes to the wilderness tabernacle, the precursor to the Jerusalem temple (Exod 25:9), as well as to the Shekinah, the term that refers to God's dwelling among his people (here Reinhartz cites Tg. Onq. Deut 12:5), while reference to the "glory" (δόξα) of the Logos may allude to Exod 16:10 (where כָּבוֹד, "glory," is translated δόξα in the LXX). The assertion in John 1:18 ("No one has ever seen God; the only Son, who is in the bosom of the Father, he has made him known") creates a contrast between Moses in Exod 33–34, whose request to see God's face was denied, and Jesus, who as the Logos resided eternally in a face-to-face relationship with God.

Every point in Reinhartz's interpretation is correct. Nowhere does she appeal to gnostic docetism as providing part of the backdrop of John 1:14, 18, or any part of the prologue.[5] The background to John's prologue is Judaic, seen through the lens of faith in Jesus as the Logos who became fully human and lived in Israel. Reinhartz's understanding of the whole of the Fourth Gospel is consistent with her comments on the prologue. Throughout she finds points of contact with first-century Jewish life and Judaic tradition.

Reinhartz questions Martyn's argument that the three expulsion passages in the Gospel of John reflect the revision of the twelfth benediction. She finds "no evidence that the Gospel in fact encodes the history and experience of the community in its story of Jesus" (2011b, 153). At this point her perspective is consistent with Bernier's thesis mentioned above. Commenting on John 9:22, where the parents of the healed blind man fear being cast out of the synagogue, Reinhartz states: "Exclusion of Christ-confessors from the synagogue would be anachronistic for the time of Jesus." Here Reinhartz's perspective is at variance with Bernier's thesis. She does not think John 9:22, or the other two passages (12:42 and 16:2), reflects synagogue policy at the end of the first century either. Having rejected Martyn's semiallegorical reading of the Fourth Gospel and apparently not

5. The classic presentation will be found in Rudolf Bultmann, who for a generation was followed by many German scholars and a few Anglo scholars. See Bultmann 1971, 61, where he speaks of the "gnostic Redeemer-myth" and the "mythological language of Gnosticism." Elsewhere in a piece of remarkably tortured linguistic reasoning (74 n. 2), Bultmann claims that "it is not possible" to explain John 1:14 in reference to Exod 34:6. More will be said below about Bultmann's interpretation.

open to Bernier's reading, Reinhartz is therefore unable to account for the claims of these three passages.[6]

Now I readily admit that the solution is not simple, but I find myself still drawn to aspects of Martyn's hypothesis.[7] After all, both additions to a revised form of the twelfth benediction ("Let the Nazarenes and Minim be destroyed in a moment" and "let them be blotted out of the book of life and not be inscribed with the righteous") seem to be reflected in the Johannine writings. Contrary to the "benediction," John assures those who believe in Jesus that they will not perish (or "be destroyed"), as in John 3:16 (μὴ ἀπόληται), even if they are expelled from the synagogue. The Revelation of John asserts that those who remain faithful to the risen Jesus will not have their names blotted out of the book of life (ἐκ τῆς βίβλου τῆς ζωῆς). Rather, Jesus will confess their names before his heavenly Father (Rev 3:5). It is hard not to see in these Johannine affirmations a counterthrust of some sort directed against synagogue practice somewhere, a practice that in time came to expression in the revised twelfth benediction.[8]

---

6. The opponents of Jesus called οἱ Ἰουδαῖοι in the Fourth Gospel, especially in the second half of this work, consist principally of elders and ruling priests, all based in or near Jerusalem. On this understanding, see Bennema 2009. In response to Reinhartz, one should ask whether the Fourth Gospel really imagines a "synagogue policy" in a universal sense. The evangelist may be speaking of no more than an opposition to Jesus that was limited to Jerusalem, where Jewish authorities such as the ruling priests had power. This power is reflected in the violent opposition toward the leading followers of Jesus, as described in Acts 4–12, as well as in the eventual murder of James, the brother of Jesus, in the year 62 (as recounted by Josephus, *Ant.* 20.200). One should recall too that the influence of the Pharisees in pre-70 CE Jerusalem was such that even the Sadducees, and presumably the Sadducean ruling priests also, found it necessary to make concessions to the more popular Pharisees (so Josephus, *Ant.* 13.297–298). For further discussion, see Robinson, 1960–1961. Robinson argues that what is portrayed in the Fourth Gospel could in fact reflect a pre-70 CE setting.

7. This does not mean that Bernier's interpretation cannot also be valid. After all, the localized opposition to Jesus and his disciples centered in Jerusalem could well have spread to other parts of the Roman Empire as the Jesus movement itself spread. This means that the Fourth Gospel could reflect both the *Sitz im Leben Jesu* and at the same time apply to the situation that the Johannine Christians faced outside the land of Israel at the end of the first century.

8. The nature of the Johannine scriptural apologetic seems very much designed with a skeptical synagogue in view. For details, see Evans 1993. Moreover, the understanding of "signs" (σημεῖα) also seems to reflect the function of the prophetic sign (אות) of the Old Testament prophets, which again suggests an apologetic designed for a skeptical synagogue. On this point, see Förster 2016.

The Epistles of John from a Jewish Perspective

The introductions and annotations relating to the epistles of John in *JANT* are by Michele Murray (2011), Julie Galambush (2011), and Jonathan Brumberg-Kraus (2011). Murray (2011, 448) comments that 1 John "shares much of the vocabulary, and a number of themes, with John's Gospel" and "does not reflect a polemical attitude toward Jews." She draws attention to the old/new commandment articulated in 2:7–10. The "old" commandment (v. 7: ἐντολὴν παλαιὰν ἣν εἴχετε ἀπ' ἀρχῆς) harks back to the words of Jesus in the Fourth Gospel: "A new commandment I give to you [Ἐντολὴν καινὴν δίδωμι ὑμῖν], that you love one another; even as I have loved you, that you also love one another" (John 13:34). The author of 1 John reminds his readers of this commandment, teaching: "He who says he is in the light and hates his brother is in the darkness still. He who loves his brother abides in the light, and in it there is no cause for stumbling" (1 John 2:9–10). Murray notes that love of neighbor is "one of the central tenets of Judaism" expressed in Scripture (Lev 19:18, "you shall love your neighbor as yourself"), in Jewish literature from approximately the same time as New Testament literature (e.g., T. Reu. 6:9; T. Iss. 5:2; T. Benj. 3:3), and in later Jewish sources and authorities. One immediately thinks of Rabbi Aqiba, who is remembered to have said: "Love your neighbor as yourself—this is the major principle of the Torah" (y. Ned. 9:4). As another example, Murray (2011, 448–49) compares 1 John's use of light and darkness imagery (1 John 1:5–7; 2:9–11) with the similar imagery found in some of the Dead Sea Scrolls.

Murray (2011, 451) thinks those who deny that Jesus is the Christ (or Messiah) are probably nonmessianic Jews. I agree with her. Bultmann (1973, 38), of course, understands the reference very differently. According to him, what the author has claimed "can only be understood from the standpoint that the doctrine of the heretics is rooted in the dualism of Gnosticism, which asserts the exclusive antithesis between God and the sensible world." Bultmann takes this view above all because of what is asserted in 1 John 4:2 and 2 John 7. The first passage reads: "By this you know the Spirit of God: every spirit which confesses that Jesus Christ has come in the flesh [ἐν σαρκὶ ἐληλυθότα] is of God." The second reads: "For many deceivers have gone out into the world, men who will not acknowledge the coming of Jesus Christ in the flesh [ἐρχόμενον ἐν σαρκί]; such a one is the deceiver and the antichrist." The denial that Jesus did not "come in the flesh" can only be understood in reference to docetic Gnosticism, says

Bultmann.[9] But the denial is not focused on the corporeality of Jesus; it is a denial that the Messiah has come, a denial that Jesus came as the Messiah. More will be said about these passages shortly.

Bultmann also appeals to 1 John 5:6, where we are told that Jesus the Messiah is "he who came by water and blood." For Bultmann this can only be an affirmation of the reality of the incarnation in the face of a form of docetic Gnosticism.[10] Based on his interpretation of 1 John 4:2 and 5:6 Bultmann (1973, 112 n. 4) identifies the "deceivers" with the heretics described in 1 John 2:18–27, who are of course gnostics. With regard to 2 John 9 ("Anyone who goes ahead and does not abide in the doctrine of Christ") Bultmann (1973, 113) speaks of "gnostics or gnosticizing Christians."

Murray sees nothing gnostic in most of these passages. With respect to 1 John 5:6, Murray (2011, 454) wonders whether the "water and blood" allude to water baptism and the shed blood of Jesus. But with respect to 1 John 4:2 Murray (453) wonders whether the false prophets have claimed that Jesus did not come in flesh but that his humanity was only an illusion. At this point she seems to be describing some form of docetism (and these words are not found in Murray's notes), a view that is quite similar to Bultmann's interpretation. But this understanding of 1 John 4:2, as well as 2:18–27 and 5:6, is questionable.[11]

It is not necessary to see docetism in any of these passages in 1 John. What is denied is that the Messiah has come in the person of Jesus. The true spirit, the spirit that comes from God, confesses that Jesus has truly come as the Messiah. This question has been addressed in a lengthy and learned dissertation by Daniel Streett (2011).

Streett (2011, 255) argues that that the affirmation that "Jesus Christ has come in the flesh [ἐν σαρκὶ ἐληλυθότα]" (1 John 4:2) and the description

9. Bultmann 1971, 63 n. 2: "It is not clear in what sense the Gnostics, who are under attack in I Jn. 4.1–3 and II Jn. 7, challenged the notion of the ἐληλυθέναι ἐν σαρκὶ of the Revealer; but it is clear that for the author the ἐν σαρκὶ is decisive." He adds in 1973, 38: "The decisive point is that Gnostic thought cannot comprehend the offense which the Christian idea of revelation offers, namely, the paradox that a historical event (or historical form) is the eschatological event (or form)."

10. Bultmann 1973, 80: "This obviously contradicts the gnosticizing view that the heavenly Christ descended into Jesus at his baptism, and then abandoned Jesus again before his death."

11. For a review of John and Gnosticism, see von Wahlde 2010b; repr. in von Wahlde 2015, 27–57. Von Wahlde finds that Gnosticism probably plays no role in John.

of the "deceivers" as those "who will not acknowledge the coming of Jesus Christ in the flesh [ἐρχόμενον ἐν σαρκί]" (2 John 7) are not focused on the *mode* of Jesus's coming but on the *fact* of his coming.[12] The confession that Jesus the Messiah "came in the flesh" is a confession that the Messiah has in fact come and that the Messiah is Jesus.[13] This "sarkic" language, as Streett calls it, is confessional language, and it is not distinctly Johannine, as we see elsewhere in New Testament literature. For example, Paul speaks of Jesus as "descended from David according to the flesh [κατὰ σάρκα]" (Rom 1:3). There is nothing polemical here; Paul is not countering a group claiming that Jesus did not descend from David or did so in a nonphysical manner. So also in Rom 8:3, where Paul says God sent Jesus, his Son, "in the likeness of sinful flesh." There is no hint of polemics. The confessional language of 1 Tim 3:16 is especially relevant:

> Great indeed, we confess, is the mystery of our religion:
> He was manifested in the flesh [ἐφανερώθη ἐν σαρκί],
> vindicated in the Spirit,
> seen by angels,
> preached among the nations,
> believed on in the world,
> taken up in glory. (RSV)

We find similar language in 1 Peter. In 3:18–22 the author affirms:

> For Christ also died for sins once for all,
> the righteous for the unrighteous,
> that he might bring us to God,
> being put to death in the flesh [θανατωθεὶς μὲν σαρκὶ]
> but made alive in the spirit …[14]
> who has gone into heaven and is at the right hand of God,
> with angels, authorities, and powers subject to him. (RSV)

All of this language is confessional; none of it is polemical. The later affirmation in 1 Pet 4:1 should be understand in the same way: "Since

12. For linguistic arguments that see no real difference between the phrases ἐν σαρκὶ ἐληλυθότα and ἐρχόμενον ἐν σαρκί, see Jensen 2014.

13. Compare the confession in John 20:31, Ἰησοῦς ἐστιν ὁ χριστὸς ὁ υἱὸς τοῦ θεου ("the Messiah, the Son of God, is Jesus"). For grammatical, exegetical, and contextual arguments in support of this reading, see Carson 1991, 662.

14. The tangential material in 1 Tim 1:19–21 is omitted.

therefore Christ suffered in the flesh [παθόντος σαρκὶ]..." Other confessional references to the "flesh" of Jesus could be mentioned,[15] such as Col 1:22 (ἐν τῷ σώματι τῆς σαρκὸς αὐτου); Heb 5:7 (ἐν ταῖς ἡμέραις τῆς σαρκὸς αὐτοῦ); 10:20 (τῆς σαρκὸς αὐτοῦ); Polycarp, *Phil.* 7.1 (ἐν σαρκὶ ἐληλυθέναι); Barn. 5.6–11 (ἐν σαρκὶ ἔδει αὐτὸν φανερωθῆναι / ἦλθεν ἐν σαρκί / ἐν σαρκὶ ἦλθεν) and 6.6–9 (Ἐν σαρκὶ οὖν αὐτοῦ μέλλοντος φανεροῦσθαι καὶ πάσχειν / ἐν σαρκὶ μέλλοντα φανεροῦσθαι). The point of this sarkic language is not to oppose a false teaching, a teaching that supposedly denies the fleshly reality of Jesus, but to affirm the condescension and humiliation of the incarnation.

Streett (2011, 213–14) also wonders whether this manner of speaking was perhaps suggested by Old Testament idiom, especially as seen in the Psalter. There are examples in the Greek Psalms that may have been understood by early Christians as suggesting that the Lord's faithful one (in this case the Messiah) will suffer in the flesh. We may consider the following three passages, to which Streett has drawn our attention:

> LXX Ps 26:2 When wicked people would approach me to devour my flesh [τοῦ φαγεῖν τὰς σάρκας μου]—those that afflict me and my enemies—they became weak and fell.

> LXX Ps 37:4 There is no healing in my flesh [ἴασις ἐν τῇ σαρκί μου] from before your wrath; there is no peace for my bones from before my sins.

> LXX Ps 101:6 Due to the sound of my groaning, my bone clung to my flesh [τὸ ὀστοῦν μου τῇ σαρκί μου].

It is in this light that the quotation of Ps 16:9–11 in Acts 2:26–27 should be understood. Jesus has suffered in the flesh, but in his flesh he will be vindicated. The righteous sufferer declares: "Therefore my heart was glad, and my tongue rejoiced; moreover, my flesh will dwell in hope [ἡ σάρξ μου κατασκηνώσει ἐπ' ἐλπίδι], because you will not abandon my soul to Hades or give your holy one to see corruption" (Ps 15:9–10 LXX).

In light of the context of 1 John 4:2 and the sarkic language found in the LXX and in early Christian literature in reference to Jesus, Streett concludes, rightly in my view, that the secessionists are best understood as Jews who have left the Johannine community and have returned to the synagogue. They have not introduced a docetic heresy into the community.

15. All of the passages that I have cited here are discussed in Streett 2011, 204–13.

Rather, having at one time believed that Jesus was the Messiah, they now no longer believe that he is the Messiah (Streett 2011, 110–11, 171–72). In departing from the community, they demonstrated that they really were not believers in Jesus (1 John 2:19). One might say, from the Johannine perspective, that they had revealed their true colors.

The Revelation of John from a Jewish Perspective

David Frankfurter (2011, 463–98) wrote the introduction and annotations for the book of Revelation in *JANT*. He notes that although the name of the seer ("John"), the reference to Jesus as the "Lamp," and some other shared vocabulary and images "might suggest some relationship to the 'Johannine tradition,'" the "language and interests of Revelation bear little in common with" the gospel and the epistles (463). The last statement, however, requires qualification, for aspects of the language, including shared vocabulary, leave open the possibility that the author of the book of Revelation was in some way linked to the community that produced the gospel and epistles of John.[16]

In a recent major study of Revelation, Gerhard Maier (2009–2012, 1:28–29, 41) has argued, contrary to Frankfurter and the majority of Revelation scholars, that the points of contact between Revelation and the Fourth Gospel are so close and at such key points of doctrine, such as Christology, that one must conclude that the two works arose from the same author. For the present purposes, of even greater importance is that Maier (2009–2012, 1:49) argues that Revelation must be interpreted

16. For an assessment of vocabulary and linguistic data, see Charles 1920, xxix–lv; Frey 1993. Both Charles and Frey conclude that the book of Revelation was in some way linked to the Fourth Gospel and the so-called Johannine writings. See also Smith 1999, 34: "some remarkable points of contact or similarities." On the question of a Johannine community or "school," one must consult Culpepper 1975. Published the same year, but preferring to speak of a "Johannine Circle," is Cullmann 1975. It is widely agreed that the author of the Gospel of John was not the author of the Revelation. What remains disputed is how and whether these authors were connected. See the succinct summary in Aune 1997, liv–lvi. Aune (lvi) concludes that the "unknown author of Revelation … was probably a Palestinian Jew who had emigrated to the Roman province of Asia." In "The Quest for the Johannine School: The Apocalypse and the Fourth Gospel," E. S. Fiorenza (1977) long ago suggested that the author of the book of Revelation was not part of the Johannine school but knew of it and had access to its writings.

against a Jewish background, a background that includes a sophisticated interaction with the Old Testament.

However we should understand Revelation's relationship to the other Johannine writings, we are interested in the religious and social background of this book, especially with regard to the question of its relationship to the Jewish people. At least here there is wide agreement that the work throughout reflects the world of the Old Testament and Jewish ideas.

Frankfurter believes the John of the book of Revelation was a Jewish seer, a believer in Jesus who, among other things, was critical of people who claimed to be Jewish but "are not." These false Jews make up "synagogues of Satan" (Rev 2:9; 3:9). Frankfurter (2011, 464) concludes that "Revelation shows no sense of a Christianity, or even of Jesus-devotion, unmoored from Judaism."

The evidence in support of Frankfurter's position is substantial. Although it is hard to find an actual quotation of Jewish Scripture, the book of Revelation is laced throughout with words and phrases from Scripture. Everywhere the prophets are echoed. But more important is the nature of the polemic found in the letters to the seven churches (Rev 2–3). Every letter contains Jewish traditions, traditions that either commend the church or condemn it or false teachers within it. I shall briefly survey this evidence.

First Letter: To the Church of Ephesus (Revelation 2:1–7)

The risen Christ acknowledges the endurance of the church at Ephesus and its vigorous opposition to "evil men," as well as its testing of "those who call themselves apostles, and they are not, and you found them to be false" (v. 2). But the church has lost its first love (v. 4). If it does not repent and once again do the works it did at first, its lampstand will be removed (v. 5). This church hates "the deeds of the Nicolaitans" (v. 6). Those in this church that hears the word of Christ and conquers will be granted "to eat of the tree of life, which is in the paradise of God" (v. 7).

These exhortations contain several Jewish elements. The false apostles are almost certainly Jewish[17] and are probably to be identified with the

---

17. The concept of "apostles," or "sent ones," is right at home in the Jewish world. The prophets are *sent* by God (e.g., Isa 6:8; 61:1). Moses is God's sent one (שליח) in the rabbinic and Samaritan traditions (Mek. Simeon ben Yohai on Exod 3:10–11; Exod. Rab. 3:14 [on Exod 4:10]; Memra Marqa 5.3; 6.3). This is why those appointed by

Nicolaitans, who in turn are to be identified with the followers of Balaam, as seen in Rev 2:14 (more on Balaam below). The threat of removal of the lampstand is quite significant, recalling that what is in view here is the menorah, the seven-branched candelabrum, perhaps the best known Jewish religious symbol in late antiquity. If the church at Ephesus does not repent, its menorah will be removed, and its removal means a loss of Jewish identity as much as its loss of Christian witness in the city. But those who repent will "eat of the tree of life, which is in the paradise of God." The allusion here is to the famous garden of Eden, in which was the tree of life, whose fruit was denied to fallen Adam and Eve (Gen 2:9; 3:22, 24). The hope of regaining paradise, as well as the tree of life, is deeply rooted in Jewish eschatology (see 1 En. 25.5; 3 En. 23.18; T. Levi 18:11; Apoc. Mos. 28.4; 4Q385a 17a–e II, 3).

Second Letter: To the Church of Smyrna (Revelation 2:8–11)

The polemic in the letter to the church of Smyrna is sharp and angry: "I know your tribulation … and the blasphemy by those who say they are Jews and are not, but are a synagogue of Satan" (v. 9). Modern readers will be tempted to hear in this outburst Christian anti-Semitism. But this misses the mark widely. It is a reflection of intramural Jewish dispute. The Jewish believers in Messiah Jesus make up the true people of God, not the Jewish congregation that blasphemes by denying that Jesus is the Messiah[18] and claiming that they—those who reject the Messiah—are the true Jews. On the contrary, the risen Christ says, they are a "synagogue of Satan."[19] This is not anti-Semitic slander, as Frankfurter (2011, 469) rightly maintains, but an intramural struggle among those who confess Jesus. Frankfurter thinks the "synagogue of Satan" is made up of Pauline-influenced Christians who are lax with regard to food and purity laws (as in 1 Cor 7–8; see Rev 2:14,

---

Jesus and sent to proclaim his message are called apostles. Jesus himself is sent by his heavenly Father (see John 13:16; 20:21).

18. We have important coherence here with the opposition described in 1 John 2:22–23. It is the parallel with 1 John that clarifies the point of the blasphemy (or slander) emanating from the synagogue of Satan.

19. Remember that the meaning of *satan* is "opponent." Accordingly, the "synagogue of Satan" opposes the teaching of John the seer. On synagogues in Asia Minor, see Trebilco 1991.

20, where the author inveighs against teachers who encourage the consumption of meat sacrificed to idols).

Those who are faithful in the face of persecution will be given the "crown of life" (Rev 2:10) and will not be hurt by the "second death" (v. 11). The metaphor "crown of life" and close approximations have their roots in early Judaism (see Jas 1:12 "crown of life"; T. Levi 8:2 "crown of righteousness"; T. Benj. 4:1 "crown of glory"; T. Job 4:10 "receiving the crown"; Jer 13:18 LXX and Lam 2:15 LXX "crown of glory"). The expression "second death" appears to have developed in the Aramaic-speaking synagogue, as we see in the Aramaic paraphrases of Scripture or targums (e.g., Tg. Onq. Deut 33:6 "May Reuben … not die a second death"; Tg. Isa 22:14; Tg. Jer 51:39, 57).

Third Letter: To the Church of Pergamum (Revelation 2:12–17)

The letter to the church of Pergamum acknowledges the challenges the struggling community faces. It is, after all, the place where "Satan dwells." In contrast to the "synagogue of Satan" in verse 9, the "throne of Satan" (v. 13) in the letter to the church of Pergamum probably refers to Roman, not Jewish, opposition to the Christian movement.[20] Nevertheless, the author, writing from a Jewish perspective, makes use of this ancient Semitic term, which traditionally referred to the evil, sometimes personified, that opposes the will of God.

The major complaint is that members of the Pergamum church "hold the teaching of Balaam" and the "teaching of the Nicolaitans" (vv. 14–15). In Jewish Scripture (Num 22:5–8 and throughout) and lore (4Q339 I, 1–2; b. Ber. 7a; b. Sanh. 106a), as well as in Jewish-Christian teaching (Jude 11; 2 Pet 2:15–16), Balaam rises to the level of an all-time villain who sought to destroy the Jewish people (see Vermes 1973). This Balaam, of course, "taught Balak to put a stumbling block before the sons of Israel, that they might eat food sacrificed to idols and practice immorality." Our Jewish author is much stricter in matters of *kashrut* than what we see in Paul (1 Cor 8:1, 4, 7, 10; 10:19). Paul, of course, is primarily concerned with the "weak" Christian, whose superstitions regarding pagan gods and idols make it impossible for him with a clear conscious to eat meat sacrificed to idols. Here in Rev 2:14 the idea of eating meat sacrificed to idols is

20. For a survey of possible references, see Aune 1997, 182–84.

repugnant in any situation and in any frame of mind, much as we see in the case of the Maccabean martyrs, who refused to eat pork and take part in Seleucid sacrifices (2 Macc 6–7).

The one who conquers these temptations will receive "some of the hidden manna" (Rev 2:17). Manna, of course (from the Hebrew, literally meaning "What is it?"), is the famous food provided the Israelites during their wilderness sojourn (Exod 16:4–36). In Jewish interpretation this food took on all sorts of interesting properties and associations. In some traditions it is the heavenly bread that will be provided in the age to come (2 Bar. 29:8; Gen. Rab. 82:8 [on Gen 35:17]), for it will convey eternal life (Jos. Asen. 16.14, "everyone who eats of it will not die for ever").

The faithful will also be given a "white stone." Although the precise meaning here is uncertain, in light of the context, it is probable that it was understood as a token of innocence and guarantee of membership in the congregation of the faithful.[21] Not only is a stone received, but it has one's name written on it, a "new name," for confidentiality. This makes the best sense in light of the synagogue's efforts to "blot out" the names of the Christians from the membership book (see Rev 3:5 below).

Fourth Letter: To the Church of Thyatira (Revelation 2:18–29)

In this letter the congregation is admonished for tolerating "the woman Jezebel, who calls herself a prophetess, and she teaches and leads astray" (v. 20). Jezebel, of course, was the infamous Phoenician princess who married Israel's King Ahab (1 Kgs 16:29–31), promoted the worship of Baal (1 Kgs 16:31), murdered many of Israel's prophets who had remained faithful to Yahweh (1 Kgs 18:4, 13), and goaded her husband into murdering Naboth so that he might take possession of the man's property (1 Kgs 21:5–16). In fulfillment of the word of a prophet, the evil woman was murdered, and dogs ate her corpse (2 Kgs 9:30–37).[22] It is no surprise that Jezebel was vilified in later Jewish traditions (e.g., in 2 Bar. 62:3 we hear of the "curse of Jezebel" in reference to Israel's tragic legacy of idolatry).[23]

---

21. The options are surveyed in Hemer 1986, 96–104.

22. From a Jewish point of view, Jezebel's end was horrible, as in the prophetic word: "The dogs shall eat the flesh of Jezebel; the corpse of Jezebel shall be as dung upon the face of the field in the territory of Jezreel." That is, Jezebel was eaten, then defecated.

23. For a convenient summary of rabbinic legends about Jezebel, which for the

As in the letter to the church at Pergamum, here the risen Christ inveighs against the "Jezebel" of Thyatira, who encourages believers to "eat food sacrificed to idols" and to "commit adultery" (Rev 2:20). Whereas the charge of engaging in πορνεία is probably metaphorical (as in Judg 2:17; 8:27, "Israel played the harlot"; 2 Kgs 9:22, "the harlotries and the sorceries of your mother Jezebel"), the reference to eating the meat sacrificed to idols should be taken literally (see comment on Rev 2:14 above).

The warning that the Lord "will strike her children dead" (v. 23) is the harshest in the seven letters. These children should be understood as Jezebel's followers, not her literal children. There is no hiding from the Lord, for he "searches the mind and heart," as he always has done (1 Chr 28:9, "the Lord searches all hearts").

He who overcomes the temptations and false teaching of the false prophetess Jezebel will be given "power over the nations" (Rev 2:26), and "he shall rule them with a rod of iron, as when earthen pots are broken in pieces" (v. 27). These words unmistakably allude to Ps 2:8–9, the psalm that celebrates the victory the Lord's Messiah has over the nations, which he will "break with a rod of iron, and dash them in pieces like a potter's vessel." The risen Christ will also give to him "the morning star" (Rev 2:27). Here we may have an allusion to the morning star of Isa 14:12, which in Judeo-Christian interpretation was understood as Satan (or Lucifer). If so, perhaps the believer is assured that he will have power over Satan. But the morning star of Rev 2:27 may refer to the messianic star (Num 24:17; T. Levi 18:3; Matt 2:2). If so, this may mean that Christ will share with his followers his messianic power and glory.[24]

Fifth Letter: To the Church of Sardis (Revelation 3:1–6)

The risen Christ assures the faithful person of Sardis that he will be clad in "white garments" (v. 5a). Given the eschatological context of the book of Revelation, it is likely "white" is best understood in the light of Daniel, who says the righteous will "purify themselves, and make themselves white" (Dan 12:10; see 11:35), perhaps even as the Ancient of Days is himself clad

---

most part accentuate her evil and idolatrous habits, see Ginzberg 1909–1938, 4:188–89.

24. See also Jos. Asen. 14.1, "So the Lord God listened to my prayer, because this star rose as a messenger and herald of the light of the great day" (trans. Burchard, *OTP* 2:224).

"white as snow" (Dan 7:9; see Eccl 9:8; 1QM VII, 10). The faithful person may be assured that his name will not be blotted out of the "book of life" (Rev 3:5b). The tradition of a book from which one hopes not to have one's name blotted out originates in Exod 32:32 (where Moses is willing to be blotted out of God's book, if in exchange God will forgive Israel's sin). In time this "book" was referred to in various ways, among them "book of life" (Jos. Asen. 15.3, "your name is written in the book of life"; Ordinances of Levi 59, "carried in the book of remembered life"; T. Benj. 11:4, "he will be inscribed in the holy books").

For Jewish Christians ejected from the synagogue (as in John 9:22; 12:42; 16:2), which would result in loss of membership and their names struck from the roll, Christ's promise that their names will not be blotted out of the book of life would have been very reassuring.

Sixth Letter: To the Church of Philadelphia (Revelation 3:7–13)

The risen Christ lodges no complaints against the church of Philadelphia. There is again reference to opponents as "those of the synagogue of Satan who say they are Jews and are not, but lie" (v. 9). Christ describes himself as the one who "has the key of David, who opens and no one shall shut, who shuts and no one opens" (v. 7). We have here a clear allusion to Isa 22:22 ("I will place on his shoulder the key of the house of David; he shall open, and none shall shut; and he shall shut, and none shall open").

The interesting references to the "temple of my God," "city of my God," and the "new Jerusalem"—imagery that recalls Ezekiel's vision of the new Jerusalem—have been thrown into a new light thanks to the discovery of the new Jerusalem texts at Qumran (1Q32; 2Q24; 4Q554; 5Q15; 11Q18). At the very least it shows how important this theme was to Jews who longed for Israel's redemption.

Seventh Letter: To the Church of Laodicea (Revelation 3:14–22)

The risen Christ describes himself as "the Amen, the faithful and true witness, the beginning of God's creation" (v. 14). The word amen (אמן/ἀμήν) occurs more than two dozen times in the Old Testament. It is even more frequent in the targums. The words "faithful and true" (πιστὸς καὶ ἀληθινός) are part of the meaning of "amen." One sees this in Isa 1:21, when the prophet laments over Jerusalem's sinful condition: "How the faithful [נאמנה/πιστή] city has become a harlot." The description "beginning of creation" immediately recalls Gen 1:1, as well as John 1:1. Of course, as the eternal Son of God, who existed in the very bosom of the Father (John 1:18), Christ may be compared to Wisdom, who was in God's presence before the "beginning of the earth" (Prov 8:22–23).

Recalling the words of Prov 3:12, Jesus tells the church of Laodicea: "Those whom I love, I reprove and chasten" (Rev 3:19). Although they are lukewarm, he urges them to be zealous and to repent, assuring them: "Behold, I stand at the door and knock; if any one hears my voice and opens the door, I will come in to him and eat with him, and he with me" (v. 20). These words may allude to the beckoning call of the lover in the Song of Songs: "Hark! my beloved is knocking: 'Open to me [κρούει ἐπὶ τὴν θύραν ἄνοιξόν μοι]' " (Song 5:2).

Those who respond, those who conquer, will sit with Jesus on his throne, just as he conquered and sat on the throne of his father (Rev 3:21). This remarkable promise takes us back to the words of Jesus, who promised his disciples that someday they would sit on twelve thrones, judging the twelve tribes of Israel (Matt 19:28; Luke 22:28–30; see Dan 7:9; Ps 122:1–5), and who threatened his priestly accusers: "You will see the Son of man seated at the right hand of Power, and coming with the clouds of heaven" (Mark 14:62; see Dan 7:13; Ps 110:1). These dominical utterances, spoken before Easter and spoken in a new way decades after Easter, are firmly rooted in the Scriptures of Israel.

Concluding Remarks

Given the Judaic orientation of much of the polemic in the letters to the seven churches and its coherence at points with the Fourth Gospel's apologetic that is clearly oriented toward the synagogue, I am convinced that we need to take a fresh look at the references to the opponents and false teaching in the Johannine epistles. These opponents are not gnostics or Hellenizers; they are Jewish skeptics and members of synagogues who reject the claims that Christian Jews make about Jesus, or, as perhaps obtains in the case of the churches of the book of Revelation, their opponents are liberal Pauline Christians who hold to lax views of food and purity.

The affirmation in the Gospel of John, that the "Word became flesh and dwelt among us" (John 1:14), is not a counterthrust against docetic Gnosticism. It is an affirmation that the eternal Logos of God, God's wisdom, has, in a manner not unlike the very glory of God descending and occupying the leather tent of Exod 40, entered into the human realm as a human being.

The opponents of the Johannine community, as reflected in the Johannine epistles, are not docetic gnostics, who reject the corporeal reality of Jesus; they are Jews who deny that the Messiah has come at all. They deny Jesus. They assert that the Messiah has in fact not come in the flesh. In short, he has not arrived! This is the meaning of 2 John 7, "Many deceivers have gone out into the world, who do not confess Jesus as the Messiah having come in the flesh." This is the meaning of 1 John 2:22, "Who is the liar, other than the one who denies, [by saying,] 'Jesus is not the Messiah.'" These liars and deceivers are those who deny the messianic identity of Jesus. They simply reject the affirmation of John 20:31, which declares: "These things are written that you believe that the Messiah, Son of God, is Jesus." This confession is affirmed in 1 John 4:2, "By this we know the Spirit of God: Every spirit that confesses Jesus as the Messiah having come in the flesh is of God."

The struggle seen in the Gospel of John, in which those who confess Jesus are threatened with expulsion from the synagogue, continues in the epistles of John and in the Revelation of John, particularly as seen in the letters to the seven churches. To be sure, the book of Revelation is very concerned about state persecution, but the most troubling difficulty facing these struggling churches is the opposition of synagogues that simply do not believe that Israel's Messiah has come and that the Messiah is none other than the crucified and resurrected Jesus of Nazareth.

Before bringing this essay to a close, it is necessary to respond to recent calls for dating the Fourth Gospel much later. In essays that have appeared in the last few years, John Kloppenborg (2011; 2015, especially 234–35) has asserted that the Fourth Gospel should be dated to the second half of the second century. Indeed, he even goes so far as to say: "My guess is that in the not-too-distant future we will see a commentary on John that returns to the late dating of F. C. Baur, or at least a date around mid-century" (235). Kloppenborg's forecast is truly astonishing. Will we really see scholarly commentaries on the Fourth Gospel published in the not-too-distant future that will offer interpretations of John based on the assumption that this gospel was composed no earlier than the 170s, the date that Baur proposed almost two centuries ago?[25] I find that most unlikely.

25. Baur 1847, 239; 1878–1879, 1:177–81. Baur could date John no later than the

Kloppenborg believes scholarly acceptance of a late date of John is around the corner because a few scholars have recently called into question the early date of 𝔓[52]. Andreas Schmidt (1989) and Brent Nongbri (2005) have argued that the Manchester fragment of John 18 should be dated to the *late*, not *early*, second century (see Orsini and Clarysse 2012). If so, then this witness no longer requires John to be dated to the end of the first century or the very beginning of the second.

Even if a later date of 𝔓[52] is accepted—and it is in fact not accepted by a number of papyrologists and textual critics[26]—this hardly clears the way for a much later dating of the Fourth Gospel. Papias, writing no later than the 120s, refers to John the evangelist (frag. 3.5, "John … clearly meaning the evangelist"), which surely implies awareness of the Fourth Gospel. Ignatius, writing about the same time, perhaps earlier, alludes to passages from the Fourth Gospel (e.g., John 1:14; 3:8; 6:33; 10:7, 9; 14:10; 15:19) in some of his letters (e.g., *Rom.* 3.3, "he is in the Father," "hated by the world"; 7.3, "the bread of God, which is the flesh of Christ," "for drink I want his blood"; *Eph.* 5.2, "bread of God"; *Phld.* 7:1, "the Spirit … knows from where it comes and where it is going"; 9.1, "door of the Father"). In his *Dialogue with Trypho*, written circa 155, and *1 Apology*, written circa 160, Justin Martyr explicitly quotes passages from the Fourth Gospel.[27] Tatian, writing in the late 160s or early 170s, harmonizes John with the Synoptic Gospels in the *Diatessaron*, and Irenaeus, in his *Against Heresies*, written circa 180, recognizes John as one of the four authoritative gospels. Finally, one should mention p. Egerton 2, which most agree dates to the second century, perhaps as early as the mid-second century. This papyrus, which may be a gospel harmony of some sort, draws on the Fourth Gospel. Surely the Fourth Gospel predates this work by at least a few decades.

Another point needs to be raised concerning the proposal of a later date for 𝔓[52]. If this fragment is dated to the very end of the second century, is it

---

170s because of Irenaeus, whose *Against Heresies*, which affirms the authority of John, was penned circa 180. Cooke (2009, 333) speculates that had it not been for Irenaeus, Baur would have argued for a third-century date for John.

26. See the critical assessment in Porter 2013, 71–84. Nongbri and others are reacting, in part, to apologetically driven attempts to date 𝔓[52] and other papyri to very early dates.

27. See *Dial.* 91, where Justin interprets John 3:14 ("Moses did not teach us to believe in the serpent"); and *1 Apol.* 61, where Justin quotes John 3:5 ("Unless one is born of water and the Spirit, he cannot enter the kingdom of God").

realistic to think that the Fourth Gospel was composed no earlier than the 160s or 170s? This would mean that we have a fragment of a gospel that dates to within twenty or thirty years of the autograph. How likely is that?[28] So even if we date 𝔓[52] to the late second century, in itself that hardly recommends dating the Fourth Gospel to the time proposed by Baur.

It is hard to see how the Fourth Gospel could have achieved this widespread recognition of authority had it been penned in the middle of the second century, never mind as late as the 170s. If Ignatius in fact does allude to the Fourth Gospel in his letters, then the gospel must have been in circulation no later than the beginning of the second century. Finally, given the topographical, geographical, and cultural verisimilitude exhibited throughout the Fourth Gospel, a mid- or late second-century date seems most unlikely.

The Fourth Gospel reflects a period of tension within the Jewish community that arose in the aftermath of the capture of Jerusalem and the destruction of the temple. It reflects the intramural conflict that at points recalls the conflict the Jewish people experienced in the second century BCE at the time of the Maccabean revolt.[29] The crisis of the destruction of the temple led to a conflict of ideologies and strategies as various groups called on the Jewish people to repent and embrace their respective theologies and religious practices. It is in this Jewish mix that the Johannine Christian community, as seen in the Fourth Gospel, should be viewed.[30]

28. This would be like finding a fragment of Romans that dates to the 70s or 80s.
29. As has been argued recently by Ripley 2015.
30. For a recent assessment of the date of the Fourth Gospel, see Porter 2016.

Johannine Christian and Baptist Sectarians within Late First-Century Judaism

Joel Marcus

Since the publication of J. Louis Martyn's *History and Theology in the Fourth Gospel* in 1968, study of the Fourth Gospel vis-à-vis first-century Judaism has been dominated by the attempt to situate the Johannine community in relation to Pharisaism and the nascent rabbinic movement. In my opinion (here I differ from Jonathan Bernier, Jörg Frey, and Adele Reinhartz in this volume), there is no going back from Martyn's insights, which are firmly rooted in literary features within the Johannine text, such as the way in which the healing story in 9:1–12 morphs into the hostile dialogue between the formerly blind man and the Pharisees in 9:13–17, which in turn morphs into an inquisition of the man by οἱ Ἰουδαῖοι in 9:18–34.[1]

At the same time, however, Reinhartz (2001a, 41–48) has made important observations about the way in which the positive portrayal of the Jews in John 11 qualifies Martyn's picture of a Johannine Christian group in conflict with the larger Jewish community. These confusingly mixed signals, however, can be reconciled if we posit that, in John's local environment, the Pharisaic movement was in charge of significant Jewish institutions, including the synagogue,[2] but that John still held out hope for the conversion of the larger Jewish populace. This hope comes to the fore in passages such as 11:45–48, where the Jewish leadership frets that the excitement created by Jesus's Lazarus miracle will make everyone believe in him, and 12:19, where the Pharisees, worried by the size of the crowd Jesus has attracted at his triumphal entry, say to one another, "You see

1. For a defense of Martyn's use of Birkat Haminim, the rabbinic cursing of heretics, which has been especially attacked by his critics, see Marcus 2009.

2. Notice that I say that "*in John's local environment*" the Pharisees were in control of the synagogues. The situation elsewhere may have been different; see Cohen 1999b.

how you can do nothing; look, the world has gone after him."[3] As Philip Alexander (1992) has argued, the fear that the Jewish world would defect to Jewish Christianity was a realistic one in the early Tannaitic era, when it was not yet clear whether the Pharisaic/rabbinic form of Judaism or the Christian one would prevail.

But besides the Pharisees and the larger Jewish populace, the Johannine narrative presents another Jewish actor: John the Baptist and his disciples. We are only six verses into the gospel before we get our first reference to John, and that an insistent one: "There was a man sent from God, whose name was John. He came for testimony, to bear witness to the light, that all people might believe [in Jesus] through him. He was *not* the light, but [he only came] in order to bear witness to the light" (1:6–8).

The author, then, is accenting the point that Jesus rather than John is the true light who enlightens every person coming into the world. He seems to have inserted both this passage and verse 15 into a preexistent form of the prologue, since they break the poetic structure and flow of thought with their references to the Baptist (see Brown 1966, 1:21–23, 27–28). Both of these inserted passages seem designed to put John in his place—namely, beneath Jesus.

In the continuation of the gospel, the evangelist mobilizes the Baptist himself to testify to his own inferiority, making him acknowledge that he is neither the Messiah, nor Elijah, nor even a prophet (1:19–20); that he is unworthy to bend down and untie the sandal of "the Coming One" (1:26–27); that the whole purpose of his baptismal ministry has been to reveal Jesus to Israel (1:31); and, climactically, that Jesus's influence must increase while his own must decline (3:30). These protestations are emphatic, and all except one (1:27) are unparalleled in the Synoptics. A similar diminution of the Baptist with regard to Jesus is both implicit and explicit elsewhere in the gospel. When Jesus begins his own baptizing ministry, he makes and baptizes more disciples than John (3:26; 4:1). John performs no miracles, whereas Jesus accomplishes a plethora (10:41–42). The point of all of this is that Jesus, not John, is the one to be followed.

As has been recognized since Wilhelm Baldensperger's 1898 dissertation, the most logical explanation for this insistence on the Baptist's inferiority to Jesus is that the Fourth Gospel is pushing back against

---

3. Translations of New Testament texts are my own, though they often reflect contemporary translations, esp. RSV.

followers of the Baptist who are proclaiming the opposite: *John* is the light, perhaps even the Messiah, whose superiority to Jesus is shown by his preceding him in time (see "the one coming after me" in 1:15, 30).[4] Baldensperger (1898, 59) calls particular attention to the repetition in John 1:20: "And he confessed, and he did not deny, and he confessed: 'I am not the Christ,'" which Oscar Cullmann (1956, 178) terms an "emphatic insistence which can only be explained as aimed at an assertion to the contrary."[5] As Walter Wink (1968, 98) points out, moreover, the gospel itself inadvertently testifies to the existence of advocates of John's messiahship when it has the Baptist pointedly say to his disciples, "You yourselves bear me witness, that I said, I am not the Christ…" (3:28)—a "reminder" that makes most sense if there were followers of the Baptist in John's environment who maintained the opposite. Probably a large part of the Fourth Evangelist's purpose was to transfer the allegiance of such adherents of the Baptist to Jesus, as happens in the paradigmatic scene in 1:35–41. One of the ways in which he does so is to demonstrate that while, in one sense, John preceded Jesus, in another sense Jesus preceded John, since Jesus was and is the eternal word (1:15, 30; see 1:1; 8:58; Cullmann 1956, 180–82).

Baldensperger himself, and subsequently Martin Dibelius in his breakthrough monograph of 1911, found other evidence throughout the New Testament for the influence of, and Christian competition with, the Baptist sect. Most important here is Paul's encounter in Ephesus in Acts 19:1–6 with disciples of John who have never even heard of Jesus. They are quickly converted when they hear the good news preached by Paul, and they receive the Spirit in confirmation that Jesus rather than John is the one who should be followed. The note of competition here has been rightly emphasized by Ernst Käsemann (1964). Matthew, similarly, inserts a mini-dialogue into the scene of Jesus's baptism by John, in which John says to Jesus, "*I* need to be baptized by *you*—and do *you* come to *me*?" (Matt 3:13–

---

4. On the principle that the better proceeds the worse, see Cullmann 1956, Thomas 1935 (125 n. 1), and von Dobbeler 1988 (229), who cites Odes Sol. 28:17–18 (= Charlesworth [1983–1985, 2:760–61] 28:18–19). Satan uses similar logic in LAE 14:3; see also Moses's superiority to Joshua and Peter's preeminence among the disciples of Jesus.

5. Although ὁμολογεῖν = "to confess" in the New Testament often has the nuance "to declare publicly" and can lack the note of admission of an uncomfortable truth, its three Johannine usages (1:20; 9:22; 12:42) all seem to strike this note (see Heb 11:13 and BDAG, s.v. "ὁμολογέω," §3).

15). This invented dialogue is designed to ward off the assumption that the baptizer (John) must be superior to the baptizand (Jesus), since he confers on him a spiritual blessing (see Heb 7:7).[6] Dibelius (1911, 50) even thinks that the Q logion in which Jesus comments on John's status in the kingdom of God had been influenced by early Christian competition with the Baptist movement: the first part, in which Jesus acknowledges that John is the greatest of those born of women, goes back to Jesus; but the second, in which he ranks John below "the least in the kingdom," reflects a later Christian need to put John down (Matt 11:11 // Luke 7:28).

Nor is the evidence that these and other scholars adduce for the existence of Christian competition with the Baptist movement confined to the New Testament canon or the first century. Cullmann (1966; 1976) calls particular attention, as background for his reconstruction of the Johannine community, to passages in the Pseudo-Clementine *Homilies* and *Recognitions*, which attained their present form in the fourth and fifth centuries but which probably incorporate Jewish-Christian sources from second- and third-century Syria (see Strecker 1981; Jones 1995, 166; Reed 2003, 197; Wehnert 2011, 1073–77). One early passage (*Rec.* 1.60.1) depicts a disciple of the Baptist saying that John rather than Jesus was the Christ and adducing the first part of the Q passage just cited to prove it. Another (*Rec.* 1.54.8) mentions a group of John's disciples who separated themselves from the people and proclaimed their master as the Christ.[7] Since Walter Bauer (1971, originally published in 1934), we have learned to read such denunciations of schismatics through a hermeneutic of suspicion: they often mask a situation in which the so-called separatists are actually the majority and the "orthodox" an embattled minority. The Pseudo-Clementine literature, correspondingly, protests too much, and the truth seems to be that, at least in second-century Syria, the followers of the Baptist were in a strong position vis-à-vis the followers of Jesus.

Although these *Recognitions* passages charge John's followers, not John himself, with asserting messianic claims for him, other Pseudo-

6. Morton Smith (1965, 737–38) notes that in Acts 8:9–24 Simon Magus is similarly inferior to Philip, who baptizes him.

7. Strecker (1981, 221–54) identifies the source used in these passages, the *Ascents of James*, with *Rec.* 1.33–71 and locates it at Pella in the second half of the second century CE. Van Voorst (1989, 157–68) identifies it with *Rec.* 1.27–71 and thinks it was written under the name of Matthew by a Jewish-Christian author around the year 200, "quite possibly in Judaea or Jerusalem."

Clementine texts, perhaps from a later phase of development, are not so gentle. Various passages in both the *Homilies* and the *Recognitions*, for example, turn John into a false prophet, the founder of a heretical sect, and the demonic counterpart of his paired opposite, Jesus, on the unusual principle that the worse precedes the better (*Hom.* 2.17, 23; 3.22–23 // *Rec.* 2.8).[8] Here again, the Q logion is invoked, but in a sharpened way: John is one of those born of *woman*, and that puts him on the demonic side of the cosmic ledger, whereas Jesus is from the male, divine side of things.

The mirror image of this denigration of John vis-à-vis Jesus is found in the Mandaean literature, which makes *Jesus* into a false prophet and *John* into the true one (for representative texts, see Lupieri 2002, 224–53; for a more extensive sampling and analysis, see Lupieri 1988, 195–395). Rudolf Bultmann (1923; 1925; 1971, 17–18), as is well known, foregrounded Mandaean texts, which he traced backed to the original Baptist sect, in his reconstruction of the background of the Fourth Gospel; and the gnostic nature of the theology of the Mandaean texts helped him argue that the gospel was strongly influenced by Gnosticism. Bultmann was harshly criticized for this hypothesis and his use of late Mandaean texts to support it (see already Lietzmann 1958, originally published in 1930). The view of recent scholars, as epitomized by the careful study of Rudolph, is that the Mandaeans are not *direct* descendants of the Baptist sect. Their writings show little sign of contact with the historical Baptist but are fantastic and legendary in their descriptions of John. Moreover, although baptism is central to the Mandaean religion, Mandaean baptism differs greatly from what we know about John's baptism: it is neither an initiation nor once and for all but a constantly repeated rite and includes unparalleled features such as the drinking of baptismal water (Rudolph 1960–1961, 1:67–68, 76; Lupieri 2002, 15–22). Such differences, however, should not lead to a denial of all connection between the Mandaeans and the Baptist sect. The Mandaeans may not be direct successors to the Baptist movement, but they probably had contact in second-century Syria with the sort of followers of the Baptist who are polemicized against in the Pseudo-Clementines (see Rudolph 1960–1961, 1:72, 75).

---

8. This is a reversal of the usual principle that the better precedes the worse; see above, n. 4.

If there is so much indirect evidence of competition between early Christians, especially Johannine Christians, and the Baptist sect, why has scholarly interest faded in the hypothesis that this competition had a decisive influence on the composition of the Fourth Gospel? Partly because Bultmann overplayed his hand and thereby discredited the hypothesis, and partly because of Martyn's move toward seeing the background of the gospel in the conflict with Pharisaic/rabbinic Judaism. But the two hypotheses are not mutually exclusive, and it now remains to ask how they might be integrated.

It is immediately obvious that John expresses no bitterness toward the followers of John the Baptist comparable to that he shows toward the Pharisees, who, as pointed out above, are equated in some key passages with the Jews. Manuel Vogel (2015, 78) goes so far as to speak of the early Christian relation to followers of the Baptist as a "*friendly* competition." This is probably an overstatement, but it contains an element of truth. The Baptist is never designated a false Messiah or false prophet in the New Testament (as he is in the Pseudo-Clementines), even in John 1:8a—it is just that he is not (as some apparently were claiming) the *true* Messiah. Indeed, the Fourth Evangelist acknowledges in the context that John was "sent from God" (1:6; see 3:28)—a designation that elsewhere in the gospel applies only to Jesus (3:17, 34; 5:36, 38, etc.) and the Paraclete (14:26; see Theobald 2009, 292). As Wink (1968, 104–5) puts it in his unsurpassed little book on the Baptist in gospel traditions:

> Polemic and apologetic directed at contemporary "disciples of John" clearly seem to be present, yet Baptists are not the chief opponents of the Evangelist's church. The prime target is Pharisaical Judaism, with the Baptist community deployed to one side, and somewhat closer to the church than to the emergent "normative Judaism" of the Jamnian scholars. This is not surprising, since in the eyes of the Pharisees both Baptists and Christians belonged to the heretical sectarian baptist movement, and both paid allegiance to John. Apparently the Fourth Evangelist is still in dialogue with these Baptists, countering their hyper-elevation of John and wooing them to the Christian faith.

Although this conclusion exaggerates the extent to which "normative Judaism" existed in John's time (see Neusner 1980; Barclay 1996, 83–88), Wink's overall thesis seems valid. In the eyes of the Fourth Evangelist, Baptists are not enemies in the same way that Pharisees are; they are, rather, a mission field to be cultivated. As Philipp Vielhauer (1965, 45) puts it, "The missionary church indeed battled against the Baptist sect, but not against, but rather for, the Baptist, and therefore finally not against, but rather for, his adherents."

But although Wink, Vielhauer, and Vogel are right to emphasize that the New Testament attitude toward the Baptist and his followers does not break out into open enmity, the term "friendly competition" may mislead. Even "friendly competition" is still competition, and there may be resentment without overt hostility. Open refutation or abuse is not the only way to deal with a troublesome rival, who may instead be won over—a better result if the competitor is also a predecessor with whom one wishes to assert continuity. Bultmann (1963, 164) puts it nicely:

> The Christian attitude to John the Baptist is a divided one: while some passages make the Baptist appear as a confederate in Christian affairs, others emphasize his inferiority to Jesus. Understandably, for both points of view were occasioned by the anti-Baptist polemic.

To draw an analogy, in the Qur'an, Muhammad is to Jesus as, in the Fourth Gospel, Jesus is to the Baptist; and Muhammad's relation to Christians and Jews roughly corresponds to the relation of the Johannine author to the Baptist sectarians and οἱ Ἰουδαῖοι = Pharisees. The competition between the new prophetic movement led by Muhammad, on the one hand, and the older communities of Christians and Jews, on the other, was intense, especially after the *hejirah* from Mecca to Medina in 622 CE. Of these two groups, the Jews were the more adamant in their rejection of Muhammad, whereas he seems to have gained something of a foothold among Medinan Christians. His attitude toward Christians, in consequence, is more mixed than his attitude toward Jews. He can be fierce in his denunciations of some of their doctrines, especially belief in the Trinity and the divinity of Jesus, but he can also be surprisingly sympathetic, even imagining that Christians' eyes will overflow with tears of repentance when they hear the true message preached and that they will end up asking to be enrolled as Muslims (Q Maida 5:83). As David Marshall (2001, 22–23) puts it, "Behind the apparently conflicting positive and negative material on Christians there is a coherent qur'anic attitude: on the assumption that they are ready to believe in the Qur'ān, Christians are seen positively; where they disappoint that expectation, they are seen negatively." Correspondingly, while Muhammad criticizes latter-day Christian doctrines, he never criticizes Jesus but incorporates him into a history of salvation that culminates in himself: Jesus is the prophetic forerunner who points towards Muhammad's own position as "the seal of the prophets."

This comparison alerts us to the fact that muted criticism does not necessarily indicate a lack of competition. It may, on the contrary, coexist with intense competition; the criticism is muted not because there are no competitors around but because the mission field is still in play. It is easy to imagine that Christians such as the author of the Fourth Gospel hoped for and expected a response such as that described in Q Maida 5:83: the eyes of Baptist followers overflowing with tears as they recognize the truth that their commitment to their master has led them to a better and living master.

How then can we characterize the Baptist sect in relation to Johannine Christians and other Jewish groups in the dynamic environment of late first-century Judaism? Clearly the Pharisees were in the ascendant, at least in John's area, and they were probably suspicious of all messianic and eschatologically oriented groups that might challenge their influence with the populace and their attempt to get along with the Romans (see John 11:47–50)—including not only the Christians but also the followers of the Baptist. It is no accident that, in John 1:19–25, the delegation deputed to quiz John about his claims consists of Pharisees. Already synoptic passages such as Mark 11:27–33 and Matt 21:31–32 // Luke 7:29–30 reflect the tendency of Jewish groups more central to the power structure, including (after 70) the Pharisees, to see the two messianic movements as related, to reject their claims across the board, and to fear their influence among the populace. This attitude of Pharisaic suspicion and hostility may have helped bring together the two messianic groups, on the principle that the enemy of my enemy is my friend. They were also, of course, historically linked by the memory that Jesus had begun his ministry within the Baptist movement. But that memory, along with the fact that Jesus eventually struck out on his own, also sowed the seeds of tension between the two messianic movements—and this we also see reflected in John's Gospel.

In the Johannine environment, the Christians were probably the stronger group than the followers of the Baptist; otherwise we would expect more direct and fiercer Johannine polemic against the Baptists. No charge is made, moreover, that the Baptist or his followers have colluded in the persecution of Jesus and the Christians that is ascribed, for the most part, to the Pharisees. But it is also true that the Baptist is a major concern in the Fourth Gospel, in a way that he is not in the first three. In fact, there are almost as many usages of John's name in the Fourth Gospel as there are of the term Φαρισαῖος (eighteen versus twenty), although, if we recognize that οἱ Ἰουδαῖοι is often a cipher for "the Pharisees," the latter still remain the dominant concern. There may, then, be a relation between the strength of the polemic against the Pharisees and the urgency of the Johannine appeal to the Baptists: thrust out of the centers of Jewish institutional power in their area, the Johannine Christians could not afford to be weakened further by an exacerbation of the split in messianic ranks. One of their hopes for the future, rather, was to absorb the Baptist movement in which their founder had begun his career.

The Shema in John's Gospel and Jewish Restoration Eschatology

Lori Baron

In the Synoptic Gospels, Jesus cites the Shema, along with the injunction to love one's neighbor, as part of the Great Commandment: "Hear O Israel, the LORD our God, the LORD is אחד, one. And you shall love the LORD your God with all your heart, and with all your soul, and with all your might" (Deut 6:4–5).[1] Although John's Gospel lacks such a citation, the Shema is woven deeply into the fabric of John's narrative and is central to John's Christology and to the shape of his community (Barrett 1947, 161–62). In this paper, I argue that John makes use of an eschatological interpretation of the Shema at the heart of the vision of national restoration found in the Hebrew prophets. Drawing on this hope, John includes Jesus within the divine unity and portrays Jesus's disciples as the united, eschatological people of God. This use of the Shema to characterize both Jesus and the believing community is plausible in the context of the late first century, when tensions were high between Jewish believers in Jesus and the synagogue to which they had once belonged. The Johannine Shema contains within it the seeds of tension that would lead to continued and escalating strife between church and synagogue and ultimately to their separation. The problematic implications of the Johannine Shema for John's relationship to Judaism will be considered briefly in the conclusion.

1. Translation mine. Deut 6:4 is cited only in the Gospel of Mark. Deut 6:5 appears in the Synoptic Gospels with significant variations (Mark 12:30, 33; Matt 22:37; Luke 10:27). For a discussion of these variants, see my forthcoming monograph *The Shema in the Gospel of John* (WUNT 2).

The Shema in John 10

The theme of Jesus's unity with the Father is prominent in the good shepherd discourse (John 10:1–21). The passage in the Hebrew Bible most often cited in connection with this text is Ezek 34, where the prophet condemns Israel's leaders as false shepherds who feed *themselves* but starve the sheep who are in their care (see, e.g., Brown 1966, 398; Barrett 1978, 373; Dodd 1953, 358–62; Manning 2004, 111–35; Smith 1999, 205). Israel is a scattered flock, led astray by its leaders, but God promises to rescue them as their shepherd: "I myself will be the shepherd of my sheep" (Ezek 34:15).[2]

In Ezekiel, the shepherd is "one," a descriptor highly suggestive of the Shema (Deut 6:4). God proclaims, "I will set up over them *one shepherd*" (Ezek 34:23a; εἷς ποιμήν/רעה אחד), and "they shall all have *one shepherd*" (Ezek 37:24; ποιμὴν εἷς/רועה אחד). In ancient Near Eastern inscriptions and literature, the language of oneness is used to connote the supremacy of a god or king (Lohfink and Bergman 1974, 1:194–95; see also Weinfeld 1991, 338, 350–51; M. S. Smith 2008, 144–45). Furthermore, in this same literature and in the Hebrew Bible, the image of the shepherd connotes divine kingship. In Ezekiel, these features are joined to produce a vivid image of eschatological deliverance: Adonai, Israel's one God, delivers his people from destruction as a shepherd rescues his sheep. So it is striking that, in John 10, when Jesus speaks of the ingathering of sheep to the fold, he applies the image of the shepherd along with the word "one"/εἷς to himself: "So there will be one flock, one shepherd" (10:16; μία ποίμνη, εἷς ποιμήν). Jesus's attribution of the word "one" to himself effectively unites him with God, Israel's one Shepherd and King.

But the prophetic picture is a bit more complicated. Ezekiel and Jeremiah also describe an agent standing in for the Divine Shepherd:

> I will set up over them *one shepherd* [ποιμένα ἕνα / רעה אחד], my servant David, and he shall feed them: he shall feed them and be their shepherd. And I, the LORD, will be their God, and my servant David shall be prince among them; I, the LORD, have spoken.... You are my sheep, the sheep of my pasture, and I am your God, says the LORD. (Ezek 34:23–24, 31, emphasis added; see also 37:24)

2. Unless otherwise specified, Scripture quotations in this essay are from the NRSV.

In addition, and striking in its affinities with John 1, Philo refers to the shepherd's stand-in as the Logos:

> Thus, indeed, being a shepherd is a good thing, so that it is justly attributed, not only to kings, and to wise men, and to souls who are perfectly purified, but also to God, the ruler of all things.... For God, like a shepherd and a king, governs (as if they were a flock of sheep) the earth, and the water, and the air, and the fire, and all the plants, and living creatures that are in them ... appointing, as their immediate superintendent, his true Logos and first-born son [ὁ ὀρθός αὐτοῦ λόγος καὶ πρωτόγονος υἱός], who is to receive the charge of this sacred company, as the lieutenant of the great king. (*Agriculture* 50–51; trans. Yonge 1854–1890; slightly abridged; see also *Posterity* 67–68; noted by Dodd 1953, 56–57)

Like the Davidic ruler of Ezekiel, the Logos is deputized by God to superintend God's created order or "flock." Moshe Greenberg (1983–1997, 2:708) observes that, in ancient Near Eastern literature and in the Prophets, "The meaning of the epithet [shepherd] vacillates between the owner of the flock (as in the case of a god) and the agent of the owner who is responsible to him." The attribution of God's authority, whether to a future Davidic figure, as in the Hebrew prophets, or to the Logos, as in Philo, thus anticipates John's portrayal of Jesus, who is both λόγος and θεός (John 1:1).

The parallels between Ezekiel and John 10 are readily apparent: just as God castigates the false leaders in Israel and vows to care for his people, so Jesus rails against the Pharisees and promises to protect *his* sheep. When this imagery is applied to Jesus in John 10, it more than hints at Jesus's unity with God; it invites the reader to see Jesus in the role of God, who delivers his people from the grasp of false leaders bent on their destruction. When Jesus utters his climactic statement, "I and the Father are one" (John 10:30), his opponents fully comprehend the audaciousness of this claim; they pick up stones to kill him for blasphemy, for "making himself God" (10:33). The significance of this declaration can hardly be overstated: the author invokes the word "one" (ἕν) a key word in the Shema, explicitly locating Jesus within the divine אחד. For John, believing in Jesus is no violation of monotheism; Jesus has not "made himself" God's equal, nor have his followers made him so. Rather, Jesus is the unique Son, authorized and sent by the Father to speak God's words and perform God's works. The Johannine Shema thus serves to counter claims of ditheism: Jesus is no threat to the divine unity—he exists within it.

Corresponding to the notion of one Shepherd or one King, both Ezekiel and John assert that God's people will be unified as one entity. Ezekiel 37:21–28 reads:

> I will take the people of Israel from the nations among which they have gone, and will gather [συνάξω] them from every quarter, and bring them to their own land. I will make them *one nation* [ἔθνος ἓν/גוי אחד] in the land, on the mountains of Israel; and *one king* [ἄρχων εἷς/מלך אחד] shall be king over them all.… And they shall all have *one shepherd* [ποιμὴν εἷς/רועה אחד].… I will make a covenant of peace with them; it shall be an everlasting covenant with them; and I will bless them and multiply them, and will set my sanctuary among them forevermore.

The "one nation" in this passage represents the reunification of the northern and southern kingdoms. This is spelled out when Ezekiel portends national reunification in a symbolic action in which he unites two sticks representing both kingdoms. God commands the prophet: "Join them together into one stick [ῥάβδον μίαν/עץ אחד], so that they may become one [ἔσονται ἐν/והיו לאחדים] in your hand" (Ezek 37:17; see 37:19).[3] The prophet thus envisions a renewed covenant and Israel's restoration as *one* people (37:17, 19) under *one* king (37:22), with *one* heart (11:19; see also "new heart" 18:31; 36:26),[4] worshiping in *one* place (37:27–28). Ezekiel's word of reunification harks back to the Shema, to the one God who had created Israel as his one people. So the promised restoration recapitulates the Shema as it anticipates a renewed covenant in which the one Shepherd and his flock are reunited.

Jeremiah uses similar language when he writes of the ingathering of Israel. In a surprising twist, the prophet reverses the terms of the Shema. Following the covenantal affirmation, "They shall be my people, and I will be their God" (Jer 32:38; see also Ezek 37:27), the Lord proclaims that Israel will be אחד, one, undivided in its faithfulness to God: "I will give them one heart and one way [לב אחד ודרך אחד] that they may fear me

3. The LXX reads ἔσονται ἐν τῇ χειρί σου, most likely due to confusion over the breathing mark or over a double εν in a putative Ur-text (ἔσονται ἕν ἐν τῇ χειρί σου; suggested by Joel Marcus).

4. In the LXX, לב אחד is translated καρδία ἑτέρα, probably due to the similar appearance of אחד and אחר. Greenberg (1983–1997, 1:190) comments that אחר "is a possible Hebrew reading, but it lacks the rich overtones of the reading ʿeḥad."

for all time" (Jer 32:39a).[5] Restored Israel will be one people with one heart. The divine response to Israel's renewed faithfulness echoes Deut 6:5, applying its terms to God: "I will rejoice in doing good to them, and I will plant them in this land in faithfulness, *with all my heart and with all my soul*" (בכל־לבי ובכל־נפשי; Jer 32:41, emphasis added).[6] God thus reaffirms his covenant faithfulness toward Israel, reversing the terms of the Shema in the process: God is devoted to his *one* people with all *his* heart and with all *his* soul. As was the case with Ezekiel, a renewed covenant necessitates a renewed Shema.[7]

Zechariah, too, envisions a day of restoration expressed in terms of the Shema: "And the Lord will become king over all the earth; on that day the Lord will be one and his name one" (יהוה אחד ושמו אחד; Zech 14:9). It is not surprising that the themes of "one shepherd" (or one king or Lord) and "one heart" or "one flock" are found in oracles of future restoration, as the renewal of the covenant is at the heart of these passages, and the Shema is at the heart of the covenant. The Shema is thus reinterpreted in light of Israel's exile and is the foundation on which Israel's hopes for renewal rest.

John 10:16 resonates with this prophetic imagery—the unity of God's people as "one flock" under the rule of the one Shepherd. This suggests that John understands believers in Jesus as Israel restored (see also Manning 2004, 127; Kysar 1986, 163). For the Hebrew prophets, the vision of restoration contains a renewed Shema in which the one God will be worshiped by a united people. For John, prophetic eschatological restoration is now becoming a reality for followers of Jesus.

Evidence of themes related to prophetic restoration elsewhere in John reinforces the significance of this theme in John 10 and in the Fourth Gospel as a whole. For example, in John 11:52, the narrator reinterprets the high priest's cynical remark about the necessity of Jesus's death as a prophecy that Jesus will die for the nation and gather *into one* the dispersed children of God. The verbs διασκορπίζω and συνάγω are used frequently in Zechariah, Jeremiah, and Ezekiel (LXX) to refer to the scat-

5. Jer 39:39 LXX reads ὁδός ἑτέρα καὶ καρδία ἑτέρα, probably due again to the similar appearance of אחד and אחר; so Lundbom (2004, 519).

6. This echo of Deut 6:5 was recognized by Janzen (1987, 288–91); see also Lundbom (2004, 521).

7. Jer 3:10; 24:7; 29:13 also speak of returning to YHWH or seeking YHWH with all one's heart.

tering of the people of Israel among the nations for their disobedience and God's regathering of them *into one*.[8] The presence of this language in John undergirds the idea that the Fourth Evangelist sees the regathering and restoration of Israel as integral to his narrative about Jesus and those who believe in him.[9]

The Shema in John 17

The prophetic, eschatological Shema is foregrounded in John 17, where the Johannine Jesus prays for the unity of those who will believe in him through the word of his disciples, presumably those who are alive at the time of the writing and experiencing persecution:[10]

> Holy Father, protect them in your name that you have given me, *that they may be one, as we are* [ἵνα ὦσιν ἓν καθὼς ἡμεῖς].... I ask not only on behalf of these, but also on behalf of those who will believe in me through their word, *that they may all be one* [ἵνα πάντες ἓν ὦσιν]. As you, Father, are in me and I am in you, may they also be[11] in us, so that the world may believe that you have sent me. The glory that you have given me I have given them, *so that they may be one, as we are one* [ἵνα ὦσιν ἓν καθὼς ἡμεῖς ἕν], I in them and you in me, *that they may become completely one* [ἵνα ὦσιν τετελειωμένοι εἰς ἕν], so that the world may know that you have sent me and have loved them even as you have loved me. (John 17:11b, 20–23, emphasis added)[12]

Here, the repetition of the hope "that they may be one [ὦσιν ἓν]" echoes Ezekiel's repeated statement concerning the unification of the kingdoms of Judah and Joseph, "that they may be one" (Ezek 37:17, 19 והיו אחד).

---

8. E.g., διασκορπίζω (Zech 2:2, 4 LXX; Jer 9:15 LXX; 23:1, 2; Ezek 5:10; 12:15; 22:15); συνάγω (Zech 2:10 LXX; Jer 23:8; 38:10 LXX; Ezek 11:17; 28:25; 39:27).

9. On Jesus as prophet of eschatological restoration, relying primarily on the evidence of the actions of Jesus in the Synoptic Gospels, see Sanders (1985).

10. Hints that the disciples represent persecuted believers after the time of Jesus: Jesus has guarded them and kept them from perishing (17:2); he explains that the world has hated them and that they need protection from the evil one (17:14–15; see also 15:18–24).

11. ℵ A C^3 contain ἕν here, while P^{66vid} C* D lack it.

12. On the giving of the divine name to Jesus in John 17 as the transmission of the divine life from Father to Son to believers, see Shirbroun (1985).

But John 17 and Ezek 37 do not merely agree verbally; they share contextual affinities as well. In John 17, the unity of the disciples suggests that they share in Jesus's mission: as one people, Jesus's followers participate in the divine work of eschatological judgment and reconciliation. The expression "that the world (or the nations) may know" is common to both Ezek 37 and John 17; in both writings, the unity of the people is a witness to God's kingship (which is implied in the Shema) and God's mission to the world. Knowledge of God is a theme that recurs throughout Ezekiel and the prophets. For example, Israel's dispersion among the nations and regathering occurs so that Israel will know that the Lord is God: "And *they shall know that I am the Lord* [καὶ γνώσονται διότι ἐγὼ κύριος], when I disperse them among the nations and scatter them through the countries" (Ezek 12:15, emphasis added). So, too, the nations will know that the Lord is God when they see Israel regathered: "and *the nations shall know* [γνώσονται τὰ ἔθνη] that I am Adonai, says the Lord GOD, when through you I display my holiness before their eyes" (Ezek 36:23). At the culmination of the oracle in Ezek 37, God promises to reaffirm the covenant with Israel as one nation with one king, declaring: "Then *the nations shall know* [γνώσονται τὰ ἔθνη] that I the LORD sanctify Israel, when my sanctuary is among them forevermore" (Ezek 37:28). God's restoring of Israel and dwelling among them will cause all people to *know* that Adonai is the one, true God.

In John, the disciples' unity is *also* a testimony to the world. Their mission mirrors that of Jesus: just as the Father sent Jesus into the world for eschatological judgment and reconciliation ("I came into this world for judgment so that those who do not see may see, and those who do see may become blind"; 9:39; see also 15:22), the disciples are sent into the world for the same purpose. This point is made through the use of multiple ἵνα or purpose clauses. Jesus prays for his disciples:

- "*that* they may all be one. As you, Father, are in me and I am in you,
- *in order that* they may also be in us,
- *so that the world may believe* that you sent me" (17:21; alt. trans., emphasis added).

"The glory that you have given me I have given them,

- *so that* they may be one, as we are one, I in them and you in me,

- *in order that* they may become completely one,
- *so that the world may know* that you have sent me" (17:22–23, emphasis added).

The goal, the purpose of the "oneness," is *in order that* the world may know and believe in Jesus's unique relationship with the Father. John stresses that the unity of Father, Son, and believers is for the sake of the world. In the Fourth Gospel, however, the world does not know God or the Logos, nor do Jesus's own people recognize him: "He was in the world, and the world came into being through him; yet *the world did not know him.* He came to his own, and his own people did not accept him" (1:10–11). By contrast, Jesus's disciples both "believe" and "know" that Jesus is from God: "We have believed and known that you are the holy one of God" (6:69, my translation). The unity of the disciples is a testimony to the unity of the Father and the Son: just as the presence of "one king" and "one people" testifies to the nations that God is sovereign (Ezek 37), so the disciples' unity with the Father, the Son, and one another signals the in-breaking of God's kingly rule in Jesus. Thus the Johannine Jesus prays for the unity of his people, that they might be bound up into the mission of the Father and the Son "in order that the world may believe and know" Jesus as the *one* Lord and King.

Conclusion

It is fitting that Ezekiel, in particular, provides the background for the Johannine Shema; the prophet writes under the influence of the trauma of the exile, proclaiming that Israel's fate is a consequence of disloyalty to God's covenant and yet that there remains a hope for redemption and restoration.[13] If, in fact, Johannine believers in Jesus were forced out of the local Jewish community to which they once belonged, they would readily identify with the exiled people of the past and apply the biblical imagery of restoration to themselves. Just as the prophets take up and transform the idea of covenant—with the Shema at its core—making it relevant to new historical situations, so, too, John transposes both the covenant and the Shema, but he does so *christologically*: believers in Jesus constitute the

13. For introductory matters on Ezekiel, see Greenberg (1983, 12–17); Zimmerli (1979, 9–16).

one flock of God, united to one another through the one Shepherd. This move transforms expectations with an apologetic and christological twist: followers of Jesus represent the hoped-for messianic unity, while nonbelieving Jews are excluded from that unity. John gets to have the last word: some Jewish authorities may have expelled Jesus believers from their midst, but now *they* are the outsiders. The good news for the disenfranchised has itself become a rhetorical weapon of exclusion, a weapon that has proven deadly in a later context, in the hands of a powerful church against a Jewish minority.

Anyone who interprets the Fourth Gospel must exercise great caution not to step carelessly on any of its polemical land mines and thereby perpetuate the legacy of Christian anti-Judaism. John's christological reinterpretation of the Shema may have been an anchor for a struggling community in the first century and provided a narrative of empowerment to those who felt themselves to be exiled, but to apply John's condemnation of some Jewish authorities of his day to present-day Jews or Judaism is to misread the contemporary situation. As J. Louis Martyn, of blessed memory, observed, history and theology are always intertwined. Teachers and preachers of the Fourth Gospel must therefore discern their own place in history in order to make theirs a theology that gives life and hope to all people (Deut 30:16; John 10:10).

Tensions in Matthean and Johannine Soteriology Viewed in Their Jewish Context

William R. G. Loader

Soteriology is an area of controversy in relation to both the Gospel according to Matthew and the Gospel according to John, two rather different gospels, but sharing what many would indeed see as a strongly Jewish background. This paper will explore the divergence among scholars concerning soteriology in each before turning to an approach that seeks to move beyond that divergence to an understanding that is rooted in the strongly Jewish spirituality that informs both gospels, though in different ways.

Matthew and the Saving Death of Jesus

At first sight Matthew's Gospel appears to give a very clear answer to the question about soteriology when in 1:21 it has the angel declare: "You shall call his name Jesus; because he will save his people from their sins." Accordingly, for many interpreters Matthew is thereby pointing forward to the cross as an act of atonement.[1] Accordingly, he is doing so also in taking over Mark's logion about Jesus's coming to give his life a ransom for many (Matt 20:28; Mark 10:45).[2]

The early claim of redaction analysis that Matthew had omitted Mark's description of John's baptism as a baptism of repentance for the forgiveness of sins and transferred it to the last meal scene confirms this for many (so Hummel 1966, 101; Meier 1979, 184; 1983, 319). Thus William Davies

1. So Kingsbury 1976, 82, 85, 117; Meier 1979, 143–44, 183–84; 1983, 24, 229, 319; Hagner 1993–1995, 1:19; 2:582–83, 773; Repschinski 2006, 265.

2. Meier (1979, 184; 1983, 319), against, for instance, the claim of Gerhardsson (1974, 25) that this is not in the context of atonement and so refers to the "spiritual service of sacrifice."

and Dale Allison (1988–1997, 1:292) write: "If John had preached a baptism for the forgiveness of sins, Jesus' baptism would have been all the more troublesome for Matthew than it already is."[3] Accordingly, to Mark's account, "This is the blood of the covenant poured out for many" (Mark 14:24), Matthew appends "for the forgiveness of sins" (Matt 26:28). Thus, it is argued, for Matthew, forgiveness of sins is now only through Jesus's shed blood, and so for Matthew the cross as an act of atonement is at the heart of Matthew's soteriology. As John Nolland (2005, 41, emphasis original) puts it, "Matthew clearly intended Jesus' death to be viewed as a saving event, as *the* saving event" because "the pouring out of Jesus' blood in death is … the means of forgiveness of sins." This is a strong case.

John and the Saving Death of Jesus

We have a similar situation in John's Gospel, where also in the first chapter John the Baptist declares to onlookers: "Behold the lamb of God, who takes away the sin of the world" (1:29; see detailed discussion in Loader 2017, 136–48). Most see this, too, as pointing forward to Jesus's death as an act of atonement and therefore as the hermeneutical clue for interpreting all subsequent references to Jesus's dying, however one understands the imagery of lamb, an issue of contention itself. John the Baptist, accordingly, has nothing to do with forgiveness of sin (Bieringer 2007, 224; Theobald 2009, 170). That role is to be fulfilled by Jesus, it is argued, through his death on the cross as the lamb of God.

Jesus's last words on the cross, "It is finished" (John 19:30), mean, accordingly, that the act of taking away sin has been achieved (Schnelle 2007, 242–55; Müller 1966, 34, 50, 74, 130–31; Thüsing 1979, 68–69, 100) or, strictly speaking, is about to be achieved in his death, which immediately follows, and is reflected for some in the symbolism of the flow of water and blood from his side (19:34; Thüsing 1979, 161, 164, 324; cf. Loader 2017, 185–87).

Much can be cited in support of these conclusions, including key texts found in the body of the gospel (discussed in detail in Loader 2017, 169–80). One is 6:51c, "The bread which I give is my flesh for the life of the world," coming in the context of what are most likely allusions to

3. Similarly 1:300–301; 3:474; Gundry 1991, 65; 1994, 43; Repschinski 2006, 258, 260–61; 2009, 74; Gurtner 2007, 134.

eucharistic tradition about eating the flesh of the Son of Man and drinking his blood. The shepherd discourse has Jesus speak of laying down his life for the sheep (10:11, 15, 17, 18). John 15 has Jesus speak of laying down his life for his friends. The high priest's rationale for Jesus's execution to rescue the nation from Roman suppression becomes an inspired allusion to Jesus's saving death for all (11:50–52; 18:14). The gift of eternal life promised after the lifting up of the Son of Man in 3:14–15 and his death as God's act of giving up his Son in love so that all who believe in him may have eternal life seem indeed to underline the centrality of the cross as the act that makes salvation and eternal life possible according to John, just as the Baptist had announced.

Pressed to its logical conclusion, such an interpretation implies that only after Jesus's death was salvation possible and eternal life available. Any allusions to Jesus's bringing life during his ministry are accordingly to be read as proleptic. Thus Jörg Frey (1997–2000, 2:282) writes:

> Nach johanneischer Auffassung ist der wahre Gottesdienst ebenso wie die geistliche Totenerweckung allein durch Christus und in seiner Gegenwart möglich. Insofern Johannes die Heilswirklichkeit der nachösterlichen Zeit proleptisch bereits im Verlauf des Werkens Jesu zur Darstellung bringt, hat das *kai nun estin* auch in der Sprechperspektive des irdischen Jesu seine Berechtigung.[4]

Marianne Meye Thompson (2001, 178) explains:

> The actual reception of life seems to be deferred until after Jesus' death. Consequently when Jesus speaks of giving life (e.g., 3:5–8; 6:63), he speaks proleptically of a situation that will obtain only after his death.... What also needs to be emphasized is that what happens *after* Jesus' death also happens *because of* Jesus' death, whether that be the conferring of life or the giving of the Spirit. (emphasis original)

Accordingly, it is argued, the author could not have meant that Jesus gave life before he had achieved the basis for it by his atoning death. This, too, is a strong case.

---

4. See similarly Haenchen 1980, 109; Schillebeeckx 1980, 405–6, 410–11; Schnackenburg 1977, 217; but see Schnackenburg 1967, 208.

Matthew and the Saving Life of Jesus

If we return to Matthew, the notion that there, too, salvation, or at least forgiveness of sins, becomes possible only after Jesus's death runs into some difficulty when Matthew's narrative of Jesus's ministry is taken into account. Matthew takes over Mark's report of the healing of the paralytic, which includes a declaration of forgiveness of sins (Matt 9:2–8; see Mark 2:1–12). Matthew's additional comment that the authority to declare forgiveness would be given to human beings (Matt 9:8) clearly points beyond Jesus's death, but the declaration and its effect also clearly show that Jesus, the Son of Man, was already authorized to forgive sins during his ministry—before his death.[5] This can hardly be dismissed, as does John Meier (1983, 91; similarly Hagner 1993–1995, 1:234; Gundry 1994, 154–80), who argues that Jesus's healing of the paralytic in Matthew (9:2–8) is christological, not soteriological, in nature, as it focuses on Jesus's authority, not on forgiveness of sins itself. The Sermon on the Mount includes the Lord's Prayer and the associated saying about forgiving and being forgiven. Nothing suggests that this could apply only after Jesus's death or that it is to be dismissed as being concerned with judgment and reconciliation rather than forgiveness (Harrington 1991, 94–95, 122, 125, 270; see Davies and Allison 1988–1997, 1:616–17, 2:796–99).

The argument based on omission of "for the forgiveness of sins" and its addition to the last meal narrative is also not as cogent as it might seem. For in place of Mark's words, "preaching a baptism of repentance for the forgiveness of sins," Matthew reads: "saying, 'Repent, for the kingdom of heaven is at hand'" (3:2). Matthew rewrote Mark's account of John, importing Mark's summary of Jesus's proclamation (Mark 1:15) into it as now also a summary of John's preaching, identical to the summary of Jesus's message. He retains, however, the detail that people came to be baptized by John, confessing their sins (Matt 3:6). The most natural reading of Matthew's account is surely not that they confessed their sins without any prospect of forgiveness until after Jesus's death but that forgiveness accompanied what the washing and immersion symbolized in that act.[6]

5. Harrington 1991, 121–23; France 2007, 347, 350–51; Hasitschka 2008, 92; Davies and Allison 1988–1997, 100, 474–75; Nolland 2005, 294, 504–6, 753–62, 1082; Luomanen 1998, 222, 224–30; Carter 2000, 99, 533; 2004, 115, 142–43, 147, 177.

6. So Hagner 1993, 47; Harrington 1991, 52, 122–25; Luz 2002a, 205; Nolland 2005, 1081 n. 135; see Davies and Allison 1988–1997, 300–301; Repschinski 2009, 74.

The call to repentance, identically expressed by both John and Jesus, surely promised forgiveness of sins there and then. A contemporary Jew would hardly have understood otherwise.

If one moves beyond forgiveness of sins to obtaining eternal life, then it is incontrovertible that Matthew portrays Jesus as declaring that one inherits eternal life by keeping the commandments, the torah, every stroke, as interpreted by Jesus (Matt 5:20; 19:16–22; Harrington 1991, 281; 1992, 1431–32). This is a promise not just for the future, a key theme associated with judgement in all five main discourses (Luz 2007a, 37), but also for the present and by implication already during Jesus's ministry. In addition, Jesus's saving people from their sins clearly must include aspects of Jesus's ministry of healing (Meier 1983, 85–86, 91; Harrington 1991, 116–17, 287)—before his death. Daniel Harrington (1991, 123) sees Jesus's saving power also in the stilling of the storm. As Anthony Saldarini (1994, 166) puts it, Jesus saves his people "by his teaching and healing and pre-eminently by his death, which leads to his resurrection (chaps. 26–28) and the ultimate vindication of the just at the final judgment (25:31–46)."[7] The case therefore for claiming that in Matthew Jesus brings forgiveness of sins already during his ministry is also strong.

It is therefore not surprising that some identify a major tension in Matthew's soteriology: between statements that suggest that Jesus's death achieved forgiveness of sins, salvation, and those that suggest that he already offered this in his life; some seek some way to reconcile the two, while others simply ignore the issue. To this we shall return, but first let us observe the similar situation in John.

John and the Saving Life and Person of Jesus

The Fourth Gospel portrays Jesus as the Word made flesh who in his person offers life. Differently from Matthew, who make Jesus torah's champion, John portrays God's gift of torah as foreshadowing the coming of an even greater gift, namely, the coming of the Messiah, who in John's terms is none other than God's Son, eternally with God from the beginning (see detailed discussion in Loader 2017, 282–303, 321–22, 443–52). What had been images of torah, including word, wisdom, water, bread, light, and life, are now transferred to Jesus. The temple and its feasts point to and

7. Similarly Stanton 1992, 376; 1982; Senior 1997, 89, 114.

are fulfilled and superseded—I think that is what John means—by a new temple, in whom is the water of life, the true manna, the true light and life, and who is the true vine (Loader 2017, 443–52; 2012, 143–58). For all the statements that speak of the gift of eternal life in the future—and they are there in John, though not many (John 3:14–15; 6:27, 51–58; 7:38–39; see Loader 2017, 190–93; de Boer 1996, 103)—there are many more that, consistent with the logic of John's Christology, portray Jesus in his person as offering life already during his ministry (Loader 2017, 194–202).

While one might cite the significance of John the Baptist's statement about the lamb as coming so early in the gospel and allegedly defining how the gospel should be read, this is even more so with the prologue (Loader 2016). Furthermore, whereas the last of the few references to Jesus's vicarious death comes in chapter 11, with possibly one in 15:13, the notion of salvation being in the person of Jesus and what he gave in his ministry dominates the final chapters, not least Jesus's final prayer. Sanctification in relation to Jesus in 10:36 and 17:19 and to the disciples in 17:17–18 is about setting people apart in a state of holiness for some special task or action. The special task or action need not be cultic or have to do with sacrifice, and ἁγιάζω is not sacrificial in the LXX.[8] Furthermore, "it is finished" (19:30) connects intratextually not with references to vicarious death but with references to finishing the work he had been given to do during his ministry, to make the Father known (4:34; 17:4; 13:1; Loader 2017, 187–90).

Some have, of course, pushed the logic of this position to the extent that for John Jesus's death became simply the point of exit, his revealing work having been done.[9] That, of course, will not do, as many have pointed out. For John depicts the "hour," the death, with typical irony as both a lifting up on a cross and lifting up to God, as glorification, which has to include the total event reaching its climax in his returning to the glory of the Father, as his ascension and as his return to the Father (discussion in Loader 2017, 213–81). This event complex clearly marks not just the end (*Ende*) but the turning point (*Wende*; Blank, 1962, 282; see also Bultmann 1941, 330), especially as this is enunciated in the last discourses, because it makes possible the sending of the Spirit to empower the disciples for the mission of offering eternal life to all in his name and so to do greater works

8. De la Potterie 1977, 761–62; Chanikuzhy 2012, 382; Loader 2017, 181–83; see Bultmann 1941, 391; 1953/1977, 407; Beasley-Murray 1999, 301.

9. Käsemann 1971, 23, 49 n. 53, 124, 135; Lattke 1975, 142; Müller 1975, 54, 65, 68; Appold 1976, 52, 103, 123, 135; Becker 1979–1981, 406–7; Langbrandtner 1977, 97.

than Jesus himself (14:12–17). It is also the event that exposes both Jesus's vindication and the world's sin, in that sense disempowering the world's ruler, judgment (16:8–11; 12:31; 14:30; 16:33).[10] As I have noted elsewhere (Loader 2017, 199),

> It is a mark of the extent to which expiatory and vicarious death and its effects are not central that nowhere in the accounts of the passion, indeed from chapter 12 onwards, do we find any reference to what Jesus' death achieved expressed in those terms. The only explanation, significantly, relates to the judgment of the ruler of this world (12:31; 14:30; 16:11), a moment of realised eschatology typical of the author, so that what was expected at the end of time has now happened in Jesus' death.

It is thus possible to give a coherent account of John's soteriology on the basis of its depiction of both Jesus's ministry and his death as expressions of his offering life and love to the end (13:1–2). "In him was life" (1:4), in his person and so in encounter with him, already during his ministry. One should not confuse our historical awareness that such beliefs were developed primarily through the post-Easter period with what the author apparently would have believed and articulated (see Bornkamm 1968, 114; Frey 2013d, 506; 2013b, 646). T. Onuki (1984, 206) speaks of a paradox that saving knowledge of Christ's divinity is possible only after his resurrection and yet is mediated by his earthly ministry, but this, like many of the approaches mentioned, confuses the process of growth of awareness in history (our insights into how Christology developed) with the evangelist's understanding that in the person of the earthly Jesus, life was already offered. Jörg Frey (1997–2000, 3:254–56, 266, 268, 281) notes the merging of horizons in the last discourses, and also in John 3:11 and 9:4a, but wrongly denies the application of "now is" to the pre-Easter earthly Jesus except proleptically (3:281; see Loader 2017, 198). John Ashton (2014, 41) writes: "In spite of an occasional wobble the evangelist makes an absolute principle of his distinction between all that transpired in Jesus' lifetime—both words and actions—and the quite different situation after his death and resurrection." Similarly Larry Hurtado (2007, 212):

> John distinctively emphasizes the contrast between the cognitive possibilities in the pre-resurrection and post-resurrection situations,

10. See Müller 1990, 76; Rusam 2005, 60–80; Dennis 2006a, 208; 2007, 677–92; Kovacs 1995, 227–47; Ashton 2013, 13.

> indicating more explicitly than in the Synoptic Gospels, that in his earthly ministry Jesus did not reveal all that came later to be known of his divine significance.

The author indeed shows awareness of historical development in the disciples' recognition of who Jesus was and how biblical texts applied to him (John 2:22; 7:39; 12:16), but what they came to realize was what he actually was (14:26; see also 15:26; 16:12–15), not what he became only after Easter and after the Spirit finally enabled them to see this. The Spirit similarly enabled the gospel author to portray Jesus as the source of life and light and salvation in his person from the beginning, thus already during his ministry, not just when the disciples came fully to realize it, after Easter. This case is surely also strong, indeed, compelling.

Saving Death and Saving Person in John?

What then does one do with 1:29 and the references to Jesus's laying down his life? We cannot discuss the complex issues surrounding 1:29 in detail here. As Frey (2013a, 525, 527) notes, it is not possible to reach a definite conclusion concerning its background. Some connect the lamb image to the strongly messianic motifs in the context and so see it as depicting Jesus's removal of sin through his ministry, a messianic role being to remove sin. Thus John Painter (2004, 293; see also Hurtado 2003, 359) writes: "The best we can do with this text is to suggest that it refers to Jesus as the messianic deliverer of his people, indeed, of the world. Nevertheless, the text raises a question that it does not answer. *How* does the Lamb of God take away the sin of the world?" As Mavis Leung (2011, 53) notes, "It is sufficient to note that despite the limited pre-Christian evidence of the use of 'lamb' as a messianic title, the strong messianic tenor surrounding the Baptist's testimonies in John 1:29 and 1:36 suggest that these testimonies most likely pertain to Jewish messianic hopes." Reading "who takes away the sin of the world" in the light of the context is less clear except that in the immediate context it stands in parallel to baptizing with the Spirit (so Bieringer 2007, 218; Rusam 2005, 75).

Others note problems in reading the lamb imagery as vicarious or atoning. The Passover lamb is frequently proposed as background.[11] It is

11. Porter 2015, 207–11; Beasley-Murray 1999, 24–25; Bultmann 1941, 66–67; 1977, 406.

not, however, a sacrifice for sins, nor usually was the daily sacrifice.[12] Not lambs but goats bear sins on Atonement Day (see Busse 2014, 130–31; Lee 2011, 16–17; Keener 2003, 456).

An allusion to suffering like a vulnerable lamb in Isa 53 need not be vicarious. Given the allusion to Isa 42:1 in the tradition, the use of the "lamb" image to convey vulnerability may well have evoked the allusion to the vulnerability of God's servant as a "lamb" (ἀμνὸς) in Isa 53:7. The use of Isa 53:7 to convey suffering without any explicit reference to vicariousness is present elsewhere (Acts 8:32), so it should not be automatically assumed here (Porsch 1974, 40–42; Jeremias 1968, 702; Burge 1987, 61). It could, of course, be so.[13] The story of Isaac's offering speaks of a ram, not a lamb.[14]

The case for allusion to Jesus's death as atoning in John 1:29 is at least not as straightforward as Christian scholars steeped in their own traditions are wont to assume. Frey (2013e, 581–82; see also 2013d, 492–96) argues conversely that dogmatic concerns have led others to deny that such motifs play a role in John. One of the major contribution of Bieringer's (2007) study of 1:29 is that he insists that it be read in its literary and traditio-historical context. I have argued that one must read 1:29 in the light of its context from the prologue onwards (Loader 2017, 148–68; see also Rusam 2005, 72).

On the other hand, any discussion must take into account not only traditional Jewish imagery, as if that were the only influence, as sometimes appears to occur, but also the elaboration of such imagery in Christian-Jewish contexts, such as is reflected in the—in my opinion—slightly later 1 John, an observation well made by Frey (2013a, 286; 2013d, 522, 530; 2013e, 581; see also Loader 2017, 194–202). We must therefore take into account the inevitable merging of metaphors brought about by the fact that they are all seeking to interpret the same event. Thus Bauckham (2015,

12. On the Passover lamb as not a sacrifice for sins, see Loader 2017, 158–66; Hahn 2002, 1:633; Ashton 2007, 80, 163; 2014, 143; Frey 2013d, 519, 527; 2013e, 582; Knöppler 1994, 86–89; Lincoln 2005, 113; Weidemann 2004, 423; Metzner 2000, 22–23, 132–37. For this passage as a daily sacrifice, see Painter 2004, 292; Frey 2013d, 527.

13. So Barrett 1978, 176; Schnackenburg 1968, 300; Brown 1966, 61–63; Beasley-Murray 1999, 24–25; Hahn 2002, 1:633; Dietzfelbinger 2004, 1:53; Schnelle 1998, 49–50; Lincoln 2005, 113; see discussion in Loader 2017, 166–68.

14. See Vermes 1961, 223–24; Le Déaut 1963, 158; Thyen 2005, 119–23; Coloe 2001, 191–92.

156–57) most recently assumes an allusion that associates both Isa 53 and the Passover lamb together with Isaac typology within Christian tradition.

Similarly, dismissing 1:29 or the other allusions to vicarious death in John as relics of tradition will also not do.[15] Neither do suggestions that these are either the author's late additions by the author or a redactor take us further, especially if our concern is with the received text.[16] Ashton (2007, 162, similarly 466), for instance, sees 1:29 as having been part of a signs gospel where it had no relation to Jesus's death and suggests that the words about taking away sin are "a later addition" on the basis of 1 John 3:5. Martinus C. de Boer (1996, 103) observes that both 3:14–15 and 6:27, 53, 62 "stand awkwardly in their immediate literary context," and writes that "6:51c–56, along with 6:27 and 6:62, may with some confidence be assessed as secondary elaboration (Jn III) of the Bread of Life discourse" (226). Such developments are certainly possible, but our concern is with the received text. It is better, with Barnabas Lindars (1990, 82; see also Müller 1990, 73; Culpepper 1983, 87–88), to recognize that "John also carries forward the traditional interpretation of Jesus' death as an atonement sacrifice which belongs to earliest Christianity (cf. 1 Cor. 15.3), and which is accepted in the Johannine church (1 John 2.2)." Frey (2013a, 499–500) prefers to speak of "relecture," a category developed by Jean Zumstein and Andreas Dettwiler.

While John 10:17 somewhat undermines the emphasis on vicarious death by having Jesus declare that the reason why he laid down his life was to be able to take it up again, and 15:13 may just be about loving even to the point of death, the case for claiming that the author knows and affirms the belief that Jesus's death was vicarious, possibly also as sacrificial in a cultic sense, is not to be dismissed in the interests of avoiding the tension that such texts appear to present when set alongside others that declare the gift of life as something Jesus gave already during his ministry. At the same time, one should acknowledge the relative weighting given to such statements within the text. Thus de Boer (1996, 280, similarly 234; Moloney 1998, 59) observes that "the idea that Jesus' death is being regarded as a blood sacrifice expiating sins is not clearly discernible in 1:29 and has very little support (in the remainder of the Gospel, including in ch. 19)." Similarly Jan G. van der Watt (2005, 116) writes: "Although John does not

15. Käsemann 1971, 23 n. 7; Haenchen 1980, 166–67; Müller 1975, 63; Forestell 1974, 15–16.

16. See Becker 1979/1981, 91–92; Theobald 2009, 1:65.

emphasize or focus on substitution or sacrifice, there are some insinuations in that direction. However, these references do not come into focus at all. They are secondary to the revelatory function of the cross events."[17] D. Moody Smith (1997, 116) observes that it is "surprising that such an understanding and interpretation of Jesus' death does not find a larger place in the Gospel of John. Yet several passages in the Gospel clearly allude to the primitive Christian interpretation of Jesus' death as a vicarious sacrifice."

Beyond the Impasse

We appear, then, to have evidence in both gospels that many sense as contrary or inconsistent and that, when not ignored, has led to various attempts to diffuse the tension by explaining away the evidence for one or the other side of the argument. It is interesting that in his discussion of soteriology in John Talbert ignores this tension by discussing soteriology almost entirely on the basis of enabling indwelling as reflected in John 15:1–17, not once addressing 15:13. Similarly Charles Talbert's (2011, 95–118, 176–91) chapter in the same volume, "Indicative and Imperative in Matthean Soteriology," cites neither 1:21 nor 26:28. By contrast, the review of research on Jesus's death by John Dennis (2006b) exposes the current impasse.

Frey's (2013e, 561) discussion of the various ways in which the author depicts the significance of Jesus's death as seen from a post-Easter perspective cautions against making any single motif the key to unlock all the others and clearly identifies the tension:

> Wird dem *Tod* Jesu bei Johannes eine eigenstständige *Heils*bedeuting beigemessen oder gründet das Heil nach johanneischer Auffassung wesentlich oder primär in einem anderen Akt als in dem Akt seines Sterbens im *Ostergeschehen* oder bereits in seiner *Sendung* bzw. seiner *Menschwerdung*? (2013d, 492, emphasis original)

Posing the question in terms of *Akt* already, however, distorts the issue in favor of his resolution focusing on the cross. The alternatives are not so much two events but an event/transaction and a person who in himself brings salvation because of who he is.

---

17. So also Rensberger 2001, 19; Schnackenburg 1993, 314–15.

One can seek to dissolve the tension by explaining away some of the data. For instance, one can explain away allusions to expiatory or vicarious death, or minimize their significance, or deny them altogether, a response documented already by such scholars as G. B. Stevens (1889, 224–33; Scott 1908, 207–12). On the other hand, one can argue that once one finds a single indication that the author viewed Jesus's death as expiatory or vicarious, then this understanding must for the hearer fill out the substance of all allusions to Jesus's death (so Frey 2013e, 576). As an argument this does not hold, if it is used to claim that expiatory or vicarious death is the center of the author's soteriology, and certainly not if it is used to dismiss the offer of life that the Son brings in his ministry. It is, nevertheless, a valid observation, to the extent that once we can establish it as one way that the author (and potentially his hearers) saw Jesus's death, then it should at least be taken into account in considering other texts. Dennis (2006a, 353) goes further arguing that "the burden of proof, I believe, remains squarely on those who argue that Jesus' death in John's Gospel has nothing to do with *Jewish* atonement theology or the elimination of sin." However one resolves the tension in relation to forgiveness of sins, it is clear that the author sees the cross as at least an act of exposure and judgment in relation to the ruler of this world. That is not inconsistent with an understanding of forgiveness of sins being already implied in the offer of life through Jesus already during his ministry.

In the final brief section of this paper I want to suggest that a resolution of this tension lies not in playing one side of the argument off against the other, nor in pressing the logic of some statements to the exclusion of others (see also Loader 2017, 202–3). Rather, I believe that it is important to take into account the strongly Jewish background of both documents: Matthew, whose author still wants to hold a place within the Jewish community despite the pain of conflict and failure, and John, having made its own way with pain and conflict because of its extreme christological claims but, with all that behind it, still needing to justify itself in largely Jewish terms.

If we begin with forgiveness of sins, in the range of Jewish communities of the time, one could assume that God forgives sins. That might be in response to actions that included sacrifice and prayer, or just prayer, or one's own death, or the death of another, the latter reflected already in Isa 53 but also in the retelling of the Maccabean martyrs. We do not find evidence of attempts to play these off against each other. At most we find controversy surrounding John the Baptist's novel approach, but not as an issue of law.

At the level of forgiveness, it would have been explicable that believers in Matthew's community, for instance, could see Jesus's death as for the forgiveness of sins without having to deny other means of forgiveness. I suggest that the same is true of John's Gospel. In neither gospel do we find the argument that Jesus's death thereby had to mean the end of all other sacrificial offerings, such as we find in Hebrews, or all other means of forgiveness. The latter was certainly an option, but not, I suggest, one that Matthew took. In John, Jesus replaces the temple, but even so, nowhere do we find Jesus's death used against all other means of forgiveness.

In the broader sense, in neither gospel do we exhaust the meaning of salvation by talking about forgiveness of sins. Sin is always important, but in the forms of Judaism that we know from the time the ongoing relationship of faithfulness and obedience toward God expressed in the keeping of torah is much more important. Soteriology is in that sense theocentric, and this is why one might even consider replacing the word "soteriology" with "spirituality." This is also true in Matthew: salvation, which in Matthew certainly has a strong future dimension related to the judgment day, is essentially hope and belonging based on faithfulness and obedience to Torah as expounded by Jesus. Matthew's Jesus, miraculously conceived, is God's authorized agent. Matthew's soteriology, spirituality, is fundamentally theocentric and in that sense typically Jewish. Claims about the special status of the agent mark the point of tension with other Jews, not issues of torah, at least not as Matthew sees it.

In John, the christological claims were for most contemporary Jews over the top, and clearly soteriology is intimately bound up with believing its claims about Jesus. John's soteriology includes forgiveness of sins, and sin and sins remain important, as John 8 shows, but salvation is always about more than that. Much more significantly, it entailed life and belonging based on faithfulness and obedience to Jesus. This fits both how John depicts it pre-Easter and how he depicts it post-Easter.

As many, however, have recognized, despite his high Christology and, indeed, because of it, John's soteriology is profoundly theological and theocentric. So elevated and abstracted is John's Jesus from the historical Jesus and the Jesus of the anecdotes that he is at almost every point and in every dialogue "making God known," that is to say, presenting God, a divine cipher. He is not in himself light and life and bread and water independent of the Father but portrayed as an extension of God's being. Paradoxically, one might say that he is so elevated as to disappear into the being of God, leaving the church later to resolve the conundrum through the doctrine of the Trinity.

What we see here, I suggest, is in reality a transposing and return to what is the structure of Jewish spirituality of the time: relationship, faithfulness, obedience to the Word is central, but now not as torah but as Jesus. That worked itself out therefore differently (and sometimes dangerously) and meant developing a new basis for ethics, but essentially what we have here is, I suggest, transposed Jewish spirituality. We may call it soteriology, if you like, but it is not focused solely on the cross as a singularly atoning event, nor on a single eschatological promise, but first and foremost on ongoing life in relationship through Christ with God and in community with fellow believers. In John, this is apart from torah. In Matthew, it is on behalf of torah.

Matthew and John: Reflections of Early Christianity in Relationship to Judaism*

R. Alan Culpepper

Matthew and John present an interesting pairing of two of the four gospels. On the one hand, while some contend that John knew Mark and there are tantalizing evidences of a literary relationship between Luke and John, there is little evidence of a direct relationship between Matthew and John (see, however, Barker 2015; Allison forthcoming). One notable exception is the "thunderbolt from the Johannine heavens" in Matt 11:27. Still, among the four gospels, there is less reason to posit a literary relationship, or knowledge of the other, between Matthew and John than between John and any other gospel. On the other hand, these two are both more closely related to Judaism, and perhaps more specifically local synagogues or the "Council of Jamnia," than are Mark, which by tradition was written in Rome, or Luke, which may have been written by the only gentile writer in the New Testament. Both Matthew and John, therefore, seem to belong to that period following the destruction of Jerusalem and the temple in 70 CE, when what it meant to be Jewish was being redefined both among the postwar Pharisees and Jewish Christians. Donald Senior (1999, 5; see Konradt 2014, 355) underscored the importance of these issues for understanding Matthew, claiming "that Matthew's interface with Judaism … is the fundamental key to determining the social context and theological perspective of this gospel."

Both Matthew and John seem to address an early Christian community, or set of communities, near the point of their separation from the synagogue. For this reason, both articulate the Christian gospel and retell

* This essay addresses issues to which my mentors, W. D. Davies and D. Moody Smith, devoted years of study. It is dedicated to their memory.

the story of Jesus's ministry in relation to the heritage of Judaism and the observances that defined the lives of first-century Jews. In this way, each gospel defines for its Jewish-Christian adherents how the Christian community represents an authentic extension of their Jewish heritage, if not in some sense its fulfillment, while also appealing to those who remained in the synagogue to join the Christian community. Both also reflect positive and negative assessments of the Jewish communities with which they interacted (Barrett 1975, 172; Meeks 1975, 71; Luz 1995, 12–13).

As a way of mapping the place of Matthew and John in their relationship to Judaism and enabling us to make comparisons between them, I propose to survey seven issues in each gospel: (1) Jesus as a new Moses, (2) fulfillment of the Scriptures, (3) the law, (4) the Sabbath, (5) purity issues, (6) the Pharisees, and (7) the synagogue. These topics will serve as probes that may help us understand more clearly the similarities and differences between Matthew and John as generally contemporary but different approaches to interpreting the Jesus tradition for early Christian communities still in close proximity to their Jewish origins.

1. Jesus as the New Moses

1.1 Jesus as the New Moses in Matthew

Without mentioning Moses by name, Matthew narrates Jesus's birth and infancy in such a way that the reader cannot miss the parallels that suggest that Jesus is the "one like Moses" (Deut 18:15, 18) who was to come. Both Moses and Jesus were born to families struggling under the oppression of a foreign power that held their people captive. Herod and Pharaoh were tyrants who did not hesitate to shed Hebrew blood; both ordered the killing of Hebrew children (Exod 1:22; Matt 2:16). Both stories involve flight from the tyrant and return (Exod 2:15–16; Matt 2:13–15). The flight and return of Jesus's family also reenacts the exodus experience of the Hebrew people under Moses: "out of Egypt have I called My son" (Hos 11:1; Matt 2:23). By evoking these parallels in his account of Jesus's infancy, Matthew prepares the reader to understand that Jesus fulfills the expectation of a new Moses (Deut 18:15, 18) who will lead the people of Israel.

Then, like Moses, Jesus goes up on a mountain (Matt 5:1) to deliver a new teaching on righteousness for his followers. Later, Jesus feeds a multitude (twice) and crosses the Sea of Galilee. Moses appears to Jesus on a mountain, and Jesus's disciples see him transfigured (17:1–8). In his teaching on divorce, Jesus responds that Moses allowed divorce, "for their hardness of heart" (19:8). The allusion to Moses in the Sadducees' question regarding resurrection of the dead in Matt 22:24 occurs also in Mark 12:19, but the reference to "Moses' seat" in Matt 23:2 occurs only in Matthew.

Finally, although most interpreters take issue with B. W. Bacon's proposal that the fivefold repetition of the formula "Now when Jesus had finished…," marking five sections of the gospel that contain both narrative and discourse, is an allusion to the five books of Moses, perhaps suggesting that Matthew represents a new torah for the church, the significance of these transitional markers continues to be debated.

1.2. Jesus as the New Moses in John

John's allusions to Moses are never as connected as in Matthew's birth narrative, but they are more explicit. There are twelve references to Moses in the first nine chapters of John and a reference in the added scene in 7:53–8:11 (8:5). Although most of these have a polemical tone and the progression climaxes in the debate with the Pharisees in John 9, Moses also serves typologically for Jesus's functions in the gospel and as a reference to the authority of Scripture (Harstine 2002, 74–75, 162–63).

The prologue alerts the reader to the significance of the juxtaposition of Moses and Jesus when it says, "the law was given by Moses; grace and truth came through Jesus Christ" (1:17). The comparison with Moses continues in the next verse: "No one has ever seen God. The only divine one, who is in the bosom of the father, has made him known" (1:18; see 6:46). The prologue declares "No one has seen God" (1:18; see 5:37), but Jesus affirms that the one who was with God has seen God (6:46), and those who have seen Jesus have seen the Father (14:9). These claims evoke God's words to Moses on Mount Sinai, denying his request to see God: "You cannot see my face; for no one shall see me and live" (Exod 33:20). Moses did signs "so that they may believe that the Lord … has appeared to you" (Exod 4:5; see Exod 4:8–9, 30; 7:3). The signs Jesus does are clearly reminiscent of the signs Moses performed—changing water to blood (Exod 4:9; 7:17–19), providing manna and water in the wilderness (Exod 16:12, 15; 17:6), crossing the sea (Exod 14:21–22), speaking to the people what he had heard from God (Exod 4:12; 6:28–7:2), and providing the paschal lamb (Exod 12:46). The Mosaic overtones of the characterization of Jesus in John are therefore far richer than the few explicit references to Moses suggest.

When John the Baptist denies that he is "the prophet," which is an allusion to the expected prophet like Moses (Deut 18:15, 18), he leaves the way open for the reader to understand that Jesus is the one who fulfills this role (Martyn 1978, 51–54). Jesus fulfills the role of "the prophet like Moses" (Deut 18:15, 18), but he is also greater than Moses (see Boismard 1993, 22, 25–30).[1]

Jesus is "the one of whom Moses—in the law—and the prophets wrote" (John 1:45). Like the serpent Moses lifted up on a pole, Jesus says, so the Son of Man will be lifted up (3:14). Moses is the one who accuses them—the Ἰουδαῖοι—before God. If they believed Moses, they would believe him, because Moses wrote of him (5:45–46). With this charge, John introduces the narrative of Jesus's feeding of the multitude in the wilderness at the time of Passover and Jesus's crossing of the sea in John 6. John follows this sign with a discourse on the bread from heaven, in which he contrasts the provision of the true bread with the provision of manna, which was not given by Moses but by Jesus's Father (6:32). The authorities draw the line of demarcation when they charge that the man who had been born blind was a disciple of "that one," whereas they are Moses's disciples. In their skepticism they assert that they know that God spoke to Moses, but they do not know where "this one" came from (9:28–29). On the other hand, John appeals to Moses as an important witness to Jesus. John does not accept the forced alternative of Jesus or Moses. Those who understand Moses accept Jesus.

Whereas Matthew sets Jesus in continuity with Moses as the fulfillment of the Moses typology, John reinterprets the opposition between Jesus and Moses, rejecting the forced choice required by the Pharisees in John and affirming Moses as a witness to Jesus. Matthew invites the reader to accept Jesus's teachings as the fulfillment of the law. John's use of the Moses typology is more christological and more polemical, without rejecting the authority of Moses (i.e., the law). Therefore, we may accept what Dale Allison (1993, 274) says about Matthew, while preferring to nuance his reference to John:

> All this is to be emphasized because too often the parallels between Jesus and Moses have been neglected in favor of focus on the differences. This may work with the Gospel of John, but it does not work with Matthew.

---

1. For the points of contact between the Father-Son relationship in John and the Septuagintal rendering of Deut 18:15–22, see Anderson 1999.

> In the First Gospel Jesus' superiority to Moses is not argued. Rather, it is simply assumed.

Alicia Myers (2012b, 19) offers a nuanced interpretation of John's characterization of Jesus in relation to Moses by employing the classical rhetorical convention of *synkrisis* and concludes that although Jesus is regarded as superior to Moses, "John's portrait of Jesus is *not* meant to force the audience to choose between Jesus and Moses like the Pharisees do."

2. Fulfillment of the Scriptures

2.1. Fulfillment of the Scriptures in Matthew

The fulfillment of the Scriptures in the life and teachings of Jesus is one of the most pronounced themes in Matthew.[2] In the heading and the genealogy, the narrator links Jesus to persons in the Scriptures. The gospel opens with references to Abraham and David. A major function of the genealogy is to link Jesus with Israel's scriptural heritage and thereby lead the reader to accept the claim that Jesus came to fulfill Scripture. The fulfillment of Scripture is then signaled by the repetition of fulfillment formulae early in the gospel (Matt 1:22; 2:15, 17, 23; 3:3; 4:14; see Viljoen 2007, 302–5).

Events in the story take on added meaning when viewed against their scriptural background. Like his biblical namesake, Joseph has revelatory dreams that guide coming events. The places named in the birth narrative provide a biblical geography that recapitulates much of Israel's history: Bethlehem, Egypt, Ramah, and Nazareth (see Stendahl 1964; Brown 1983, 52–54). The narrator introduces John the Baptist in the same idiom, with a formula quotation (3:3). Similarly, the first words that Jesus speaks in the gospel explain that his motive was fulfillment (3:15). The voice from heaven at his baptism echoes the words of Ps 2:7, "You are my son." Like Israel, Jesus was tempted in the wilderness, and contrary to Gerhard Kittel's (1964, 658) contention that "there are no serious reasons for making the common connection of the forty days with the forty years of Israel in the wilderness," recognition of this connection is essential for Matthew's purposes. The forty days of temptation also recall the forty days Moses was on Mount Sinai (Exod 24:18; 34:28; Deut 9:9, 18; see Gurtner 2012, 1–11), during which he

2. The section reproduces and abbreviates portions of Culpepper 2015b.

neither ate nor drank, and Elijah's forty-day journey to Mount Horeb (1 Kgs 19:8; Luz 2007b, 151; Balz 1972, 137–39), setting up Jesus's claim that he fulfilled "the law and the prophets" (5:17). Throughout its account of Jesus's baptism, temptation, calling of the disciples, and early ministry (esp. 3:3; 4:4, 6, 7, 10, 15–16), Matthew maintains the continuous underlying claim of the fulfillment of the scriptures. Jesus's arrival fulfilled the law and the prophets, and Jesus's words and actions "fulfill all righteousness."

Jesus's claim that he came not to abolish but to fulfill the law (Matt 5:17–20) is so central to Matthew's treatment of the law that it is discussed separately in the next section. The antitheses that follow in Matt 5:21–48 further educate the reader to understand Jesus's teachings as fulfilling Scripture. As F. Scott Spencer (2010, 368) aptly puts it, "above all, Matthew's Jesus emerges as the church's authoritative biblical exegete and teacher."

Matthew begins with the repeated affirmation of the fulfillment of Scripture but also its enduring authority. In the Sermon on the Mount, Jesus declares his own authority both over against and in fulfillment of Scripture. This dialectic fuels conflict over Jesus's authority, which the religious leaders challenge repeatedly. In response, Jesus asserts that if they understood the Scriptures—indeed, if they had read the Scriptures (12:3, 5; 19:4; 21:16, 42; 22:31)—they would understand that what he did fulfilled the law and the prophets. By the end of the Gospel of Matthew the transfer is complete: Jesus's words now carry the authority of Scripture (for further development of this argument, see Culpepper 2015b).

2.2. Fulfillment of Scripture in John

The theme of the fulfillment of Scripture is present in the Gospel of John, but it is handled differently. Whereas the fulfillment formula generally occurs in the first four chapters in Matthew, it occurs only in the latter half of John's Gospel (12:38; 13:18; 15:25; 17:12; 19:24, 36).

The theme of fulfillment is set up in the first half of the gospel by the reference to Moses in John 1:16–17, which is discussed below. The first scene following the prologue, the interrogation of John the Baptist by the religious authorities (1:19–23), assumes a relationship between Scriptures and the events reported in the gospel. The authorities assume the Baptist must be one of the expected figures—the Messiah, Elijah, or the prophet—and he answers by quoting the text from Isa 40:3. Fulfillment is implicit from the beginning. Allusions and titles from the Scriptures are then used for Jesus in the remainder of the first chapter, including

"Lamb of God" (1:29, 36), "Son of God" (1:34, 49), "Messiah" (1:41), "King of Israel" (1:49), and "Son of Man" (1:51), as well as "him about whom Moses in the law and the prophets wrote" (1:45). Allusions and quotations of Scripture follow as part of the vocabulary, theology, and rhetoric of the gospel.

In place of the explicit claims of the fulfillment formula in Matthew, in John one finds the fulfillment theme in the "I am" sayings and the Jewish festivals in John 2–12, with their implicit and explicit claims that Jesus fulfills what they commemorate. Jesus himself will take the place of the temple (2:21). He is greater than the patriarch Jacob (4:12). He brings healing to the man at the Pool of Bethesda at a festival (5:1–9). The Scriptures and Moses bear witness to Jesus (5:39, 46). At the time of the Passover celebration Jesus feeds a multitude in the wilderness and crosses the sea (6:1–21). He is himself the bread of life (6:35, 48). At Sukkot, with its libations from the Pool of Siloam, Jesus cries out, "Let anyone who is thirsty come to me" (7:37). Between the references to Sukkot and Hanukkah, at both of which light was prominent, Jesus declares that he is "the light of the world" (8:12), and he gives sight to a man born blind (9:1–7). He is greater than Abraham, who saw his day and rejoiced (8:53, 56), and Isaiah spoke about him (12:41). Jesus is the Good Shepherd (10:11, 14). The Book of Signs is bracketed with references to what the disciples understood only later, after study of the Scriptures and reflection on what Jesus had done and said (2:22; 12:16): "these things had been written of him" (12:16), and "the scripture cannot be annulled" (10:35). On the other hand, those who reject Jesus also fulfill the pronouncements of judgment in the Scriptures (12:36b–41).

Again, John is more polemical than Matthew. Both appeal to the Scriptures, and both engage in polemic, so comparisons must be nuanced. Nevertheless, whereas Matthew appeals to the Scriptures so that those who adhere to them might see how Jesus fulfilled them, John defends the claims for Jesus against those who do not accept him by showing how the Scriptures testify to him. John therefore assumes a dialectical situation and defends the claims for Jesus by showing how Jesus fulfilled the Scriptures, while those who opposed him were judged by the Scriptures.

3. The Law

Monographs have been written on the law in Matthew and John, so all we can attempt here is a passing overview.

3.1. The Law in Matthew

Matthew inserts references to the law that do not appear in Mark (Matt 22:36; 23:23; Barth 1963, 63). Some manuscripts also have νόμος in Matt 15:6. Matthew uses the phrase "the law and the prophets" four times (5:17; 7:12; 11:13; 22:40), and Matt 11:13 is particularly interesting because it departs from Luke 16:16 and reverses the sequence of the prophets and the law:

> Luke 16:16 Ὁ νόμος καὶ οἱ προφῆται μέχρι Ἰωάννου· ἀπὸ τότε ἡ βασιλεία τοῦ θεοῦ εὐαγγελίζεται καὶ πᾶς εἰς αὐτὴν βιάζεται.
> The law and the prophets were in effect until John came; since then the good news of the kingdom of God is proclaimed, and everyone tries to enter it by force (NRSV)

> Matt 11:12–13 ἀπὸ δὲ τῶν ἡμερῶν Ἰωάννου τοῦ βαπτιστοῦ ἕως ἄρτι ἡ βασιλεία τῶν οὐρανῶν βιάζεται καὶ βιασταὶ ἁρπάζουσιν αὐτήν. πάντες γὰρ οἱ προφῆται καὶ ὁ νόμος ἕως Ἰωάννου ἐπροφήτευσαν·
> From the days of John the Baptist until now the kingdom of heaven has suffered violence, and the violent take it by force. For all the prophets and the law prophesied until John came. (NRSV)

Why did Matthew apparently change the sequence of "the law and the prophets" in this reference? As Gerhard Barth (1963, 64) argues, the answer must be that he cannot abide the implication one might draw from Luke that the law and the prophets were superseded by the preaching of the kingdom of God after John. Hence, the prophets and the law prophesied, presumably about John, until he came. There can be no implication that their authority ended with the coming of John. John Meier likens the subordination of the law to the prophets to a "Copernican revolution." The law *prophesied*: "in Matthew's mind, the Law, in both its ethical and prophetic utterances, pointed forward to the Messianic events and teachings of Jesus" (Meier 1979, 227).

Matthew 5:17–20, the first and most important reference to the law in Matthew, is consistent with what we have seen in Matt 11:13. The dialectical construction, "not to … but to," suggests a context in which the teachings of the Matthean community have left the community open to the Pharisaic charge of antinomianism; that is, they set aside the law (see Konradt 2014, 357). Alternatively, but less likely in my judgment, Matthew may be challenging a Pauline or libertine Christian group. Matthew's

Jesus, therefore, following the Beatitudes, on the mountain, asserts that he has come not to abolish but to fulfill "the law and the prophets" (5:17). Various interpretations have been offered as to the meaning of "fulfill": "establish," "complete," "fill" (through Jesus's self-surrender), or "do" what the law commands, especially the love command ("He who loves his neighbor has fulfilled the law" and "Love is the fulfilling of the law," Rom 13:8–10; see Gal 5:14; Jas 2:8; see Suggs 1970, 116–18; Hagner 1993, 105–6). At a minimum, in this context, "fulfill" probably means (1) that Jesus has come as the Messiah, fulfilling the promises and specifically the messianic expectations based on the Scriptures; (2) Jesus's teachings provide an interpretation of the law—centered in the love command—that brings the law to full expression; and (3) by implication, those who follow Jesus's teachings will also keep the law. Further, the law abides until the end of time—not just until the coming of Jesus. His followers, therefore, are expected to keep the law in every detail (5:19). They should be more righteous—in light of Jesus's teachings on righteousness—than even the scribes and the Pharisees.[3]

For our purposes, it is significant that this opening declaration regarding the continuing validity of the law is followed by repeated warnings that disciples will be judged by what they do or do not do, and that Matthew includes instructions on a variety of specific issues: Sabbath observance (which will be considered in the next section), prayer (6:5–13; 7:7–11), fasting (6:16–18), almsgiving (6:2–4), oaths (5:33–37; 23:16–22), divorce (5:31–32; 19:1–9), tithing (23:23), and other issues addressed by the torah. Parenthetically, the situation in the Gospel of John, where there are no such specific teachings, is strikingly different. In a way not unlike the rabbis, Matthew offers guidance on the essence of the law: the "golden rule" in its positive form, which Matthew says *is* "the law and the prophets" (7:12); the greatest command—the love command (22:36–40); the "light" things of the law—tithing mint, dill, and cumin, which also ought not to be

---

3. For a helpful overview of interpretations of Matt 5:17–20 in relation to the *Sitz im Leben* of Matthew, see Viljoen 2015. W. Reinbold (2006, 61–62) concludes from a study of the law in Matthew (esp. 5:20 and 23:2–3) that Matthew maintains that the authority of the teaching of the scribes and Pharisees from the seat of Moses should be recognized and that Jesus's followers should be more righteous than the scribes and the Pharisees: "Die Jünger sollen die Tora in ihrer Auslegung durch die 'Schriftgelehrten und Pharisäer' halten, und zwar in höherem Maße als sie. Sie sollen, wenn man so will, die besseren Pharisäer sein."

neglected; and "heavy" things of the law—justice, mercy, and faith (23:23). There is no debate in Matthew regarding whether Jesus's followers ought to keep the law, only how the law is to be interpreted and what its essence is (see also Suggs 1970, 117–19). Jesus interprets—in some instances radicalizes—and prioritizes *mitzvot* (see Matt 12:5), but he does not abolish, relax, or supersede the law.

3.2. The Law in John

The relationship between Jesus and the law is important in John also, but here again the differences between Matthew and John are pronounced. The reference to the law in the prologue sets the tone for the development of this theme in later chapters.[4] The prologue declares that "the law was given through Moses; grace and truth came through Jesus Christ" (1:17).

The KJV follows the translation of William Tyndale in John 1:17, inserting a gratuitous "but" between the two halves of the verse. I say gratuitous because there is no adversative conjunction in the Greek text: ὅτι ὁ νόμος διὰ Μωϋσέως ἐδόθη, ἡ χάρις καὶ ἡ ἀλήθεια διὰ Ἰησοῦ Χριστοῦ ἐγένετο. The previous verse declares, "From his fullness we have all received, grace upon grace."[5] Verse 17 opens with a causal ὅτι, "for" or "because." The natural sense of this construction is that the law was a gift of God's grace, and "grace and truth" were further grace. Both come from the Logos. On the other hand, the adversative sense, juxtaposing law and grace, has both a long tradition of interpretation and some basis in the flow of the prologue toward verse 18.[6] As W. Gutbrod (1967, 1083) observes, however, the relationship between the law and Jesus is not simply antithetical: "Between the Law as the word of Scripture and the revelation of God in Jesus there is a positive inner connection." Both are revelatory; John treats the law as "the body of divine revelation given to Moses" (Pancaro 1975, 517). Both are also manifestations of grace (χάρις), but the law does not give life; it bears witness to Jesus, who is the giver of life (Gutbrod 1967, 1083–84; Pancaro

4. The following paragraphs, on the law in John, appear also in Culpepper 2016.

5. For a review of various interpretations of "grace upon grace," see Brown (1966, 16) and Phillips (2006, 212–13). Brown notes that the preposition ἀντί occurs only here in John and considers three interpretations: replacement, accumulation, and correspondence.

6. For a nuancing of the adversative interpretation of verse 17, see Harris (1994, 64–65, 71, 90), Smith (1999, 60–61), and Beutler (2009, 97).

1975, 537; Asiedu-Peprah 2001, 225). As Peter Phillips (2006, 214) puts it, verse 17 makes a distinction "between two graces/gifts of God and not two opposing systems of belief."[7] Nevertheless, John's christological focus relativizes the authority of the law and may intend "to shape a genuinely ambivalent attitude towards the Jewish law" (Winter 2009, 195).

James Dunn's (1991, 1998) challenge to interpreters to "let John be John" is nowhere more important than in the interpretation of the role of the law in John. As Gerhard Kittel (1967, 135) observes, "the relation between Christ and Law is a basic question throughout the Gospel." John does not set grace over against law, as Paul does. Instead, references to the law in John function to vindicate Jesus against charges brought against him by the religious authorities. It has often been noted that the discussion at the festival in Jerusalem in John 7 continues the debate over Jesus's healing of the man at the Pool of Bethesda on the Sabbath in John 5. The Mosaic law justifies Jesus's works. It is a matter of correct judgment or correct interpretation of the law, not choosing between Moses and Jesus, because Moses bears witness to Jesus. Although the people venerate Moses as the lawgiver, they do not follow the law's prescriptions (7:19). Moses gave them the rite of circumcision, and the law allows circumcision on the Sabbath (7:22). Therefore, on the basis of the principle that what is true for the lesser also valid for the greater, it is also permissible to heal the man's whole body (7:23; see below). Ironically, when the religious authorities—the chief priests and Pharisees—demean the crowd as ignorant of the law, Nicodemus confronts them with their own failure to follow legal procedure and due process by judging Jesus without first giving him a hearing (7:51). Their own law requires that charges be upheld by two witnesses (8:17; Deut 19:15). The references to "your law" in John 8:17; 10:34; and 18:31 and to "their law" in 15:25 can be interpreted to mean that the law applies to "them" but not "us," which is clearly the sense when Pilate says, "Take him yourselves and judge him according to your law" (18:31). On the other hand, when Jesus speaks of "your law" in John 8:17 and 10:34 in the context of debate with the Ἰουδαῖοι, the term drives home the inconsistency between their charge that Jesus violated the law and their failure to follow its prescriptions (the requirement of two witnesses) or note its implications (those whom God sanctifies and sends can be called "gods" or

7. See also Moloney (1998, 46) and Brown (2010, 94), who clarifies the verse, saying, "One cannot 'replace' the other. One prolongs and perfects the never-ending graciousness of God. The gift of the Law is perfected in the gift of the incarnation."

"the son of God"). Likewise, the crowd is mistaken when they stumble over Jesus's proleptic reference to his exaltation because they maintain that the law says that the Messiah will abide forever (12:34). Ironically therefore, the law defines norms and terms that vindicate Jesus when he is accused of violating it.

The final references to the law in John draw the conclusion toward which the earlier references build. The conclusion is stated explicitly in Jesus's appeal to the Psalms (35:19; 69:5; see Pss. Sol. 7:1), "They hated me without a cause." Then, by ironic implication, the same point is made when the Ἰουδαῖοι claim that according to their law Jesus ought to die because he claimed to be the Son of God (John 19:7).

When we look for commands to "do" or "keep" the law in John, such as we find in Matthew, the result is surprising. The general trajectory of the theme in John is that because Jesus does the will of his Father, his followers should follow his example and do as he commands them. Jesus's mother suggests this development when she tells the servants at Cana to do whatever he tells them to do (2:5). Jesus draws sustenance from doing the will of the one who sent him (4:34; 6:38), and he does only what his Father gives him to do (5:19–20; 8:28–29). Those who do good will be given life in the resurrection (5:29), yet when Jesus is asked what one must do to perform the works of God, his answer is to believe in the one whom God sent (6:28–29). Parenthetically, we may compare Matt 19:17, where one who asks what good deed he must do to inherit eternal life is told to keep the commandments—that is, the law!

Jesus has set the example (13:15, ὑπόδειγμα; see 13:17), and his followers should do as he did (Culpepper 1991). One who believes in him will do as he did and will do even greater works (14:12), but apart from him they can do nothing (15:5). If they do what he commands, they are his "friends" (15:14). One who loves him will keep his commandments (14:15, 21, 23, 24), and one who keeps his word will abide in his love (15:10) and never see death (8:51–52).

Matthew contains similar exhortations to act on Jesus's teachings (7:24–27) and "observe" all that Jesus commanded them (28:20), but the declaration that all authority has been given to the risen Lord comes at the climax of Matthew's juxtaposition of Jesus's authority with that of the law, which he fulfills but does not annul.

In John, as we have seen, Moses serves two primary functions: he defines the role of the expected prophet like Moses and serves as a cipher for the law (see Theobald 1988, 360–62). In both cases, within the juridical process of the gospel, Moses, like John the Baptist, serves as a witness for Jesus. The roles of both Moses and the law are therefore reframed when they are brought in relationship to the incarnation: they have become witnesses to Jesus.

4. The Sabbath

The interpretation of Sabbath law comes into focus in two passages in each of the two gospels under consideration here: in Matthew plucking grain on the Sabbath (12:1–8) and the healing the man with the withered hand (12:9–14), and in John the healing of the man at the Pool of Bethesda (5:1–18) and the healing of the man born blind (9:1–41). Both agree that Jesus healed on the Sabbath and was challenged by the Pharisees for doing so, but Jesus responds to the challenge differently in the two gospels.

4.1. The Sabbath in Matthew

Matthew follows Mark's account of the disciples plucking grain on the Sabbath (2:23–28) closely except that he omits the appended saying, "The sabbath was made for humankind, and not humankind for the Sabbath" (Mark 2:27), which may have struck Matthew as coming too close to abrogating the command to observe the Sabbath. Alternatively, this verse may be a later gloss (N. Collins 2014, 88). In place of this verse Matthew adds the following retort:

> Or have you not read in the law that on the sabbath the priests in the temple break the sabbath and yet are guiltless? I tell you, something greater than the temple is here. But if you had known what this means, "I desire mercy and not sacrifice," you would not have condemned the guiltless. (Matt 12:5–7)

This insertion fits well because it follows the reference to "the priests" in the previous verse. The challenge, "have you not read," is characteristically Matthean (19:4; 21:16, 42; 22:31). The implication of the question is that Jesus's opponents oppose him because they do not know or heed the essence of the Scriptures. The force of verse 5 is that the Sabbath command is not unqualified; other duties, such as temple service, may supersede it. Verse 6 appeals to something or someone greater than the temple (in which the priests serve, even on the Sabbath). In an impressive monograph on the Sabbath debate, Nina Collins (2014, 50) explains: "within the Temple itself it was obligatory for the priests to sacrifice a goat or lamb every morning and evening, including the Sabbath day (m. Pes 5.1)." Therefore, Collins (52) continues, "in the temple area … the only place where Temple law was in force, and thus the only place where Temple law and Sabbath law could both be in force at the same time, the conflicting demands of Temple and Sabbath law always resulted in the overriding of Sabbath law." Parenthetically, through a close examination of Matthew's form of argumentation, Collins (esp. 285–87) concludes there was a close association between Matthew and Rabbi Akiva and Rabbi Ishmael late in the first century. Matthew no doubt meant to suggest Jesus's superiority to the temple. Immediately thereafter, Jesus cites Hos 6:6, "I desire loving-kindness and not sacrifice," as a criterion, like the love command, for interpretation of the law (see Hays 2005, 180–82; Viljoen 2014a, esp. 232). Matthew is the only gospel that quotes Hos 6:6 (Matt 9:13; 12:7), which is at least interesting in view of Johanan ben Zakkai's appeal to this verse:

> Once, as R. Yohanan was walking out of Jerusalem, R. Joshua followed him, and, upon seeing the Temple in ruins, he said: Woe unto us that this place is in ruins, the place where atonement was made for Israel's iniquities! R. Yohanan: My son do not grieve—we have another means of atonement which is as effective. What is it? It is deeds of loving-kindness, concerning which Scripture says, "I desire loving-kindness and not sacrifice." (Hos 6:6; Avot R. Nat. 4 [version B 8]; see Davies 1966, 306–7; Allison 2005, 212–14)

As W. D. Davies (1966, 307 n. 1) points out, Simeon the Just's "three pillars"—torah, temple service, and deeds of loving kindness (m. Avot 1:2)—were being reinterpreted at Jamnia at the same time that Matthew was written. Dale Allison (2005, 208–15) subsequently made a persuasive case for interpreting the triadic structure of the Sermon on the Mount as based on Simeon's three pillars.

Matthew's account of the healing of the man with the withered hand also moves to the question of what is allowed on the Sabbath. Here too Matthew adds an argument not found in Mark: "He said to them, 'Suppose one of you has only one sheep and it falls into a pit on the sabbath; will you not lay hold of it and lift it out? How much more valuable is a human being than a sheep! So it is lawful to do good on the sabbath'" (Matt 12:11–12). By means of argument from the lesser to the greater (*qal wahomer*), Jesus argues that since it is permissible to help an animal on the Sabbath it is also permissible to come to the aid of a human being. In neither of these pericopae is there a hint of ceasing to observe the Sabbath, but both set the priority of mercy above Sabbath observance.

4.2. The Sabbath in John

John defends Jesus's healing on the Sabbath, but on altogether different grounds.[8] In John 5:17 Jesus defends his healing on the Sabbath by saying, "My father is still working, and I also am working." C. H. Dodd (1953, 320–23; see also Harris 1994, 162) wrote a classic exposition of the debate in John 5 regarding what is permissible on the Sabbath. When four rabbis were challenged as to whether God kept his own law, their response assumed that God continued to work but that God's work on the Sabbath did not violate the prescriptions for the Sabbath (Exod. Rab. 30:9). Philo agrees; divine rest does not mean abstention from good deeds: "The cause of all things is by its nature active; it never ceases to work all that is best and most beautiful" (*Cherubim* 87, trans. Colson 1954). In fact, Philo claims that it is impossible that God should rest because "God never ceases creating, but as it is the property of fire to burn and of snow to be cold, so it is the property of God to create … for He causes to rest that which, though actually not in operation, is apparently making, but He Himself never ceases making" (*Alleg. Interp.* 1.5–6, trans. Colson 1929). Elsewhere Philo modifies this claim, saying that God rests from creating mortal things (*Alleg. Interp.* 1.16). Later rabbis followed the same line in claiming that God ceased from some things but not others. God rested from the work of creation but not from "the moral government of the universe" (Dodd 1953, 322). The two activities that Jesus claims the Father has given to the Son are giving life and judging (John 5:21–22), and both of these activities belong the continuous work of God. Hear Dodd's (1953, 323) comment:

> John similarly speaks of two divine activities, *zōopoiein* and *krinein*. The former is clearly a function of the creative power of God, and the latter of the kingly power.… Even on the Sabbath, as always, God gives life and judges. The words which follow, *kagō ergazomai*, imply that the life-giving work which Jesus has performed on the Sabbath is an instance of the divine activity of *zōopoiēsis*, and as such is exempt from the Sabbath restrictions.

---

8. This paragraph also appears in Culpepper 2015a, 27–28.

The argument here, while it is generally rabbinic in nature, as is Matt 12:5–7, is characteristically Johannine in its christological focus: Jesus does the work the Father has given him to do. Therefore, it is permissible for him to heal (i.e., give life) on the Sabbath. The implications for Jesus's followers are less clear in John because the rationale is so peculiarly christological (see Bultmann 1971, 247; N. Collins 2014, 188–89). Jesus did not abolish the Sabbath. Rather, he established its eschatological significance for his followers. Herold Weiss (1991, 319–20) contends that the realized eschatology of the Johannine community led them to claim that "its whole life was being lived on the Sabbath." The community was therefore no longer concerned with Sabbath observance, as were the Synoptic Gospels. They perform the works of the Son every day.

John 7:23 offers a *qal wahomer* argument that if circumcision is allowed on the Sabbath, then healing a person's whole body overrides the Sabbath command also. "If a man receives circumcision on the sabbath in order that the law of Moses may not be broken, are you angry with me because I healed a man's whole body on the sabbath?" Collins (2014, 161) cites a version of the same argument attributed Rabbi Eleazar b. Azariah, who was active in the second half of the first century:

> R. Eleazar b. Azaraiah says, "As to circumcision, on account of which one overrides Sabbath [law], why is this so? It is because on account of it one is liable to extirpation [if it is done] after [the right] time. Now the matter can be decided with an argument *kal va-chomer*—If on account of a single limb of a person, one overrides Sabbath law, is it not logical that one should override Sabbath law [in order to heal and/or save the life of] the whole of him!" (t. Shabb. 15.16; see Mek. de-Rabbi Ishamel Shabb. 1)

We need not accept Collins's (2014, 160, 165) claim that John did not understand the underlying logic of R. Eleazar's argument. The provision for circumcision on the Sabbath is a legitimate precedent for healing (one's whole body) on the Sabbath. Mary Coloe's (2001; 2007) argument for the importance of the theme of Jesus's replacement of the temple in John provides further context for John's argument. Jesus is not only "one greater than the temple"; he is the one in whom God is now present with the community.

In summary, the disputes over healing on the Sabbath in Matthew and John show that both gospels were in touch with current debates among the rabbis and may have borrowed directly from them. Matthew assumes

Sabbath observance, while John does not. As Raimo Hakola (2005b, 143) concludes: "Both John 5:1–18 and 7:19–24 suggest that the gospel already reflects a situation where the non-observance was taken as self-evident." John affirms that Jesus as the Son does the life-giving work of the Father, which continues on the Sabbath. This christological affirmation dominates John's interpretation of the Sabbath. As followers of the one in whom traditional eschatological expectations are fulfilled (see Culpepper 2008), the Johannine community lives in a perpetual Sabbath, doing the work that Jesus has given them to do.

5. Purity Issues

Purity issues offer another barometer of interaction with Judaism. The Pharisees in the period after the destruction of the temple laid the foundations of classical, rabbinic Judaism (study of torah, practice of the commandments of torah, and performance of good deeds) while maintaining the earlier emphasis on tithing, ritual purity, Sabbath, and festival observance (Neusner 1973, 99, 104).

5.1. Purity Issues in Matthew

Matthew's attention to matters of purity accords well with the concerns of the Pharisees during the latter part of the first century, especially in the delicacy with which it handles Jesus's words and practice related to ritual purity. When the Pharisees and scribes ask Jesus why his disciples do not observe "the tradition of the elders" by washing their hands before they eat (Matt 15:1), Jesus's response reveals a concern not to dismiss Pharisaic tradition, a concern that is not present in Mark. Mark explains the practice of the Pharisees in an aside (Mark 7:3–4), an explanation that was apparently unnecessary for Matthew's audience, since he omits it. Citing the practice of qorban, Jesus responds that the Pharisees compromise the word of God for their tradition, quoting the pronouncement of judgment in Isa 29:13. Then he declares that it is not what goes into the mouth that defiles a person but what comes out of the mouth. Matthew adds that "the Pharisees were offended when they heard this," a comment that is not in Mark. Matthew also omits Mark's sweeping declaration, "Thus he declared all foods clean" (Mark 7:19). In doing so, Matthew shows sensitivity to the debate about food laws among the early Jewish Christians, as well as the Pharisees' observance of these laws.

When a leper comes to Jesus with the astounding request, “Lord, if you will, you can make me clean,” Jesus touches him and says, “I will; be clean” and sends him to show himself to the priest and offer the sacrifice that Moses commanded (Matt 8:1–4). The command to offer the sacrifice adds support to Jesus’s claim that he did not come to abolish the law.

The crossing of boundaries is exaggerated in the healing of the Gadarene demoniacs (Matt 8:28–34). Jesus crosses to the other side of the Sea of Galilee, where he encounters two demon-possessed, unclean, and violent men who live in tombs not far from swine. The setting aptly evokes the warning to Jacob in Jubilees:

> And you also, my son, Jacob, remember my words, and keep the commandments of Abraham, your father. Separate yourself from the gentiles, and do not eat with them and do not perform deeds like theirs. And do not become associates of theirs. Because their deeds are defiled, and all of their ways are contaminated, and despicable, and abominable. They slaughter their sacrifices to the dead, and to the demons they bow down. And they eat in tombs. And all their deeds are worthless and vain. (Jub. 22:16–17, trans. Charlesworth 1983–1985)

Jesus then eats with tax collectors and sinners, which again offends the Pharisees (Matt 9:9–13), and then comes in contact with a bleeding woman and takes a corpse’s hand—actions that normally brought uncleanness (Matt 9:18–25; Lev 15:19–33; Num 19:11–12). Later, Jesus condemns the Pharisees for whitewashing tombs, “to enable people to avoid contamination by the dead” (Matt 23:27–28; see Thompson 2017).

The point is that in Matthew Jesus cleanses others, while exposing himself to uncleanness that does not render him unclean in the process (see Viljoen 2014b; 2014c). Jesus never purifies himself after such contacts. When questioned, Jesus appeals to Hos 6:6, to the “weightier matters” of the law, and to the greater importance of “the word of God” (Matt 15:3, 6). Matthew, therefore, shows sensitivity to the issues of purity—and food laws—while demonstrating Jesus’s power over uncleanness and setting a higher value on mercy, justice, healing, and inner purity.

5.2. Purity Issues in John

John’s treatment of purity issues is remarkably different. None of the scenes in Matthew discussed above appear in John. Jesus does not heal a leper; he is not criticized for eating with tax collectors and sinners; he does not cast out unclean spirits; he is not touched by a bleeding woman; he does not touch a corpse; and he does not teach on purity, defilement, or food laws. John shows awareness of the currency of these concerns when he refers to the six stone water pots at Cana (2:6), and when John the Baptist has a discussion about purification (3:25), but John's approach to these issues lies elsewhere.

In a recent paper on baptism and purification in John, Marianne Meye Thompson (2017) shows that the Baptist's affirmations that Jesus will baptize with the Holy Spirit and that he is the Lamb of God that takes away the sin of the world are closely related. Thompson explains the connection in terms of biblical imagery:

> In the Gospel of John, washing with water now points to cleansing with the Spirit. This one "purity ritual" points ultimately to the purifier: the one on whom the Spirit remains, who baptizes with the Spirit, "the Lamb of God" who takes away the world's sin.

John is therefore not unconcerned about purity; he interprets Jesus as the one who provides true cleansing, access to God, and life. The difference between Matthew and John is that Matthew has Jesus debating with the Pharisees about their purity issues, whereas John leaves them behind, as part of the background, while presenting the cleansing available through Jesus in terms that could be understood by gentiles as well as Jews. Again, therefore, John does not appear to be engaged with Pharisaic, Jewish concerns, while Matthew does. We turn to the next diagnostic element: references to the Pharisees.

6. The Pharisees

6.1. References to Pharisees in Matthew

Graham Stanton (1997, 52) observes that "in Matthew, Jewish religious leaders and groups—and, in particular, scribes and Pharisees—are consistently placed in a negative light." Michael Cook (1987a, 191–95) cites the following examples where Matthew intensifies anti-Jewish references:

1. Mark 14:55–6 // Matt 26:59–60: Matthew inserts "false" testimony.
2. Mark 12:13–17 // Matt 22:15–22: Matthew inserts "malice" and "hypocrites."

3. Mark 12:28–34 // Matt 22:34–40: Matthew omits Jesus's commendation of the scribe.
4. Mark 15:12–15 // Matt 27:22–26: Matthew inserts "His blood will be on us and our children."
5. Matt 9:34; 22:34–35; 22:41: Matthew inserts "Pharisees."

Let us test these observations by analyzing the twenty-nine references to Pharisee(s) in Matthew. They fall into five categories, where: (1) Matthew is the same as Mark or substantially the same—six times; (2) Matthew is the same as Luke—none; (3) Matthew modifies Mark—nine times, (4) Matthew differs from Luke—seven times, and (5) Matthew's references do not occur in Mark or Luke—seven times.

6.1.1. Matthew Is the Same as Mark, or Substantially the Same

In this set of references (Matt 9:14, 34; 12:2, 24; 15:1; and 19:3) the Pharisees question or accuse Jesus on matters of fasting, casting out demons, Sabbath violation, purity, and divorce—generally (with the exception of casting out demons) matters to which the rabbinic materials devote considerable attention.

6.1.2. Matthew Is the Same as Luke

Interestingly, when Matthew includes double tradition or Q material referring to the Pharisees, Matthew modifies it. See category 4 below.

6.1.3. Matthew Modifies Mark

Mark	Matthew	
2:1: The scribes of the Pharisees	9:11: the Pharisees	
3:6: the Pharisees	12:14: the Pharisees	omits the Herodians in Mark 3:6
8:11: the Pharisees	12:38: the scribes and the Pharisees	
7:17	15:12–15: the Pharisees	

8:11: the Pharisees	16:1: the Pharisees and Sadducees	
8:15: the Pharisees and Herod	16:6: the Pharisees and Sadducees	
12:13: they sent	22:15–16: the Pharisees plotted to entrap Jesus	
12:28: one of the scribes	22:34–36: the Pharisees	
12:35: the scribes	22:41–42: the Pharisees	see the texts

What stands out from this tabulation is that Matthew occasionally sharpens the focus on the Pharisees as Jesus's interlocutors or opponents (Matt 9:11; 22:34), while at other times Matthew inserts stock phrases (scribes and Pharisees, 12:38; Pharisees and Sadducees, 16:1, 6). Matthew 22:15–16 changes Mark's ambiguous "they" to "the Pharisees" while adding that they "went and plotted to entrap him."

6.1.4. Matthew Differs from Luke

> Matt 3:7 But when he saw many *Pharisees and Sadducees* coming for baptism, he said to them, "You brood of vipers! Who warned you to flee from the wrath to come?"
> Luke 3:7 John said to *the crowds* that came out to be baptized by him, "You brood of vipers! Who warned you to flee from the wrath to come?"

> Matt 21:45 When *the chief priests and the Pharisees* heard his parables, they realized that he was speaking about them.
> Luke 20:19 When *the scribes and chief priests* realized that he had told this parable against them,…

> Matt 23:23 Woe to you, *scribes and Pharisees, hypocrites*! For you tithe mint, dill, and cummin, and have neglected the weightier matters of the law: justice and mercy and faith.
> Luke 11:42 But woe to you *Pharisees*! For you tithe mint and rue and herbs of all kinds, and neglect justice and the love of God.

> Matt 23:25–26 Woe to you, *scribes and Pharisees, hypocrites*! For you clean the outside of the cup and of the plate, but inside they are full of greed and self-indulgence. *You blind Pharisee*!

> Luke 11:39–40 Then the Lord said to him, "Now you *Pharisees* clean the outside of the cup and of the dish, but inside you are full of greed and wickedness. *You fools*!"

> Matt 23:27 Woe to you, *scribes and Pharisees, hypocrites*! For you are like whitewashed tombs.
> Luke 11:44 Woe to you! For you are like unmarked graves, and people walk over them without realizing it.

> Matt 23:29 Woe to you, *scribes and Pharisees, hypocrites*! For you build the tombs of the prophets and decorate the graves of the righteous.
> Luke 11:47 Woe to you! For you build the tombs of the prophets whom your ancestors killed.

Anti-Pharisaism can be seen most clearly in this category. The Q sayings in Matthew generally depict the Pharisees more negatively than their parallels in Luke. Matthew 3:7 makes the Pharisees and Sadducees the object of Jesus's "brood of vipers" rather than the crowds. Matthew 21:45 pairs the Pharisees with the chief priests (in place of the scribes) as those against whom Jesus told the parables. Matthew 23:23 names the scribes and Pharisees as those who tithe herbs while neglecting the weightier things and calls them "hypocrites," as do Matt 23:27, 29 and Matt 23:25–26, which also changes Luke's "you fool!" to "you blind Pharisee!"

6.1.5. Matthew's References That Are Not in Mark or Luke

> Matt 5:20 For I tell you, unless your righteousness exceeds that of *the scribes and Pharisees*, you will never enter the kingdom of heaven.

> Matt 16:11 How could you fail to perceive that I was not speaking about bread? Beware of the yeast of *the Pharisees and Sadducees*! (see Matt 16:6, 12)

> Matt 16:12 Then they understood that he had not told them to beware of the yeast of bread, but of the teaching of *the Pharisees and Sadducees*. (see Matt 16:6, 11)

> Matt 23:2 *The scribes and the Pharisees* sit on Moses' seat …

> Matt 23:13 But woe to you, *scribes and Pharisees*, hypocrites!

> Matt 23:15 Woe to you, *scribes and Pharisees*, hypocrites!

> Matt 27:62 The next day, that is, after the day of Preparation, *the chief priests and the Pharisees* gathered before Pilate …

The references in this category offer an interesting mix. By demanding that the righteousness of his disciples exceed that of the scribes and Pharisees (Matt 5:20), Jesus recognizes them as exemplary, while their efforts are inadequate. Matthew 16:11–12 castigates the teachings of the Pharisees and Sadducees. The scribes and Pharisees sit on Moses's seat (Matt 23:2). Jesus instructs his followers to do as they teach but not as they do (23:3) and then adds references to them as hypocrites (23:13, 15; see the references in the previous category where Jesus introduces the same aspersion to references in Luke). Finally, the Pharisees are paired with the chief priests as those who sought Jesus's death (Matt 27:62; see 21:45).

The two instances where Matthew refers to "the chief priests and the Pharisees" are particularly interesting, as are the occurrences of this pairing in John (7:32, 45; 11:47; and 18:3) and Josephus (*Life* 21; *J.W.* 2.409–417), because they appear to reflect a historically plausible collaboration between these two groups during the exceptional circumstances of the Jewish revolt in 66–70 CE (see von Wahlde 1996, esp. nn. 34, 43; and Tomson 2001, 323–24 n. 80).

In sum, the references to Pharisee(s) in Matthew present a mixed picture. Matthew takes over some references from Mark unchanged. Where Matthew changes Mark, it is simply a matter of changing the designation of the groups interacting with Jesus. Most interesting is the data that Matthew's rendering of the references in the Q material is always different from Luke's, and typically Matthew's references to the Pharisees are more anti-Pharisaic than Luke's. The references that appear only in Matthew offer a variety of designations of groups, and some add the invective "hypocrites."

6.2. References to Pharisees in John

There are nineteen references to the Pharisees in John (excluding 8:3).[9] Urban von Wahlde's work on the Jews and the Jewish leaders in John is helpful for our purposes, as he finds that the designation of the religious

9. John 1:24; 3:1; 4:1; 7:32 (2x), 45, 47, 48; 8:13; 9:13, 15, 16, 40; 11:46, 47, 57; 12:19, 42; 18:3. See Poplutz 2013.

authorities as "Pharisees," "chief priests," and "rulers" is characteristic of the first edition of the gospel, whereas the second edition employs the more general expression οἱ Ἰουδαῖοι (von Wahlde 2010a, 1:63). From his detailed analysis we can glean characteristics of the portrayal of the Pharisees in John, many of which apply to the chief priests and rulers also, that von Wahlde assigns to the first edition. This data is helpful because it distinguishes earlier from later strata of the Johannine tradition and therefore offers the potential for comparisons with the development of the synoptic tradition, which we have just discussed.

John refers to divisions among the Pharisees regarding Jesus but never divisions among the Jews (von Wahlde 2010a, 1:84). In the first edition, the level of hostility of the Pharisees increases progressively, while in the second edition the level of hostility of the Jews is constant throughout the gospel (von Wahlde 2010a, 1:84; Tomson 2001, 322, agrees). There are repeated reports of the reaction of the Pharisees to reports of belief among the common people (John 3:1; 7:32; 12:19), but this does not occur in later editions (von Wahlde 2010a, 1:85). These responses are generally based on belief in response to Jesus's signs (3:1; 7:32; ch. 9; 11:47–50; 12:19), but these are ignored in the later editions (von Wahlde 2010a, 1:86). The common people show no fear of the authorities in the first edition of the gospel (7:45; 9:15–17, 24–34), whereas "fear of the Jews" occurs three times (7:13; 19:38; 20:19; see 12:42) in material assigned to the second edition (von Wahlde 2010a, 1:87–88). The Pharisees exhibit a range of responses to belief among the common people, while the response of the Jews is "unanimous, unswerving" hostility (von Wahlde 2010a, 1:88). The Pharisees never dialogue with Jesus, while the Jews are almost always in dialogue with him (von Wahlde 2010a, 92). From these and other, unrelated characteristics of the first edition, von Wahlde (2010a, 1:116) concludes that

> All of this suggests that the intended audience of the first edition was a Jewish one. Almost certainly this was an audience of fellow Jews *within the synagogue*. That is, the document that served as the "first edition" of the Johannine Gospel had been composed as a way to produce evidence that would be attractive to fellow Jews.

The social location of the second edition is much different: "At the time of the second edition, the Johannine community was a Jewish-Christian group, in the midst of, or having just emerged from, a thoroughgoing conflict with its parent Jewish matrix, resulting in expulsion from the synagogue" (1:214). Von Wahlde's reconstruction of the composition history of the gospel and the parallel developments in the Johannine community, therefore, confirms the general outlines proposed by Martyn and Brown, without agreeing with either entirely, and does so on the basis of analysis of verbal, literary, and theological elements in the gospel that exhibit patterns that allow them to be assigned to one of three editions of the gospel.

> By the time of the third edition, the community is no longer part of a synagogue community but is now an independent community of persons who believe in Jesus. The tension with Judaism and the synagogue, which so dominated the second edition, is now absent. (1:367)

Our brief survey of Matthew's references to the Pharisees and von Wahlde's analysis of the role of the Pharisees in John provides another lens through which to view the development of the gospel tradition and the social location of Matthew and John in relation to Judaism late in the first century. Matthew's references to the Pharisees exhibit signs of an increasingly negative portrayal of the Pharisees (over against Mark and Luke), whereas John's shift in terminology from "Pharisees" to οἱ Ἰουδαῖοι in the later editions of the gospel points to a movement from appeal to Jews within the synagogue to conflict with the synagogue and on to a period when that conflict lay in the past (see Culpepper 1987, 282). We may therefore turn next to the references to the synagogue(s) in Matthew and John.

7. The Synagogue

7.1. The Synagogue in Matthew

The references to the synagogue(s) in Matthew pose a problem for interpreters because they reflect both the intimacy of detailed knowledge and assumed participation in the synagogues, and the distancing of condemnation, warnings, and references to synagogues as belonging to others. In Matthew, Jesus regularly teaches in the synagogues in Galilee (Matt 12:9; 13:54), and the evangelist includes references to the synagogues in the gospel's summary statements, where he characterizes them as "their synagogues" (4:23; 9:35). "Their synagogues" also appears in 10:17; 12:9; 13:54; and "your synagogue" in 23:34. A leader of one of the synagogues comes to Jesus for help when his daughter has just died (9:18), and Jesus heals a man with a withered hand in the synagogue on the Sabbath (12:9–14). At the same time, Jesus condemns the "hypocrites" in the synagogues for practicing their piety to be applauded by others (6:2, 5). That condemnation is developed far more fully in Matthew than in any of the other gospels, specifically in Matt 23.

Scholarship has been divided on the questions of the identity of those condemned in Matt 23 (fellow Christians or leaders of the synagogue) and whether this chapter represents the views of the evangelist or a pre-Matthean source (see esp. Garland 1979; Newport 1995). Readers are at least expected to be very familiar with the workings of the synagogue (Moses's seat, 23:2; instructors, 23:10; flogging, 23:34) and the practices of the Pharisees (phylacteries and fringes, 23:5; oaths, 23:18; tithing, 23:23; purity, 23:25; decorating graves, 23:29). Telling perhaps is what is not said. Matthew does not advocate dispensing with phylacteries and fringes, or tithing herbs, or washing, only that one's word be such that oaths are unnecessary (5:37). The demand is that one not neglect the "weightier" things, justice, mercy, and faith (23:23), that one's piety be genuine (23:26) and one's practice consistent with one's teaching (23:3), and that one be a servant to others (23:4, 11). Still, Jesus warns his followers that the synagogues will persecute them (10:17; 23:34).

Any discussion of the synagogue in Matthew must also take note of the fact that Matthew is the only gospel to refer to the church, giving evidence that Christians were meeting outside the synagogue and forming their own religious community (see Stanton 1997, 53–55). Commentators point out that in Matt 16:18 the reference to "my church" seems to have in view the church universal, while the two references to "the church" in Matt 18:17, in the context of instructions regarding settling disputes, speak of the individual, local community of believers.

7.2. The Synagogue in John

When we turn to the Gospel of John, the situation is both different and generally the same. Jesus taught in the synagogue at Capernaum (John 6:59) and other synagogues, where he said nothing in secret (18:20), but aside from the three references to being put out of the synagogue, these are the only references to the synagogue(s) in John. John does not convey the impression, as does Matthew, that believers are still organically related to the synagogue. Jesus frequented the synagogue, but now believers have been put out of the synagogue, and only "secret believers" remain in the synagogues. These secret believers are encouraged to confess Jesus openly, like John the Baptist (1:20) in contrast with Peter, who denied him. There is also evidence of conflict between believers and the synagogue. "The world" will hate Jesus's followers, as it hated him (15:18–25), and they will be put out of the synagogue and even killed (16:2; see 9:22; 12:42). While there are no references to the church, one can infer separate meetings of believers in the references to eating Jesus's body and drinking his blood (6:51–58), washing one another's feet (13:14–15), and Jesus's prayer for those who will come later (17:20–24). Peter and the Beloved Disciple appear to have emerged as Christian leaders, and John affirms the pastoral role of Peter while holding to the authority of the Beloved Disciple's testimony.

Daniel Harrington (1980, 105) makes the following observation about the anti-Jewish references in Matthew and John:

> The most blatant "anti-Jewish" passages in both Gospels suppose the exclusion of Jewish Christians from the synagogue and are part of the church's claim to be God's people in opposition to rival claims to the title being made by other Jewish groups. Nevertheless, neither Matthew nor John yet sees the Christian community as a new religion apart from Judaism. Their anger is over the exclusion of their community from the synagogue. Paradoxically, then, despite their strong anti-Jewish statements, they are eloquent testimony to the radical Jewishness of early Christian self-understanding.

I would qualify his comments by adding that the references in Matthew suggest a closer relationship with the synagogue, while in John the separation between the two communities is more advanced and in places characterized by exclusion or secrecy to avoid exclusion.

8. Conclusions

As a way of gathering up the key points of the foregoing analysis, we may review the conclusions drawn at the end of each section.

8.1. Jesus as the New Moses

Both Matthew and John characterize Jesus as the fulfillment of the Moses typology, but with individual differences. Matthew sets Jesus in continuity with Moses, inviting the reader to accept Jesus's teachings as the fulfillment of the law. John reinterprets the opposition between Jesus and Moses, rejecting the forced choice required by the Pharisees in John and affirming Moses as a witness to Jesus. John's use of the Moses typology is therefore more polemical than Matthew's.

8.2. Fulfillment of Scripture

Both Matthew and John appeal to the Scriptures. Affirming that Jesus fulfilled the Scriptures is a common feature in the gospels, Paul, and Hebrews. Both Matthew and John also engage in polemic, so comparisons must be nuanced. Nevertheless, recognizing the risks of generalization, it appears that whereas Matthew appeals to the Scriptures so that those who adhere to the Hebrew Scriptures might see how Jesus fulfilled them, John defends the claim that Jesus is the Christ against those who do not accept him by showing how the Scriptures testify to him.

8.3. The Law

Jesus's declaration regarding the continuing validity of the law in Matt 5:17–20 is foundational for understanding Matthew's stance. Moreover, these verses are followed by repeated warnings that disciples will be judged by what they do or do not do, and Matthew includes instructions on a variety of specific issues common in rabbinic tradition. Jesus's fulfillment of the law clearly does not mean that Matthean believers no longer need to keep the law, but it is interpreted in the light of Jesus's teachings and particularly the love command. The situation in the Gospel of John, where there are no such specific teachings, is strikingly different. Polemically, the Johannine Jesus charges that his opponents do not understand the law and do not keep it themselves, because the law bears witness to him.

8.4. The Sabbath

Sabbath observance is central to Jewish practice and a test of whether one is torah observant. Both gospels agree that Jesus healed on the Sabbath and was challenged by the Pharisees for doing so, and in both Jesus responds with arguments that echo rabbinic arguments, but Jesus responds to the challenge differently in the two gospels. In Matthew, he argues by means of argument from the lesser to the greater that since it is permissible to help an animal on the Sabbath it is also permissible to come to the aid of a human being. There is no hint that Jesus's disciples should cease to observe the Sabbath, but Jesus sets the priority of mercy above Sabbath observance. John 7 employs a *qal wahomer* argument also, based on the provision for circumcision on the Sabbath. The argument in John 5 is characteristically Johannine in its christological focus: Jesus does the work that the Father has given him to do. Therefore, it is permissible for him to heal (i.e., give life) on the Sabbath. This work is continued in the Johannine community, so nonobservance of the Sabbath is taken for granted.

8.5. Purity Issues

Matthew shows sensitivity to the issues of purity—and food laws—suggesting that at least some in the Matthean audience continue to observe these matters in fidelity to the law. At the same time, Matthew demonstrates that Jesus overcomes uncleanness and sets a higher value on mercy, justice, healing, and inner purity. John's treatment of purity issues is remarkably different. None of the scenes in Matthew that deal with purity issues appear in John. John is not unconcerned about purity, however. It interprets Jesus as the one who provides true cleansing. The difference between Matthew and John is that Matthew has Jesus debating with the Pharisees about their purity issues, whereas John leaves these issues behind. Again, therefore, John does not appear to be in close proximity to Pharisaic, Jewish concerns, while Matthew does.

8.6. The Pharisees

The references to Pharisee(s) in Matthew present a mixed picture. Matthew takes over some references from Mark unchanged. Moreover, where Matthew changes Mark, it is simply a matter of changing the designation of the groups interacting with Jesus. Most interesting is the data that Matthew's rendering of the references to Pharisees in the Q material is always different from Luke's, and typically Matthew's references to the Pharisees are more anti-Pharisaic than Luke's. The references that appear only in Matthew offer a variety of designations of groups, and some add the invective "hypocrites."

Whereas Matthew's references to the Pharisees exhibit signs of an increasingly negative portrayal of the Pharisees (over against Mark and Luke), John's shift in terminology from "Pharisees" to οἱ Ἰουδαῖοι in the later editions of the gospel points to a movement from appeal to Jews within the synagogue to conflict with the synagogue and on to a period when that conflict lay in the past.

8.7. The Synagogue

The references to the synagogue(s) in Matthew reflect the intimacy of detailed knowledge and assumed participation in the synagogues, while also including condemnations, warnings, and references to synagogues as belonging to others. When we turn to the Gospel of John, the situation is both different and generally the same. Jesus teaches in the synagogue at Capernaum (6:59) and other synagogues (18:20), but aside from the three references to being put out of the synagogue, these are the only references to the synagogue(s) in John. John does not convey the impression, as does Matthew, that believers are still organically related to the synagogue.

9. *Intra Muros* and/or *Extra Muros*

Various reconstructions of the settings of Matthew and John have sought to explain and account for the differences in the way they handle matters related to Judaism. Both the early Christian communities and their Jewish counterparts were diverse and evolving rapidly in the late first century, so interpreters must allow for ambiguity on both sides, "both from the Gospel itself [themselves] and 'mapping the complexity of Judaism and its relationship to the emergent Christian movement' " (Gurtner 2011, 31, citing Senior 2011). Current Matthean scholarship is divided over the question of whether "the community found itself in a *current* and pressing conflict with the Pharisaic opponent" (Konradt 2014, 355) or "no longer remained within the association of synagogues," although "the breach between synagogue and community lay in the relatively recent past" (Luz 1995, 14, 15). These alternatives are sometimes reduced to the metaphorical terms *intra muros* or *extra muros*, but this dichotomy may be too decisive and unambiguous to serve in untangling such a fluid historical process and such nuanced interpretations of the period. As Dale Allison (1993, 290) puts it, "Matthew was much concerned with the preservation of his Jewish religious heritage in a church inexorably becoming Gentile." On the other hand, our findings lead us to agree with Hakola's (2005b, 218) assessment that "the Johannine Christians assess various aspects of Jewishness exclusively in light of their faith in Jesus which had the effect of obliterating the relevance of these matters as fundamentals of Jewish identity."

If the data I have collected add anything to the intense discussions regarding these issues, it seems to me to incline toward distinguishing the situations of Matthew and John in relation to Pharisaic Judaism in the latter part of the first century by suggesting that Matthew is still engaged in a hermeneutic of interpreting his Jewish heritage in order to make it possible for Jewish believers to continue to live as practicing Jews while worshiping with believers in the *ekklēsia*, whereas the separation of Johannine believers from the synagogue now lies in the past, and the Fourth Evangelist and his community are engaged in a polemical hermeneutic that justifies this break and claims the spoils of Judaism for the Johannine community/ies.[10]

10. See the similar conclusion Loader reaches in this volume.

Toward Reconfiguring Our Views on the "Parting of the Ways": Ephesus as a Test Case

Jörg Frey

The present contribution aims at providing a wider framework for a more comprehensive understanding of a process that can be observed in parts of the Johannine literature: the gradual separation between Jesus followers and synagogal Jews that resulted in the later existence of two separate plants in spite of the one common root. There is much debate about that so-called parting of the ways (Dunn 1991).[1] When did it happen, and for what reason? Did the decisive split happen as early as in the Pauline mission, or earlier, with the Jerusalem "Hellenists," or even with Jesus himself? Or did the separation occur only later, after the destruction of the temple, with the decisions of Yavneh, with the Bar-Kokhba war, or with the triumph of the gentile church? Was the opposition of two separate "religions" manifest already in the second century, for example, in Ignatius, or only in the fourth century (Boyarin 2004), or did the ways in fact "never" really part (Reed and Becker 2003)? Can we identify a certain point of decision, such as, for example, the reformulation of the Birkat Haminim, often attributed to the sages at Yavneh, as J. Louis Martyn (1968) suggested with the Johannine ἀποσυνάγωγος in view? Was there a decisive stumbling stone, such the veneration of Jesus as a divine being (see John 5:17–18) or already with Paul's view of the Jewish law? Or did the processes of separation happen in a locally and temporally incoherent manner, with different factors involved in various group constellations and regions?

1. See apart from Dunn 1991; 1992 the critical survey of recent scholarship in Broadhead 2010, 354–71, also the analysis of the problems in Lieu 2002, the revised view in Dunn 2006, and the general questioning of the paradigm in Reed and Becker 2003. Concerning the issues and developments in the second century, see now Nicklas 2014.

In my view, the latter is the case, and the task of reconfiguring our views on the parting of the ways can only mean to step back from the general perspectives for a while and to look more precisely at particular authors, groups, or regions, in order to get hold of the variety of factors involved in that extended and multifaceted process.[2]

1. Ephesus as an Exemplary Test Case

Presupposing that the Johannine writings provide glimpses into a community or group of communities in Ephesus and its surroundings, we can take Ephesus as an exemplary case for describing the dynamics between synagogal Jews and various groups of Jesus followers in the first and early second century.[3]

The situation in the metropolis of Asia is particularly illuminating due to the fact that there are a number of literary sources that can be confidently related to the development of the Christian community or communities in Ephesus or its surroundings (see Frey 2013g, 237–43): (1) Paul's epistles mentioning Ephesus several times and reflecting Paul's experiences there; (2) the narrative account of Acts 18–20 about Paul's ministry in Ephesus; (3) the Johannine corpus with the gospel and the epistles; furthermore (4) Revelation mentioning the "seven cities" of Asia Minor, including Ephesus; and finally (5) Ignatius's Letter to the Ephesians. There are, of course, some uncertainties.[4] It is disputed whether Philippians can be dated to an imprisonment of Paul in Ephesus and thus serve as a source for the situation in Ephesus (Frey 2015c, 570–72; Omerzu 2009). It is uncertain whether we can also locate the deutero-Pauline letters in Ephesus, although the link of Ephesians with Ephesus and the location of Timothy in Ephesus provide at least some good reason to assume that Ephesus was a center of the further development of the Pauline tradition

2. Most significantly, Dunn (2006) now uses the plural ("partings of the ways"). See also Wander (1999), who uses the term *Trennungsprozesse* (although he only considers the time before 70 CE).

3. The present article draws in many aspects on the more detailed discussion of the development in Ephesus in Frey 2013g, where also much more scholarly literature is considered than is possible in the present framework.

4. See for discussion Günther 1995; Thissen 1995; Strelan 1996; Trebilco 2004; Witetschek 2008; Tellbe 2009. Not all of these authors include all the texts mentioned above as sources for Christian communities in Ephesus.

and possibly one of the places where Paul's epistles were collected in the time after his death. There are also some doubts whether all the Johannine writings can serve as sources of the situation in Asia Minor or whether either the gospel (Trebilco 2004, 237–41) or also some of the epistles (Thissen 1995, 111–23) should be cautiously excluded. Of course, the date of the letters of Ignatius has been disputed in recent scholarship (Hübner 1997; Lechner 1999), and we cannot enter that debate in the present context. But in spite of these uncertainties, the sources for the development of "Christian" communities in Ephesus are extraordinarily rich.[5]

From these sources, we can conclude that at least by the end of the first century there was probably a variety of Christian communities within that metropolis, with different theological profiles or identities, including post-Pauline communities, Johannine communities, and perhaps also a circle of prophets around the author of Revelation.[6] There is good reason to assume that the Jesus followers of the different groups were aware of one another. Paul Trebilco (2004, 613, 626) has coined the term "non-hostile relations," but actually this description is merely a stopgap, as we have no direct evidence about the mutual relations between those different communities or groups in the post-Pauline period. Their views obviously differ at many points, but we cannot find any direct polemic between those writings or the groups related.[7]

Given that there was also a large and self-confident Jewish community in Ephesus (see Trebilco 2004, 37–52) and that all relevant sources touch the relations between the community of Jesus followers and the local synagogue or οἱ Ἰουδαῖοι, it is possible to get at least some glimpses into the development of those relations that can help to understand the so-called parting of the ways. Given such insights admittedly taken from a particular place and region, but in view of the shortage of sources for most other cities and regions in the first-century Mediterranean world, the image we

5. There is comparable source material only for Rome, but the majority of the Roman sources are later and illuminate the situation at the end of the first and the first half of the second century.

6. Revelation is probably not addressed to communities where the authority of the author is well respected but rather to communities dominated by other theological views.

7. We should at least say that for the explicit polemic in some of those writings (in particular Revelation, 1–2 John, or the Pastorals), the exact target group remains uncertain.

get from Ephesus is extraordinarily valuable, and the local situation there can serve as an exemplary case for understanding the dynamics in the relations between the diaspora synagogue and the groups of Jewish and gentile Jesus followers.

In view of the debate between a traditional viewpoint, dating that parting rather early, and others dating at least its completion much later, and in view of tendencies in Johannine research to assume a particular incident of an "expulsion" (represented in the Johannine term ἀποσυνάγωγος in John 9:22; 12:42; 16:2), the observations from this test case can contribute to a reconceptualizing of the parting of the ways as a multifaceted process, influenced by different local and general factors and stretched over a considerable time span. It may have started quite early but was completed, if ever, rather late.

2. Glimpses into the Development of "Christian" Communities in Ephesus

I can only briefly sketch the various aspects of the development of the Ephesian communities of Jesus followers. In speaking of mere glimpses, I would like to stress that the sources are not dense enough to fully reconstruct the development in all its stages, but that there remain dark and unclear periods between the various points of information we get from our sources.

2.1. Before Paul—A Group of Jewish Followers of Jesus Instructed by Apollos

Paul was not the founder of the Ephesian community, nor was he the first Jesus follower in Ephesus. If we can follow Luke in this aspect (who narrates contrary to his usual tendencies; see Witetschek 2008, 358), another early preacher, the Hellenistic Jew Apollos, was at work in Ephesus (Acts 18:24–28) before Paul arrived there. While Paul accepts Apollos as his missionary colleague (see 1 Cor 3:5–9), Luke tries to present him as an incompletely instructed and therefore subordinate figure who needs correct instruction.[8] In view of that tendency, it seems rather remarkable that

8. The fact that he was not baptized in a "Christian" manner is only problematic from a later view, when baptism had become common. For the earliest followers, we cannot presuppose this.

Luke feels obliged to mention Apollos even decades later. Were there still traces of his mission in the post-Pauline period?

Apollos is presented as a Jew from Alexandria, well trained in speaking and educated in the Scriptures, teaching in the synagogue: a powerful missionary who engages in debates with the Jews. As we also know also from Corinth, Apollos acted as an independent missionary, unrelated to the Pauline mission, although Paul "recognized him as a co-worker" (Trebilco 2004, 116). In spite of Luke's objections, he should, therefore, be regarded as a real Christian, as "all his activity in Ephesus that we know of was as a Christian" (Trebilco 2004, 122).

At least in the Ephesian context,[9] Apollos's missionary activity was completely focused on a Jewish audience within the local synagogal community, and it seems that he had at least some success with his mission. We can, therefore, assume that there was already a group of synagogal Jews following his teaching.[10] There was a group of Jewish Jesus followers in Ephesus before Paul.

2.2. Paul, the Jewish Apostle to the Gentiles, and His Move to a "Neutral Place"

So, when Paul arrived at Ephesus, he did not find a *tabula rasa* but already a group of Jesus followers (see also Acts 19:1), instructed by another Jewish missionary and living within the context of the local synagogue. It is unclear whether those first believers in Ephesus were actually instructed incompletely, as Luke claims, or whether they should also be regarded as "real Christians." On the other hand, it is quite probable that their views differed in some points from Paul's ideas, and that their lifestyle (i.e., their practice of the Jewish law) also differed from the lifestyle Paul taught in "his" communities.

Could Paul simply join that group of synagogal Jewish Jesus followers? According to his own self-concept as a missionary, he might have sought their fellowship for his missionary work. But were they prepared to support Paul's way of preaching, especially his deliberately approaching the gentiles? Could Paul try to work within the given synagogue structures?

---

9. Due to the different structure of the community in Corinth (founded by Paul), things may have been somewhat different in the Corinthian context.

10. Some scholars see the twelve Ephesians from Acts 19:2 who had only heard about John's baptism as Apollos's converts; see Trebilco 2004, 122.

Or did his missionary strategy cause problems with the other Jewish Jesus followers in the synagogue and also with the other Jews? Did Paul's proclamation lead to a second circle of Jesus followers, still within the synagogue but more committed to Paul's views and activities and more open to the gentiles? Such a scenario is quite conceivable in view of the large Jewish community gathering in various houses or synagogues.[11] Is such diversity already a kind of the factionalism Paul criticizes in Corinth? Or is it the simple result of the fact that different preachers address different people and thus bring about circles committed to the respective teacher? Paul's criticism of the Corinthian factionalism does not rule out the possibility that his preaching in Ephesus could quite easily lead to a group that differed in its views and in its (still Jewish) lifestyle from the other Jewish Jesus followers instructed by Apollos and possibly other teachers.

We have no information about the discussions during the first period of Paul's stay in Ephesus, nor do we know anything from Paul himself about an early "separation" between the different groups. Luke narrates that Paul "examined" the disciples he found in Ephesus and discovered some insufficiency of their faith and knowledge, but this may rather be explained from Luke's interest in the superiority of Paul's mission. But even if the faith of those disciples cannot be considered insufficient, there might have been differences and disputes between the members of the two subgroups. It is not unimportant that Paul was not the founder of the community of Jesus followers in Ephesus (as he was, e.g., in Thessaloniki, Philippi, or Corinth) but had to respect an existing Jewish group of Jesus followers with a practice of (Jewish) life that probably differed from the way Paul instructed his converts.

We have some more information from the later periods of Paul's stay. From 1 Cor 16:9 we learn that, in spite of earlier difficulties, Paul's mission in Ephesus finally bore fruits. First Corinthians 16:19 mentions communities in Asia and thus suggests that Paul's strategy of using the metropolises as missionary bases was also successful in this province, so that the mission of Paul and his coworkers probably even extended to the Lycus Valley, to Colossae, Laodicea, Hierapolis, and other places. This implies that Paul did actually approach and reach gentiles, although he probably started his missionary work, as usual, in the synagogue. Luke further narrates

11. Numbers for the Jewish population in Ephesus vary between hundreds and twenty-five thousand (Strelan 1996, 181); see Trebilco 2004, 50–51. Ameling 1996 suggests that about 5 percent of the population of Asia Minor was Jewish.

that Paul's influence on gentiles even led to conflicts with pagan religious groups and, as a consequence, with the civic authorities (Acts 19:23–40). If there is some truth in that, it means Paul's missionary work was so successful that it was noticed by the non-Jewish society.

We should not ignore that an intense contact with gentiles could cause difficulties for Jews within their Jewish environment due to the steady threat of impurity (especially in common meals with gentiles participating). Moreover, Paul's mission among gentiles could not only stir up their anger against himself; it could also cause suspicion among pagan groups of the Jewish community and thus endanger the place of the Jewish community within the civic society. On the other hand, the leaders of the Jewish communities could not want the anger of pagan circles or civic authorities stirred up by such a "troublemaker" who was still a member of the Jewish community.

This may be the background of the brief but important note in Acts 19:9–10, that Paul with his group of disciples "withdrew" from the synagogue to a place called "the school of Tyrannus." Was this a room for rent, a building for public orators, or a room where philosophers used to teach? We actually know very little about that location (see Witetschek 2008, 211), and neither are we told the precise reasons of Paul's withdrawal. But rather than being expelled, Paul seems to have taken that step deliberately, by his own decision. Of course, such a move to another place was no formal separation. Paul was still a Jew, although he did not teach any more in the rooms of the synagogue. A "neutral" place could better enable him to invite gentiles and to speak to them more directly and without running into troubles with other Jews. If Paul instructed his followers at that place, the group shaped there was no longer part of the synagogal community (although some if its members still were). Instead, it was more accessible and attractive for gentiles, who could understand Paul's teaching as a kind of philosophy, as there were certainly many public speakers and philosophers active in the town. On the other hand, it is quite probable that not all the Jewish believers followed Paul from the synagogue to that neutral place. At least some of them—possibly those shaped by Apollos—stayed and met within the synagogal context.

I cannot go into the issues of Philippians here (see Frey 2015b), but if that letter can be dated to a captivity in Ephesus, Paul's lament that not all Christians at the place of his captivity support him and share the view that he really suffers for the sake of the gospel (Phil 1:16) may be explained from such a situation. Believers who did not support Paul's offensive preaching to the gentiles could easily say that it would have been better if he had not stirred up pagan sensitivities, thus troubling not only himself but also other Jesus followers and even the Jewish community. Thus, the opposition against Paul's mission, even at the place of origin of Philippians, can be explained from Jewish and Jewish-Christian distrust of Paul's mission to gentiles, which was not accepted by all Christians at that place.

Paul's withdrawal from the synagogue to the school of Tyrannus can be considered an early step toward the later split, although it might have been caused to a considerable extent by practical reasons. Although Paul was Jewish until the end of his life (see Frey 2012b, 57–62), an initial part of the parting of the ways can already be found in the context of his mission and in his withdrawal from the synagogue to a neutral teaching room.

2.3. Post-Pauline Developments and the Existence of Mixed Communities in Separation from the Synagogue

From the post-Pauline writings (Ephesians, Acts, and 1 Timothy), it obvious that in the decades after Paul's death, there were communities in Ephesus linked with Paul. This is suggested by the address of Ephesians (Eph 1:1), the mention of the Ephesian elders in Acts 20:18–36, and also later by Ignatius, who calls the Ephesians Paul's *συμμύσται* (Ign. *Eph.* 12.2).

If Ephesians is indicative of the situation in that region, we can conclude that some decades after Paul's death, there was a mixed community of Jewish and gentile believers related to Paul's mission. They are now considered a unity, although they had been separated before (Eph 2:11–18). The use of the terms *near* and *remote* still addresses the former distinction between Jews and gentiles from a Jewish perspective, but the separation is a phenomenon of the past, whereas the present is characterized by the unity in Christ. There is no evidence that the community addressed by Ephesians was still considered (or considered itself) part of the Jewish *ethnos* or the diaspora synagogue. It is a new unity, neither Jewish nor pagan, and the relationship with the Jewish *ethnos* seems not to be a major theme or even a struggle at the time of the epistle.

If Ephesians is pseudonymous, the letter most probably dates to the time after 70 CE. Thus, Ephesians already reflects the consequences of the Jewish War and the changes it brought for Jews and related groups. The same is true for the Pastorals, where the community life is also rather unrelated to the life of the synagogue. Only the opponents are linked with elements of Jewish tradition or teaching (Titus 1:14; 3:9). But the practical issues of circumcision and the practice of elements of the Jewish law seem to be unimportant in both Ephesians and the Pastorals.

It is, however, a question whether there were no longer Jewish believers in Ephesus or Jesus followers who still considered themselves part of the synagogue or kept closer connection with the synagogue. But from the fact that Luke still narrates the mission of Apollos and his instruction through Priscilla and Aquila, we may conclude that at his time there was still a group of Jesus followers related to Apollos, that is, influenced by Hellenistic-Jewish ideas and possibly more closely linked with the synagogue than the post-Pauline communities. As we do not have any written sources from those circles, our information is very meager, but in view of the large city and its extensive Jewish *ethnos*, such a diversity of groups of Jesus followers is still the most plausible option.

2.4. Revelation and the Separation of Jewish Jesus Followers from the Synagogue

Roughly the same period as in Ephesians is mirrored by the Johannine writings, the gospel, the epistles, and Revelation, and it is one of the most difficult issues of scholarship, how those writings are related to the Pauline and post-Pauline tradition. Moreover, the relationship between Revelation and the other Johannine writings is a notorious problem of scholarship (see Frey 1993; 2015a).

For the present purpose, Revelation has to be considered first.[12] It is quite clear that the book addresses the situation in communities of the province of Asia, including Ephesus. The author, however, does not simply represent the views of those communities but rather the views of a circle of prophets who are in a minority position in the respective area, strictly opposed to certain tendencies of compromising with the society around. In particular, the seven letters (Rev 2–3) take a critical stance against such a "liberal" position (represented by the Nicolaitans; Rev 2:15; see 2:6) or the prophet called Jezebel (Rev 2:20). Apart from the general charge of fornication (which possibly points to idolatry in general), Rev 2:13 and 2:20 particularly point to the problem of food offered to idols. Whereas the opponents seem to follow a liberal view prefigured already in 1 Cor 8–10, the author condemns such views as inadequate and idolatrous. We

12. See the more extensive discussion in Frey 2013g, 254–56.

cannot really decide whether Jezebel and the Nicolaitans actually drew on Pauline teachings or—perhaps also—on traditions from a Hellenistic Jewish milieu as represented by Apollos.[13] It is clear that the author takes a position strictly opposed to Paul's advice in 1 Cor 8–10. Without explicitly mentioning Paul, Revelation takes a clearly anti-Pauline stance, and in spite of the silence, we can include Paul among those condemned by the author of Revelation. On the other hand, Revelation's interest in purity, in ethical dimensions as well as in the radical distance from anything related to pagan cults, represents rather a Jewish tradition or Jewish (-Christian) mindset. Three or four decades after 70 CE, and even longer after the time of Apollos, the author of Revelation and his circle represent a kind of Jewish Christianity in Ephesus—albeit most probably in a clear separation from the synagogue.

The most difficult problems are posed by Rev 2:9 and 3:9, the strongly negative mention of the *συναγωγὴ τοῦ σατανᾶ*. If this phrase really points to the Jewish synagogue (at Sardis and Philadelphia), the author would be strictly opposed to the Jewish community, claiming that those Jews are not even real Jews, possibly due to their compromising with the civic society and the imperial cult, or even to the denunciation of Jesus followers. Unlike in the Fourth Gospel, the term Ἰουδαῖος is not used in a polemical manner but rather as an ideal that is then contrasted with the "real" synagogal community of Jews. They are said to act inconsistent with the true loyalty to Israel's God (see Koester 2014, 275). In spite of being a Jew himself, the author certainly felt opposed to that group of Jews. For him, the true followers of Jesus are Jews, and as such, they are opposed to the pagan society as well as to the contemporary synagogue.

The author's thought and theology is still strongly shaped by Jewish tradition. He can still be addressed as a Jewish Christian, albeit in separation from and fierce opposition against the synagogue. Revelation thus presupposes a certain act of separation between the local or regional diaspora synagogue(s) and Jewish followers of Jesus, although such an act of repudiation or expulsion is not reported directly in the book of Revelation.

The question about the factors that have led to the present situation (and maybe also to the anti-Jewish phrases in Rev 2:9 and 3:9) can only be answered from a broader historical view. As Peter Hirschberg (1999,

---

13. At least the name Nicolaitans seems to draw on Nikolaos, the name of one of the early Hellenists in the Jerusalem community (see Walter 2002).

106–27) and Marius Heemstra (2010, 105–33) have shown, there is good reason to assume that the events of the Jewish War and the imposition of the so-called *fiscus Iudaicus* triggered the processes of separation between Jewish Jesus followers and the local synagogues. The imposition and (particularly under Domitian) reinforced administration of that new tax only for Jews (thus replacing the former "inner-Jewish" tax to the Jerusalem temple) could cause gentile Christians and or former Godfearers to present themselves definitely as non-Jews. Jewish communities could feel obliged to distance themselves from "dubious" groups (e.g., Jewish Jesus followers, gentile Christians) in order to safeguard their own position in the provincial society after the Jewish War. Most important is a juridical change with regard to membership in synagogues: with the imposition of the *fiscus Iudaicus*, members of a Jewish community were registered in special tax lists, and thus for the first time ever membership in a Jewish community was a matter of public registers, not merely of being accepted by the community itself.

In that situation, local synagogues could follow the interest not "to be associated with a movement that caused a lot of hostility from their pagan environment, which could affect their position in a negative way as well" (Heemstra 2010, 124–25). As a consequence, Jesus followers could get into a precarious legal situation if they were no longer considered members of the traditional Jewish community but still refused participation in certain civic and cultic activities. The respective dangers are clearly expressed in the letters of Pliny to Trajan reflecting the situation in Bithynia at the beginning of the second century (Pliny the Younger, *Ep*. 10.96–97): Christians could be denounced, called to renounce their faith, forced to sacrifice to pagan deities, or even killed. It is quite conceivable that Jesus followers could interpret the distancing tendencies of local synagogues as a hostile act possibly threatening their life or just as a blasphemy. The link between the synagogue and Satan in Rev 2:9 and 3:9 is best explained in this way.

If this explanation is valid, we can see that the processes of separation between the local synagogue and (Jewish and gentile) Jesus followers was multifaceted and influenced not only by theological aspects but—perhaps even more—by wider sociopolitical and legal developments.

2.5. The Johannine Community and the Ἀποσυνάγωγος

The legal situation sketched as a background for understanding Revelation's anti-Jewish polemics is probably also valid for the communities addressed by the Johannine gospel and epistles. In the gospel (though not in the epistles) we find a similarly fierce polemic against the Ἰουδαῖοι.[14] But even more than in Revelation, the debates are strongly focused on theological issues. Reconstructing an appropriate social background is particularly difficult here, as the gospel is a narration of the story of Jesus's earthly ministry presenting the polemic within the world of Jesus and his contemporaries. On the other hand, the Gospel of John is the only New Testament writing that explicitly mentions an act of "expulsion" of Jesus followers from the synagogue, using the otherwise unattested term ἀποσυνάγωγος (John 9:22; 12:42; 16:2–3). It is quite clear, however, that such a phenomenon cannot be part of the world of Jesus and his contemporaries but only an experience of the world of the author and his readers that is now introduced into the narration of Jesus's earthly ministry.

The situation is further complicated by the fact that the Johannine epistles do not mention the Ἰουδαῖοι or related themes, so that the question arises of whether they actually represent a later situation of the community of addressees (thus Brown 1979, 171–74) or of how the difference between the epistles and the gospel can be explained. While some authors (Thyen 1988) suggest that the epistles also reflect an intense debate with synagogal Jews, others (see Frey 2013c, 349–53; Kierspel 2006) point to the fact that the dispute with the Ἰουδαῖοι in the gospel is limited to the dramatic tale of Jesus's public ministry (John 2–12) and—somewhat differently—the passion narrative but is absent in the prologue and the farewell discourses. This may point to the fact that not only the epistles but also the gospel reflect a world with Jewish and gentile opposition against the community and that the expulsion or split as referred to in the gospel is already somewhat in the past.

But due to their literary character and their mutual relationship, the Fourth Gospel and the Johannine epistles pose a number of specific problems, and their mutual relationship and thus also the history of conflicts among the addressees is somewhat unclear. Thus it is difficult to contextualize the debate with the Jews reflected in the gospel. There, the debate with the Jews is a major theme of the dramatic narrative, whereas the relation with the synagogue or Jews is totally unmentioned in the Johannine epistles. As the gospel narrates the story of the earthly Jesus, the debate

14. See on the interpretation of the term and the background of John's usage Frey 2013c.

with the Jews is presented as a debate between Jesus and his contemporary fellow Jews, although a number of terms and aspects adopted in those passages cannot be explained from the time of the earthly Jesus. Scholarship has shown, instead, that the Fourth Gospel is written in retrospect, and a number of aspects from the world of the Johannine addressees are read back into the narrative of Jesus's interaction with his contemporaries. Only on that basis can we use the gospel as a source for the relationship between synagogual Jews and Jesus followers in the time of the composition of the gospel. But we have to ask whether the Fourth Gospel simply mirrors the situation of its time, or how aspects of various developments are comprised in the gospel; it is unclear which elements can be linked with the time of composition and which elements rather reflect earlier periods of the communities or even the time and ministry of the earthly Jesus. In my view, the gospel text combines elements from the world of the earthly Jesus, elements from the world of the author and his addressees, and also elements from the history and experience of the earlier communities (and in particular the Johannine community), and it is often impossible to distinguish clearly between those layers.

While most interpreters read the Johannine corpus and in particular the gospel and the epistles only as testimony to a particular circle of communities and its inner developments, our inquiry of the parting of the ways forces us to consider also their relationship with the earlier Christian tradition, in particular the Pauline tradition and the Pauline school. But this is an even more disputed theme in scholarship.

A number of patterns have been suggested in scholarship (see Hoegen-Rohls 2004; Ueberschaer 2017), but none of them has found general acceptance. While a literary dependence on Paul cannot be demonstrated, some exegetes have pointed to a number of structural analogies between Paul's theology and the Johannine theology, which may suggest some kind of influence.[15] Most striking is the local connection: the Johannine communities developed in an area where communities were strongly shaped by Paul, his mission, and his school (Schnackenburg 1991), and it seems rather improbable that the bearers of the Johannine tradition were completely unaware of the developments based on Paul's ministry. But whereas earlier research could claim that "John stands on Paul's shoul-

15. Thus already Bultmann 1953; later Zeller 1983; Schnelle 1987; and—most recently—Ueberschaer forthcoming.

ders" (Bousset 1913, 180), the observation of the variety of communities of Jesus followers in Ephesus may call for a further distinction: Did the Johannine school really develop in the footsteps of Paul? Did Johannine teaching take control over the Pauline school? Or can we say that the Johannine school developed apart from the Pauline school, simply in its neighborhood? Could we thus reframe the image and say that the Johannine school did not actually stand on Paul's shoulders but—at most—on one of his shoulders?

The difficulties are hard to solve, as we do not have any clear sources for the origins of the Johannine school. Some of its traditions may go back to Palestine and the period before 70, but we should cautiously admit that we cannot trace back structures of the Johannine communities from the end of the first century to the period before 70 CE, or from Asia Minor to Palestine. It is hard to assume that a whole community or school, its writings or their earlier versions, migrated or were transferred from somewhere in Palestine to Asia Minor. We can only see that the traditions were shaped and finally edited there, although some of the material may be adopted from earlier groups and other areas. Thus, the language and theology of the Johannine writings was probably developed within the Ephesian region, mostly in the time after 70 CE. So it could actually adopt some of the developments of the Pauline and post-Pauline tradition.

What can we say about the history of the Johannine communities or school with regard to its connection with synagogal Judaism? The scholarly patterns established by J. Louis Martyn (1979, originally 1968) and Raymond Brown (1979) commonly presuppose that there was a Jewish-Christian community at the very beginning. At the end, with the edition of the gospel and the epistles, there is evidence for a mixed community of Jews and gentiles. The presence of gentile Christians is clearly evidenced in the Johannine epistles (e.g., the personal names of community members in 3 John, Gaius, Demetrius, and Diotrephes) but is also suggested by particular passages in the gospel such as 10:17–18 or 11:51–52. These passages clearly point to the unity of Jewish and gentile believers, thus providing an interesting parallel to the view of Ephesians (Heckel 2004). But in contrast with the later Pauline mission and school, the Johannine communities seem to originate within the framework of the local synagogue. Their early period was probably after Paul's departure, at a time when Pauline circles already lived independent from the synagogue.

In the term *ἀποσυνάγωγος* scholars have found evidence for a traumatic separation between Jewish believers in Christ and synagogal Jews.

Influential was the suggestion that such a separation was caused by a central act, a decision of leading Jewish circles, possibly in Palestine, such as the modification or rephrasing of the Birkat Haminim, the twelfth blessing of the Shemoneh Ezreh, the daily prayer. That rephrasing is attributed to the sages at Yavneh in the period between 70 CE and the Bar Kokhba war, roughly in the time between 80 and 90 CE.[16] The rephrased form of the Jewish prayer would have prohibited Jewish Christians from further participating in the synagogal service, as it contained a curse on all the "heretics" (*minim*) or, in later textual traditions, even of the *nozerim*, that is, "Christians." But the interpretation of the rabbinic tradition about the Birkat Haminim is difficult, and specialists have strongly criticized the bold suggestions regarding the effects of the decisions of Yavneh in the diaspora (see Kimelman 1981; Katz 1984; Horbury 1998). More recent scholarship, therefore, explains the expulsion mentioned in the gospel not from a central act of the rabbis in Palestine but rather from a local split between Jewish (and to some extent Johannine) Jesus followers and the local synagogue (Hengel 1993, 288–91; Frey 2013d, 246–49). Although that divide possibly happened some time before the composition of the gospel and the epistles, it still occupies the thoughts and identity discourses of (at least a considerable part of) the Johannine community members. The debate with the synagogue on Scripture, messianism, and the true identity and dignity of Jesus, therefore, still dominates the Johannine discourse, although other issues are already in view in the gospel (e.g., the farewell discourses) and—even more so—in the epistles.

But with regard to the beginnings we can say that the roots of the foundational parts of the Johannine communities (and probably of the evangelist himself) were within synagogal Judaism. This is confirmed by the christological debates in John 7–8 and 10, where Jewish debates about the Scriptures and the Messiah (see Bauckham 2006, 54–67) are adopted: Where is he to come from? What signs is he to do? What do the Scriptures really say? These textual elements point back to an earlier inner-Jewish debate about Jesus and about the true way of Israel.

The question is, however: For what reason did the split between the Johannine group of Jewish Jesus followers and the local synagogue actually happen? Which factors were decisive in that process? Did the Jews expel their fellow Jews because of their faith in the Messiah Jesus Christ? Did

16. See for discussion Frey 2013c, 346–49.

they consider a separation necessary because the Christology developed by the Jesus followers could be considered a violation of Jewish monotheism? But were there really such clear boundaries of being Jewish? Could the view of Jesus as a divine figure therefore be considered as a step beyond the boundaries of Judaism?[17] Or was the high Christology developed in the Johannine circle only a later phenomenon, a reaction to the expulsion from the synagogue (thus Martyn 1979) or even a consequence of growing pagan influence? In my view, it is more plausible that the high view of Jesus was gradually developed before the split, since all elements of Johannine Christology, including the titles (Messiah, Son of God, Son of Man, Logos), phrases ("I am"), and images (vine, shepherd, temple, etc.) used for Jesus draw on the Scriptures and other Jewish and earlier Christian traditions. If the development of a high view of Jesus as a divine figure was considered a blasphemy at least by some fellow Jews, as is confirmed by elements of the Johannine text (John 5:18; 10:33; 19:7), such a Christology can be considered to be one reason for the split between the synagogue and the Jewish Jesus followers, which was experienced as an expulsion from the body of the large Jewish community and is now reflected in the unique use of the term ἀποσυνάγωγος in the Gospel of John.

As in the case of Revelation, sociopolitical factors may have played an additional role. The *fiscus Iudaicus*, imposed on all Jews after 70 CE, with the inscription in Roman tax lists, triggered the decision regarding who was a Jew and who was not, who belonged to the synagogue and who did not. Especially for the groups in the vicinity of the synagogue, the sympathizers and Godfearers, proselytes and apostates, and thus also for the Jewish and non-Jewish Jesus followers, a kind of "official" decision was required, and we may well imagine that those who had never been Jewish could clarify that they did not have to pay the tax, but also a synagogue could indicate that it did not wish to be associated with some dubious people and did not belong to their community.

For Jewish Christians, this separation would have meant a total change in their social life. They not only had lost their social network, supply of pure food, and all the other things of everyday life, but also the relative security and privileges granted to the Jews by the Roman emperors. At a

17. The more recent views of the high Christology in the Jesus movement as a relatively early development from basically Jewish roots and traditions (Hurtado 2003) do not suggest that such a view would immediately be considered a step beyond Judaism.

distance from the synagogue, the gentile Christian influence could further intensify. An increasing number of community members might now have joined who were rather unaware of Jewish customs and had never observed the Jewish law. Such a mixed community is presupposed in the Johannine texts.

In any case, we should acknowledge that there were a variety of factors that contributed to the separation between synagogal Judaism and the (Jewish) Jesus followers. Whereas the Gospel of John focuses on the theological issues and thus suggests that the whole process of identity formation and demarcation was governed by christological aspects, other sources suggest that the influence of social and political factors was much stronger than the gospel allows.

3. The Pauline and the Johannine School: A Comparison

The further development of Christianity in Ephesus could be described up to the letters of Ignatius and, in particular, Ignatius's epistle to the Ephesians. But we have to stop here and come to some conclusions. For that purpose, we will first enter a brief comparison between the situation in the Johannine school and that in the Pauline and, in particular, the post-Pauline tradition, which is roughly contemporary to Johannine writings.

1. As far as we know, the Pauline communities were mixed communities from the very beginning. There was "neither Jew nor gentile" (Gal 3:28). This may go back to the initial development in Antioch, and Paul continued this view in his missionary enterprise. As a consequence, there was already a considerable gentile Christian influence in the communities founded by Paul, although he firmly considered himself a Jew (see Frey 2012b). In Ephesus, where Paul had not founded the first group of Jesus followers, his decision to teach not in the synagogue but in a neutral location might form an early practical step toward a community independent from the local synagogue. Notably, this was not a split or a final departure from the synagogue, neither for Paul nor for those Jewish Jesus followers who turned with him to the school of Tyrannus. But in time that step could have led to the development of a predominantly gentile-Christian community independent from the synagogue.

2. Whereas the establishment of a community independent from the synagogue can be dated to the mid-50s, and the post-Pauline development shows even stronger gentile Christian tendencies, the separation or expulsion of the Johannine Jesus believers from the local synagogue happened

later, probably only after 70 CE. But not only the time of the separation but also the reasons for the split differ: whereas Paul was concerned about the possibility of addressing the gentiles without further difficulties, the reason for the split in the Johannine circles was primarily christological but probably triggered by further sociopolitical aspects that made the split the ultimate solution of a longer conflict.

3. In the Pauline communities the issue of the Jewish law was intensely debated, at least as far as Jewish Jesus believers were involved or part of the discussion. In the deutero-Pauline epistles, instead, that issue is not a problem anymore. It is apparently solved, probably due to the fact that these communities were predominantly gentile Christian communities without close connections to the Jewish synagogue in their neighborhood. Interestingly, the issue of the law (as a body of precepts to be obeyed or fulfilled) is also almost absent in the Johannine writings. This may point to the fact that the Johannine Christians, once separated from the synagogue, could more easily adopt views and solutions already developed by other Christians, for example, from the Pauline school.

4. It is striking, however, that other issues of Scripture and messianism and thus the debate with the synagogue are still vivid in the Johannine writings. Not the law as such but its interpretation as a testimony for Christ is now disputed. The issues of the Johannine communities with synagogal Judaism differ from those Paul had to debate with his contemporary fellow Jews.

4. Reconceptualizing the Parting of the Ways

With regard to the so-called parting of the ways, we can see from those limited glimpses into the local communities and developments in the region of Ephesus that the separation between synagogal Judaism and Jesus followers was a rather incoherent process, one that happened not at one particular moment, that was influenced by various practical, theological, and sociopolitical reasons, and that differed from group to group and from place to place. While the organizational independence of the Pauline groups from the local synagogues was established rather early, the christological conflict and the separation of the Johannine groups happened considerably later. While the step to a neutral place in Paul's mission was probably a rather pragmatic decision that might not have implied a formal separation but only inaugurated an independent development, the Johannine texts give evidence of a severe conflict that remained traumatic for the Jesus believers involved.

So the very limited look at the Ephesian context can help us to see important aspects for conceptualizing that processes of separation, evaluating their facets in different group contexts and discussing the explicit and implicit reasons and factors that contributed to the final split. Of course, the evidence from other texts and other places will further enrich the picture and show that the processes took much more time: the "parting" may have begun early (at a time when its final results could not be imagined yet) but came to completion only quite late. In any case, the discussion of exemplary cases and case studies can prevent us from all-too generalizing hypotheses about "the" expulsion, as were developed in former generations of scholarship.

Part 4
Reading John as Jews and Christians

Anti-Judaism and the Fourth Gospel Fifteen Years after the Leuven Colloquium

Reimund Bieringer

> Understanding of the text is never definitive but rather remains open because the meaning of scripture discloses itself anew in every future.
> —Rudolf Bultmann, "Is Exegesis without Presuppositions Possible?"

"Anti-Judaism" in the New Testament and more particularly in the Gospel of John is a phenomenon that has been studied extensively for at least fifty years (see the bibliography in Bieringer, Pollefeyt, and Vandecasteele-Vanneuville 2001a; 2001b). Between 1998 and 2001 an externally funded research project at the Catholic University of Leuven offered a new, decidedly interdisciplinary approach to anti-Judaism and the Gospel of John. The climax of the project was an international interdisciplinary conference that resulted in the publication of two books that have become a point of reference in the recent discussion.[1] Moreover, this line of research has been continued in Leuven in the past fifteen years in various ways. This contribution will consist of two parts. In the first part, I will focus on the research project "Anti-Judaism in the Fourth Gospel and Jewish-Christian Dialogue," the resultant conference, and publications. In the second part, I will report on the developments after the conclusion of the project in the area of John and Judaism in Leuven.

---

* In memoriam C. K. Barrett (1917–2011) in the year of his one hundredth birthday

1. Our Leuven research line on anti-Judaism and the Gospel of John was conceived when I heard a paper on this topic by Alan Culpepper during the 1993 Society of Biblical Literature meeting in Washington, DC. I wish to express my gratitude to Alan for his many contributions to this subject and for the invitation to the 2015 Mercer conference on John and Judaism.

1. The Research Project (1998–2001)

In 1997 the Research Foundation Flanders approved a four-year research grant spearheaded by my Leuven colleague Didier Pollefeyt and myself as principal investigators. The grant proposal was titled "The Gospel of John and Jewish-Christian Dialogue: An Interdisciplinary Investigation of the Theology of Jewish-Christian Relations Taking John 8:31–59 as Starting Point" (FWO, 1998–2001). The two major fruits of this research grant were the Leuven colloquium in the year 2000, with its resultant publications and the doctoral dissertation by the project researcher, Frederique Vanneuville (2001; see below). The project was decidedly and deliberately interdisciplinary, and as such it was marked by a real cooperation between biblical exegetes and a theorist of Jewish-Christian dialogue who is at the same time an ethicist.

1.1. The Leuven Colloquium "Anti-Judaism in the Fourth Gospel and Jewish-Christian Dialogue" (2000)

The Leuven colloquium was one of the first conferences of the internet age, making full use of the opportunities this medium provided for the organization of conferences. The conference, which was held in cooperation with the Netherlands School of Advanced Studies in Theology and Religious Sciences (also known as NOSTER), the Institutum Iudaicum, Brussels, and the Belgian National Catholic Commission for Relations with Judaism, was characterized by a unique methodology that was so different that we did not have the courage to follow it again afterwards, even though we remain convinced that it was effective and successful. With the letter of invitation, the potential speakers received a list of eight topics for discussion (see appendix). They were asked to write a paper that would deal with a minimum of two of the eight topics. The papers (nineteen from an exegetical perspective and six from a Jewish-Christian dialogue perspective) of the twenty-five presenters who accepted the invitation[2] were

2. The exegetical papers were by C. K. Barrett, J. Beutler, J. H. Charlesworth, R. F. Collins, R. A. Culpepper, M. C. de Boer, H. J. de Jonge, J. D. G. Dunn, J. Lambrecht, J. Lieu, M. J. J. Menken, S. Motyer, A. Reinhartz, J.-M. Sévrin, P. J. Tomson, G. Van Belle, J. W. van Henten, U. C. von Wahlde, and J. Zumstein. The papers in the field of Jewish-Christian dialogue were by R. Burggraeve, J. Denker, H. H. Henrix, R. Hoet, B. Klappert, and S. Schoon.

collected before the conference, and two-volume sets of the bound hard copies and were distributed to the presenters before the conference. Meanwhile in Leuven, Didier Pollefeyt, Frederique Vandecasteele-Vanneuville, and I spent several weeks reading the papers and identifying key quotations in their texts. We looked for similarities and differences, on the basis of which we determined a structure in and among the papers. This work resulted in a PowerPoint presentation of the core points of all the papers and their contributions to the discussion.

At the conference itself, which was held from January 17–18, 2000, three papers were presented in full during the public opening session, those by James D. G. Dunn (2001), R. Alan Culpepper (2001b), and Simon Schoon (2001). After this the colloquium continued as an expert seminar in the presence of a smaller number of interested students and colleagues who joined the presenters around a big oval table in the senate room of the rector of the Catholic University of Leuven. What was most characteristic for the methodology of the seminar was the fact that the participants did not read their papers, but their positions were presented by Pollefeyt and myself by means of the abovementioned PowerPoint presentation. This allowed us to discuss the content according to the central themes represented in the papers, which became the backbone of our introductory article in the book (Bieringer, Pollefeyt, and Vandecasteele-Vanneuville 2001c; 2001d). By virtue of this methodology, the discussion was very focused, and the invited scholars enjoyed extended time for seminar discussions among one another and with the audience.

The Leuven project was characterized by a strongly interdisciplinary perspective, which resulted in the need to supplement historical and literary-critical studies of the Gospel of John with a hermeneutical approach. This challenge is also present in the collection of contributions, which was published immediately after the colloquium.

1.2. The Publications titled *Anti-Judaism and the Fourth Gospel* (2001)

After the conference our research team, Pollefeyt, Vandecasteele-Vanneuville, and I, composed the introductory article of the planned volume of the conference papers (Bieringer, Pollefeyt, and Vandecasteele-Vanneuville 2001c; 2001d).[3] As none of us had participated in the colloquium with a

3. An adapted and abridged version of the introductory article is also available

paper, in this introductory article we presented our position in dialogue with all the papers to be published in the book. The full book with all the twenty-four contributions plus our introductory article was accepted for publication by Deo Publishing, a new publisher that worked closely with NOSTER at the time. When the book was first published in 2001 it had become volume one of the Jewish and Christian Heritage series published by Royal Van Gorcum. Since then the book has migrated to Brill (Bieringer, Pollefeyt, and Vandecasteele-Vanneuville 2001b). In addition to the hardcover edition, a concise paperback edition with thirteen of the twenty-five contributions (all taken from the exegetical part) was published by Westminster John Knox on the basis of an agreement between publishing houses and with no involvement of the editors of the volume. We were not consulted in the decision about which articles were to be taken up into the original edition (Bieringer, Pollefeyt, and Vandecasteele-Vanneuville 2001b). The book publication was supported by a website featuring the bibliography, the table of contents of each edition of the book, a list of book reviews, and an excerpt of the introductory article (Bieringer, Pollefeyt, & Vandecasteele-Vanneuville 2001c; 2001d).[4] Between 2001 and 2005 about twenty-five book reviews appeared in a broad spectrum of exegetical journals.[5]

The impact of the book is very difficult to gauge. To be sure, it appears in a large number of bibliographies and in many synthetic bibliographical footnotes as an informative volume on John and anti-Judaism. For some time and sometimes still today it has been referred to as a book that offers the state of the question. As such it seems to be a welcome reference work that saves many authors the work of a composing a *status quaestionis* on the subject. The diversity of the contributions of the book offers a broad spectrum of positions that has something to offer for everyone. While the

---

online: Reimund Bieringer, Didier Pollefeyt, and Frederique Vandecasteele-Vanneuville, "Wrestling with Johannine Anti-Judaism: A Hermeneutical Framework for the Analysis of the Current Debate," http://tinyurl.com/SBL0398b.

4. "Ancient Judaism and the Fourth Gospel" n.d.

5. De Kruijf 2001; Lincoln 2002; Senior 2002; Burnett 2002; Danker 2002; Gutiérrez 2002; Ashton 2002; Kysar 2002; Edwards 2002; van Tilborg 2002; Porter 2002; Smalley 2002; Scholtissek 2002; 2003; 2004; Fuchs 2003; Köstenberger 2003; de Ruyter 2003; Good 2003; Labahn 2003; van der Watt 2004; Chilton 2004; Devillers 2004; Gourgues 2005.

general references to the book are mostly in summary fashion, the specialized academic interaction is focused on individual scholars' contributions.

The actual contribution of the volume to the scholarly discussion on John and anti-Judaism can perhaps be summarized in the following five points:

1. The volume documents the great variety of positions among contemporary scholars concerning the issue: Is/was the Gospel of John anti-Jewish?
2. The volume clearly illustrates the choice before which the gospel places every reader/interpreter, namely: Do we defend John or consider John as part of the problem (dangerous potential)? Here again the book is a mirror image of the great diversity of answers among contemporary scholars.
3. The book is a strong plea for contextualizing the problem of John and anti-Judaism, and as such it is a warning against all those who use decontextualized readings to construct a clear allegedly Johannine position, either to use it in support of their own highly problematic views or to condemn the alleged Johannine anti-Judaism.
4. The volume also is a clear witness to the need of hermeneutics in any exegetically and theologically responsible approach to John and anti-Judaism. This remains true even if we have to admit that the specific hermeneutical approach spearheaded in the introductory article of the book was far from gathering a following.
5. The volume prefigures the subsequent shift of focus from "John and anti-Judaism" to "John and Judaism," which is the consequence of the realization that before one wants to speak in earnest about John and anti-Judaism, one needs to pay close attention to John and Judaism.[6]

We also need to ask what got lost or was opposed as much as what was not taken note of and continues to be a challenge fifteen years later. We have identified five areas to be discussed here: the interdisciplinary approach, the interfaith dimension, the ecumenical dimension, the theological challenge, and the need for hermeneutics. First and foremost, we

6. It may be noted that the analogous publication to *John and Anti-Judaism* about Paul, which was edited by Bieringer and Pollefeyt, follows this trend and is titled *Paul and Judaism* (Bieringer and Pollefeyt 2012a).

need to mention the interdisciplinary character of the conference and the volume. This clearly was one of the most important challenges that the conference and the volume offered. It is symptomatic that this interdisciplinary character was already lost in the paperback edition where only contributions from one discipline, namely, biblical exegesis, were retained. Even the complete volume seems to have been received more strongly in exegetical circles than in those of Jewish-Christian or Christian-Jewish circles. Despite the efforts of the project and the colloquium, we do not see a lasting effect of interdisciplinary dialogue and cooperation on this topic, which is needed more today than ever before.

There was also an initial, timid interfaith dimension, which was most clearly reflected in the concluding ritual of the conference. This dimension has since then increased in international critical scholarship (see, e.g., Donahue 2005) and is thankfully also an important dimension of the present volume.

In fact, the colloquium and the book had a stronger albeit implicit intra-Christian ecumenical dimension, which admittedly, however, did not transcend what is (and was already fifteen years ago) a reality in academic circles of New Testament scholars, namely, that scholars from different Christian traditions freely communicate and exchange scholarly views without all too quickly focusing on what divides them. Neither the interfaith nor the inner-Christian ecumenical dimensions of this issue have received much attention in the past fifteen years. The attempts noticeable in some parts of the conference and the book to suggest that an exclusively historical contextualization of the problem is not sufficient for a scholarly debate on "John and Anti-Judaism" already met with a certain skepticism during the conference. This has not changed in the fifteen years of effects of the book on scholarship.

Our research project and our contribution to the conference volume started from the premise that in a theological perspective readers of the Gospel of John who accept that it has a revelatory authority have to choose between three possibilities: (1) John is anti-Jewish (supersessionist), and this is authoritative for believers; (2) John is not anti-Jewish (supersessionist), and this is authoritative for believers, and (3) John is anti-Jewish (supersessionist), and this is not authoritative for believers.[7] To our

7. The fourth logical possibility (John is not anti-Jewish [supersessionist], and this is not authoritative for believers) is not considered in the discussion. It would imply

knowledge in academic scholarship there is no one who holds that those who consider the Gospel of John to have revelatory authority need to be anti-Jewish or supersessionist. They reach this goal by either claiming that the gospel is not anti-Jewish or by holding that the gospel is anti-Jewish but that these anti-Jewish aspects themselves have no revelatory authority and are therefore not binding for believers. Most of scholarship has invested its efforts in trying to demonstrate that the gospel of John is not anti-Jewish. But as scholarship in general and the Leuven colloquium as well as the collection of essays in particular demonstrated, there are also those who admit that there are issues or problems in the gospel but try to explain them as not binding for the contemporary reader since they were contextual elements of a particular conflict situation between the first-century synagogue and the church that have since changed, or they were part of an inner-Jewish dispute. However, the research project, the introductory article, and the dissertation that was completed as part of the project research came to the conclusion that there is a dangerous potential in the theology of the Gospel of John that goes beyond the first-century conflict and inner-Jewish dispute, a dangerous potential that continues to be an issue in the world before the text and that can only be addressed adequately in a hermeneutical approach. After fifteen years we need to face the fact that this aspect of the project has hardly been engaged in research, which has only tended to revisit previous positions.

Finally, we also note that our plea for a theological-hermeneutical reading of the issue of anti-Judaism and the Gospel of John that follows, builds on, or replaces the historical-hermeneutical readings that have generally been practiced went largely unheeded. This is, of course, closely related to the previous point. The conviction that historical criticism can solve the issue has continued to be the prevalent position in the time since the colloquium. Theological-hermeneutical studies, if they are at all seen as necessary, are considered to be the responsibility of systematic theologians, not of exegetes.

Looking back over the past (more or less) fifteen years of research in the area of John and (anti-)Judaism we realize that despite the frequent references to the collective volume *Anti-Judaism and the Fourth Gospel*,

---

that people are defending being anti-Jewish or supersessionist against the Gospel of John, which they understand as not anti-Jewish or not supersessionist.

the unique contributions of the book have not had a lasting effect on the ongoing research in this area.

2. Ongoing Research in the Area of John and (Anti-)Judaism in Leuven (2000–2016)

In the second part of this contribution we shall give an overview of the continuation of the research carried out in Leuven in the area of John and (anti-)Judaism since the Leuven colloquium in 2000. This section will be subdivided into two parts. The first will focus on the last part of the project research until about 2005. The second part will treat the continuation and new developments in Leuven research in this area.

2.1. Research in the Period Immediately Following the Colloquium (2000–2005)

In addition to composing their own introductory article for the collection of the colloquium papers and editing those papers for publication, the researchers of the project made two important additional contributions to the research, the completion of a doctoral dissertation and the drafting of a comprehensive article.

In the year after the colloquium, project researcher Vanneuville (2001) completed and defended her doctoral dissertation, titled "Jesus and 'the Jews' in John 8:31–59: An Interdisciplinary Investigation into the Problem of Anti-Judaism in the Gospel of John." This historical and literary-critical study of John 8:31–59 in light of the anti-Jewish potential of this text includes a hermeneutical approach. In the epilogue the author writes:

> Our main concern was to develop a Christology that is not supersessionist and not simply exclusivist, consciously taking into account the Jewish perspective, in order to deal with the potential violence towards Judaism in Christian identity affirmation as developed by the Fourth Evangelist. In the present study we have been looking for the key to such a hermeneutics in the theology of the Fourth Gospel itself.

At the end of the epilogue she concludes: "In this study we have argued that John's gospel itself contains elements that can overcome its exclusivist claims in order to restore the primacy of God's dream of salvation for all in his message" (222–23).

The concluding article of the project, authored by Pollefeyt and myself, was published in the *Festschrift* for Johannes Beutler in 2004.[8] In this contribution we attempt to make a synthesis of the findings of our project and in important points go beyond our introductory article to *Anti-Judaism and the Fourth Gospel.* We argue that in the context of this gospel, the term οἱ Ἰουδαῖοι has a very specific, unprecedented meaning. It is clear that the polemic that is expressed by means of this term does not go against οἱ Ιουδαῖοι as an ethnic designation or against Judaism as a faith. Rather, the evangelist frequently refers to οἱ Ἰουδαῖοι as people who share the same ἔθνος and faith tradition as he but who fundamentally differ from him by not becoming disciples of Jesus as the Christ and the Son of God. It is against these people that the evangelist uses the expression οἱ Ἰουδαῖοι. In fact, the evangelist considers himself and the disciples of Jesus to be more faithful to the faith tradition of his own Jewish people than those who do not follow Jesus. In the words of the 2004 article:

> we note that the fourth gospel is in no way opposed to Judaism as an ethnic or racial entity nor to Judaism as a religion as such. The gospel of John is never critical of all[9] the Jews of his time or of previous centuries. His distinction within the Jewish people between those who are faithful to God's covenant and those who are not reminds us of a central feature of the Biblical tradition where the Israelites or the Jews are constantly

8. For other contributions of the same period, see a short entry on "Hoi Ioudaioi" in the *Dictionary of Jewish-Christian Relations* (Pollefeyt and Bieringer 2005). See also Pollefeyt 2001, 2002.

9. It should, however be noted, that, by using οἱ Ἰουδαῖοι about seventy times in his gospel, by using it with frequently changing referents, and by often using it in a negative sense, the evangelist has created a potentially dangerous expression. For the frequency of the expression and its general undifferentiated semantic quality facilitate the formation of stereotypes and generalizations. When using the expression οἱ Ἰουδαῖοι with a negative connotation, he restricts it to one group within Judaism, namely, his own contemporaries and neighbors who did not believe in Jesus. By using such a general expression for such a specific group, he creates the danger that his statements might be generalized to all the Jews of all places and times. Perhaps we even need to admit that it would be in keeping with the logic of the gospel (though not consciously intended) to transfer the statements about οἱ Ἰουδαῖοι to all the members of the Jewish people (of all places and times) who decide not to believe in Jesus. It is for this reason that the problem of John and anti-Judaism cannot simply be solved by placing the anti-Jewish statements into their original historical context.

> reproached for their infidelity to the covenant with God. (Bieringer and Pollefeyt 2004, 20)

The most important implication of this is that it would be more precise to speak of "anti-unbelievers-in-Jesus-ism" instead of anti-Judaism.

In addition to this terminological clarification, in our article we also discuss whether this interpretation of οἱ Ἰουδαῖοι makes John's polemic any less dangerous. The result of our line of argument is that this "anti-unbelievers-in-Jesus-ism" has at least as much dangerous potential as what is called anti-Judaism.[10] The problem is that the sole criterion for dividing the Jews into good ones (disciples) and bad ones (unbelievers) is whether they believe in Jesus or not. The Fourth Evangelist proves to be incapable of thinking of any explanation for Jewish unbelief in Jesus except their alleged moral corruptness and their lack of understanding of or their infidelity to their own Jewish faith.[11]

We state in our 2004 article:

> Faith in Jesus thus becomes the litmus test for any faithful Jew. Thus the fourth gospel leaves no room for the possibility of people who are faithful to their Jewish faith but do not believe in Jesus. In addition and closely related, the Gospel of John gives as the deepest reason for a person's refusal to believe in Jesus human sinfulness.[12] In this way of thinking, all those who refuse to believe in Jesus prove by their refusal that they are morally corrupt.[13] Virtuous unbelievers (in Jesus) are unthinkable in

10. "Our interpretation of the fourth gospel also implies that the harsh reproaches which the Johannine Jesus addresses to 'the Jews' are, in John's perspective, not addressed to Judaism as such, but to those whom the evangelist considers to be unfaithful to their own Jewish faith. He could have addressed most of those reproaches to many Jews of the pre-Jesus period as well" (Bieringer and Pollefeyt 2004, 20). For instance, they do not keep the law (7:19); have never heard God's voice or seen his form and do not have God's word abiding in them (5:37–38); do not know God (7:28; 8:19–55; 15:21; 16:3); are from below (8:23); do not know the truth (8:32), are from their father, the devil, and choose to do their father's desires (8:44); and hate the Father (15:23–24).

11. See, however, Rom 11:11, where the apostle Paul understands Jewish unbelief in Jesus as part of God's plan to bring the gentiles into the church.

12. See "Christology and anthropology are thus inseparably linked in the Fourth Gospel. Who people are is determined by their response to Jesus" (O'Day 1995, 553). The surprising thing is that she does not seem to see anything wrong with this.

13. In later theological debates about this issue, provision was made for the pos-

> such an approach. This religiously and ethically disowns and disinherits all those Jews who decide not to believe in Jesus and leaves no room for any authentic Jewish faith for those who have chosen not to become followers of Jesus. (Bieringer and Pollefeyt 2004, 21–22; for a similar argument see also Bieringer 2005)

It is clear that all those who follow this line of argument by allowing their own faith perspective to be challenged by the faith of Jewish believers are faced with very fundamental questions concerning the ethical foundations of their own faith documents and ultimately faith itself. In 2004 we formulated it as follows,

> A challenge for Jewish-Christian dialogue is how it is possible to develop a Christology which does not continue to establish the authenticity of the Christian faith in Jesus at the cost of authentic Jewish faith. In the same way, Jewish-Christian dialogue will only be possible if Jewish believers are found ready to accept that scripture allows for the possibility of authentically embracing faith in Jesus as Messiah and Son of God. (Bieringer and Pollefeyt 2004, 22; see also Reinhartz 2001a, 88–95; Diefenbach 2002, 258–62)[14]

---

sibility that a person who rejects faith in Jesus might ultimately be guided by a misunderstanding, so that the person de facto is not rejecting Jesus but an erroneous image of Jesus. This position assumes that any virtuous person who would come to know Jesus truly and without distortions would come to faith in him. The question must be raised whether we need to go one step further and assume that it is also possible that under certain circumstances a person who is morally good and has a correct image of Jesus might still not believe in Jesus as Messiah and Son of God.

14. Reinhartz (2001a, 89) works out "the Jews' point of view" in John 8:31–59 along the lines of monotheism and monolatry and identifies "the basic issue at stake" as "whether or not Jesus and the claims made for him are an enhancement of monotheism, that is, a 'new and improved' but fundamentally recognizable revelation or, conversely, a radical infringement on this basic Jewish belief" (95). We are convinced that the challenge is for Jews and Christians to accept that the respectively other arrives at opposite answers to this question and has, at least in their own judgement, authentic reasons for doing so. See also the section "3.2.3.2 Der exklusive Glaubensanspruch Israels" in Diefenbach 2002, 258–62. In an attempt to understand how contemporary Jewish believers at the time of Jesus might have reacted to the claims of Jesus he arrives at the conclusion: "'Die Juden' wollten so einerseits den exklusiven monotheistischen Glauben Israels nach innen wahren und andererseits sich als Glaubensgemeinschaft konsolidieren. Denn die obsolete inklusive Glaubensüberzeugung Jesu, er sei der 'Sohn Gottes' und Gott Jahwe sein Vater, musste den 'Juden' zur Zeit Jesu als nicht

Finally, we also dealt with the question of what responsible but honest interpreters can be expected to do with the problematic, potentially violent dimensions of authoritative texts of their own (or others') traditions. The final point that we reached in this article is put into words as follows:

> we are convinced that one may not reduce the Gospel of John to its anti-Jewish dimensions, nor overlook the universal concern of God's saving love, expressed so eloquently by the Fourth Evangelist. The Johannine Jesus says about himself: "I came that they may have life and have it abundantly" (John 10:10). God's ultimate concern is life and salvation for the world in an all-inclusive sense. We understand God's desire of salvation for all to be so strong that the rejection of Christ as mediator of salvation is not necessarily a reason for excluding people from salvation. (Bieringer and Pollefeyt 2004, 31–32; see also Bieringer, Pollefeyt, and Vandecasteele-Vanneuville 2001c, 38–44)

In the first years after the scheduled end of the funded research project, very significant developments happened in a few additional publications. A more nuanced understanding of both the semantics of οἱ Ἰουδαῖοι and the theological background of the alleged Johannine anti-Judaism was proposed. Finally, the biblical hermeneutics of the project were deepened as a hermeneutics of life. In this period the foundations were deepened for our research of the following ten years.

2.2. Continuation of the Leuven Research after the Completion of the Project (2006–2016)

In the period between 2006 and 2016 (and beyond) we distinguish two phases. In the first we turned to the letters of Paul with analogous research questions (2006–2011), only to return to different aspects in Johannine studies that continued and deepened the earlier project (2011–2016).

2.2.1. Paul and Judaism

In 2007 both the Research Council of Katholieke Universiteit Leuven and the Research Foundation Flanders approved a research project titled

---

thorakonform erscheinen" (260). This, however, raises the question how it was possible that some Jews were able to accept Jesus's claims and believe in him.

"New Perspectives on Paul and the Jews: A Critical Investigation into the Significance of the Letters of Paul in Light of the Historical Parting of the Ways between Judaism and Christianity with Particular Attention Paid to 2 Cor 3:6.7–18 in Light of Jewish-Christian Dialogue." The project was again directed by Didier Pollefeyt and me (Bieringer and Pollefeyt 2007–2010). We conceived this research project in close continuity with the previous project.

In the project proposal we wrote the following:

> The intended project is a logical continuation of our earlier research in so far as we shall concentrate on the role of the theology of Paul in the process of early Christian self-definition in relation to contemporary Judaism. The research gives special attention to 2 Cor 3:6.7–18, a text which has not played an important role in the context of research on Paul's relationship to the Jewish people (cf. Duff 2004).

We formulated the research question as follows: What does 2 Cor 3:6, 7–18 tell us about the continuity or discontinuity between Paul's own "Jewish faith" and his newfound faith in Jesus? We described the significance of this project as follows: "The answer to this question has significant implications concerning the crucial question for Jewish-Christian dialogue, namely whether Paul became the founder of Christianity in this process of separation while Jesus had stayed completely within the boundaries of Judaism." In an initial way we described the intended contribution of the project as follows:

> The innovative nature of this project is to be found in the critical rejection of the prevalent paradigm which dissolves the tension between Paul and Judaism by understanding Paul exclusively as being in harmony with his Jewish background (much of the so-called "New Perspective"). In the alternative position which our research shall develop it is, however, not our intention to support reactionary tendencies which deconstruct the "New Perspective" in order to simply reaffirm Christian identity against Judaism (cf. Gundry, 2005).

This research project was again characterized by a strong interdisciplinary dimension and by a decidedly hermeneutical approach. It resulted in two conference volumes (Bieringer and Pollefeyt 2012a; Bieringer et al. 2014) and two essentially interdisciplinary doctoral dissertations, one with a strong focus on the study of Christian-Jewish dialogue (Bolton 2011) and one with a primarily biblical-hermeneutical approach (Nathan 2010; see also Nathan and Bieringer 2011).

The interdisciplinary and hermeneutical preferences of this project and of its research results are evident in the concluding section of the introductory contribution by Pollefeyt and me in the first conference volume:

> In our understanding, from a Normativity of the Future approach, we are encouraged by our vision of the future to position ourselves on the borderlands of inclusivism-pluralism, certainly as it concerns the Jewish-Christian relationship. God is in a permanent relationship with the Jewish people. That guarantees their salvation. Where Paul lost sight of that in his writings, the contemporary church community needs to enter into constructive dialogue with him in light of his own future vision. We can also agree with those who, like Sanders, critique the all too common power plays attendant to soteriological debates. Christ does not need to save everybody directly in order for him to remain as the Christ. God has many ways to express his commitment and love to creation. Regaining a theocentric vision, the real *telos* of Paul's new creation, is actually continuing the Pauline project and exploring further the avenues he all too vaguely mapped out. (Bieringer and Pollefeyt 2012b, 14)

By way of conclusion we would like to stress that the "Paul and Judaism" project benefited enormously from the preceding "anti-Judaism and the Fourth Gospel" research. At the same time its focus almost automatically became broader as the narrow focus on anti-Judaism or anti-Jewish potential was replaced by the new focus on Judaism as a whole. This widened perspective became crucial for the research of the following years.

2.2.2. The Return to the Gospel of John

After a five-year excursus into the realm of Paul and Judaism, our research returned to the Gospel of John by many avenues and in a much broader perspective. Our research reached its broadest perspective in our attempt to earn research funds through a GOA[15] grant from the Research Council of Katholieke Universiteit Leuven. The project proposal was titled "Dialogue as Future—The Future of the Dialogues: Towards an Adequate Hermeneutics of Sacred Texts in Jewish-Christian, Ecumenical and

15. GOA stands for "geconcerteerde onderzoeksactie," i.e., concerted research programme.

Christian-Muslim Dialogues." In this interdisciplinary research program Pollefeyt and I proposed to cooperate with Peter De Mey, a specialist in inner-Christian ecumenical theology, and Maha El Kaisy, a researcher in Islamic studies. This proposal was not able to garner support from the funding body and as a result was never carried out. The intended research was described as follows in the research proposal:

> We will investigate *how* Jewish-Christian and ecumenical dialogues are impacted by interpretations of the Bible and the way in which this can *mutatis mutandis* also be said of the Qur'an in Christian-Muslim dialogue. But we will also examine the ways in which religious concepts of the future function or might function in biblical studies/Qur'an studies and how a future-oriented hermeneutics can inform the study of Jewish-Christian, ecumenical and Christian-Muslim dialogues. Conversely, we will analyse how research on these dialogues informs, challenges and possibly transforms the future-oriented biblical hermeneutics. *Four research groups*—which are embedded in biblical theology, pastoral theology, systematic theology and religious studies respectively—plan on following the thematic framework of the future-oriented hermeneutics as a means of focusing and structuring their research in the coming years, while employing the expertise and critical mass they have already acquired in previous years.

With this proposal our research agenda had reached its broadest perspective. Its goals were only partially realized in a much smaller research project, which we shall describe in the next section.

2.2.3. The Dialogues Project

In 2013 the Research Council of the Catholic University of Leuven approved a four-year interdisciplinary project titled "New Hermeneutics for Renewed Dialogues. A Catholic Perspective on Crucial Theological Issues in Jewish-Christian and Ecumenical Dialogues in the Perspective of a Future-Oriented Interpretation of Key Johannine Texts" (2013–2016). The promoters of this project were Pollefeyt (Jewish-Christian dialogue), De Mey (ecumenism), and I (exegesis). There were three researchers working in this project: Viorel Coman (2016) worked on the issue of the *filioque*, including its postulated Johannine background, in an Eastern Orthodox-Roman Catholic dialogue perspective. Laura Tack (John and Jewish-Christian dialogue) and a postdoctoral researcher, Marilou Ibita, concentrated on the dimension of Jewish-Christian dialogue, education, and exegesis. In what follows, due to our focus in this contribution, we shall focus on the work of Tack and Ibita.

Tack (2015) wrote her dissertation on John 14:6 in exegetical and Jewish-Christian dialogue perspective. She interprets the "way" in Johannine, synoptic, and Philonic perspective as the way to the Father and as such as relational. According to her, an isolated reading of "the way" in 14:6 as a proof text is particularly dangerous because the role of the Father in the process of salvation is not focused on (see, however, 6:44) and because nothing is said about the Spirit in this verse. "Truth" is equally interpreted as relational, as the truth concerning Jesus's identity, which is shaped in relationship with the Father. Tack interprets "life" as a gift that comes forth from the loving union between the Father and the Son. As relational terms, "way," "truth," and "life" are thus not to be read as exclusively referring to the Son but as relational, demonstrating how the Son is way, truth, and life in relation to the Father, illustrating their unity in diversity. Tack notes the significant absence of the Spirit or Paraclete in this context.

Tack further argues that the "I am" sayings and 14:6 in particular are not to be understood as theophanic or epiphanic, nor as identification formulae (A = B) but as metaphoric (A is B and is not B), which implies that in John 14:6 Jesus is not presented simply as identical with way, truth, and life in the literal sense. Tack interprets the *καί* between way, truth, life as epexegetic. This implies that the nouns "truth" and "life" explain in which way Jesus is seen as the way. Moreover, the tension and ambiguity created by the metaphors suggest in the context of the entire gospel that Jesus's identity is shaped by his relationship with the Father, that Jesus is part of the dynamic and relational unity in diversity between Father and Son. By formulating 14:6 in a christocentric way, however, without making explicit the relations of the Son with the Father and the Spirit, the author of this verse created a dangerous potential of Christomonism. Tack tries to counter this dangerous potential in her hermeneutical part by thoroughly contextualizing the verse and reading it in light of the vision of 14:2–3, the many "mansions" in the Father's house, which she reads as inclusive.

In a recent contribution by Ibita (2015b; see also Ibita 2014; 2015a; 2017), under the title "The 'I Am' Sayings at the Johannine Farewell Meal: Exploring the Possible Influence of Segregative Association Meals and the Implications for Jewish-Christian Dialogue," she studies the statement "no one comes to the Father except through me" in John 14:6b in its literary context of a meal. She applies Claude Grignon's concept of "segregative commensality" to John 14:6b. "This kind of exclusivity in a segregative meal can help provide the context in understanding Jn 14:6, a part of the Johannine Farewell Discourse located in a meal setting" (2015b, 11). Ibita understands these exclusive claims as a strong affirmation of the identity of the Johannine community. This need to affirm their identity can explain the exclusive claims of 14:6b, but its dangerous potential for later readers needs to be dealt with separately. Ibita tries to achieve this by following the future-oriented hermeneutics that we developed in the introductory article in *Anti-Judaism and the Fourth Gospel* (see also Bieringer and Elsbernd, 2010).

2.2.4. The Docetism Project

In 2013 the Research Foundation Flanders approved a grant proposal submitted by my Leuven colleague Joseph Verheyden and me and titled: "Hunting Down a Ghost: A Critical Study of the Concept of Docetism and Its Use and Abuse in Ancient and Modern Discussions on Early Christian Christology and Soteriology." In the grant proposal we wrote:

> the hypothesis that will be defended here is that "Docetism" is only a useful term if it is understood to denote a "range" of phenomena, teachings and arguments, not the name of a heresy or a clearly defined group of people. While this hypothesis was not proposed here for the first time, it has never been tested in detail nor has it been systematically worked out taking into consideration the latest developments in research.

While this project is mainly focused on the second-century evidence (the doctoral research of this project concentrates on the letters of Ignatius), there is also a Johannine dimension. The project proposal describes the goal of this part as follows:

> The central question will be whether at the background of certain … Johannine texts, the alleged "docetic" controversies or sensitivities could have played a role.… Concerning the Fourth Gospel and 1–2 John … [we] will investigate certain texts which some scholars perceived (rightly or wrongly) as "docetic" (cf. Käsemann 1980) or "anti-docetic" (Schnelle 1987).… We will study whether "docetism" is nothing more than a projection by modern scholars. If the latter is the case, we need to study the conditions and reasons of the origin of such allegations.

In this project Ines Luthe (now Jäger) (2013–2017) is preparing a doctoral dissertation with the working title “In Search for Docetism: A Critical Study of the History of Research, with Special Attention to Ignatius of Antioch and the Johannine Literature.” While not directly related to anti-Judaism, the question of a docetic or antidocetic understanding of the Gospel of John has obvious important implications for the issue of John’s relationship to Judaism (see appendix, no. 3, p. 263).

At the 2014 joint meeting of the international Society of Biblical Literature and European Association of Biblical Studies we organized a workshop on docetism and the Gospel of John. In December 2014 we held an expert seminar on docetism titled “The Quest for an Elusive Phenomenon: Docetism in the Early Church” (Leuven, December 3–5, 2014). During the Oxford Patristics Conference in August 2015 we organized a workshop on early-Christian Christologies with special focus on docetism. The papers of both seminars have been collected in a publication (Verheyden et al. 2017). In my own contributions to the project I have studied John 1:14 and the passion narrative and reached the preliminary conclusion that these Johannine texts do not have anything to do with what has been called docetism (Bieringer 2017).

2.2.5. The Kosmos Project

While the meaning of οἱ Ἰουδαῖοι has been frequently and extensively studied, the same cannot be said for *ὁ κόσμος* (see Kierspel 2006). This doctoral project, which is being carried out by Joan Infante (2017), investigates the meaning of *ὁ κόσμος* against the background of conflict studies from a social-science perspective. The results of this project will have important implications for the understanding of οἱ Ἰουδαῖοι and for the ethnic versus transethnic debate (see below).

2.2.6. The Ethnicities in the Gospel of John Project

The most recent project intends to focus on the concept of ethnicity in the Gospel of John. The goal is to study how the Fourth Gospel constructs ethnicity in comparison to Paul in his letters. Special attention will be given to the question how the concept of ethnicity (Fortes 2016–2019; Buell 2005; 2010, 159–90; Nasrallah and Fiorenza 2010; Wan 2010, 129–58; Töllner 2007; Hall 2002) can help or hinder the understanding of οἱ Ἰουδαῖοι in the Gospel of John. This will require a study of Ἰουδαῖοι in comparison to the

Samaritans (4:1–42), the Ἕλληνες (7:35; 12:20), the Romans (11:48), and the *κόσμος* (esp. 12:19). A careful analysis of 11:47–52 will also be required in comparison to Gal 3:28. In his Society for New Testament Studies main paper in Amsterdam, David G. Horrell (2016) spoke of "a recurring and persistent depiction—namely a dichotomy between an ethnically particular Judaism and a trans-ethnic, inclusive universal Christianity" and concluded, "its basic form and prominence seem to endure, up to the present-day." The main question will be how this lens of ethnicity and of the ethnic versus transethnic dichotomy can contribute to the John and anti-Judaism debate.

3. Conclusion

The goal of the Leuven colloquium was to foster dialogue between representatives of the major positions and approaches to the issue of "anti-Judaism in the Gospel of John," both in the perspective of exegesis and in Jewish-Christian dialogue. At the same time, in our research team in Leuven, we had a clear position of our own, which we presented in the introductory article of the book and which we developed further after the conference. In this contribution we opted for a position that accepts that there are anti-Jewish elements in the Gospel of John but at the same time tried to show that these elements are in tension with the inclusive future horizon or vision that, at least in our reconstruction, the gospel projects. In a later publication we nuanced this position considerably. We emphasized that John's anti-Judaism is a dangerous potential. We tried to give a more precise description of the meaning of "anti-Judaism," which in our conviction was not ethnic, nor religious, but rather what one might call ethical(-religious), as it distinguishes between genuine and not genuine Jews, admitting that this understanding uncovers a potentially even more dangerous dimension of Johannine "anti-Judaism." Finally, we discussed the inclusive potential of the gospel on a deeper theological level.

Since then in Leuven we have been involved in research that intends to contextualize the issue of "anti-Judaism and the Fourth Gospel" by comparing it to the letters of Paul, by viewing it in the context of John's use of *κόσμος*, by relating it to the docetism discussion, and by seeing it in light of constructions of ethnicity. In addition, we have continuously developed the future-oriented hermeneutics that we proposed in 2001 as a way of confronting the anti-Jewish potential on a theological level.

One other element that this overview of the past years brought to my awareness is how difficult it is to work in a truly interdisciplinary way. It seems that sixteen years after the conference the contributions of the Jewish-Christian dialogue scholars have receded into the background—not the least since they are only found in the much less accessible full edition of the papers. If the impact of the papers of the conference on exegetical research is already difficult to measure, as we have seen, their impact on the study of Jewish-Christian dialogue is even more difficult to gauge. Then we are not even focusing on the question of the impact on preaching or catechesis or Christian-Jewish/Jewish-Christian dialogues as such. It is, however, a long-term effect of the Leuven colloquium that I have been asked to become a member of the "Promise, Land and Hope Project: Jews and Christians Seeking Understanding to Enable Constructive Dialogue, within the International Council of Christians and Jews."

My last remark is focused on the future. In her contribution to this volume, Adele Reinhartz moves from a purely past-oriented, static understanding of the reconstruction of the Johannine community to a future-oriented, dynamic reading of what the author of John would envision the Johannine community to be. If I understand correctly, her future-oriented reading of the Johannine community is author-centered. In our introductory article to *Anti-Judaism and the Fourth Gospel*, which was published in both volumes, we proposed a future-oriented or vision-oriented reading of the elements of anti-Judaism in the Fourth Gospel. I would call our future-oriented hermeneutic reader-centered. This proposal did not have any real impact on the scholarly echoes of the Leuven colloquium over the past sixteen years (if at all, it met with irony). It is clearly a neglected factor. With the distance of fifteen years I realize that our reader-centered approach needs to be preceded by an author-centered and a text-centered approach and that any future-oriented reading needs to have a stronger awareness of the dangerous potential that is present in any future vision. But this, it seems to me, makes a future-oriented reading of authoritative texts, and John's Gospel in particular, all the more important.

Appendix: Topics for Discussion for the Leuven Conference 2001

1. Are the anti-Jewish elements that allegedly are found in the Fourth Gospel rooted in the spirit of the interpreters, or do the texts themselves contain such elements? If the latter is the case: Are they concentrated in specific passages (such as John 8:12–59) and on specific themes (e.g., the disputes between Jesus and the Jews), or do they penetrate the entire gospel?

2. Did the Fourth evangelist intend to present a historical conflict between Jesus and the Jews? Or do we have to consider this conflict in the Fourth Gospel as a product of John's creative mind, a literary means of presenting his high Christology?

3. Is affinity of John's Gospel with Gnosticism a possible (partial) explanation for his anti-Jewish statements?

4. Does the Christology of the Fourth Gospel include salvation for nonbelievers (esp. for the Jews)?

5. How does the Fourth Evangelist differ from the other so-called anti-Jewish New Testament writers?

6. What role did the effective history of the Fourth Gospel play in the development and legitimation of anti-Judaism and anti-Semitism?

7. What does canonicity of biblical texts mean, taking into consideration passages that present Jews in a way that is seen as ethically problematic in our time? How can divine revelation take place in texts that are considered to be unacceptable? Is the canonicity of biblical texts still a basic criterion for their authority for theology today? Do theologians have the freedom or even the duty to practice *Sachkritik*?

8. What is the relationship between Jewish-Christian dialogue and the exegetical study of the Gospel of John and other Christian Scriptures?

Anti-Semitism and Religious Violence as Flawed Interpretations of the Gospel of John

Paul N. Anderson

While it is a tragic fact that the Gospel of John has contributed to anti-Semitism and religious violence during some chapters of Christian history, John is not anti-Semitic. It was written by a Jewish writer, about a Jewish messianic figure, targeted first toward convincing Jewish audiences that Jesus was indeed the Jewish Messiah. Salvation is "of the Jews," according to the Johannine Jesus, and each of the "I am" sayings embodies a classic representation of Israel. John is no more anti-Semitic than the Essene community or the prophetic work of John the Baptist. On the other hand, the Jews sometimes typify the unbelieving world and are portrayed as primary adversaries of Jesus and his followers, despite the fact that some are also presented as coming to faith in Jesus. The Ἰουδαῖοι in John can be seen to represent several associations, ranging from the Judeans (suggesting north-south divisions) to the religious leaders in Jerusalem (or locally in a diaspora setting), who actively oppose Jesus and the growth of his movement. The main problem is with interpreting John wrongly or with allowing flawed interpretations to stand.[1] When read correctly, the Fourth Gospel not only ceases to be a source of religious acrimony; it points the way forward for all seekers of truth to sojourn together, across the boundaries of religious movements, time, and space.

A few years ago, on display at Yale's Beinecke Rare Book and Manuscript Library was the block-print collection of Fritz Eichenberg's works,

1. As important books and collections on the subject have shown: Culpepper 1987; Dunn 1991/2006; 1992; 1999; Kysar 1993; Rensberger 1999; Bieringer, Pollefeyt, and Vandecasteele-Vanneuville 2001a; Reinhartz 2001a; 2001b; 2001c; Lieu 2002; Pesch 2005; Heemstra 2010; Donaldson 2010; Trachtenberg 2002; van Belle 2013; Frey 2013c; Nicklas 2014.

and of prime notoriety within the collection was a striking print of a Jewish Holocaust victim on a cross. This haunting image (*The Crucifixion*, 1980) highlights ironic tragedies on several levels, making its prophetic points along the way.[2] The onlooking guard at the crucifixion is not a Roman soldier but a Nazi SS officer. The Golgotha site is not a hill in Jerusalem but a death camp adorned with jagged barbed wire in the foreground and a menacing guard-tower beacon in the background. Central within the print, however, is the tragic figure of a man on a cross wearing the Jewish Star of David on his jacket. As a Jewish European himself, Eichenberg portrays this figure not only as a tragic victim in the singular but as a typological representation of the mass victimization of the Jewish nation at the hands of Nazi Germany in particular, condemning also Christians and others for their anti-Semitism on the global stage in general. Ironically, Jesus of Nazareth came to break the cycles of violence in the world, but movements in his name have too often dreadfully failed to carry out that mission faithfully.

It is a sad fact that just as the Old Testament conquest narratives have been wielded by interpreters somehow to overturn the clear teachings of Jesus on peace and nonviolence,[3] the Gospels of Matthew and John have been used to instigate and further anti-Semitism and religious violence by Christians and others. The vexing presentations of the Jews as the killers of Jesus at the hands of the Romans in these two gospels have become fodder for prejudicial platforms against those of Semitic origins, sometimes motivated by political or economic reasons, and the voices of the wise and the discerning have too often gone unheeded. This is terribly sad, given the tragic outcome for the Jewish nation and the history of religious violence in Western society. One's first reaction might thus favor banning these or other religious documents from the marketplace of ideas altogether.[4]

2. Fritz Eichenberg, a Jewish German-American who escaped Germany in 1933, contributed dozens of wood-block ink prints to *The Catholic Worker*, edited by Dorothy Day. This image, first published in his *Dance with Death* (Eichenberg 1983; see Ellsberg 2004, 95), is also featured online in Hammond 2000.

3. If the Johannine Gospel is concerned with the revelation of truth, such cannot be furthered by force or violence (with de la Potterie 2007). Thus, Miroslav Volf's (1996, 264–68) work on exclusion and embrace and Stephen Motyer's (2008, 163–67) analysis of truth in John see John's promise of liberation and redemption (John 8:32) as being rooted in truth rather than force. On the conquest narratives, Jesus, and nonviolence, see Anderson 1994; 2004b; 2004c.

4. This comes close to Maurice Casey's approach to the truth of John's Gospel. In Casey's (1996) view, because John is anti-Semitic it conveys no historically worthy

Censorship, however, would produce a new set of prejudicial disasters, as inquisitions and book-burning schemes always create more problems than they solve.

Questions remain, however, as to whether the Gospel of John was indeed anti-Semitic in its conception and development, or whether such is a flawed reading of the text altogether. Exegesis trumps eisegesis when it comes to the responsible interpretation of biblical texts, and especially on world-impacting subjects it deserves to be applied. The thesis of this essay is that while John has played a role in anti-Semitism and religious violence, such influences represent the distortion of this thoroughly Jewish piece of writing, which actually provides ways forward for all seekers of truth and inclusivity if interpreted adequately. The Fourth Gospel represents an intra-Jewish perspective, standing against violence and force, forwarding a universalist appeal to all seekers of truth, while also documenting the dialectical engagement between revelation and religion.

1. The Phenomenology of the Issue and Various Approaches

Of several approaches to the problem of the presentation of Ἰουδαῖος and οἱ Ἰουδαῖοι in John, a variety of solutions have emerged. Given the facts that Jesus is undeniably presented as a Jew in John 4:9, that salvation is "of the Jews" (4:22), that the evangelist displays evidence of being Jewish, and that his goal is to show that Jesus is the Jewish Messiah/Christ—fulfilling Jewish Scripture—it cannot be said that the Johannine narrative is ethnically anti-Semitic. Then again, the narrator shows Jesus referring to religious authorities as bound to "your law" in John 8:17 and 10:34 and to "their law" in 15:25, so some individuation between Jesus of Nazareth and religious authorities in Judea is suggested by the text.[5] The question

content regarding Jesus of Nazareth, and it is to be disregarded by all persons with moral sensibilities and historical interests. Of course, Casey's first inference is flawed exegetically (Just 1999), and few of his other views are critically compelling.

5. For instance, if references to "your" and "their" law represent John's total rejection of the Torah and thus Judaism (Ashton 2007, 23), why does John's story of Jesus feature no fewer than a dozen references to central passages from the Torah being fulfilled in Jesus either implicitly and typologically or explicitly and prophetically (see Anderson 2011b, 83–85)? Typologically, the Torah is fulfilled in Jesus in multiple ways: Gen 1:1–2:4/Prov 8:22–30 → John 1:1–18; Gen 12–22 → John 8:12–59; 12:20–21; Gen 28:12 → John 1:51; 4:5–12; Exod 20:1–18 → John 1:17; Num 21:8 → John 3:14; Exod 16:4/Ps 78:24–25 → John 6:1–13; Exod 14 → John 6:16–21; Deut

centers on the character of what that individuation might have been, how it developed, and whether it reflects an intra-Jewish set of tensions or an extra-Jewish set of engagements between the emerging Jesus movement and its parental Judaism.

One approach is to see the Gospel of John as *theologically anti-Jewish*. John's presentation of Jesus as the Jewish Messiah is seen by some interpreters as Christian supersessionism. Jesus not only fulfills the typologies of Israel, but he virtually becomes the new Israel, displacing the need for the other. Within this approach John is seen as being written against Jewish people and/or members of the Jewish religion, seeking to supplant one religion with another. Therefore, this form of anti-Semitism may or may not be ethnocentric, but it certainly is religiocentric for holders of this view. The problem with that, however, is that John's soteriology is also a universal one. The light enlightens everyone (John 1:9), Jesus's reign is one of truth (18:36–37), and the true sign of discipleship is love, which knows no religious bounds (13:34–35). Authentic worship is neither in Jerusalem nor Samaria; rather, it transcends particular religious forms, locations, and expressions (4:21–24). John's presentation of Jesus as the Messiah shows the Revealer to be challenging all that is of human origin, including Christian religion and power, as well as Jewish and Roman renderings of the same. John's Jesus sets up no cultic meals of remembrance (John 13), and he himself did not baptize, despite his followers' having done so (4:2). Therefore, John's Jesus challenges creaturely religious practices rather than setting up one religion over against another. John's scandal is not that it is supersessionist—challenging Judaism; it is that it is it is revelational, challenging all that is of human origin as an affront to human-made religion, proper.

A second approach is to read οἱ Ἰουδαῖοι as a reference to "the Judeans" (southerners versus Samaritans or Galileans) within Palestine or the Levant in general. These themes thus represent a *regional struggle*

18:15–22 → John 5:46; 18:9. Prophetically, the Torah is cited as being fulfilled by Jesus in John: John 1:45; 5:39 → Deut 18:15–22; John 6:31 → Exod 16:4; John 8:17 → Deut 17:6; 19:15; John 19:31–36 → Exod 12:10, 46; Num 9:12. In addition to Torah references, other passages from Hebrew Scripture are also employed in John's story of Jesus, implicitly and explicitly, including: 1–2 Kings (2), Nehemiah (1), Psalms (11), Proverbs (1), Isaiah (4), Ezekiel (1), Daniel (1), Micah (1), Zechariah (4). According to Manns (1988, 30), despite the fact that John's Jesus seems to distance himself from Jewish leaders, Jesus is still presented as fulfilling the heart of Jewish ideals.

between a province and the center of the Jewish religious and political world. Certainly, Jewish people traveled to and from Jerusalem, and extensive evidence in the text bolsters such a reading. The Jewish nation would obviously have thought of Jerusalem as its center, so Jerusalocentricism may be a helpful way to understand the Johannine use of the term Ἰουδαῖοι as referring to *Judeans* in particular, not *Jews* in general. Thus, the "Jerusalemites" (7:25) are presented among the "Judeans" who were seeking to kill Jesus (7:1, 19, 25). As a northern-Palestinian narrative about its Mosaic prophet having been rejected by the leaders in Judea, north-south dialogues certainly would have reflected also a variety of regional and ideological concerns. This approach works fairly well for most of John's presentations of οἱ Ἰουδαῖοι, and this is where most of the Johannine analysis should focus its attention. Yet, associations extend beyond Judean-Galilean regional struggles to larger issues of centralized religion versus its challenges from the periphery. As with the rich and poignant tradition of the Jewish prophets before Jesus's day, Jesus is not the first progressive figure to encounter an uneven reception at the center of Jerusalem's religious elite. Thus, John's north-south tensions reflect a series of dialectical engagements between the cult-oriented center of Jerusalem-based religion and the charisma-oriented periphery of first-century Galilean Judaism.

A third approach is to take οἱ Ἰουδαῖοι to mean "particular Jewish authorities" who wanted to do away with Jesus, described as *a struggle between the unauthorized prophet and official religious authorities*. It certainly appears to be the case that in John (as well as in the other gospels) religious authorities are presented as the ones most threatened by Jesus. Whether he was challenging their religious institutions, such as temple worship and its sacrificial systems (let alone the money-changing operations), or challenging the legalistic approaches to the Mosaic law erected by Scripture lawyers and scribes, Jesus is indeed remembered as evoking controversy among the religious leaders of his day. In that sense, John's story of Jesus reflects an autonomous historical memory of the ministry and last days of Jesus, developed in theological reflection. Thus, Jerusalem's chief priests, rulers, and Pharisees demand to know Jesus's authorization, which leads to pointed debates over Abrahamic, Mosaic, and Davidic authority. Then again, even in the way Caiaphas, the chief priests, the Pharisees, and the called council are presented betrays political interests. Their willingness to "sacrifice" the Galilean prophet reflects an endeavor to prevent a Roman backlash against the Jewish populace (11:45–53). Of course,

Judean-Galilean tensions between the Jesus movement and the Jerusalem authorities did not begin with his ministry or end with his death. Regional tensions are clear in the Johannine narrative, and later struggles between followers of Jesus and Jewish authorities are by no means late and only late. The ways that these groups are portrayed in John as being threatened by Jesus and his followers, including their reactions, might even reflect several phases of debates within the developing Johannine tradition, as Urban von Wahlde, Raymond Brown, and others have suggested.[6]

A fourth approach considers the presentation of religious authorities in John as narrative characters who represent the ambivalent relationships with local Jewish authorities by Johannine Christians in a diaspora setting, as they sought to convince family and friends that Jesus was indeed the Jewish Messiah, sometimes to no avail. This would involve *a reflection of evolving religious dialogues* within Johannine history and theology—a multilevel reading of the text. Plausibly, post-70 CE Johannine Christianity may originally have had a home within one or more synagogue communities within a Hellenistic setting, leading to some followers of Jesus being eventually distanced from the synagogue (ἀποσυνάγωγος; see John 9:22; 12:42; 16:2) because of their willingness to confess Jesus openly. The Birkat Haminim (the curse against the heretics, effecting removal from the synagogue of followers of "the Nazarene") likely represents an orthodox attempt to discipline perceived ditheism within the Jesus movement, even if the primary interest was something short of expelling all Jesus adherents

6. In Brown's (1979; 2003) paradigm, the pregospel stage of John's composition involved tensions between Judeans, Samaritans, and Galileans (ca. 50–80 CE), while the stage in which the gospel was written involved at least six sets of dialogues within the Johannine situation (ca. 90 CE): dialogues with "the world" (unbelieving gentiles), οἱ Ἰουδαῖοι (members of local synagogues), adherents of John the Baptist (even in Asia Minor), those Brown calls "crypto-Christians" (ones who remained in the synagogue as secret believers in Jesus), those he calls "Jewish Christian churches of inadequate faith" (those not accepting the divinity of Jesus or the Eucharist as the true flesh and blood of Jesus), and "apostolic Christians" (Petrine-hierarchy institutional Christian leaders, who did not appreciate the spiritual work of the risen Christ through the Paraclete). Von Wahlde (1979; 1996; 2000; 2010a) sees gradations of difference between the ways that religious leaders are portrayed in John, arguing that the earliest edition of John referred to Jewish leaders as "Pharisees," "chief priests," and "rulers," while the second edition referred to the adversaries of Jesus as οἱ Ἰουδαῖοι. The latter term represents engagements with local synagogue leaders in the Johannine situation, according to von Wahlde's paradigm.

from all local synagogues. Such a view overstates likely realities. However, when Jesus adherents became distanced from local synagogues and joined in with local gentile believers in Jesus, it appears that some of them were courted back into the synagogue on the basis of Mosaic authority and Abrahamic blessing—contingent upon their diminishing or denying their belief in Jesus as the Messiah/Christ. This appears to represent the schism in the Johannine situation reported in 1 John 2:18–25.[7] From this perspective, the narration of Jewish leaders' acceptances and rejections of Jesus in earlier time periods serves to explain how things had come to be the way they were in later generations, including the inconceivable theological problem of how Jewish leaders would continue to reject their own Jewish Messiah.[8]

A fifth approach is to view John's presentation of οἱ Ἰουδαῖοι as *archetypes of the unbelieving world*: ὁ κόσμος. As the Revealer from God, Jesus reveals nothing except that he is from God (according to Rudolf Bultmann[9]), and this brings a crisis of faith for the world. Humans must be willing to accept the Revealer, but in doing so, they must forfeit their attachments to creaturely wisdom and the worldly scaffolding of human-made religion. Therefore, inauthentic existence is replaced by authentic, believing response to the divine initiative, and this is the *crisis* effected by the incarnation. The Jewish leaders opposing Jesus in the Johannine narrative thus represent human hopes in creaturely sufficiency, complete with its conventional successes, and this is why "the world" finds the coming of Christ an offense and a scandal. In this sense, the Johannine critique of οἱ Ἰουδαῖοι implies more than a contextual critique of religious antipathy to Johannine believers; it more generally and universally denotes the confrontation of humanity's devised religious approaches to God by the

7. Note the antichristic errors of interpretation, as well as the distinctive errors of the Johannine antichrists; Anderson 2007a; 2007c.

8. This is precisely the sort of issue faced by Paul a generation earlier in his writing of Rom 9–11, as Krister Stendahl's (1976) treatment of Paul among the Jews and the gentiles reminds us, although the tables by now have been turned. Instead of gentiles feeling inferior to more established Jewish members of the Jesus movement, the Johannine Gospel asserts the Jewishness of Jesus for the benefit of his audiences, whether they be Jewish or gentile.

9. Jesus is the Revealer without a revelation (Bultmann 1955, 66); it is the "thatness" (*die Dass*) of God's saving-revealing activity that calls for a response to the divine initiative rather than being concerned with the "how" or the "wherefore." Or, as de la Potterie (2007, 78) puts it, "John's theology is above all a theology of revelation."

eschatological advent of the Revealer. If the divine initiative scandalizes all that is of human origin—religious and political ventures that are creaturely in their character rather than of divine origin—the Johannine Jesus as the Christ must be seen as confronting Christian scaffolding and investments as well as Jewish and Roman ones. As the universal light, available to all (John 1:9), Jesus comes as the light illuminating those who walk in darkness (8:12; 9:5; 11:9), but they also must respond to the light even if it exposes the creaturely character of their platforms (3:18–21). In that sense, Jesus as the life-producing "bread" brings a crisis to the world: a crisis of decision as to whether one will make a stand for or against the Revealer.[10] Yet, as John is highly theological, its content cannot be divorced from its originative and developing contexts. Thus, abstraction and particularity in John are inextricably entwined.

A sixth approach is to see John as *pro-Jewish*. After all, nearly all persons and groups mentioned in John, except for the Romans, are either Jewish or Semitic, and Jesus is presented pervasively as the Jewish Messiah-Christ. Jesus is Jewish, and so are all of his disciples; those touched by his ministry—whom he heals, teaches, feeds, and challenges—are all Semitic or Jewish. While some of the Ἰουδαῖοι in Jerusalem mount opposition to Jesus, many of them also believe in him, and this fact has gone strangely unnoticed among several interpreters.[11] Further, some leaders among the Jews also come to believe in Jesus, and others offer support to the grieving family of Lazarus. Even the Samaritans receive Jesus as the Messiah and welcome him to stay with them; despite his rejection in Nazareth as presented in Mark 6, many receive him in Capernaum—even within the household of the royal official (John 4:43–54). Greeks desire to meet Jesus in John 12:20–26, and this fulfills his sense of mission, as the blessings of Abraham are availed to the world. Climactically, the fulfilled word of Caiaphas, that the sacrifice of Jesus would gather the scattered children of God in the diaspora, is presented as an unwitting prophecy by the high priest in John 11:49–52, extending the blessings of Judaism to the

10. Thus, Jesus's claiming to be the life-producing bread in John 6:35 invites audiences to make a stand "for or against the Revealer" (Bultmann 1971, 213).

11. As demonstrated below, in over a dozen instances Jews in Jerusalem are presented as believing in Jesus in the Gospel of John. While Griffith (2008) suggests that some of these may have turned away, accounting for some of the Johannine acrimony, the link between John 6:60–71 and 8:31–59 is not entirely certain; nonetheless, echoes of 1 John 2:18–25 are palpable in the narration of John 6:66 (Anderson 1996, 258).

world. Therefore, while some of "his own" rejected Jesus as the Christ, and even though some of his disciples abandoned him and followed him no more (John 6:66), as many as received him are welcomed into the divine family as children of God simply by believing in his name (John 1:10–13).

In addition to these particular approaches, it could be that οἱ Ἰουδαῖοι in John can be used meaningfully in more than one of these categories or that there may be other ways of understanding the use of the term in John besides the above options.[12] Adequate interpretation of John and Judaism would thus involve *a synthesis of multiple factors*, and it is likely that at different stages of its development the Johannine tradition possessed distinctive approaches to the Ἰουδαῖοι in the Johannine situation. Thus, the literary contexts of the term's usage must be considered in the light of what may be inferred about the history of the text and the history of the Johannine situation before constructing an exegetical appraisal of the best meaning(s) of the term originally and thus for later generations. This forces an evaluation also of the history of interpretation, and it calls interpreters to make responsible judgments regarding the adequacy of interpretive applications in later generations.

2. Religious Violence as a Flawed Interpretation of John

While religious violence has sometimes been evoked by distortive readings of the gospels, Jesus commands Peter to put away the sword in John 18:11, just as he does in the Synoptics (Matt 26:52; Luke 22:38). While John's Jesus is portrayed as driving sheep and cattle with a whip of cords, the dove sellers are expelled with words, not force—not exactly a license for resorting to physical violence, and certainly not lethal force, against humans (John 2:15–16). Further, Jesus declares that his kingdom is one of truth; it is not of this world, which explains why his disciples cannot fight (18:36–37). It is not that truth *may not* be furthered by violence, a factor of permission; it *cannot* be furthered by violence, a factor of possibility.[13]

---

12. There may also have been disagreements in the late first century as to what it meant to be Jewish—full stop (see Cohen 1993; 1999a). In de Boer's (2001) view, while issues of identity and behavior would also have been key, there might have been disagreement over those very measures. Therefore, confusion in later generations of interpretation may reflect a historic reality: things were confusing back then, as well.

13. An important feature within treatments of John's dualism, determinism, universalism, and particularity: Anderson 2011b, 34–38, 183–86.

Rather, truth is furthered by convincement, not coercion, and the Holy Spirit—the Spirit of truth—convicts persons of sin, righteousness, and judgment (16:8). The truth is always liberating (8:32). Yes, John's narrative carries a good deal of religious invective—a factor of heated debates with religious leaders in Jerusalem and/or a diaspora setting—but one must go against the clearly counterviolent presentation of Jesus in John to embrace any form of religious violence. Therefore, resorting to violence cannot be supported by an exegetically faithful reading of the Gospel of John. It goes directly against the Johannine stance against violence, corroborated also by the clear teachings of Jesus in the Synoptics (Anderson 1994).

A further consideration involves John's presentation of Jesus as combatting the spiral of violence of his day, every bit as pointedly as does the Jesus of the Synoptics.[14] From the perspective of Jonathan Bernier (2013), a strong case can be built that the issues related to the ἀποσυνάγωγος passages of John 9:22; 12:42; 16:2 were early rather than late. According to Bernier, they reflect tensions in Jerusalem rather than in the diaspora, and they are political in character rather than theological. Following the insurrection in Sepphoris—near Nazareth—after the death of Herod in 4 BCE, when Judas the son of Hezekiah raided Herod's palace and confiscated weapons, Varus of Syria marched in, putting down the rebellion and crucifying two thousand Jews (Josephus, *Ant.* 17.295; *J.W.* 2.75). A decade or so later, when Judas the Galilean launched a revolt against Roman monetary taxation, founding the "fourth philosophy" Zealot movement, political tensions again arose in Galilee. Therefore, the Birkat Haminim may have emerged as a disciplining of perceived zealotry within Judean synagogues, lest, as Caiaphas worried in John 11:48–50, the Romans should step in and "destroy our place and nation." Indeed, the Birkat is clearly referenced later in Justin's *Dialogue with Trypho* (ca. 150 CE), where curses against Christians in the synagogues are referenced half a dozen times or so (Horbury 1998). Also, Gamaliel II is associated with introducing the Birkat during the Jamnia period (70–90 CE), but those later tensions with followers of the Nazarene (Jesus) may have originated with concerns over Roman retaliation against messianic

14. Richard Horsley (1987) argues compellingly that Jesus of Nazareth sought to reverse spirals of violence endemic in the Levant over this period of time. Walter Wink (1992) contributed particular understandings to how Jesus offered a "third way" in dealing with the fight-flight dichotomies of domination (Anderson 2014c, 34–38).

pretenders such as Judas the Galilean, the Samaritan, Theudas, or the Egyptian.[15]

That being the case, the nearness of the Passover in John 2:13; 6:4; 11:55 is not mentioned with theological significance in mind, but it references political tensions related to Roman sensitivities regarding Jewish uprisings during Judaism's greatest nationalistic celebration, the Passover.[16] In John 2 Jesus predicts the tearing down of the temple and its rebuilding—a reference nonetheless to the resurrection and not the temple's eventual destruction in 70 CE. In John 6:14–15 the crowd wishes to rush Jesus off for a hasty coronation as a prophet-king like Moses—an honor Jesus eludes by escaping into the hills. In John 11 Caiaphas and the chief priests "sacrifice" Jesus politically as a means of staving off a Roman backlash (vv. 48, 50). Despite these politically laden tensions, however, John's Jesus eschews violence and popularistic acclaim. Rather, he confronts authorities—both Jewish and Roman—by appealing to truth. He offers his followers unworldly peace (14:27), not a worldly kingdom (18:36–37). In postresurrection appearances, Jesus then bestows peace on his followers (20:19, 21, 26), and as Jesus's kingdom is one of truth, despite tribulation experienced in the world, his disciples are promised peace because he has overcome the world (16:33). Therefore, on the basis of a clear and straightforward reading of the text, one cannot adequately base violent actions on the presentation of Jesus in the Fourth Gospel; to do so violates the text exegetically.

3. Anti-Semitism as a Flawed Interpretation of John

Despite the fact of John's contributing to anti-Semitism, this is not to say that such is a sole or even a primary cause of anti-Semitism.[17] It is to say, however, that unwittingly or otherwise, anti-Semitic attitudes have either

15. This represents a more dialectical view of the Johannine-Jewish history of engagement in longitudinal perspective. Rather than seeing the issue as being early only (Bernier 2013) or late only (Martyn 1968), it may have involved earlier and later engagements, even over different issues (Anderson 2014c, 52–55, 133).

16. Anderson 1996, 184; 2014c, 147–48.

17. Indeed, anti-Jewish measures precede Christianity by many centuries (see 2 Macc 6), and even in the Common Era, anti-Semitic thrusts have come from many directions besides Christian ones. See, for instance, John Gager's (1983) book on the origins of anti-Semitism exogenous to Christianity as well as endogenous to it. Roman anti-Semitism is also apparent in John and in other Greco-Roman sources (Meeks

emerged from readings of John or have resulted in the employment of John to support anti-Semitic agendas. It is a troubling fact, for instance, that Martin Luther's theologization of the Jews as villains of the faith contributed to German anti-Jewish sentiments and preaching, which later played roles in the tragic unfolding of the Holocaust (Probst 2012). Luther, of course, is not alone in that matter. Samuel Sandmel reminds us of the anecdote he heard as a child: a man was beating up on Jewish people after attending a Christian worship service.[18] When a policeman stopped him and asked him why he was doing so, he replied, "Because the Jews killed Christ." The policeman said, "But that was two thousand years ago," to which the man responded, "That may be so, but I just heard about it today!"

This story points to problems of contemporary influence regardless of what a biblical text originally meant and what it authentically means hence. It is what people make of a text and what people do in response to their understandings of it that present real problems, not just imaginary ones. A further distortion continues, however, in that some Christian catechisms have included derogatory portrayals of the Jews as a feature of theological anti-Semitism with profound sociological implications.[19] The Jewish law is juxtaposed to the grace of God availed through Christ (John 1:17), and Christians all too often bolster their religious commitments by disparaging other religions, including their parental Jewish faith. My contention is that such approaches misunderstand what the New Testament writings are claiming with regard to Jesus and to Judaism.[20] All of its writers were Jewish, and to develop out of them an anti-Jewish worldview goes against

---

1975; Daniel 1979). On Luther's anti-Semitism and its trajectories of influence, however, see Töllner 2007; Probst 2012.

18. Rendered in print in several ways; see Sandmel 1978, 155.

19. For the devastating ecumenical implications of theological anti-Semitism see Banki 1984; Leibig 1983; Radford Reuther 1979. Then again, the best hope for building better ecumenical and interfaith relations hinges on clarifying what the Gospel of John is saying, as well as what it is not; see Knight 1968; Cargas 1981; Cook 1987a; Kysar 1993; Beck 1994.

20. In his book on Jesus and the transformation of Judaism, John Riches (1982) argues compellingly that the goal of Jesus of Nazareth was neither to do away with Judaism nor to displace it; it was to restore it to a better vision of itself. Likewise, Richard Horsley and Tom Thatcher (2013) argue that the original Johannine vision was the vitalization of Israel, not its supplanting with a new movement. What we see in the Johannine reflection on the movement's uneven reception within its own ambivalent history is an overall failure—at best only a partial success—in extending the grace of

the religion of Jesus, Paul, John, and the heart of the New Testament. Jesus, Paul, and John were thoroughly *Jewish*—full stop.[21] Thus, anti-Semitic views among Christians might not have primarily emerged from reflective Bible study or exegetically adequate Christian teaching. More often than is acknowledged, anti-Semitism has been evoked from nonreligious sources, and for political or economic reasons that are then supported by the flawed citing of Scripture or religious stances. Likewise, those disparaging Christianity might do so for political rather than religious reasons, so the fact of political and economic intrusions into religious dialogues and interfaith discussions merits critical analysis.

A less obvious yet sinister fact thus involves the wresting and employment of religious authority or motifs for the purposes of co-opting society into the toleration of, and even the conducting of, evil. Here religion itself becomes both a *pawn* and a *victim*, and in particular, the Gospel of John. Religious and nonreligious leaders alike resort to yoking sources of rhetorical equity to their programs, and religious authority is all too easily co-opted unwittingly. "God, Mom, and apple pie" get yoked to war efforts and marshaled nationalism, but is apple pie *really* the cause of militarism? Of course not, and neither are mothers or God. Thus, the authority of religion in general, and of the Fourth Gospel in particular, get used as pawns by the cunning in ways that are often undetected. Religious people must be skeptical of such ploys, especially because the religious tend to be more trusting, and uncritically so. Politically motivated leaders have and always will yoke religious values to their causes, whether or not they are personally religious, using societal authority to motivate audiences to do their bidding. This is especially the case if it involves the exalting of the home group and the villainizing of others. Inevitably, when resorting to violence is then rightly criticized, those who have used religion as a pawn then tend to blame it as a scapegoat. In blaming religious values for atrocities otherwise legitimated by such persons, they deflect the blame away from themselves, hoping to emerge personally unscathed. Thus religion in general, and the Fourth Gospel in particular, get blamed as scapegoats. This sequence characterizes the modern era extensively, and many a co-opting or critique of religion should be seen as the misappropriation of its

membership in the divine family to all who might respond in faith to the divine initiative (Culpepper 1980; Anderson 2011b, 22–23, 35–38, 183–90).

21. Falk 1985; Frey 2012b; Anderson 2014c, 46–47, 171–76, 208–13.

authority, especially if followed by its denigration, rather than representing the heart of authentic religious faith on its own (Anderson 2004c).

A parallel example involves the presentation of Israel as God's chosen people in the Bible, which has then yoked Christian fundamentalism to the Israeli cause against the Palestinians, many of whom are Christians. This has led to America's providing billions of dollars in military aid to Israel's use of violent force against populations internal and external to its borders, including Christians, bolstered by simplistic biblical reasoning. Such appropriations of Gen 12–17, however, do not prove the Bible is anti-Christian, and neither does the fact that negative portrayals of the Ἰουδαῖοι in Matthew and John have contributed to anti-Semitic views historically prove these gospels are anti-Semitic. The fault lies with anachronistic and inadequate interpretations of the Bible, including the fact that political uses of biblical themes at times function to demarcate opponents and to marshal support for causes in ways partisan. Just because religious texts possess authority, however, this does not mean that they will be employed in rhetorically adequate ways. Their misinterpretation and misuse must thus be challenged with rigor by serious scholars if exegetical integrity is to be preserved.[22] Such is the goal of the present essay.

4. Anachronisms Then and Now

Despite the fact that John's presentation of Ἰουδαῖος and οἱ Ἰουδαῖοι has contributed to anti-Semitism, though, the question remains as to whether the category "anti-Semitic" is appropriate for discussing religious tensions within the first-century Jesus movement. If meant by anti-Semitic is "against the Jewish people" within the first century and later eras, the answer is definitely "No." Such a label is entirely anachronistic. The evangelist was himself Jewish, as were the leaders and core members of the Johannine situation. It would be akin to claiming the Essenes or John the Baptist were anti-Semitic in their vitriolic judging of the Judean status quo, or that the Pharisees were anti-Semitic because they opposed the Sadducees. Would any genuine scholar argue such a thesis? Obviously not! If Christianity had not separated from Judaism over the next century

22. With Sean Freyne (1985), only as we examine closely the historical contexts of the developing Jesus movement, appreciating impassioned ideals and experienced losses, can we appreciate what is meant by Matthean and Johannine polemic regarding Jewish leaders, and more importantly—I would add—what is *not*.

or more, the Johannine dialectical presentation of the Ἰουδαῖοι would not even be an issue—or, at least not an interfaith one.

Another unattended factor in the discussion is the modest beginnings of the Jesus movement followed by the growth of Christianity over the centuries. If the Jesus movement had not outgrown its parental Judaism in terms of size and reach, the Jesus movement would likely have been experienced simply as an irritating sect rather than a societal majority. In fact, the emerging Jesus movement was largely a fledgling stepsister to Judaism until several decades into the Constantinian era. It was only around 350 CE that its numbers within Western society broke the 50 percent mark, according to Rodney Stark (1997), and Christianity did not become the official religion of the Roman Empire until the Edict of Thessalonica in 380 CE under Theodosius.[23] Therefore, it is anachronistic to envision followers of Jesus in the Johannine situation as anything but the smaller of competing religious groups.

On this account, Brown's (1979) analysis of the Johannine community reflecting fledgling bands of believers seeking to negotiate the worlds of their Jewish background and emerging fellowship with gentile believers in Jesus makes sense. With some of their membership participating in synagogue worship on the Sabbath, with some meeting in house churches for first-day worship along with gentile believers, and with some participating in both venues of worship, Jesus adherents within the post-70 CE Johannine situation must have been stretched in their capacities to manage community life effectively. They still appealed to Jewish family and friends that Jesus was the Jewish Messiah/Christ, and yet they also sought to extend the blessings of Judaism to gentile audiences within the Roman imperial world. Thus, Johannine believers were fledgling minorities, not dominant majorities; so to read their community investments as oppressing minority groups is anachronistic and wrong.[24]

---

23. Assuming a 40 percent growth rate per decade, Stark estimates the numbers of Jesus adherents or Christians at the following dates to be: 40 CE—1,000; 50 CE—1,400; 100 CE—7,530; 150 CE—40,496; 200 CE—217,795; 250 CE—1,171,356; 300 CE—6,299,832; 350 CE—33,882,008 (p. 7). These figures, of course, are estimations based on Stark's informed calculations.

24. On this anachronism the views of numerous interpreters founder; see, for instance, William A. Johnson (1989), who, on assuming John to be anti-Semitic and levied against Judaism as an extra-Jewish movement, finds his own suspicions confirmed without challenging the frailty of his initial assumptions.

That being the case, it is also wrong to compare Johannine Christianity too closely with Qumranic sectarians, although some features of Jewish motivational dualism cohere between Qumran's War Scroll and Community Rule and the ethos of the Johannine Gospel and Epistles. The light-darkness thrust of the Johannine writings, however, is also explanatory as well as motivational; it is Hellenistic as well as Jewish.[25] It therefore does not simply chastise religious leaders for their failure to embrace the sapiential teachings and prophetic actions of the Revealer; it also calls for embracing the values of Judaism within a diaspora setting in terms of Jewish faith and practice. This is precisely what is going on in the later Johannine situation, where traveling ministers, likely two or three decades into the Pauline mission, are teaching assimilation and cheap grace rather than cultural resistance and costly discipleship.[26] From the perspective of the Johannine Elder, the second antichristic threat was not a matter of secessionism; it involved the threat of invasive false teachings, advocating easy codes of discipleship supported by docetizing Christologies. This is why Ignatius called for the appointing of a singular episcopal leader in every church as a means of facilitating church unity against the rabid bites of those who would divide Christian communities by their false teachings (Anderson 1997; 2007c).[27] Thus, rather than seeing Johannine Christi-

25. Contra Ashton 2007, who sees Qumranic ethos "in the bones" of the Johannine evangelist, John's rendering of Jesus and his ministry is crafted for reception in a Hellenistic setting (Anderson 1997; 2007d; 2016). Therefore, John's explanatory dualism follows Plato's Allegory of the Cave (*Resp.* 7), showing that those rejecting Jesus sought to remain in the dark rather than coming into the light, lest it be exposed that their platforms are rooted in human origin rather than divine initiative (John 1:10–13; 3:18–21). John's dualism is also motivational (like that of the Essenes) in that it calls for audiences to embrace the way of life, light, and truth rather than the ways of death, darkness, and falsity (Anderson 2011b, 187–90; 2011a).

26. In particular, the invitation to ingest the flesh and blood of Jesus calls for embracing the way of the cross, as the bread that Jesus offers is his flesh, given for the life of the world; Forestell 1974; Anderson 1996, 207–9.

27. Ignatius thus corroborates similar crises, or dialectical engagements, within the later two phases of the Johannine situation (70–85 and 85–100 CE). First, he describes visiting Judaizers (see Barrett 1982); second, he references the divisive impact of docetists (see Goulder 1999), who proselytize and bring false teachings among the churches of Asia Minor; third, he calls for faithfulness to the way of Christ for those living under the hegemony of the Roman Empire (see Cassidy 1992); fourth, in addressing these threats, he advocates appointing a single bishop in every church as a means of dealing with internal and external threats to church unity—a move that in

anity as a backwater sect, its struggles reflect engagements with Jewish communities, Greco-Roman culture, and emerging centers of the Jesus movement, rooted in seeking to maintain basic standards of Jewish ethos while also embracing newcomers to the faith from outside Judaism. In that sense, they were more cosmopolitan than sectarian—even more cosmopolitan than their synagogue-abiding counterparts.[28]

Nonetheless, the diaspora-setting tensions between Johannine believers and synagogue leaders still appear to reflect a set of intra-Jewish struggles over the heart of Judaism rather than the periphery. John's narrative is written by a Jew, about Jesus the Jew, who is believed to be fulfilling Israel's divine vocation and global mission as a light to the nations and a blessing to the world. Thus, in no way can the thoroughly Semitic Gospel of John, the most Jewish of the gospels, be considered anti-Semitic. If anything, John represents a radical view of the Jewish vocation, in that it sees Jesus as the embodiment of typological Israel as a means of blessing the nations. As being a descendent of Abraham means receiving a blessed inheritance, so any who believe in Jesus receive the power to become children of God (John 1:11–13).[29] As the law came through Moses, grace and truth came through Jesus as the Jewish Messiah/Christ (1:16–17).

Therefore, the central struggle between the Johannine leadership and local synagogue leadership in the 80s and 90s of the first century CE

---

turn leads to further tensions between Johannine leaders and other Christian groups in the region (see Käsemann 1968). Whereas Martyn engaged only one primary threat in his reading of John 9, all four of these dialectical engagements are clearly evident in a two-level reading of John 6 (Anderson 1997, 24–57).

28. Here I take issue with the thesis of Wayne Meeks (1972) that Johannine Christianity was sectarian. If John's sector of early Christianity included Jewish and gentile believers within an urban setting of the second-generation Pauline mission, they would have been more cosmopolitan than sectarian. *That* was their challenge: how to help gentile believers aspire to basic codes of Jewish faith and practice, being *in* the world but not *of* the world (John 17:15–16; 1 John 2:15–17; 5:21; Anderson 2007c). See also Kåre Fugsleth's (2005) thesis, challenging sectarian appraisals of the Johannine situation within its diaspora setting.

29. With Culpepper 1980; Pancaro 1970; de Jonge 1978; and van der Watt 1995, inviting audiences into the divine family is the center of the Johannine prologue and the rest of the gospel. As a communal response to John's story of Jesus (see 1 John 1:1–3), the Johannine prologue reformulates the Jewish agency schema of the Johannine narrative (rooted in Deut 18:15–22) in a Hellenistic-friendly way, welcoming later audiences into the divine family across cultural bounds as an invitation of grace (Anderson 2016).

involved struggles regarding how to actualize the blessings of Judaism as extensions of grace to the world. It is out of this contest over the heart of Judaism that the Johannine tensions with Jewish communities grew. Like the author of Revelation, who disparaged religious sibling rivals as "those who claim to be Jews but are not" (Rev 2:9; 3:9), so the Johannine evangelist heralds Jesus as fulfilling the heart of Jewish ideals; his is a radically Jewish vision. Therefore, just as John cannot be considered anti-Semitic, neither can it rightly be considered anti-Jewish in the general sense, even if it betrays tensions with particular Jewish groups during its Palestine and diaspora settings. John's presentation of Jesus as the Jewish Messiah/Christ reflects an intra-Jewish debate wherein the evangelist's radical Jewish messianism is only partly compelling, eventually leading to the parting of the ways with its parental Judaism. That eventuality, however, is only prefigured in the Johannine writings, not yet actualized.[30]

5. John's Dialectical Presentations of Jesus and Judaism

Before searching out the "correct analysis" of the Fourth Gospel's stance on Judaism, however, it must be acknowledged that the presentation of οἱ Ἰουδαῖοι in John is itself a dialectical one, not a monological rendering.[31] C. K. Barrett pointed out long ago that unless the dialectical character of the evangelist's thought and presentation of content is considered adequately, interpreters are likely to misconstrue the overall Johannine presentation of any given subject.[32] Jesus is portrayed in John as the most human as well

30. Contra Meeks (1985) and others who overread Johannine individuation from Judaism, the actualized parting of the ways before some time into the second century (and even so, unevenly) is critically questioned by recent scholarship: Lieu 2002; Nicklas 2014; Reed and Becker 2003; Dunn 2006; Shanks 2013; Charlesworth 2013. And the reason that Katz (1984) argued against Martyn's expulsion theory was the fact of Jewish-Christian closeness of fellowship well into the second century CE, around the time of the Bar Kokhba rebellion in 132 CE.

31. Note the highly dialogical character of a dozen of John's key theological subjects in especially presentations of the Ἰουδαῖοι. Even in John's construction of the "I am" sayings material, we see presentations of Jesus as fulfilling typological associations with the true Israel (Anderson 2011b, 190–93). Therefore, it is no surprise that first-rate scholars such as Zimmermann (2013) struggle with how to render John's complex presentation of οἱ Ἰουδαῖοι within its narrative.

32. Given that Barrett (1972) argues compellingly that the Fourth Evangelist was a dialectical thinker (see Anderson 1996, 136–65; 2004a), unless the evangelist's

as the most exalted, as equal to the Father as well as subordinated to the Father. Both sides of John's presentations *must* be considered in performing an adequate analysis of any Johannine subject. If not, the interpretation will be inevitably flawed. This is especially true on the subject of Jesus and Judaism within the Gospel of John.[33]

On one hand, some of the Jews in John are presented as archetypes of the unbelieving world. They reject Jesus as the revealer of the deity, and the evangelist portrays them as those who remain in darkness instead of coming to the light—those who love the praise of men rather than the glory of God, whose father is not Abraham or Moses but the devil (John 8:44). Robert Kysar (1993) and John Painter (1989) have pointed this out effectively, and John's presentation of quest and rejection stories reflects some of the agony within the only partly successful Johannine mission. Then again, John's tradition is pervasively Jewish, and it presents a Jesus who embodies the heart of the true Israel, declaring, "Salvation is of the Jews" (John 4:22). It is also a fact that some of the Jews explicitly believe in Jesus, so they are not presented in a totally negative light (8:31; 11:45; 12:11). This fact has often gone unnoticed by scholars, and all of Jesus's followers and faithful associates in John *are* Jewish. Therefore, it cannot be said that John is monologically anti-Semitic or anti-Jewish, or even that it is largely so. Despite tensions between Jesus and Jewish leaders in John, the majority of Jewish and Semitic figures in John (which includes the disciples, women, and even Samaritans) become faithful followers of Jesus, even if it happens in a processive way. That is a textual fact.

Another point also deserves mention, which is that negative judgments are not reserved exclusively for οἱ Ἰουδαῖοι in John; disciples and members of Jesus's band are also judged harshly. First, those unwilling to ingest the flesh and blood of Jesus—a reference to assimilating the death of Jesus on the cross as a call to martyrological faithfulness (as in Mark

multivalent presentations of the issue at hand are considered (with Meeks 1972; see Anderson 2011b, 25–43), one cannot claim to have interpreted the Fourth Gospel adequately.

33. According to Zimmermann (2013), John's presentation of οἱ Ἰουδαῖοι is uneven and highly problematic if a singular impression is sought, making a simplistic judgment—positive or negative—likely erroneous. Thus, the polyvalence of the Johannine narrative must be considered by interpreters if John's theological, historical, and literary riddles are to be assessed adequately (Anderson 2008; 2011b, 25–90), and on this subject, all references to the word must also be accompanied with analyses of related Jewish themes (Lieu 2008).

10:38–39)—have no life in themselves (6:51–54).[34] Second, even some of Jesus's disciples are scandalized by his hard saying, calling for embracing the way of the cross,[35] and they abandon him and walk with him no longer (6:60–66). Third, Peter (or someone among the Twelve) is also labeled by the evangelist as "a devil" (6:70), although the redactor clarifies that he must have meant Judas, the member of the Twelve who would betray Jesus later (6:71; 12:4; 13:2, 26; 18:2–5; Anderson 1996, 221–50; 2007e). Fourth, Jesus's followers (including Peter) are presented as miscomprehending, which is always rhetorical and deconstructive in narrative (13:6–12; 14:5, 8–9, 22; 16:17–18; 21:15–17; Anderson 1996, 194–97; 1997, 17–24). While Judas Iscariot is indeed presented as the clear villain in the text, it would be wrong to say that John's Jesus is anti-Kerioth (the hometown of Judas, 6:71; 12:4; 13:2, 26), despite Kerioth's being in the south and the fact that Judas is the only member of the Twelve who is explicitly referenced as being from Judea. Still, the negative judgment about Judas regards his acts of betrayal, not his place of origin. Nor should the Johannine Gospel be considered anti-Petrine or antiapostolic because some disciples abandon him and he calls Peter a devil.[36] It is the particular actions of those unwilling to embrace the way of the cross, or of those miscomprehending the character of servant leadership, that John's Jesus rebukes, not individual or groups of disciples overall.

So it is with some of the Ἰουδαῖοι and some Jewish leaders in John. While a leader of the Jews in Jerusalem, Nicodemus, is presented as initially not understanding Jesus in John 3, he comes around and stands up for Jesus in 7:50–51. He even helps to bury Jesus in 19:39–42, along with Joseph of Arimathea. Thus, it is particular actions or the lack thereof that are challenged by the Johannine Jesus, not generalized people groups.

---

34. The content here is martyrological, not ritually sacramental; with Borgen 1965; Anderson 1996, 110–36, 194–220.

35. The flesh profits nothing (John 6:63; Anderson 1996, 210).

36. On this account, I believe Raymond Brown is wrong to distance the Johannine evangelist from Peter and the apostolic band, changing his position on his being the son of Zebedee to an unknown eyewitness figure—not one of the Twelve. The Johannine critique of Petrine leadership is just as easily viewed as a dialectical engagement within the core of Jesus's closest followers rather than from the outside (Anderson 1991; 1996, 247–77). Thus, seeing the Fourth Evangelist as challenging hierarchical developments from within the Twelve, in the name of a more primitive understanding of the intentionality of Jesus for the movement following his wake, has great implications for ecclesiology and ecumenicity: Anderson 2005.

While Pilate is presented as an outsider to the truth in John 18–19, the royal official and his household come to believe in 4:46–54. Likewise, the Greeks aspire to see Jesus in John 12:20–21, and the woman at the well becomes the apostle to the Samaritans in 4. Therefore, the fact of positive presentations of Jewish individuals and groups must be held in tension with their negative or ambivalent portrayals, just as the negative portrayals of some of Jesus's disciples in John must be held in tension with their positive presentations elsewhere.

Given the dialectical character of John's renderings of different individuals and groups, it is a flawed inference to assume that all Jewish people are portrayed negatively, when most Jewish people in the Gospel of John respond to him positively and believe in him. The Samaritans and the Galileans welcome Jesus (4:39–45), and in Jerusalem the Pharisees dismay because "the whole world" is going after Jesus (12:19). Likewise, Peter's confession is followed by Jesus's statement that one of his followers is a devil (not simply a child thereof), and Judas is called the son of perdition. Note also that even the brothers of Jesus do not believe in him (7:5); this does not reflect, however, an antifraternal thrust. Thus, close followers of Jesus are not portrayed with general positivity, and Jewish actants within the narrative are not portrayed with pervasive negativity, despite the fact that Judean religious authorities are presented as opposing Jesus and threatening others within their reach. Therefore, the fact of Johannine dialectical presentations of key subjects must be taken into account before assuming too facilely a monological Johannine thrust.[37]

6. Ἰουδαῖος and Ἰουδαῖοι in the Fourth Gospel: Positive, Neutral, Negative, and Ambivalent Presentations

As the above analysis suggests, John's seventy-two references to Ἰουδαῖος and Ἰουδαῖοι deserve a closer analysis than simplistic judgments have allowed.[38]

37. For a polyvalent analysis of the Johannine narrative, see Anderson 2008.

38. With Lieu 2008. Thus, the translating of Ἰουδαῖος and Ἰουδαῖοι in John is a notoriously challenging task (Bratcher 1974). The contextually sensitive approach of Stephen Motyer (2008, 152–53) works fairly well, as he renders these terms "these Jews, passionate about legal observance" (5:18); "the Jews there, whose opinion was highly regarded in all matters to do with the Law and its observance" (7:15); "the more hard-line Jews in the synagogue leadership" (9:22); and "those Jews who want to kill me" (18:36).

These terms are used both positively and negatively in the Johannine narrative, and distinguishing the focus with regard to general-religious associations (hence referencing "Jew" or "Jews") and particular-geographic associations (hence referencing "Judean" or "Judeans") is essential for understanding explicitly what John is saying, and even more importantly, what he is not. With reference to Judaism in general, and also to "Israel" in particular, the following associations are found in the Fourth Gospel.

- Oἱ Ἰουδαῖοι—the Jewish religion in general—*positive*
    - "Salvation is of the *Jews*" (Jesus, 4:22).
- Oἱ Ἰουδαῖοι—the Jewish religion in general—*neutral*
    - Purification jars used by the *Jews* are referenced at the Cana wedding (2:6).
    - The Passover of the *Jews* is at hand (2:13; 6:4; 11:55).
    - "How is it that you, a *Jew*, ask a drink of me, a woman of Samaria?" (4:9).
    - *Jews* do not share things in common with Samaritans (4:9).
    - An unnamed festival of the *Jews* is mentioned (5:1).
    - The *Jewish* Festival of Tabernacles is near (7:2).
    - Pilate and the soldiers refer to Jesus mockingly as the king of the *Jews* and affixes a multilingual titulus on the cross: "Jesus of Nazareth, King of the *Jews*," evoking objections by the Judean leaders (18:33, 39; 19:3, 19, 21).
    - Pilate asks, "I am not a *Jew*, am I?" (18:35).
    - It is the Day of Preparation for the *Jews* (19:31, 42).
    - The burial customs of the *Jews* are described (19:40).
- Oἱ Ἰουδαῖοι—the Jewish religion in general—*negative*
    - No references
- Oἱ Ἰουδαῖοι—the Jewish religion in general—*ambivalence*
    - No references
- Presentations of "Israel" or "Israelite" in the Fourth Gospel—*all neutral or positive*
    - John the Baptist comes to reveal Jesus as the Messiah to *Israel* (1:31).
    - Jesus extols Nathanael as an *Israelite* in whom there is nothing false (1:47).
    - Nathanael lauds Jesus as the Son of God and the King of *Israel* (1:49).

- Nicodemus, as a teacher of *Israel*, should understand the spiritual character of God's workings (3:10).
- The Jerusalem crowd welcomes Jesus as the blessed one coming in the name of the Lord, the King of *Israel* (12:13).

From this analysis four things are clear. First, some references to Ἰουδαῖος and Ἰουδαῖοι imply the Jewish religion and its adherents in general, but these references comprise only eighteen of the seventy-two references—a small minority. Second, one of these references is positive, but the rest are neutral—simply explaining Jewish customs and practices to non-Jewish audiences. Third, *none* of these references are negative or ambivalent.[39] Fourth, the positive or at least neutral presentation of Judaism in the Gospel of John is all the more apparent when uses of "Israel" are analyzed. In all five instances, Israel-identity is presented as highly valued, and in two of them Jesus is proclaimed the King of Israel.

Therefore, there are absolutely no pejorative statements about the Jewish religion, Israel in particular, or Jewish persons in general in the Gospel of John, as opposed to Judean or Jerusalem-centered Jewish leaders and groups who are opposed to Jesus the Galilean prophet. Thus, it cannot be claimed exegetically that the Johannine narrative disparages Judaism as a religious faith, or its adherents, overall. If anything, references to Jewishness and to "Israel" convey pervasively positive associations, and this is a textual fact in John's story of Jesus.

By contrast, however, when Ἰουδαῖος or Ἰουδαῖοι occur with reference to particular religious leaders in Judea or in association with Jerusalem, the following positive, neutral, negative, and ambivalent associations are found in John's narrative. This is where the analysis will be telling.

- "Judeans"—Jewish leaders and persons in Jerusalem and Judea—*positive*

39. Assuming the two references to οἱ Ἰουδαῖοι in John 6 refer to Judeans, despite the fact that the debate in the Capernaum synagogue occurs in Galilee. As in Mark 7:1, it could be that religious leaders from Jerusalem had come to Galilee to examine Jesus and the authenticity of his ministry. They could also be a reference to Jewish authorities in general (with von Wahlde 1982), as John 6 was likely added to the narrative in a later, diaspora setting (Lindars 1972, 46–63; Anderson 1996, 205–8).

- The *Judeans* are astonished at Jesus's teaching because despite not having a formal education, no one has ever taught as he does (7:15).
- Jesus says to the *Judeans* who had believed in him, "If you continue in my word, you are truly my disciples; and you will know the truth, and the truth will make you free" (8:31–32).
- Many of the *Judeans* have come from Jerusalem to console Mary and Martha about their brother, showing empathy and love (11:18–19, 31).
- Jesus is moved when he sees Mary weeping and the *Judeans* with her also weeping (11:33).
- The *Judeans* are deeply moved at how much Jesus loved Lazarus—seeing him weeping (11:35–36).
- A great crowd of *Judeans* comes also to see Lazarus, and many of the *Judeans* are deserting the Jerusalem-based opposition to Jesus and are believing in him (12:9–11).

- "Judeans"—Jewish leaders in Judea—*neutral*
  - The *Judean leaders* send priests and Levites from Jerusalem to ask John, "Who are you?" (1:19).
  - Nicodemus is described as a leader among the *Judeans*; he is initially miscomprehending though interested in Jesus (3:1).
  - A discussion about purification arises between John's disciples and a *Judean leader* (3:25).
  - The healed lame man goes and tells the *Judean leaders* that Jesus has made him well (5:15).
  - The *Judeans* gather around Jesus and ask, "How long will you keep us in suspense? If you are the Messiah, tell us plainly" (10:24).
  - As Jesus has told the *Judean leaders*, so he also tells his disciples, "I am with you only a little longer. You will look for me.… Where I am going, you cannot come" (13:33).
  - Caiaphas is the one who has advised the *Judean leaders* that it is better for one person to die for the sake of the people (18:14).
  - Jesus claims to have spoken openly to the world, having taught in the synagogues and the temple—where the *Judeans* gather (18:20).
- "Judeans"—Jewish leaders in Judea—*negative*
  - The *Judean leaders* challenge Jesus, asking what sign he will

do regarding the destruction and rebuilding of the temple, as they claim it has been under construction for forty-six years (2:18, 20).

- The *Judean leaders* begin persecuting Jesus because he is healing on the Sabbath (5:16).
- The *Judean leaders* seek to kill Jesus because he is also calling God his Father, making himself equal to God (5:18; 7:1, 11; 10:31–33; 11:53).
- The *Judean leaders* question how Jesus can be the bread that has come down from heaven, and how he can give of his flesh for people to eat (6:41, 52).
- People in Jerusalem, the parents of the blind man, Joseph of Arimathea, and Jesus's disciples are afraid of the *Judean leaders* (7:13; 9:22; 19:38; 20:19).
- The *Judean leaders* fail to understand Jesus's saying that people will not be able to find him and that they cannot join him, wondering whether he will go to the diaspora or whether he will commit suicide (7:35–36; 8:22).
- *Judean leaders* accuse Jesus of being a Samaritan and having a demon (8:48, 52), misunderstanding his statement about his relationship to Abraham (8:56–57).
- The *Judeans* take up stones to kill Jesus for blasphemy (8:59; 10:30–33; 11:8).
- The *Judean leaders* do not at first believe the blind man has received his sight (9:18).
- The *Judean leaders* have already agreed that anyone who confesses Jesus to be the Messiah will be put out of the synagogue (9:22; see 12:42; 16:2).
- The *Judean leaders* negotiate with Pilate the death of Jesus, ironically accusing him of blasphemy and then committing the same, confessing they have no king but Caesar (18:31, 36, 38; 19:7, 12, 14, 20–21).

- "Judeans"—Jewish leaders in Judea—*ambivalence*
  - Nicodemus, a leader among the *Judeans*, comes to Jesus "by night," exposing his miscomprehension of the Spirit and being born from above (3:1–8), and yet he later stands up for Jesus among the Jerusalem leaders (7:50–51) and helps to bury Jesus after his death on the cross (19:39–40).

- Jesus is wary of going to Judea, where the *Judean leaders* are seeking to kill him, while his brothers encourage him to go and perform signs so that people will believe in him (7:1–10).
- The *Judeans* are divided, with some saying, "He has a demon and is out of his mind. Why listen to him?" Others are saying, "These are not the words of one who has a demon. Can a demon open the eyes of the blind?" (10:19–21).
- Jesus wants to go to Judea, but his disciples warn that the *Judeans* are wanting to stone him (11:7–8).
- Many of the *Judeans* who saw Jesus raise Lazarus believe in him, but others go to the Pharisees and tell them what he has done (11:45–46).
- Jesus no longer walks among the *Judeans* but stays with his disciples in Ephraim near the wilderness (11:54).

In analyzing the presentations of Ἰουδαῖοι as Judean religious leaders and Jerusalemites (7:25), several things are clear. First, in over a dozen instances, many of the Judeans believe in Jesus, and they are presented as comforting Mary and Martha over the death of Lazarus; Nicodemus begins his dialogue with Jesus in the dark, but he eventually stands up for Jesus in the face of strong opposition. Second, eight neutral references to the actions or customs of the Judeans inform the backdrop in socioreligious perspective regarding what happens within the narrative. Third, approximately three dozen (half of the references) to the Ἰουδαῖοι in John refer to Judean religious leaders, who question Jesus's disturbance in the temple, his healing on the Sabbath, his claiming to be acting on behalf of the Father, and his garnering a following. They begin plotting to kill Jesus early on, and eventually they turn Jesus over to Pilate, who sentences to death the one he labels "the king of the Jews" (19:19–21). Fourth, ambivalence on this score is palpable in two ways: there are intense divisions among Judean leaders over Jesus, as some believe in him and others oppose them for doing so; and Jesus and his companions express disagreement and ambivalence over whether to travel to Judea, where the religious authorities are known to be seeking to kill Jesus. Fifth, some of these references could be considered Jews rather than Judeans: those questioning Jesus in 6:41 and 52 appear to be from Judea, although the discussion is set in the Capernaum synagogue; the places where the Judeans gather (synagogues and the temple) in 18:20 could also be taken to refer to Jewish places of worship more generally, although that saying is delivered in Jerusalem.

The result of this analysis is that while many among the Judeans believe—as did also the Galileans, the Samaritans, and the Hellenists—half of the Ἰουδαῖοι references in John are to Judean leaders who question Jesus, fail to embrace his works and teachings, and seek to do him in. They see him as an affront to temple money-changing and animal-selling enterprises, and his healings on the Sabbath violate the Mosaic law. In challenging a legalistic interpretation of Mosaic authority, Jesus appeals to the Mosaic prophet schema rooted in Deut 18:15–22, whereby he is accused of being the presumptuous prophet, who speaks on his own behalf. Jesus responds that he says or does nothing except what the Father commands, which leads to his being accused of making himself equal to God, claiming God as his Father.[40] Jesus predicts things in advance to show that he is the authentic Mosaic prophet, but ironically, he is then accused of blasphemy by those committing blasphemy before Pilate, claiming to have no king but Caesar.

Palpable here also is the concern that if a popular uprising should threaten Roman concerns for security, especially during Passover festivities, the Romans will exact a preemptive backlash, causing hundreds or thousands to suffer or die. Therefore, the concerns of Judean leaders are not simply over halakic interpretations of the Mosaic law; they have been on edge also about John the Baptist, and they appear threatened by the groundswell around the John-and-Jesus movement. They also may wish to preserve their place within society, so John's references to people privileging the praise of humanity over the glory of God reflect a critique of religious leaders seeking to preserve their societal status rather than being open to new revelations of God's truth (5:41–44; 7:17–19; 8:50–54; 12:43). Further, in defending a legalistic understanding of Sabbath observance, Judean leaders are overlooking the love that is central to the healings. In terms of corroborative impression, as does the synoptic Jesus, the Johannine Jesus also emphasizes the heart of the Mosaic law by his deeds and words. The center of God's concern is love, and those rejecting Jesus and his mission do so because God's love is not abiding in their hearts (5:42).

40. Wayne Meeks (1990) shows how this Jewish agency schema accounts for Jesus in John claiming to be equal to God as well as evoking a typical Jewish countermove: challenging divine agency with allegations of one's being the presumptuous prophet, also forewarned in Deut 18 (Meeks 1976).

These themes are spelled out further in an analysis of other Jewish players in the narrative, even if they are not referenced as Ἰουδαῖος or Ἰουδαῖοι explicitly.

- The chief priests and high priest
  - One of them, Caiaphas, who is the *high priest* at the time, declares that it is better for one man to die on behalf of (instead of) the nation; from then on they seek to put Jesus to death (11:49–53).
  - The *chief priests* seek to put Lazarus also to death (12:10).
  - Pilate claims Jesus's own nation and the *chief priests* have handed him over to him (18:35).
  - The *chief priests* and police call for Jesus to be crucified (19:15).
  - The *chief priests* of the Judean leaders ask Pilate to change the titulus to "This man said, I am King of the Jews" (19:21).
- The Pharisees
  - People questioning John's authority were sent by the *Pharisees*, who later learn that Jesus is making more disciples than John (1:24; 4:1).
  - Nicodemus, a leader among the Judeans, is a *Pharisee* (3:1).
  - The *Pharisees* challenge the crowd for their believing in Jesus and claim they have been deceived; none of the *Pharisees* believe in Jesus (7:32, 47–48).
  - The *Pharisees* claim that Jesus is testifying on his own behalf—implicitly the presumptuous prophet of Deut 18:15–22 (8:13).
  - The *Pharisees* question the man born blind, claiming that Jesus cannot be legitimate because he is a "sinner"—having performed a healing on the Sabbath (9:13–16).
  - Some of the Judeans report the raising of Lazarus to the *Pharisees* (11:45–46).
  - The *Pharisees* exclaim in dismay that "the whole world" has gone after Jesus (12:19).
  - Residents of Jerusalem refuse to confess adherence to Jesus openly for fear of the *Pharisees*, lest they be put out of the synagogue (12:42).
- The chief priests and the Pharisees
  - The *chief priests and the Pharisees* send the temple police to arrest Jesus, although they are later asked why they did not do so themselves (7:32, 45).

- The *chief priests and the Pharisees* call a meeting to decide what to do about Jesus, and they command people to inform them about where Jesus is so that he can be arrested (11:47, 57).
- Soldiers and temple police are sent by the *chief priests and the Pharisees* to arrest Jesus in the garden (18:3).

- The authorities
  - The Jerusalemites are baffled because *the authorities* who have been trying to kill Jesus allow him to continue speaking; they wonder whether they have come to believe in Jesus (7:25–26).
  - The Pharisees question whether any of *the authorities* or the Pharisees have come to believe in Jesus (7:47–48).
  - Many of *the authorities* believe in Jesus, but they are afraid to say so because of the Pharisees, lest they be expelled from the synagogue (12:42).
- The crowd
  - While not named as "the crowd," Jesus's disciples believe following his first sign in Cana of Galilee, and many in Jerusalem believe in Jesus early in his ministry, on account of his signs (2:11, 23).
  - Jesus disappears into the *crowd* in Jerusalem; many believe in him on the basis of his signs, yet others claim that he is deceiving the *crowds* and that he has a demon—the *crowd* is divided on Jesus (5:13; 7:12, 20, 31–32, 40, 43).
  - The *crowd* in Galilee follows Jesus, interested in his works, though even some of his disciples abandon him and walk with him no longer (6:2, 5, 22, 24, 66).
  - Many in the Jerusalem *crowd* believe that Jesus is indeed the Mosaic prophet; they are accused of not knowing the Mosaic law and declared to be accursed by the Judean leaders (7:40, 43, 49).
  - While not described as "the crowd," many in Judea come to believe in Jesus as he revisits the baptismal site of John's ministry, believing on account of his signs (10:40–42).
  - Jesus speaks for the sake of the *crowd* in Bethany, that they might believe, and many come to see Jesus and Lazarus after the sign (11:42; 12:9, 12, 18).
  - The *crowd* in Judea testifies to the raising of Lazarus and the thundering voice from heaven, and yet they also question the

> meaning of Jesus's words regarding the uplifting of the Son of Man (12:17, 29, 34).

From the characterization of these groups of people, several associations become clear. First, the chief priests in Jerusalem plot to kill Jesus, and not only do they hand Jesus over to Pilate to be crucified, but they also plot to kill Lazarus, lest his testimony be compelling. Second, the Pharisees are presented as seeking to retard the popularism of John the Baptist and Jesus—alleging the crowd has been deceived—accusing Jesus of being the presumptuous false prophet as well as a sinner. They intimidate believing authorities and others with threats of synagogue expulsion if they confess Jesus openly. Third, the chief priests and the Pharisees collaborate (likewise in Matt 21:45; 27:62) in seeking to have Jesus arrested, and they call a meeting in Jerusalem to decide what to do about the rise of the Jesus movement and the fear of Roman retaliation. Fourth, unnamed authorities are presented as ambivalent. On one hand, they seek to have Jesus killed; on the other hand, some of them become secret followers of Jesus. Fifth, the crowd is presented as especially interested in the signs of Jesus, and they come to believe that he is the prophet predicted by Moses despite being accused by the Pharisees of being ignorant of the law and accursed.

From the above analysis of the characterization of Judaism, Jewish individuals, and Jewish groups in the Fourth Gospel, there is no negative presentation of Judaism in itself. Nor are individuals or groups maligned simply for being Jewish. Rather, those who welcome Jesus and believe are commended (all of them are Semitic or Jewish), and those who question Jesus, rejecting his words and works, are disparaged. Jesus is received and rejected in both Galilee and Judea, although his rejection in Galilee is minimal (some of his followers abandon him, and the Judeans question him in John 6), and his rejection in Jerusalem is most severely pronounced. There it is that the chief priests and the Pharisees are synonymous with the Ἰουδαῖοι who challenge Jesus and endeavor to put him to death. These Judean religious leaders also intimidate the Jewish crowds and other authorities, accusing them of being accursed and threatening people with synagogue exclusion if they confess Jesus openly. The crowds are impressed with Jesus's signs, and they identify him with the prophet predicted by Moses, whose words come true and who speaks authentically the message that God has instructed. The Pharisees are threatened by Jesus's popularity; they are offended by his healings on the Sabbath and scandalized by his claiming to be one with the Father. This is why they collaborate with the chief priests to put Jesus to death.

7. Jesus and the Judean Leaders in John: An Intra-Jewish Set of Tensions

As is clear from the above analysis, the engagements between Jesus and the Ἰουδαῖοι in John reflect largely, if not solely, tensions between the Jesus movement and the Judean religious leaders, even if they are narrated in a later setting. It is thus anachronistic to infer an actualized parting of the ways, as the Johannine Jesus movement is still grounded within the Jewish family of faith, though seeing Jesus the Christ as extending the blessings of Abraham and Moses to the rest of the world beloved of God. In that sense, the Gospel of John deserves to be regarded as reflecting "Johannine Judaism" perhaps even more fittingly than "Johannine Christianity." John's Jewish center of gravity is evidenced in its thoroughly Jewish presentations of the Johannine Jesus, differing emphases within its earlier and later material, and developing sets of engagements within the evolving Johannine situation. Therefore, rather than seeing the relation between Jesus and the Judean leaders in John as anti-Jewish, here we have *an intra-faith set of tensions, not an interfaith set of dialogues*. The Fourth Gospel's intra-Jewish character and radically Jewish thrust can thus be seen in the following ways.

7.1. John's Gospel: The Most Jewish Piece of Writing in the Entire New Testament

This is because John represents a radical view of the Jewish vocation, even though it is clearly in tension with the views of those managing the Jerusalem temple and its cultic practices (the chief priests) and those appealing to Scripture-based understandings of the Jewish covenant (the Pharisees). This is why the engagements between the Galilean prophet and these formidable groups in Judea are especially pronounced in the Johannine narrative, and therein lies the bulk of John's negative presentations of Jewish leaders. The uneven acceptance and rejection of Jesus and his vision of the heart of the Jewish vocation is narrated alongside a robust appeal for Jewish and gentile audiences alike to receive Jesus as the Messiah-Christ, availing inclusion in the divine family to any and all who respond to that message (1:10–13). Thus, contra the two-level approaches of J. Louis Martyn, Brown, and others,[41] John's story of Jesus appears to convey more about the first level of history than later levels of theology.[42] More specifically, most of John's presentation of the ambivalent reception of Jesus by the Judean leaders coheres with topographical, religious, and sociological knowledge of pre-70 CE Jerusalem, and more specifically, it coheres with the time period of Jesus's ministry. Therefore, John's story of Jesus, while conveying constructed theology in a narrative mode, also conveys remembered history within a theological appeal (Anderson 2006a, 175–89). On the first level of history, the Galilean prophet was indeed unevenly received in Jerusalem, where he was finally killed at the hands of the Romans, aided by the religious establishment.

In that sense, just as the Qumran community's pitting of the Wicked Priest in Jerusalem against the Teacher of Righteousness poses a means of bolstering its vision for the heart of Judaism, John's memory of Jesus performs something parallel. An example of this pro-Jewish set of commitments is the fact that John identifies Jesus as the Jewish Messiah. Each of the "I am" sayings in John bears associations with a typological image of the essence of Israel—within the vineyard of Israel, Jesus is the true vine; alongside the light on the hill of Zion, Jesus is the light of the world; among the shepherds of Israel, Jesus is the true shepherd, who lays down his life for the sheep; in addition to the bread that Moses gave—via the wilderness and in the torah—Jesus is the heavenly bread that God now gives, and so forth. Nathanael is the "true Israelite in whom no falsity exists," and even the sonship of Jesus is portrayed in the trajectory of the authentic Israel. Jesus in John not only comes as the anticipated Jewish Messiah and the authentic Mosaic agent of Yahweh, but he also embodies the heart of "a nation of vision," Philo's description of Israel.[43]

41. In addition to the long-running critique of Martyn by Adele Reinhartz (1998; 2001a), note also critiques of the Brown-Martyn two-level reading of John overall: Klink 2009; Hägerland 2003. Then again, D. Moody Smith (1996) affirms the overall sketching of the Johannine situation as set forth by Martyn and Brown, although not all of John's riddles can be explained on the basis of a single dialogue with the local Jewish presence in a diaspora setting (Smith 1984).

42. Interestingly, the Gospel of John features more topographical and archaeologically attested details than all the other gospels put together: von Wahlde 2006; Anderson 2006a. See the contributions of vols. 1–3 in the John, Jesus, and History Project: Anderson, Just, and Thatcher 2007; 2009; 2016.

43. See Borgen's engagement of Richter along these lines: Anderson 1996, 55–57.

In addition, the Fourth Evangelist reflects notably Jewish forms of exegetical operation in his presentation of Jesus's ministry. First, as Peder Borgen has shown, John's expansion on the ministry of Jesus in ways cohering with Palestine-based midrashim and Philo's homiletical expansions on biblical texts reflects a thoroughly Jewish pattern of operation.[44] Second, Jesus is also presented in John as fulfilling the prophecy of Moses in Deut 18:15–22, confirmed by his words coming true. Therefore, the Father and the Son are connected in John because the Son does only what the Father commands.[45] Third, Jesus fulfills the typology also of Elijah/Elisha in the performing of his signs; thus, Moses and Elijah are not prefigured by John the Baptist in the Fourth Gospel but by Jesus.[46] Fourth, John's Jesus fulfills Jewish Scripture in the *typological* sense as well as in the *predictive* sense. In that sense, John's Scripture-fulfillment constructions reflect a distinctively Jewish pattern of worship and instruction designed to affirm the fulfillment of Jewish Scripture in the ministry of Jesus.[47] Fifth, John's presentation of Jesus as the Son of Man also fulfills the typologies of the true Israel, confirmed likewise by the "I am" sayings attributed to him by the evangelist.

In 1924, an orthodox Jewish scholar of rabbinics at the University of Cambridge made the remarkable statement: "To us Jews, the Fourth Gospel is *the most Jewish of the four*" (Neill 1988, 338; emphasis mine). J. B. Lightfoot (2015, 41–78) and C. K. Barrett (1975) likewise considered John

44. Following the lead of Nils Alstrup Dahl (1997), Peder Borgen (1965) identifies numerous parallels between the Johannine development of the manna motif in Exod 16:4 (and Ps 78:24–25) and its developments in the Palestinian midrashim, targumic literature, and the writings of Philo.

45. For compelling treatments of the Johannine presentation of Jesus as fulfilling the Mosaic prophet typology of Deut 18:15–22, see Borgen 1997; Reinhartz 1992. See Anderson 1999 (and the third printing of *The Christology of the Fourth Gospel*, 2010, lxxix–lxxviii), where twenty-four parallels with this passage are found in John—especially Jesus's word coming true, showing that he is indeed the authentic prophet, of whom Moses wrote.

46. Wayne Meeks (1967) shows the many ways in which the typologies of Elijah and Moses are embellished and fulfilled in Samaritan literature and in John's presentation of Jesus (Anderson 1996, 174–76, 192). This may also explain why the Fourth Gospel presents John the Baptist as denying that he is either Elijah or the Prophet (Moses)—contra Mark (Anderson, Just, and Thatcher 2007, 20–21).

47. The Gospel of John features dozens of implicit and explicit fulfillments of Jewish Scripture in the ministry of Jesus (Anderson 1996, 20–21; 2011b, 83–85).

the most Jewish of the gospels, so a nuanced analysis is required before ascribing the Fourth Gospel an anti-Semitic label. It is precisely John's pro-Jewish thrust that evoked consternation among competing visions of Jewishness with the developing Johannine tradition, and that is why tensions continued later within the emerging Johannine situation.[48] Territoriality exists only between members of like species, and this is why Jesus adherents within the Johannine situation were subjected to discipline as their Christologies rose higher and as their movement gathered strength. Thus, tensions with Jewish leaders in a Hellenistic setting shifted from the operations of the temple and healings on the Sabbath to monotheism versus ditheism and the inclusion of gentiles within the Abrahamic family of faith.

7.2. The Development between John's Earlier and Later Material

Assuming that some later material was added to an earlier stage of John's narrative composition and that the Johannine Epistles were likely composed between the first edition of John's narrative and its finalization, some interesting features of John's Jewishness emerge.[49] Of all John's composition theories, the most convincing is a modification of Barnabas Lindars's view,[50] which accounts for all the major aporias in John with

---

48. On the pervasively Jewish background of John, see W. D. Davies 1996, who sees John's assertion of a radically Jewish vision of Jesus and his mission as the reason that it received such strong opposition among some Jewish audiences. Put otherwise, territoriality exists *only* among members of like species, and more specifically, within the same gender.

49. This was the emerging consensus among several leading Johannine scholars in their analyses of the place of the Johannine Epistles as having been written within the composition process of John's Gospel. See Culpepper and Anderson 2014. For instance, von Wahlde (2010a) follows Brown (2003) in seeing the Johannine Epistles being written in Ephesus between the second and third (final) editions of John's Gospel.

50. John Ashton and I came to the same judgment independently: Ashton 2007; Anderson 1996. For a fuller development of John's dialogical autonomy and composition, see Anderson 2011b, 125–55; 2015. Within such an approach, (1) a first edition of John's narrative (concluding with 20:31) may be seen as an alternative to Mark (ca. 80–85 CE); (2) the Beloved Disciple continues to teach and preach, and the Johannine Elder writes the three Johannine Epistles as a circular (1 John), an epistle (2 John), and a letter (3 John), building on the themes of the earlier narrative material (ca. 85–95 CE); (3) following the death of the Beloved Disciple, the Elder adds to a first edition (or stage) of John's narrative the Logos hymn as an engaging introduction (similar to

minimal speculation. While more complex theories abound, a basic two-stage approach (although there may have been multiple stages within the material's development and composition) fits well within the strongest of composition theories. It also accounts for similarities between some of the gospel's later material and that of the epistles, as we see a shift in the meaning of "belief" between these two sets of materials. For the first-edition material, to believe in Jesus as the Christ is to receive him as the Jewish Messiah/Christ. Within the later material, believing is more closely associated with abiding in Christ and his community of faith. Therefore, we see a shift from an apologetic interest to a pastoral concern between the earlier and later editions of the Johannine story of Jesus.[51]

Significant for the present study, however, is an observable shift in emphasis between John's presentation of Jesus and Jewish subjects. Given that an interesting set of distributions emerges between the material in the two editions, an analysis provides insights into the community's history and resultant meanings of the material:

1. First, the most intense presentations of the *Judean leaders* occur within the first stage of the material's development. This implies a remembered set of tensions between the Galilean prophet and the religious authorities of Jerusalem.[52] As an augmentation of Mark, John's presentation of the early ministry of Jesus shows his work alongside that of John the Baptist as *a challenge to temple-centered practices in Jerusalem and the performing of early prophetic signs in Galilee* (2:11; 4:54)—before those rendered in Mark 1. John also includes *three signs of Jesus performed in Jerusalem and Bethany*, beyond the Galilean miracles presented in Mark—Sabbath healings and the raising of Lazarus—a total of five signs not included in Mark. The rhetorical thrust of this selection thus poses five prophetic signs of Jesus alongside the five books of Moses as a Jewish-friendly apologetic narrative. Therefore, the early stage in John's narrative

---

1 John 1:1–3), eyewitness and Beloved-Disciple references (esp. 19:34–35), and chapters 6, 15–17, and 21, circulating it among the churches as a complement to the other gospels (ca. 100 CE).

51. For an analysis of the strengths and weaknesses of over a dozen leading theories of John's composition leading to a new overall theory, see Anderson 1996, 33–68; 2011b, 95–170; esp. 2015.

52. Tensions between followers of the Galilean prophet and the Jewish establishment in Jerusalem are palpable in sources beyond the Johannine tradition, and hence John's story of Jesus receives corroborative support within its Palestinian phase of development (Reicke 1984).

development presents Jesus as the Jewish Messiah, inviting audiences in a Hellenistic setting to believe in him as such and to be welcomed into the blessings of the Jewish faith by believing in Jesus of Nazareth.[53]

2. Within this material, *the authorization of Jesus* (and lack thereof) is key within his engagements with the Judean leaders. While the Galilean visitors to Jerusalem are impressed with his prophetic challenge to the marketization of institutional temple practices (2:13–25; 4:45), the Judean leaders not only seek to dampen the appeal of his work, but they begin planning to put Jesus to death because of a threefold offense: the temple disturbance, healing on the Sabbath, and making God his Father (5:18). Mosaic authority is here levied, as Moses gave the law regarding the forbidding of work on the Sabbath (Exod 20:8–11), and the Shema reminds Israel that the Lord God is *one* (Deut 6:4). To these challenges, Jesus is presented as appealing to an alternative Mosaic authority—*the prophet-like-Moses typology*, rooted in Deut 18:15–22 (John 5:16–30; 7:14–30; 8:12–20), bolstered by *Danielic Son-of-Man apocalypticism* (John 5:27; 8:28). This, of course, raises further consternation over Jesus's emphasis on the unity of the Son with the Father, which then leads to charges of blasphemy and its capital penalty (8:59; 10:33). In Johannine perspective, the religious authorities do not sense God's love, which was central to the Sabbath healing, and while they may know the Scriptures, they do not see that they point to Jesus as the one of whom Moses wrote (5:31–46—a reference to Deut 18:15, 18). While Jesus spiritualizes the water-libation theme of Sukkot, they anticipate a Davidic Judean leader and are blind to the possibility that a messianic leader might come from Galilee (John 7:37–52).

3. Resulting tensions between would-be followers of Jesus and the Judean authorities are then referenced in a variety of ways, and palpable is the sense that these tensions continued for several decades after the ministry of Jesus. First, *fear of the Judean leaders* keeps people from expressing openly their allegiance to Jesus (7:13; 19:38), and even after his death the followers of Jesus meet behind closed doors as a factor of that intimidation (20:19). Second, this fear is named more specifically as being felt by oppressed-though-believing Jewish authorities, who fear the Pharisees' endeavors to put open confessors of Jesus *out of the synagogue* (12:42). The parents of the man born blind are also subjected to this intimida-

53. Thus, John's apologetic thrust is designed to lead audiences into belief in Jesus as the Jewish Messiah/Christ on the basis of the witnesses, the signs, and the fulfilled word (Anderson 2000).

tion, as the Judean leaders "had already decided" that any who confessed Jesus to be the Messiah would be put out of the synagogue—an existential reality earlier and later (9:22). In the second-edition material, this threat is reflected on more generally in the later stages of the Johannine situation, as those who do not know the Father or the Son will put people out of the synagogue, leading possibly to their death (16:1–4—perhaps at the hands of the Romans if they do not confess Caesar as Lord under Domitian's reign). While theories of mass expulsions are unlikely, the Judean leaders' investment in dampening the Galilean Jesus movement during the Palestinian phase of the Johannine situation continues on within its Hellenistic phase, involving the understandable attempt to discipline perceived ditheism within diaspora synagogues. Even if Bernier's thesis is correct, that the Birkat against the *minim* began as a political concern close to the time of Jesus's ministry, it later came to function as a means of disciplining aspects of Jewish faith and practice, which would have targeted perceived ditheism in post-70 CE Judaism.

4. While Martyn disparaged links between the Johannine Gospel and Epistles, they actually bolster his theory in a general sense, even though tensions with local synagogues were not the most acute set of crises faced by Johannine believers in the 80s and 90s. The Johannine Epistles thus reflect some of the internal difficulties faced by the Johannine community and neighboring ones. First, there is *disagreement over what is sinful and what is not*. Gentile believers might not share the same convictions as to what is appropriate and what should be eschewed, having become part of the Jewish family of faith. The final chapter of 1 John clarifies that death-producing sins are not options for believers, and the last word coheres with the first word: *stay away from idols!* (1 John 1:5–10; 5:21). That would have been especially relevant during the reign of Domitian (81–96 CE), when subjects of the Roman Empire were expected to reverence Caesar or suffer the consequences.[54] Being "out of the synagogue" also meant that while believers did not have to pay the *fiscus Ioudaicus* (the two-drachma tax exacted on all Jewish subjects in the empire—to be paid to Jupiter Capitolina, Josephus, *War* 7.218), they were expected to reverence Caesar one way or another. Second, some have apparently *abandoned the Johannine community*, deciding to recant their confessions of Jesus as the Christ,

---

54. See the compelling argument by Richard Cassidy (1992) and the work of Tom Thatcher (2008); see also Anderson 1996, 221–51; 1997, 41–50.

reflecting acquiescence to the continuing effect of synagogue disciplining endeavors reflected in John 9:22 and 12:42. This is less of a schism and more of a defection, as Jewish members of John's community find themselves courted back into the religious certainty and sociological homogeneity of the synagogue. The appeal of Jewish family and friends would also have been strong. Here the Elder counters by denying their central interest—preserving Jewish monotheism—claiming that those denying the Son will forfeit the Father, but those who receive the Son also maintain the Father's embrace (1 John 2:18–25; Anderson 1997, 32–40; 2007c). While the proselytizing defection crisis is somewhat past, however, a third crisis is on the way: *the false teachings of traveling docetizing prophets and teachers, who deny that Jesus came in the flesh* (1 John 4:1–3; 2 John 7). While the term ἀντίχριστοι is also used to describe these teachers, this crisis is altogether different from the Jewish departures. One threat is past, the next one is impending; one threat involved secession, the later involved visitation; one threat denied Jesus's being the Jewish Messiah/Christ, the later one denied his humanity. Yet the main interest of the docetizers was probably more practical than theological—the legitimizing of assimilation to culture over against maintaining Jewish standards of faith and practice. In terms of local pagan festivals, reverencing Caesar's image, and "loving the world," a nonsuffering Jesus alleviates the need for his followers to embrace costly discipleship. A fourth crisis in the later Johannine situation involved *tensions with emerging institutional hierarchical leaders in neighboring Christian communities*. Here, the primacy-loving Diotrephes has not only forbidden Johannine believers from visiting his community, but he threatens his own church members with expulsion if they take them in (3 John 9–10; with Käsemann 1968 and others). The Elder has written to "the church" about Diotrephes, whose proto-Ignatian approach to church unity is being experienced adversely by at least one neighboring community. This leads the Elder, then, to finalize the testimony of the Beloved Disciple (after his death—around 100 CE) and to circulate it among the churches as a manifesto of Jesus's will for the church—a spirit-based and egalitarian approach to believers' unity in Christ, the Jewish Messiah.

5. In the later material added to the Johannine Gospel, several operations and interests are evident. First, the Jewish agency motif rooted in the Mosaic prophet typology of Deut 18 has been transformed *into a cross-cultural Logos hymn designed to include gentile believers alongside Jewish followers of Jesus* (John 1:1–5, 9–14, 16–18; note parallels to 1 John 1:1–3; see Anderson 2016). Therefore, by extending the blessings of Abrahamic

faith to the nations, despite the uneven reception of Jesus among "his own," as many as believe receive adoption into the divine family as children of God (John 1:10–13). Second, the addition of John 6 features the only occurrences of Ἰουδαῖος/Ἰουδαῖοι found in the supplementary material, and two of these are simply within dialogues with Jesus in John 6:41 and 52, where Οἱ Ἰουδαῖοι (or Judeans) do not understand what Jesus has been saying. They are miscomprehending but not intensely adversarial here. The Passover feast of the Jews is also mentioned as locating the time of the feeding in 6:4, which is presented neutrally. What this later material suggests is that the intensity of debates with local Jewish communities has waned; the thrust of the later material is more pastoral than apologetic. It calls people to abide in Jesus and his community in the face of hardships under empire. A third feature within this later material is that it displays virtually all of the incarnational material in the Fourth Gospel, reflecting an antidocetic thrust: the Word became flesh (1:14), believers must ingest the flesh and blood of Jesus—a reference to the way of the cross (6:51–58), tribulation in the world is predicted (chs. 15–17), water and blood poured forth from the pierced side of Jesus (19:34–35), and the martyrological death of Peter is predicted (21:18–23). This thrust replicates the interest in staving off the docetists referenced in 1–2 John.[55] A fourth interest furthers John's egalitarian and spirit-based ecclesiology by presenting Peter as affirming the authority of Jesus (6:68–69; a dialectical engagement of Matt 16:17–19?), featuring Jesus's teaching on the accessibility of the Holy Spirit to all believers (John 15–16), and asserting the priority of loving the flock in the ambivalent reinstatement of Peter (21:15–17). These features in the Beloved Disciple's later ministry would have been important for the Johannine Elder to assert, especially in his dealing with Diotrephes and hierarchical developments within proto-Ignatian Christianity, following the death of the Beloved Disciple.

7.3. Closer Foci on the Palestinian and Diaspora Settings of the Evolving Johannine Situation

As a result of this overview, the developing engagements in Jesus-Judean and Johannine-Jewish engagements are evident within the evolving history

55. So argues Borgen 1965, and this accounts for elements of John's antidocetic emphases on the fleshly incarnation of Jesus, with Schnelle 1992.

of the Johannine situation. On this score, Martyn's earlier view that there was a singular dialectical relationship within the Johannine situation—with the local synagogue in a diaspora setting—is far too limited. That was one of the dialectical engagements within the Johannine situation, but it was not the only one, and in the later phase it was not even the primary one. Brown's multivalent dialectical approach is more realistic, although it also fails to account for the Roman presence under Domitian, and it makes too much of Samaritan inferences.[56] Assuming a move to Asia Minor or some other diaspora setting during the Roman invasion of Palestine from 66–73 CE, the following Jesus-Judean and Johannine-Jewish tensions are plausible.

7.3.1. Palestine-Based Tensions between the Jesus Movement and the Judean Leaders

- Jesus follows the lead of John the Baptist in challenging the institutions and religious practices of Galilee and Judea, leading off with the temple incident, performing healings on the Sabbath, and creating cognitive dissonance with his words and deeds; this evokes opposition by Judean leaders, who challenge his authorization.
- In response to Mosaic-law and institutionalized-religion challenges, Jesus defends his authorization, citing the Mosaic prophet typology (with his word being fulfilled) and Son of Man apocalyptic agency (Borgen 1997; Reinhartz 1989, 10).
- Jesus and his followers encounter resistance in Judea, leading to the chief priests and Pharisees plotting to put Jesus to death at the hand of the Romans, which indeed eventuates.
- If an early Birkat Haminim was operative in Jerusalem during the ministry of Jesus and following, it could reflect resistance against Jesus for political reasons, disparaging Galilean political-messiah insurrectionism out of fears of a likely Roman backlash.
- Competition with followers of John the Baptist is palpable within the Johannine narrative, as John is presented as being the key witness to Jesus—yoking his popular authority to the Jesus movement.

56. For a fuller analysis of the Johannine community that Raymond Brown left behind, see Anderson 2014a.

- Continuing tensions between followers of Jesus and Judean leaders are also evidenced in the Johannine narrative, as the disparaging of Galileans and Samaritans by the Jerusalemites continues.

7.3.2. Diaspora-Based Tensions between Johannine Believers and Jewish Communities

- With the movement to Asia Minor or another diaspora setting around 70 CE, the Johannine leadership joins the local synagogue, likely worshiping with Jewish community members on the Sabbath and with gentile believers in Jesus on First Day—plausibly reflecting the fruit of the Pauline mission.
- As Johannine believers witness to their conviction that Jesus is the Jewish Messiah, this appeal is partially compelling; some come to believe in Jesus, but others see the Father-Son relationship claims as a blasphemous development.
- The blessing against the heretics bolsters the disciplining of perceived ditheists, as the use of the Birkat Haminim becomes a codification of local concerns, leading, perhaps unwittingly, to the departure of some Johannine believers.
- Following a partial separation from the synagogue, some Johannine community members are apparently proselytized back into the synagogue if they are willing to diminish their beliefs in Jesus as the Messiah—embracing something like an Ebionite Christology; John's leadership calls for solidarity with Jesus and his community.
- As traveling gentile-Christian prophets and teachers come within reach of the Johannine situation, the Johannine leaders assert Jewish-based convictions against their assimilative teachings—including admonitions regarding staying away from idols, resistance to worldly customs, and refusing to offer emperor laud.
- As monepiscopal structures of hierarchical leadership emerge within proto-Ignatian Christianity, the Johannine approach to community organization maintains its Jewish egalitarian and presbyter-based approach to discernment and leadership.

Within these developments in the Johannine tradition and situation, it is clear that John's presentation of Jesus never really departs from its Jewish origin and ethos. As the Martyn paradigm too easily dismisses the first levels of history in the Johannine tradition, a more nuanced view of John's historical memory sees most of its narrative as reflecting an intra-Jewish perspective on what happened to Jesus "back then" and therefore "why it matters" in later settings. While Martyn's overall view that synagogue disciplining—leading to at least some departures or perceived expulsions—has not been overturned by scholars claiming close relations between Christians and Jews in the second century,[57] flaws in this approach are threefold. First, Martyn wrongly follows a form of the earlier Bultmannian view that the Johannine narrative was constructed on an alien source; it did not have its own historical memory to develop.[58] This inference has been overturned by the fact that Bultmann's own evidence for a diachronic origin of John's material is completely lacking.[59] Thus, the historical character of John's memory of Jesus's ministry deserves renewed critical consideration on the *einmalig* level of the events reported.[60] Second, Martyn wrongly discounts the Johannine Epistles as having anything to do with the Johannine situation in which the Johannine Gospel was finalized. This may have been a factor of the difficulty in dealing with the docetizing antichrist figures within his John-Jewish paradigm, but if the secessionists in 1 John 2:18–25 returned to religious security of the synagogue having

---

57. For instance, while Reuven Kimelman (1981, 232) questions inferences of mass expulsions from late first-century synagogues, he does acknowledge that the Birkat Haminim would have been targeted at Jesus adherents within Jewish communities in Palestine, based on the report of Rabbi Issi of Caesarea: "From this it is clear that *minim* can include at least Jewish Christians. Hence it is safe to conclude that the Palestinian prayer against the *minim* was aimed at Jewish sectarians among whom Jewish Christians figured prominently."

58. Thus, Martyn supervised Robert Fortna's (1970) doctoral work on the identification of a signs gospel as the primary source underlying the Johannine narrative, allowing him to focus on the second level of John's story of Jesus, having eliminated the Johannine character of its origin, following Bultmann's lead.

59. In the analyses of Smith 1965; van Belle 1994; Anderson 1996, the stylistic, contextual, and theological bases for inferring alien material underlying the Johannine narrative are not only inconclusive but nonexistent (Anderson 1996, 70–136; 2014b).

60. For a schematic outline of the Johannine situation sketching six or seven crises over the same number of decades, see Anderson 2006b, 196–99. With Goodenough 1945, John contains a good deal of primitive memory as well as later developments. See also the work of the John, Jesus, and History Project from 2002–2016 (Anderson, Just, and Thatcher 2007; 2009; 2016) and Charlesworth's (2010) acknowledgment of a paradigm shift within New Testament studies since the turn of the millennium.

first been distanced from it, the Johannine Epistles would actually bolster Martyn's overall theory. A third error with Martyn's earlier work is that it tends to confine the crises in the Johannine situation to a single set of issues, when real life rarely affords such a luxury. Martyn actually modified his view later, taking note of John's gentile mission in addition to Jewish engagements, further noting signs of Johannine engagements with other Christian communities (Martyn 1996; 2007). Over seven decades, ample evidence reflects at least six crises with other groups within the evolving Johannine situation, including two crises within its pre-70 CE Palestine setting (phase 1: Judea-Galilee tensions; Baptist-Jesus tensions), two crises within its early diaspora setting (phase 2, 70–85 CE: synagogue-Johannine tensions; imperial-Jewish tensions), and two crises within its later diaspora setting (phase 3, 85–100 CE: docetizing-Johannine tensions; Christian institutionalizing-Johannine tensions). A running set of dialogues with Markan and Matthean traditions is also palpable from the earliest to the latest stages of gospel traditions, reflecting a seventh set of dialectical engagements (Anderson 2002; 2013).

The significance of this analysis for the present study is that it can no longer be claimed that the Johannine presentation of Jesus and the Ἰουδαῖοι is confined to theological construction in the late first-century Johannine situation as a projection of Johannine theology with no historical memory behind it. Rather, the opposite is more likely the case. John's presentation of Jesus and his ministry conveys an autonomous memory of Jesus's works and teachings, reflecting real tensions between a Galilean prophetic leader and religious authorities in Jerusalem. While that memory is narrated later, coming into its written formation later in the history of the Johannine situation, its content did not originate there. As an alternative to Mark, John's story of Jesus includes material that augments Mark's narrative, reflecting acute tensions between Jesus and the religious leaders of Jerusalem. In terms of primitivity, critical realism, and corroborative impression, John's socioreligious presentation of religious challenge, disputed authorization, popularist sentiment, and concerted opposition with relation to the engagements of Jesus in Jerusalem, John's story of Jesus is far more rooted in early historical memory than modern critical scholarship has allowed.[61] In that sense, continued opposition by religious leaders

61. Thus, John and Mark are best seen as the Bi-Optic Gospels—two distinctive perspectives from day one: Anderson 2001; 2013.

in the second generation of the Pauline mission reflects secondary concerns, not primary ones. Even in the light of an uneven reception among Jewish family and friends within that diaspora setting, John's story of Jesus is that of the Jewish Messiah/Christ, offering Abrahamic blessing to the rest of the world. Therein lay its promise and its later challenges.

8. Final Reflection: The Fourth Gospel as an Antidote to Provincialism and Prejudice, Christian and Otherwise

Like John's rendering of so many other themes, John's presentation of οἱ Ἰουδαῖοι is highly dialectical.[62] This is a point too often missed by those studying John's tensions between Christianity and Judaism. On one hand, as we have seen, Jewish leaders are portrayed as being threatened by Jesus and opposing him and his movement. On the other hand, Jesus is presented as fulfilling many of the central typologies of Israel itself, even representing the Father's sending of the Son as the prophet anticipated by Moses in Deut 18. The negative references to the Ἰουδαῖοι in John are almost exclusively confined to particular *Judean religious authorities* who engage Jesus pointedly in adversarial ways. Granted, he calls them "children of your father, the Devil" in confronting their claims to be children of Abraham and never to have been in bondage (an ironic claim, given histories with Egypt, Assyria, Babylon, and Rome). They, in turn, claim Jesus has a demon and that he is a blasphemer, deserving of being put to death (see Lev 24:16). These invective slams are neither anti-Jewish nor anti-Christian; such inferences are thoroughly anachronistic. Rather, John's Jesus declares that *salvation is of the Jews* and presents Jesus as fulfilling Israel's historic typologies in eschatological ways.[63] This cannot be considered anti-Semitic, and John's

62. As with other tensive presentations of John's key subjects (Anderson 2011b, 25–43), the epistemological origins of John's theological tensions includes: the creative work of a dialectical thinker, forwarding his understanding of the divine-human dialogue (revelation and its uneven responses), within a dialectical and evolving Johannine situation, by means of crafting a narrative designed to engage targeted audiences in imaginary dialogues with Jesus—the subject of the narrative (Anderson 1996, 252–65). These four dialectical operations are also evident in the Johannine prologue, which was added to the final stages of the narrative in order to create an experiential response to John's story of Jesus (Anderson 2007d).

63. As John Painter (1978) notes, "Israel" in the Fourth Gospel is never identified specifically with believing Jews or other groups. Embrace within the flock of the shepherd is simply a factor of receptivity and responsiveness to the voice of the shepherd.

author and compiler, its subject (Jesus), and a good portion of its audience were all Jewish. Therefore, John's story of Jesus—in tension with Judean authorities, some of whom indeed believe in Jesus—must be seen as an intra-Jewish set of engagements. Just as John's narrative cannot be used as a basis for violence, nor can it be read responsibly as advocating any form of anti-Semitism. It is radically Jewish in its self-understanding, even if that inference is contested.[64]

John's presentation of Jesus as the Revealer, however, does challenge religious and political bastions of power and authority, yet these challenges extend beyond first-century Judean leadership and ancient imperial Rome. They also apply to modern and postmodern institutions and authorities, whether they be Christian, secular, political, economic, or ideological. On these and other subjects, the best antidote to wooden interpretations of John is the balancing of particular claims with others found within the same gospel narrative. The best corrective to John, in other words, is John. Does John portray Jesus as overturning Jewish religious structures and forms *only to set up "good Christian ones" in their place*? Absolutely not! True worship takes place irrespective of place and regardless of cultic form (4:21–24); it must be in spirit and in truth. In that sense, the Johannine Jesus not only challenges Jewish dogmatism and religiosity, but it also challenges Christian instantiations of the same. The truth in John is not a new set of notions to be assimilated intellectually; it is a spiritual reality, revealed by the divine agent and communicated by the Spirit of truth. Likewise, to be a seeker of truth is to be open to the enlightening work of the eternal Christ in whatever form or from whatever sector it may be found. John's Gospel, as well as the greatest source of Christian exclusivism (John 14:6), is also the greatest source of Christian universalism (John 1:9; 6:45).[65] In that sense, John's presentation of Jesus, because it challenges as contingent all that is worldly and partial, challenges all religious dogmatism, if understood adequately. Because the Spirit of truth is available to all, each person has the privilege

---

64. Given evidence of encounters between Pharisaic and Christian Judaism in the late first century CE (Wild 1985), it is no surprise that a good deal of Pharisaic tradition is present within John's story of Jesus. Additionally, the Jewish feasts in John are remembered with energetic vitality (Yee 1988), showing another side of John's radical Jewishness.

65. Anderson 1991; see also Alan Culpepper's (2002) important essay on inclusivism and exclusivism in the Fourth Gospel.

of engaging the spiritual presence of God and testifying to what one has seen and heard (John 3:32; Acts 4:19–20; 1 John 1:3). When this happens, people not only are enabled to listen to one another; they are better enabled to listen together, with one another, to the subtle promptings of the divine. Harking back to Isa 54:13, Jesus declares in John 6:45, "they shall all be taught by God." Thus, the greatest Johannine scandal is not its exclusivism but its universal inclusivism, which defies religious, political, and societal bounds.

So, what do we do with anti-Semitism, religious violence, and the Gospel of John? First, while it is true that John has contributed to anti-Semitic tendencies in Europe, America, and elsewhere, this is not the same as deeming John to be an anti-Semitic document in terms of its origin and character. John is thoroughly cosmopolitan in its ethos and rhetoric, and to fail to acknowledge that fact is to make an egregious interpretive error. Also, John will not go away. Sacred Scriptures are here to stay, and the problems they evoke must be addressed with exegetical acuity rather than anachronistic eisegesis. Therefore, what we see about οἱ Ἰουδαῖοι in John is not a prejudice against a race or a particular religion but a set of reflections and engagements rooted in a community's tumultuous history, reflecting its own struggles and alienation from its parent religious movement, while also seeking to extend the blessings of Judaism to the greater world beyond. Wrongly or rightly, this is seen as a liberal fulfillment of Israel's vocation rather than its more conservative appropriations.

While none of the general references to the Jewish nation or the Jewish religion are negative, John's Jesus is opposed by particular religious leaders and groups in Judea, and within that memory lies the heart of its adversarial struggle. John's tradition does not respond, however, with the supersession of one religion over another. Here Bultmann's insight relates powerfully. It is not Jewish religion proper that the saving/revealing initiative of Jesus as God's agent in John confounds; it is all that it scandalizes all that is of creaturely origin, including the religious platforms and scaffolding of Christianity, political and social empires, and even irreligion as a human construct. The reader is thus invited to be a seeker of truth, and such is the means of liberation, the character of authority, and the center of authentic faith commitments (8:32). The truth is especially liberating when it comes to correcting flawed interpretations of classic religious texts. The Fourth Gospel may be wrong, or misguided, in heralding Jesus as the Jewish Messiah/Christ, but it is neither anti-Semitic nor proviolence in doing so.

As Professor Henry Cadbury used to say to his students at Harvard Divinity School, "It may take us five hundred years to get the interpretation right on this particular text, but we're going to start today." May it be so in our careful readings of this polyvalent text.

Seed of Abraham, Slavery, and Sin: Reproducing Johannine Anti-Judaism in the Modern Commentaries on John 8:31–34

Ruth Sheridan

Any discussion of the topic "John and Judaism" requires some consideration of what is often designated as the Fourth Gospel's distinctive "anti-Judaism." Although the latter nominal term suggests an opposition to Judaism as an established religion in the late first century CE—and is thus rightly questioned for its descriptive value on the grounds of anachronism (see Dunn 1999, 200)—it is used here to describe the gospel's persistent and increasingly pejorative presentation of a group of characters bluntly called Οἱ Ἰουδαῖοι (Sheridan 2012, 46).[1] Although the Jews of John's Gospel are not exclusively depicted in a negative light—occasionally as a character group they appear receptive to Jesus (see 4:9, 11; 8:31; 11:19)—the pejorative contexts do outnumber and overshadow the positive ones (see Wilson 1995,

* This essay is a revised version of a paper I delivered at Yale University's annual Program for the Study of Anti-Semitism in September 2014. I would like to thank Professor Harold Attridge for the invitation to speak and to thank Adele Reinhartz, Hindy Naijman, and Maurice Samuels for their perceptive insights and probing questions.

1. This antagonistic element of the gospel's characterization has received considerable attention in the scholarship, and the literature to date is vast. For bibliographical summaries, see von Wahlde 2000; Bieringer, Pollefeyt, and Vandecasteele-Vanneuville 2001a; Beutler 2006. I do not use quotation marks around the term "the Jews" because this marking of the gospel text is a product of recent scholarly interests, and it did not preoccupy commentators of previous centuries (and decades), whose work I deal with here. Omitting the marking shows just how damaging is the commentating elision between the Jews of John's text and the Jews of the commentator's social world. In this respect, quotation marking the term, although well-meaning for this very reason, when overused and underinterrogated, can appear blithe, as if conveniently whitewashing the gospel's power to damage. For more on this, see Reinhartz 2001c.

74; Wheaton 2015, 43). For example, the Jews are depicted as hostile toward Jesus, as refusing to believe in him, and as actively seeking his death (1:19; 2:28; 3:25; 5:10, 15–16, 18; 6:41, 52; 7:1, 11, 13, 20; 8:31, 37, 40, 48, 52, 57; 9:18, 22; 10:24, 31, 33; 11:8, 53–54; 18:28–32, 35–38; 19:7, 12, 14, 38; 20:19).

Although ostensibly an historiographical narrative (Bauckham 2007, 17–36), these aforementioned connotations suggest that the theological motifs informing John's symbolic world are relevant to his presentation of the Jews (see Lieu 2008, 171). As a character group, the Jews are associated with traits that reputedly arise from a love of "darkness" and "evil" (see 3:19–21). The gospel's soteriology is framed around "contrasting states of being, such as light/darkness, life/death, from above/below, being from God or not being from God" (Reinhartz 2001c, 215). These "states of being" give rise to contrasting activities with respect to Jesus and God—for example, believing or not believing, loving or hating (215). While this contrastive soteriological schema of the gospel does not equate to a fully fledged ontological dualism, it considerably compounds the force of the Jews' negative characterization. This, combined with the fact that John otherwise exhibits a solid knowledge—and a noncontroversial depiction—of first-century Jewish life in Palestine, has led to the scholarly commonplace that John's is, paradoxically, the "most and least Jewish" of the four canonical Gospels (Barrett 1947).

There is one infamous text in John's Gospel that, arguably, represents the most vitriolic strain of Johannine anti-Judaism—John 8:31–59 (see Pedersen 1999, 172–93; Motyer 1997). This text centers on Jesus's debate with the Jews—albeit those who are described as having "believed" in Jesus—about the significance of Abraham for their respective self-understanding. Each reference to Abraham embroils Jesus and the Jews in deeper polemical disputation: the Jews claim to be "seed of Abraham" in reply to Jesus's implication that they are enslaved (8:31–33). Jesus warns the Jews that although they are Abraham's offspring, they are not children of Abraham, for they are murderous (8:37) and do not do Abraham's "works" (8:39–40). Ultimately, Jesus implies superiority to Abraham (8:53) on the basis of preexistence (8:56–58). In the midst of the debate, Jesus tells the Jews that they neither "see" (5:38) nor "know" (8:55) God; that they come "from below" (8:23), are fathered by the devil (8:44), and will "die in their sin" (8:24; see 9:13–17; Sheridan 2012, 65).[2] Notoriously, the particular reference to the

2. All quotations of the New Testament are taken from the NRSV.

Jews as children of the devil (8:44) has had a long and damaging reception history in Western culture. Some scholars have traced aspects of this reception history from antiquity to modernity (see Trachtenberg 2002; Reinhartz 2007, 193–94). But other features of John 8:31–59 have been comparatively neglected in the analysis of their reception.

The feature that forms the focus of this essay is John 8:32–33, specifically as it has been received in the scholarly commentary tradition. My aim is to explore how commentators have interpreted John 8:32–33 to pejoratively characterize the Jews, effectively exacerbating their already negative portrait in much of the gospel. In the course of my research, I perceived an interpretive trend on John 8:32–33 that I found alarming both for its prevalence and its longevity; it appears to have become partially entrenched in the commentary genre but, I suggest, has its roots in anti-Semitic systems of theological rationality that emerged in early modern Europe.[3]

Before developing these claims and presenting the evidence, it will be necessary to look at John 8:32–33. The passage begins with a debate between Jesus and "the Jews who had believed in him" (8:31). Jesus promises them that if they continue to "abide" in his word, they will "come to know the truth," and the truth will "set them free" (8:32). The Jews reply, "We are seed of Abraham and have never been slaves to anyone—how can you say, You will be set free?" (8:33). Jesus replies, "Anyone who commits sin is a slave to sin" (8:34).[4] The trend I noticed in the scholarly commentaries focuses mainly on the Jews' response to Jesus in verse 33 ("We are seed of Abraham and have never been slaves to anyone"). I found that multiple commentators characterize the Jews' response in 8:32 as something more than mere indignation—and certainly something other than a legitimate counterclaim—indeed, their response is deemed to be a perverse embodiment of Jewish nationalism, pride, privilege, and prejudice. In effect, this commentarial interpretive trend reproduces, even unnecessarily extends, the anti-Judaism present

3. Of course, there are exceptions to this trend, and I will discuss these also. It is important to note that the range of gospel commentaries is very extensive and that this essay contains the results of only those commentaries I have managed to consult. This includes a substantial range of texts from the period in which the "modern" or "critical" biblical commentary emerged and later evolved. Many of these commentaries are considered "standards" in the field and have had a high impact on Johannine studies, which signals their importance as objects of study in their own right.

4. Some manuscripts omit "to sin"; see Aland et al. 2001, 351.

in John 8:31–59. It also raises the important question of whether Johannine anti-Judaism is a function of the text or of its interpretation—the well-worn dichotomy of the text's original "intention" versus its subsequent "use," or indeed, the question of whether subsequent uses of the text are in fact abuses of interpretation. This is a question to which I shall return at the close of this essay.

A final caveat to address is that modern critical commentaries are not regularly considered to be part of New Testament reception history. They are metaliterary in form and function, part of academic discourse; they are not creative transformations of the primary text and as such (presumably) deserving of careful analysis in the manner of a painting, story, or sculpture (see Edwards 2004, 4).[5] Yet I would challenge this intuitive point to claim that the gospel commentary genre ought to be studied and theorized. Indeed, it is precisely the commentary's status as a metatext that sharpens the problem I am addressing: the commentary genre asks to be read as an exegetical tool and as a resource; it presents as a standard reference work. The commentary thus functions as a complement to the gospel text, almost of necessity, adopting a "compliant" reading position with respect to the text, parsing the normativity of the canonical text in positive terms.[6] The commentary augments the gospel text, quantitatively adding to it, explicating it, and transforming its meaning (adapting Genette 1997, 228; 239–41, 254, 260, 310, 370, 395–400). It also acts as a supplement to the gospel text—maybe even replacing a reading of the gospel for many students (again, adapting Genette 1997, 202–3). Its supreme metatextual status announces a type of authoritativeness that is taken for granted; the commentary retrieves the past for the sake of the present (Hughes 2003, 157). Members of the scholarly guild, students and pastors alike, rely on the biblical commentary (Hartman 2009, 394), and the religious commentary speaks to a "fellowship of readers" (adapting Gardner 1998, 401). It is therefore troubling to find that so many commentaries adopt the stereotypical reading of the Jews in John 8:33, but it is also partially to be expected given how often commentaries pass through multiple editions and updating (see MacDonald 2007, 314). This reveals an important issue that must be openly examined in Johannine scholarship, namely, that the commentary's generic veneer of meticu-

5. The technical language here is derived from Gérard Genette (1997).

6. The language of "compliance" comes from Reinhartz (2001a, 19–25).

lous objectivity simultaneously permits the importation of ideology and obfuscates author bias.

1. Characterizing the Jews in John 8:31–33: Pride, Privilege, and Prejudice

Some of the earliest modern commentaries, written in the mid-nineteenth and early twentieth centuries, evince the above line of interpretation with respect to the Jews in John 8:32. British theologian Brooke Foss Westcott, bishop of Durham in the nineteenth century, is the first example. Westcott (1892, 133) comments that the Jews' response to Jesus in 8:32 reveals their claims to "religious privilege," which, rather than demonstrating their spiritual "freedom," actually shows them to be captive to something more sinister, namely, "a close affinity with the powers of evil." Additionally, Westcott assumes that the Jews' response to Jesus arises solely from "their inveterate prejudices and most imperfect faith" (133). The Jews' reply is, in Westcott's words, their "national boast" and a claim to "sovereignty of the world … assured by an eternal and inalienable right" (134).

In the same era, Ernst Wilhelm Hengstenberg, a leading German Lutheran theologian and commentator, finds the Jews of 8:32 to be full of "empty pretensions," inasmuch as they "boasted of their freedom, whilst they found themselves in the vilest slavery—the slavery of sin." In his view, the Jews "had arrogated freedom to themselves" on the basis of being the "seed of Abraham" (Hengstenberg 1865, 453). Thus, Jesus's words to the Jews would have "greatly humbled" them because they, as "the supposed lords of the world," needed to be "delivered from slavery by Jesus" (450). Jesus's words constituted "an annihilation of their high-minded pretensions" and pulled them down to the level of the gentiles (451). It is not hard to detect, in both Westcott and Hengstenberg's texts, traces of the anti-Semitic theory of a *Weltjudentum* found in the political propaganda of the *fin de siècle*. In that worldview, "pretentious" Jews apparently aspired to plutocratic domination of the world, if they did not already engineer global events insidiously, behind the scenes.

Some decades later, John Henry Bernard, an Irish Anglican bishop born in 1884, wrote a two-volume commentary on John's Gospel for the International Critical Commentary Series. Bernard's comments on John 8:32 echo the same kind of judgmental assessment of the Jews' psychology present in the examples already mentioned. Thus, Bernard (1928, 306) ascribes negative traits to the Jews on the basis of their response to Jesus: being "seed of Abraham" "was the proudest boast of the Jews." Bernard infers a measure of self-delusion on the part of the Jews: "they would not admit, even to themselves that they were not a free people," and "their petulant retort really marked" their "uneasy consciousness" in this regard (306).

Several highly influential commentaries on the gospel were written around the middle of the twentieth century and up to the 1960s. These commentaries generally shed the trappings of anti-Semitic cultural stereotypes (e.g., *Weltjudentum*) but persist with the theme of the Jews' overt pride and privilege. Rudolf Bultmann, the major German Lutheran theologian of the twentieth century, writes on John 8:32 that Jesus's offer of freedom, if refused, "entails a judgment upon [the Jews]." In accordance with his presuppositions about the individual assent to historical revelation, Bultmann (1971, 437, originally published in 1941, my emphasis) comments that freedom comes only by way of Jesus's "eschatological gift"; instead the Jews "hold that it [i.e., freedom] is the characteristic of *the Jew*, who already has it in his possession in virtue of his being a child of Abraham." Furthermore, Bultmann comments that the Jews "commit themselves to their lost condition" and that they are "blind men who think that they see" (433). Bultmann's theological existentialist leanings produce comments on the Jews of John's text that appear deeply judgmental; but these comments also subtly merge the Jews of John's narrative with caricatures of the universal "Jew" (by way of the notable singular) that resonates with propagandistic notions of *der ewige Jude* in 1940s Nazi Germany.[7]

Raymond Brown (1966; 1970), American Catholic priest and New Testament scholar, wrote a judiciously exegetical two-volume commentary on John's Gospel for the Anchor Bible series. Yet even Brown's (1966, 355) language when commenting on the Jews' reply in 8:32 veers towards pejorative judgment, when, for example, he writes about the "ill-founded boast" of the Jews and that they see themselves as "the privileged heirs to the promise to Abraham." Brown's German Catholic contemporary, Rudolf Schnackenburg (1968; 1980), who also employs the historical-critical method, wrote a three-volume commentary on John's Gospel, although his tone, when commenting on verse 8:32, is comparatively sharper than Brown's. Schnackenburg (1980, 207) comments that the Jews reveal their "incomprehension" of Jesus's words, which had "wounded their religious

---

7. On the Nazi propaganda film *Der ewige Jude*, see Welch 1983.

and national pride." Schnackenburg also finds that "the Jews' pride and complacency are clean contrary to the attitude which would make them receptive" to Jesus's message (207). To be descendants of Abraham, notes Schnackenburg, was "the Jews' pride, and one reason for their assurance of salvation" (207).

Another "classic" commentator in this period, Charles Kingsley Barrett, was a distinguished professor of divinity at Durham, ordained Methodist, and fellow of the British Academy. Barrett's (1978) commentary on John's Gospel uses historical criticism and theological analysis and focuses on the Greco-Roman literary background to the text. Commenting on John 8:32, Barrett maintains an important distance between what the Jews of Jesus's time actually said or thought and what John the evangelist imputed to the Jews of John 8:31–59. For example, Barrett (1978, 345) writes, "It is probable that the claim John puts into the mouth of the Jewish objectors is not that they have never been in political subjection (which would have been absurd) but that they have never lost their inward freedom of soul." This comment represents an advance on the standard interpretive trend to judge the Jews' psychological motivation behind their reply in 8:32; in addition, Barrett's comment endows John's Jews with some legitimacy insofar as their claim is positively regarded as referring to inward freedom. Unfortunately, Barrett's contribution is marred by what immediately follows, where the trope of Jewish pride is reiterated: "this very claim, uttered in human pride over against the representative of God himself, is an instance of the bondage referred to in v. 34" (345).

This cumulative commentarial trend carried no small amount of clout—a spate of Johannine commentaries produced in the 1970s and 1980s followed suit. Barnabas Lindars, a Cambridge academic and Anglican priest, wrote a short commentary on John's Gospel in 1972. Lindars (1972, 325) comments briefly on 8:32 to the effect that the Jews unreasonably "boasted" in their descent from Abraham. In his 1984 commentary written to appeal both to an academic and nonspecialist readership, Catholic lay exegete Peter F. Ellis (1984, 153) uses similar language. Ernst Haenchen, the prominent German Protestant and professor of systematic theology, published a commentary on John for the respected scholarly series Hermeneia in 1984 (translated) just before his death. Haenchen's (1984, 28) comment on John 8:32 implies that the Jews were deluded in their reply to Jesus: the Jews "appear to be free, but they will really be free only as Christians." In addition, Haenchen surmises that while the Jews face "condemnation," on the other hand "only Christ and Christians need not fear [condemnation]" (28). Haenchen's anachronistic terms ("Christ" and "Christians") actually flow from an impressionistic reading of John 8:31–59, where Jesus appears differentiated from the Jews to the point that he seems non-Jewish, indeed, that he appears to be the first "Christian." Yet Haenchen's anachronism has the problematic effect of extrapolating to contemporary Jews, implying that their salvation rests in their conversion to Christianity.

Another major commentator of this period was George Beasley-Murray, a British Baptist minister and academic who taught at a number of seminaries and colleges in the United Kingdom and the United States.[8] Beasley-Murray wrote a commentary on John in 1987 for the evangelical Word Bible Commentary series. Concerning John 8:30–59, Beasley-Murray (1987, 133) comments that the text represents "a typical statement of Jews coming to faith in Jesus; they are instructed by him as to what true discipleship means, and there follows a mass of typical Jewish propaganda calculated to destroy faith in Jesus." The *Sitz im Leben* of the passage, continues Beasley-Murray (133), was not a conflict with "Judaizers, but the conflict with Judaism." The Jews' response to Jesus in 8:32, he comments, was "the boast of the rabbis," unfounded, because the Jews were really slaves in Egypt and Babylon in the earlier history they claimed as their own. Problematically, Beasley-Murray's language of "typicality" with respect to the Jews of John 8:32 ultimately conjures the stereotypical.

The final period of analysis (1990–2000) has been a most prolific time in terms of the production of Johannine commentaries. This period has also yielded unexpected results. After the paradigm shift heralded by E. P. Sanders's (1977) work on Christian stereotypes about early Judaism, one might expect the majority of commentators to be more aware of the perils of anti-Jewish exegetical interpretations, but this does not seem to be the case with respect to John 8:32–33, although there are certainly exceptions to the trend.

Donald A. Carson, a Reformed evangelical Canadian professor of New Testament, wrote his gospel commentary in 1991. Carson's (1991, 348) comments on John 8:32–33 imply that the Jews are self-deluded because of an unwillingness to "recognize their own slavery to sin" or indeed, "the fickleness that oscillates between hero-worship and massive discontent." On the Jews' specific response in 8:33, Carson notes its "ugly, challenging tone,"

8. See Beasley-Murray's obituary online (P. Beasley-Murray 2000).

adding that the Jews' "sense of inherited privilege is so strong that they can neither acknowledge their own need nor recognize the divine Word incarnate before them" (349). Carson's interpretation of Jesus's understanding of "slavery" is particularly problematic for its embellishments that actually appear to take aim at secularist modernity: "A vicious slavery to moral failure, to rebellion against the God who made us. The despotic master is not Caesar, but shameful self-centredness, an evil and enslaving devotion to created things at the expense of worship of the Creator" (350). Carson then ascribes a "fickle mob psychology" to the Jews, because they apparently serve Jesus only when "his teachings do not clash with their prejudices" or their "fundamental religious biases" (352). Because the Jews display antipathy toward Jesus in John 8, Carson ultimately determines that "they have no real heart for God, no sensitivity to his voice" (352). Several summative suggestions can be made about Carson's commentary. First, his language is redolent with evangelical presuppositions, also betraying a sense of pathos wholly absent from John 8 (human need for a savior, etc.). Second, his pastoral application of the text has the effect of extending the comments about the "evil" and "self-centred" Jews of John 8 to present day nonbelievers, those whom Carson deems guilty of "moral failure." Third, Carson assumes that the Jews' claim to be seed of Abraham is a "mere religious bias" that should give way in Jesus's presence and not a legitimate claim to covenant with God. Carson's text strongly reproduces and expands the anti-Jewish perspective of John 8: the Jews come to symbolize elements of sinful humanity—chiefly, self-centeredness and idolatry.

Similarly, Herman Ridderbos, a Reformed Dutch theologian and New Testament exegete, wrote what he termed a "theological commentary" on the gospel in 1996. Ridderbos (1997, 309) reflects on the Jews' characteristic "limitations" in 8:32:

> It becomes immediately clear … what is lacking in their [the Jews'] faith in Jesus. They were prepared to accept him and grant him credence when he spoke to them of God (cf. 3:2). But that faith had to fit into the framework of their Jewishness and could not be allowed to violate what was fundamental for them in that Jewishness.

Such a comment might, at first glance, seem innocuous. After all, Ridderbos also states that the Jews "rightly sensed" that accepting Jesus's challenge of discipleship would involve violating their core belief in monotheism (309). But Ridderbos considers that the Jews' objection "arose from a sense of spiritual superiority as children of Abraham chosen by God out of all the nations, and thus a sense of being exempt from any servant relationship to others" (309).[9] Ridderbos identifies the Jews' supposed "superiority" with the lived "illusion" adopted by (modern) people who think that they can "manage" their lives "free of all ties" and who think they have within themselves genuine freedom and autonomy (308–9). That Ridderbos understands the Jews' "limited" guiding framework in this regard to be their "*Jewishness*" only highlights the issue that this essay addresses: in the attempt to make relevant theological or pastoral points, commentaries conflate modern "sinful" concerns not just with the gospel's Jews but with their very *Jewishness.*

This trend of psychologizing the Jews' response according to modern concerns is also clear in a commentary on John written by a Catholic priest and professor at Australian Catholic University, Francis Moloney. For Moloney (1998, 275), "the Jews" of John 8 are "unable to look beyond what they can control and understand."[10] Moloney earlier uses similar terms to describe the Pharisees in John 8:12–18, who "are not prepared to move away from their traditions and their sense of self-righteous control" (255). Both "the Jews and Pharisees," Moloney writes, "are unable to go beyond external appearances because they stop at the fleshly Jesus, what their eyes can see," a trope that unwittingly recalls early Christian stereotypes of "carnal Israel" (266–67). Moloney characterizes the Pharisees of John 7–8 as "close-minded," "ignorant," and "violent" (267).

Arguably the most disparaging commentary on John 8 in this period comes from Thomas Brodie, an Irish Catholic of the Dominican Order who wrote what he titled a "literary and theological commentary" on the gospel. Published by Oxford University Press in 1993, Brodie's commentary has all the exterior markings of respected, authoritative scholarship. But his comments on John 7–8 repeatedly fall prey to the crushing convenience of old-fashioned anti-Jewish stereotypes. Brodie (1993, 328–29) characterizes "the Jews who had believed" in Jesus (8:31) as superficial believers, who profess to follow Jesus while "following the enslaved tradition of Judaism." Brodie extrapolates to interpret the Jews of 8:31 as representing "*all* those who abuse religion, and all who, in place of genu-

9. Ridderbos's citations as evidence include Matt 3:9 and Rom 2:17–20.

10. Moloney makes a strong point of using quotation marks around the gospel's term "the Jews" for the admirable purpose of circumventing anti-Semitic interpretations, and so I retain that usage here.

ine believing, substitute some form of triviality, superstition, idol or lie" (emphasis added) (329).[11] To substantiate this claim, Brodie adduces an uncited "proverb": "the corruption of the best is the worst: it shows that the corruption of religion and religion—like beliefs provides a place where evil may flourish" (329). It is hard to comprehend how such injudicious language could have escaped the editorial red pen, connoting, as it does, the stereotypical *Spätjudentum* conceived as a "corrupt" devolution. But the most destructive aspect of Brodie's text is his depiction of the Jews as "evil"—an inexcusable interpretive option in light of the history of Western anti-Semitism, which routinely associated Jews with the devil. The implication of Brodie's text is that the rejection of Jesus's offer of "freedom" indicates a human propensity toward evil.

Commenting on John 8:32, Brodie (329) adds,

> humans tend to become enslaved by a variety of idols or lies—unreal expectations, empty roles, hollow prestige games, nationalistic nonsense, dehumanizing practices and dependencies—and that it is only by recognizing these various things for what they are, as enslaving lies, that one can achieve basic freedom. In the words of the modern slogan: "Addiction is slavery."

Beneath Brodie's pontificating language one glimpses some typical problems already encountered in his earlier discourse. The above quote concludes with a "modern slogan," uncited like his previous "proverb." Brodie's proverbs and slogans have no ostensible source—they pretend to be self-evident and thus beyond falsification. Brodie's comments also imply that the Jews of 8:31–32 are not merely slaves; they are addicts and therefore to some degree culpable for their obduracy. Yet here we see a catalogue of things moderns would recognize: "unreal expectations," "empty roles," "hollow prestige games." The last two examples use alliteration to attract the reader ("nationalistic nonsense," "dehumanizing … dependencies"); and the former of these may well draw on anti-Jewish stereotypes such as that Jews were obsessively nationalistic.

---

11. Brodie's source at this point is a best-selling work of popular psychology called *The Road Less Travelled*, written in 1983 by M. Scott Peck. It is a curious choice that compromises his reading of the gospel, enabling Brodie to transform the Jews of John 8:32–33 into representatives of real people who abuse religion and who are defined by superstition, idolatries, and lies—the very things real Jews have historically and religiously stood against.

Throughout the final period of investigation (between 2000–2015, the present), I noticed fewer examples of these interpretations in the commentaries—indeed some of the most recent German-language commentaries written in this period actually turn this interpretive trend upside down, insisting on the legitimacy of the Jews' covenant with God inherent in their claim to be "seed of Abraham." But residues of the anti-Jewish interpretation are still evident—one example comes from a recent commentary written by Frederick Dale Bruner, an American Reformed Protestant theologian and biblical scholar. Bruner (2012, 531), who describes his aim in the commentary's introduction as writing for the church, interprets the Jews of 8:31 as wavering disciples of Jesus. Bruner's text oscillates between technical commentary and psychological application:

> These "believers" bring too much self-confidence to their "conversion." They don't think they *have* many problems, or at least, any bondage at all. Indeed, they don't bring problems into their new relation with Jesus so much as (they so confidently assert) they bring pedigree and privileges of the highest sort. These converts don't *need* Jesus' promised freedom; they already have it in Abraham. (532)

From this exposition Bruner derives a lesson for his readership such that "we are not in good shape" before "we meet Jesus" and that to think otherwise is to "fool ourselves" (532). Other commitments, such as "nation, race and spirituality" must give way before allegiance to Jesus (532). Bruner then poses a rhetorical question about the Jews, "Don't they know that they had been living a sinful life?" They had put their trust not in Jesus, but in their "prior heritage" and believed themselves to be their own "savior[s] and lord[s]" (532). The Jews thus have to be "converted from their righteousness to a confession of their ties to sin" (532). There is an unmistakable theological commitment to evangelicalism, evident in catchphrases such as "confession of sin," "conversion" from belief in "self-righteousness," and belief in the "savior." Most problematically, Bruner implicates the Jews in self-idolatry—an elaboration of 8:32 that is hardly warranted by the text itself.

2. Exceptions: Recent German Commentaries and Others

Although the exegetical trend I have identified is prevalent in the commentaries, there have been and continue to be a number of exceptions. Many other commentators avoided imputing overtly negative traits (such as pride and complacence) to the Jews in John 8:32. In the early period, notable exceptions are the commentators C. H. Dodd (1953) and Edwyn Hoskyns (1947); later exceptions are found in commentaries by Michael Theobald (1983), Mark Stibbe (1993), Ben Witherington (1995), Gail O'Day (1995), Bruce Malina and Richard Rohrbaugh (1998); and from the year 2000 onward, exceptions are more or less the rule in commentaries written by Craig Keener (2003), Andrew Lincoln (2005), Mark Edwards (2004), Hartwig Thyen (2005), Urban C. von Wahlde (2010a), and Joann Brant (2011). These exceptions suggest that the commentary genre does not necessarily invite compliant readings of the gospel that denigrate the Jews, extending or reproducing the text's own anti-Jewish polemic.

There are a number of factors that could explain why some commentators adopted the anti-Jewish interpretation at 8:32, while others avoided it. But the range of variables makes generalizations difficult. There are factors unique to the commentator to consider, such as gender (almost statistically negligible in this case), country of origin, and personal religious affiliation. Then, there are factors unique to the commentary, such as the date and place of publication, the status or reputation of the publisher, the audience for whom the commentary was written (scholars, students, pastors, laity, all of the above?), and the exegetical method or approach employed in the commentary. Of these factors, two appear to be influential—although not necessarily causative—and about them some observations can be made. The first pertains to exegetical method, and the second to the date of the commentary and the sociohistorical context of the interpreter, especially with respect to recent German commentaries on John.

As to method, it is evident from this sample survey that gospel commentators utilize a range of exegetical methods and theoretical approaches. Although space does not permit a comprehensive engagement with the numerous English-language commentaries that avoid reproducing the anti-Judaism of 8:32 (mentioned above), methodologically they have one thing in common: the maintenance of critical distance in the course of interpretation. One may object that "critical distance" qualifies as an interpretive "stance" more than a governable "method," but the absence of anti-Jewish interpretation is nevertheless *most* evident in the commentaries that employ a form of historical-critical methodology that we might call *comparative criticism* (not source criticism exactly, but the practice of adducing multiple "parallel" texts from the ancient sources to substantiate each verse of the gospel). The very process of adducing ancient textual comparators entailed the production of this critical interpretive distance, making the commentary significantly less likely—in fact almost wholly unlikely —to fall into anti-Jewish readings. The parallel texts from the ancient sources themselves function as explication; there is no room, as it were, for extraneous exposition. In some cases (see Keener's commentary), this approach becomes almost mere annotation (the listing of parallels side-by-side with John 8:32–33), but its virtue lies in the invitation offered to the reader to consider that the Jews might be articulating something similar—and therefore, in its own way, legitimate to other texts in antiquity. We have seen in the analysis above that both Brown and Barrett's commentaries maintain something of this type of critical distance when commenting on John 8:32 but that eventually the stereotypical reading of the Jews as "boasting" creeps into their discourse ever so slightly.

I would therefore posit that the contextual field provided by historical analogy is indispensable for the commentary genre. The incorporation of "background" material for comparative purposes can prevent (although not always) the imposition onto the text of idealistic or theological concepts governing the author's own "horizon" of understanding. The choice of a comparative critical method can allow for neutrality (not "objectivity") in judgment. By contrast, the many examples of theological or pastorally oriented commentaries presented in this essay demonstrate a stronger inclination to reproduce anti-Jewish readings of John 8:32. In these cases, the commentator's concern with rendering the remarks relevant to the present can lead to the interpretive fallacy of "presentism"—although this issue is always complicated by the purportedly sacred nature of the gospel text to a Christian readership that views the text not only as normative for faith but capable of speaking to every human experience across times and places. Nevertheless, with respect to the Jews in John 8:32, these commentaries are much more likely to pronounce that all manner of human sin and psychological ills can be represented by the Jews response to Jesus. This is problematic in that the Jews retain their characteristic Jewishness and are not subsumed under, or replaced by, the anachronistic theological or psychological symbolism developed around notions of freedom and slavery.

As to the date and cultural context of the recent commentaries that refrain from anti-Jewish interpretation, some pertinent remarks are also in order. The increasing number of English-language commentaries that fall into this category is impressive and could be the effect of the passage of time, such that denigrating readings of Jesus's narrative antagonists are no longer de rigueur in academic parlance, nor indeed in a wider intellectual context increasingly more informed by the fruits of Jewish-Christian dialogue. But the specific case of recent German commentaries on John 8:32 effectively extends this welcome abstention to the point of actually reinforcing the legitimacy of the Jews' voice.

Representative of this position is Christian Dietzfelbinger in his 2001 commentary on John's Gospel published by Theologischer Verlag. Dietzfelbinger's approach to the text is unusual; in order to explain his understanding of what the Jews are voicing in 8:32, Dietzfelbinger (2001, 1:251) directly imputes further speech to them, thus carrying the narrative mode of the gospel over into his own commentary:

> We, Jesus' interlocutors, live in the Abrahamic covenant, and say that we are already free, and do not rely on another kind of freedom.... For liberating truth is already contained in the Abrahamic covenant, not in the Word of the Son, but in the great traditions of Israel from which we have come from and which we do not wish to leave.[12]

Likewise, Dietzfelbinger adds that the Jews' reference to freedom

> does not mean an external, political freedom, but expresses the dignity [*die Würde*] of Israel as God's "first-born son" (Exod 4:22; cf. Hos. 11:1), their covenant which, throughout each age, cannot be forfeited, and through which they maintain their inner freedom. (1:251)

Dietzfelbinger's paraphrase of the Jews' response in 8:32 is crafted in their defense, so to speak. Instead of producing a compliant reading of the gospel that effectively belittles the Jews for their perceived obduracy, Dietzfelbinger importantly expresses a resistant reading that draws out the theological legitimacy of the Jews' response.[13] This new interpretive tradition is continued in the 2005 commentary of Hartwig Thyen, published by Mohr Siebeck. Thyen's approach is to defend the Jews' objection on the grounds of logic and reasonableness (as we have seen, several prior commentators were inclined to judge the Jews' response as a characteristically Johannine "misunderstanding" reflective of their obtuseness). Like Dietzfelbinger, Thyen also remarks on the covenantal self-understanding

12. All translations of the German into English are my own.

13. The terms *compliant* and *resistant* are Reinhartz's (2001a).

of the Jews' reference to freedom in Abraham. Thyen (2005, 437) writes that the Jews' reply

> does not refer to political freedom, nor does it suggest that they have in mind their past slavery in Egypt or the Babylonian captivity; it does not imply they have conveniently forgotten even their present hardships under Roman dominion. On the contrary, they speak of their sense of religious freedom which redounds to them as the chosen, covenant people of God, something that almost goes without saying.

Finally, Michael Theobald develops this line of interpretation in his 2009 commentary on the gospel published by Regensburg Press. Theobald offers what we might call a resistant reading of John 8:32 on two levels. At the level of the text, like Thyen, Theobald grants that the Jews understand Jesus rightly, inasmuch as both parties speak of an internal freedom—the Jews do not "lie" in the face of their prior historical conditions of political servitude. But Theobald (2009, 592) is also conscious of the metatextual level that has formed the reception history of this passage, and it is with this tradition that he further contends, instead of assenting to it. Theobald insists that the Jews' position in 8:32 "cannot be *morally* discredited." In relation to this claim Theobald (592–93) cites two of his German predecessors, both of whom had written influential commentaries on John's Gospel, and both of whom judged the Jews of 8:32 pejoratively—Rudolf Schnackenburg, who wrote of the Jews' "pride and self-praise" (*Stolz und Selbstruhm* [!]);[14] and Ludwig Schenke, who wrote that the Jews' "self-confidence is delusional" (*ihr Selbstbewusstsein ist Wahn*). It is this troubling reading that Theobald identifies and consequently disputes. In place of it, Theobald (2009, 592–93) suggests that the exchange between Jesus and the Jews in 8:31–34 be understood as "two *theological* convictions that are brought together: being children of Abraham—participating in the freedom afforded by their covenant with God—and faith in Jesus as the Messiah."

These recent German commentaries (Dietzfelbinger, Thyen, and Theobald) almost present an overcorrection of the previous interpretive trajectories advanced on John 8:32–33. Ultimately, as in the remarks of Theobald above, these more positive readings move in the direction of a two-covenant theology that attempts to endow the Jews' objection with its

14. The exclamation mark is Theobald's.

own legitimacy for what it represents (Israel's original covenant with God) while maintaining the implicit legitimacy of Jesus's own claim and what it represents (i.e., messianic faith). One could therefore understand these alternative readings as an effort to bridge the impasse often mandated by the gospel's inherent binary logic—or "monologic" rhetoric—requiring an "either/or" stance toward its kerygmatic proclamation (see Sheridan 2013). That is, rather than offering a "compliant" reading of the gospel that reinforces the status of the Jews as the "other" *or* offering a straightforwardly "resistant" reading that affirms the Jews' position at the expense of Jesus's claims, these German commentaries try to find a way to admit both perspectives. As to *why* these commentaries take such a concerted position at this point is open to surmise, but it is probable that they function as part of a conscious reassessment of the past, as an acknowledgment of the role that German theologians and exegetes had in fomenting anti-Semitism by wedding it to traditional Christian anti-Judaism in the Third Reich, and as a means of establishing an alternative exegetical engagement leading to interreligious repair (see Heschel 2008).

Finally, one must note that the denigrating interpretive trend that I have analyzed in this essay has become, through the scholarly commentary tradition, part of the accreted meaning of John 8:32. This bears significant implications for the field of New Testament studies as a discipline, which is becoming more aware of the need to understand the reception history of the text as part of the text's total (if not "original") meaning. Yet this pejorative reading of the Jews in John 8:32 (i.e., as boastful, proud nationalists) is not a necessary interpretive move, as the various exceptions in the commentary tradition demonstrate. It is therefore important to ask about the possible sources of this anti-Jewish trope, although the scope of this essay permits only brief suggestions by way of conclusion.

In an exhaustive study of German biblical interpretation (from 1738 to 1952), Anders Gerdmar (2009, 609) decisively demonstrates that pejorative ideas about Jews and Judaism formed "part of the warp that runs through the European and German cultural fabric." Gerdmar investigates two dominant "research traditions" of this period—the Enlightenment tradition and what Gerdmar calls "the salvation-historical" tradition. Both traditions espoused views about Judaism that are entirely consonant with the negative interpretive tropes found in the commentaries on John 8:32–33 as analyzed here. For example, the Enlightenment valuation of inner freedom went hand in hand with opposition to a perceived "external," legalistic Judaism and the construction of a symbolic Jew who was a slave to his *mitzvot* (Gerdmar, 2009, 588). On the other hand, the "salvation-historical" tradition that arose from Lutheran pietism was intrinsically tied up with missionary activity toward Jews that ultimately sought their conversion. In this latter tradition, ambiguity was rife: Jews were often positively portrayed in New Testament research, but when *actual* Jews did not accept Jesus as the Messiah, their contemporary presentation altered drastically (590).

Gerdmar (2009, 246) cites numerous examples of New Testament exegetes and theologians from both research traditions that claimed Jews characteristically assert their guarantee of salvation with misplaced pride, hindering their ability to embrace "true" salvation in Jesus. These theologians often spoke of the Jews' "aristocratic pride" (*Adelsstolz*) at being God's chosen people, a motif that was particularly popular in the *Kaiserreich* (247). Interpreters of the era saw the Jews as embodying "national pride" and a false sense of emancipation in the political sense (229). These views were not necessarily connected with the exegesis of John 8, but they were part of the general theological stance toward contemporary Jews, and the presence of politically based anti-Semitism within these views is not difficult to detect. This intellectual and cultural background informing theologically minded biblical exegesis, I would suggest, paved the way for the tropes of "Jewish pride" and "false freedom" to merge with John's hostile portrayal of the Jews in John 8:31–34 within the modern exegetical commentary, which was newly developing as a genre.

This European cultural context forms a theological backdrop to the pejorative readings of John 8:32 presented in this essay. Thenceforth, the interpretive trope was repeated from commentary to commentary. We could understand the case of commentary readings on John 8:32 as a mixing of cultural anti-Semitism and contextually aware Johannine anti-Judaism, with the two ideologies reinforcing each other. This deleterious combination of ideologies is ultimately evident in the words of Gerhard Kittel (1946; in Eriksen 1985, 42), written in his own defense during his de-Nazification process: "Never has a … more negative characterization of the Jewish religion as a religion of privilege [been made] than that found in John 8." These disturbing examples together suggest that there is a fine line between the so-called (purist) use of the gospel text and its (biased) abuse. Of course, Kittel's understanding of John 8 may not reflect the evangelist's real, original intention, but how can such an intention be definitively and objectively gauged in any case? We can easily decry these pejorative, nay, anti-Semitic, readings of John 8:32 as abuses of the text, pointing to exceptions and recent German commentaries that provide corrective readings to affirm that the stereotypes are unnecessary interpolations. But we could just as legitimately say that the gospel's anti-Jewish perspective lends itself to these problematic commentary readings by virtue of its own agenda, its ideological point of view, and its invitation to readerly compliance. The commentaries sampled in this essay would then constitute instances of the *reproduction* of Johannine anti-Judaism on a contemporary scale. Not an abuse—as though such moral valence should be ascribed to interpretive reception history—but a use of the text in keeping with the narrative and theological direction of the gospel with respect to the Jews.

Although this stereotyped interpretive trend is waning, it nevertheless continues to be expressed in some commentaries on John 8:32—and indeed, it has morphed into newer, more troubling manifestations in a specific few. The longevity of this motif should be cause for concern in light of the unique authoritativeness deriving from the commentary genre, particularly in its function as a standard reference work or supplement to the primary text of the gospel. Perhaps the heightened authority pertaining to the commentary's function also entails a deeper sense of responsibility in its composition: traditional interpretive tropes need to be critically questioned, not thoughtlessly replicated. In short, we need to ask from whence these tropes have come and to where they are going—and to seek alternatives to them when we can.

The Place of John in Christian-Jewish Relations Fifty Years after *Nostra Aetate*

Noam E. Marans

In October 2015 we celebrated the fiftieth anniversary of the promulgation of *Nostra Aetate*—"In Our Time"—by Pope Paul VI (1965). By "we celebrated" I mean not only Catholics and Jews who were freed by the document to pursue a path of reconciliation; not only Christians and Jews, who through denominations or as individuals emulated *Nostra Aetate*'s gold standard; but also all peoples who are committed to seeing the "true and holy"—*Nostra Aetate*'s phrase—in the other's religious expression. For Jews, the "Declaration on the Relation of the Church to Non-Christian Religions," the official title of *Nostra Aetate*, represents an interreligious transformation without parallel in Jewish history, perhaps without parallel in all of religious history. It marked an unprecedented turnaround in interreligious relations. In a post-Holocaust self-reflection, the Catholic Church, whose antipathy toward Jews and Judaism had contributed to hate and violence directed at Jews—pogroms, ritual murder accusations, inquisitions, ghettos, and the Holocaust—reversed itself and rejected two millennia of anti-Jewish sentiment, establishing a new way. *Nostra Aetate* teaches that Jews are not collectively responsible for the death of Jesus. Jews are not to be portrayed as accursed. Anti-Semitism is unacceptable. God's covenant with the Jewish people is eternal. Christianity's roots lay in Judaism.[1]

Nostra Aetate posits that renewed interpretation of Scripture, of the New Testament in general and the gospels in particular, is crucial to a new era in Christian-Jewish relations. When the declaration calls for "mutual understanding and respect which is the fruit above all, of biblical and

1. Excerpted and adapted from Marans and Rosen 2015.

theological studies," it recognizes the essentialness of biblical scholarship to the betterment of interreligious relations. The document addresses New Testament passages directly. When *Nostra Aetate* asserts, "True, the Jewish authorities and those who followed their lead pressed for the death of Christ," it cites John 19:6—"When the chief priests and the police saw him, they shouted, 'Crucify him! Crucify him!' Pilate said to them, 'Take him yourselves and crucify him; I find no case against him.'" But then, *Nostra Aetate*, demonstrably, importantly, and immediately distances itself from the classic deicide charge and protests, "Still, what happened in His passion cannot be charged against all the Jews, without distinction, then alive, nor against the Jews of today."

Fifty years ago *Nostra Aetate* allowed the contradictions to linger, to be resolved for a later day. Although the declaration is transformational, it is not perfect. On the one hand, it states that "the Jews should not be presented as rejected or accursed by God, as if this followed from the Holy Scriptures," and yet asserts—perhaps contradictorily—that "catechetical work" and "preaching … not teach anything that does not conform to the truth of the Gospel and the spirit of Christ." Maybe the "spirit of Christ" does not demonize Jews or Judaism, but the "truth of the Gospel" sometimes does. Can you conform to the truth of the gospel and avoid presenting Jews as rejected or accursed by God?

While acknowledging that interpretation of the Gospel according to John remains fluid and far from resolved, John has been perceived over time as the gospel most belligerent toward the Jews and is the source for the painful and lasting portrayal of the Jews as children of the devil. In this case, that is, in John, or in the way John has been nefariously used, the challenge of reconciling a new teaching regarding Judaism and the Jewish people while maintaining "the *truth* of the Gospel" is painfully clear.

This challenge was not lost on succeeding generations who were tasked with a robust implementation of *Nostra Aetate*. The *Nostra Aetate* implementers understood that a key element of their work would be focused on reconciling anti-Jewish sentiment found in the New Testament with this new era of rapprochement. In many ways John would be ground zero in that travail. Although multiple post-*Nostra Aetate* documents address this challenge broadly, there are several in particular that drill down more deeply on this issue. The most relevant among them is the 2002 publication from the Vatican Pontifical Biblical Commission titled "The Jewish People and Their Sacred Scriptures in the Christian Bible." Regarding the Gospel of John, the commission suggests:

> It has been noted with good reason that much of the Fourth Gospel anticipates the trial of Jesus and gives him the opportunity to defend himself and accuse his accusers. These are often called "the Jews" *without further precision*, with the result that an unfavorable judgement is associated with that name. (Pontifical Biblical Commission 2002)

The Vatican's description of the problem—a generalized, imprecise, and negative usage of "the Jews"—is better than its apologetic solution, which reads as follows: "But there is no question of anti-Jewish sentiment, since—as we have already noted—the Gospel recognizes that 'salvation comes from the Jews' (4:22)." I am not sure that solution works.

The same publication recognizes "a more serious accusation made by Jesus against 'the Jews' … of having the devil for a father (8:44)." Again, the solution offered is less than satisfying. "It should be noted," says the Vatican Biblical Commission, "that this accusation is not made against the Jews insofar as they are Jews, but on the contrary, insofar as they are not true Jews, since they entertain murderous intentions (8:37)." That solution certainly does not work.

In fairness, and in an attempt to minimize these less than helpful analyses, I would say that Catholic-Jewish relations have progressed much better than this biblical exegesis might reflect.

How far could or would the Catholic Church go toward reconciling a new teaching regarding Judaism and the Jewish people while maintaining the "truth of the Gospel?" In "The Jewish People and Their Sacred Scriptures in the Christian Bible," the church apparently went as far as it was able, albeit not as far as some might have liked.

Modern scholars of John and of the New Testament in general—you—have contributed mightily to furthering the goals aspired to by *Nostra Aetate*. The academic study of Scripture—scientific, historical, philological, literary, and so on—has provided a helpful contextual understanding to many of the New Testament passages most threatening to Christian-Jewish relations. Scholarship does this, for example, by clarifying that a seemingly anti-Jewish sentiment often needs to be understood as an internecine debate within the Jewish community[2] and/or as a self-conscious attempt to separate early Christians or, better said, the forerunners of

2. See Craig A. Evans, "Evidence of Conflict with the Synagogue in the Johannine Writings," in this volume above.

Christianity, from their Jewish forebears.[3] Many other new understandings are being uncovered in real time.

Modern scholarship, by its very nature and commitments, has a tendency to undermine the previously untouchable sanctity and integrity of Scripture. Once religious leadership embraces the academic/scientific study of the Bible, as the Catholic Church has mostly done, acknowledging in the "Notes on the Correct Way to Present the Jews and Judaism" that "the Gospels are the outcome of long and complicated editorial work" (Commission for the Religious Relation with the Jews 1985, IV), the poisonous impact of anti-Jewish statements can be softened. But there are Catholic limits. Although the 1985 "Notes" document acknowledges that the gospels have been edited, it steps back a bit and says, "But always in a fashion that they told us the honest truth about Jesus." There may be honest capital *T* Truth in the Bible, meaning spiritually profound messages, but it is not necessarily lowercase *t* truth, meaning historical fact. We know that Truth is often more potent than truth. But when something is not true as historical fact, it is, or could be, or should be, weakened as the foundation for stereotypes, in this case for prejudicial anti-Judaism.

All this has had practical application in the laboratory of Christian-Jewish relations. The infamous Oberammergau passion play, the mother of all dramatizations of Jesus's last days, has served as a living laboratory for the implementation of *Nostra Aetate*. Both in the Middle Ages and well into modernity, passion plays often served as particularly heinous devilish characterizations of the Jewish people, sometimes leading to spontaneous or premeditated violence directed at Jews. Usually performed during Holy Week, contiguous with Good Friday prayers for the conversion of the perfidious Jews, these plays instigated the most hateful anti-Judaism.

Inaugurated in 1634, the Oberammergau passion play has become the gold standard by which all other plays of the genre are measured. What happens in Oberammergau is not only relevant to the half-million Christians who today come to see the play performed during decennial and fiftieth anniversary years but also for all other passion plays seeking to emulate the best in the business.

It is Adele Reinhartz's summary introduction to John in *The Jewish Annotated New Testament* that helps me describe the now better, but not yet fully redeemed, version of the Oberammergau passion play. She writes,

3. See Jörg Frey, "Aspects of the 'Parting of the Ways,'" above.

"John's Gospel has been called the most Jewish and the most anti-Jewish of the Gospels" (2011b, 152). If those of us who are committed to Christian-Jewish relations cannot defeat the latter—John's anti-Jewishness—then maybe we need to embrace the former—John's Jewishness. It is harder to purge early Christian texts of anti-Jewish sentiment than to neutralize those texts by asserting the inherent Jewishness of the environment in which they were written, by making clear that most of the players on the gospels' stage are Jews; they live as Jews and fight intracommunal battles as Jews.

Christian Stuckl, the director of the three most recent versions of the Oberammergau passion play, has purged the play of many of its anti-Jewish stereotypes, but it is his portrayal of Jesus as Jew, of Jesus as rabbi, that has made the most compelling difference in mitigating the anti-Jewish elements of the play. In 2010, Stuckl added a completely new scene to a play whose supporters do not suffer easily any divergence from the music and text transmitted from one generation to the next. In his break with play tradition, Stuckl has Jesus holding aloft a facsimile of an unfurled Torah as hundreds of actors—Oberammergau townspeople—sing a newly composed version of Shema Yisrael, the central Jewish prayer of Deut 6:4, "Hear O Israel, the Lord our God, the Lord is One." The Shema is sung in the original Hebrew, not in the play's usual German. When Jesus is portrayed so Jewishly—could anything be more Jewish than chanting the Shema from a raised Torah as the faithful join in?—we begin to undermine the historically absurd understanding of New Testament narrative as Jews murdering the first Christian, a sentiment quite current in the pre-*Nostra Aetate* world and still far from extinct today. When the story of Jesus's life is told as that of reformer rabbi challenging the Jewish establishment, the classic deicide charge and its fellow travelers have weaker legs to stand on.

After viewing the 2010 version of the Oberammergau passion play with American Jewish Committee leadership, the archbishop of New York and future cardinal and president of the US Conference of Catholic Bishops, Timothy Dolan, rightfully said that the play "is a paradigm for the friendship of Jews and Catholics; it has shown low points in their relations in the past, but now it has also become a sign of great progress."

So what do we do with an imperfect John, which is not easily shoehorned into a new era of Christian-Jewish relations? We illuminate through scholarship that which can mitigate the blunt force of anti-Judaism. But we also admit that none of the Western religions—Judaism, Christianity, or Islam—have been spared the albatross of offensive, xenophobic, intolerant, and hateful texts, and that our respective enlightenments, reformations, and course corrections have been uneven, to say the least. It is not our job or even possible to expunge offense from sacred texts. It is our responsibility, however, to contextualize them and undermine their historicity, as a sacred obligation to elevate the overwhelming good in the religious expression of our traditions.

We are called to be foundationalists, not fundamentalists. Fundamentalists make the mistake of empowering selectively one, two, or several verses as the sole message of a book. By contrast, if we are foundationalists, we take up the whole text and discredit that which offends, and we emphasize the overriding messages of love, hope, and redemption that characterize the foundation of sacred religious texts.

Finally, it is certain that interpretation of the Gospel of John and evaluation of both the context and meaning of its anti-Jewish passages will continue to evolve. That is the nature of the business. In fact, it is what keeps the business, your business, going. Not all is known and understood and agreed on in the study of John, and it is extremely unlikely that we will ever reach a point where there is nothing left to debate. What is less open to debate is that John and other texts were marshaled over centuries for demonization of Jews and Judaism.

Nostra Aetate and its lesser parallels have begun to turn that curse into a blessing. Pope Francis's theologian of the moment is Cardinal Walter Kasper. Kasper served for the first decade of this century as the Vatican point man on religious relations with the Jews. He has written poignantly that *Nostra Aetate* and its many positive achievements must not be perceived as the "beginning of the end" of religiously motivated anti-Semitism but rather as the "beginning of the beginning" of developing positive relations between two of the world's oldest faith communities, Christians and Jews.[4]

4. Jim Rudin, Religious News Service, October 26, 2015.

Afterword: What Have We Learned? Where Do We Go from Here?

R. Alan Culpepper

Tom Thatcher opened this extraordinary collection of essays quoting the line that John is both "the most Jewish and the most anti-Jewish" gospel in the New Testament (Thatcher, 6).[1] At the end of this volume, we may therefore ask what we have learned about the Gospel of John's fraught relationship to Judaism, its Jewishness and its anti-Jewishness, and then reflect on avenues for future exploration. The essays in this volume consider three facets of the relationship between John and Judaism: (1) the gospel's Jewish context and what can be learned about it from the Gospel of John, (2) John's relationship to Judaism and Jewish Christianity, and (3) reading John as Jews and Christians, the continuing legacy of the gospel's anti-Jewish references.

The issues related to the setting of the gospel are inherently difficult because we know virtually nothing about the origin of the gospel, its Jewish context, or its author(s), and what we know about first-century Judaism confirms that it was varied and changing. Most Johannine scholars now embrace the view that the gospel was composed in stages over a period of years. Such theories open the possibility that John was related in different ways to different Jewish contexts during the process of its composition. For example, were the carriers of the Johannine tradition and the

1. C. K. Barrett (1975, 71) observes that "John is both Jewish and anti-Jewish." Wayne Meeks (1975, 172) sharpens the observation: "The Fourth Gospel is most anti-Jewish just at the points it is most Jewish." John Ashton (1994, 13) uses this specific formulation while discussing Karl Bornhäuser (1928), and it is repeated by Johannes Beutler (2006, 176) and by Adele Reinhartz (2011b, 152). At the same time, others have labeled Matthew as "the most Jewish and anti-Jewish" of the Gospels (France 1989, 19; Hamm 2000, xv; Miller 2004, xxii).

shapers of the gospel influenced by a particular form of Judaism or various types of Judaism? Was John composed in Judea or the diaspora, or both? How typical was this Judaism of its time, and how relevant are our sources (Qumran, Philo, rabbinic materials) for understanding the character of Judaism known to John?

In the first two essays Thatcher and Jan G. van der Watt offer orientation points around which the relationship between John and Judaism can be situated. Thatcher notes first the historical context in which the discussion occurs—fifty years after the publication of *Nostra Aetate* called for and introduced a historic reassessment of Christian attitudes toward Jews and Judaism—and then reviews current responses to the question of who are the Jews in the Gospel of John. The latter is closely related to evaluations of the Martyn-Brown hypothesis that by the time the Gospel of John was completed Johannine believers had been put out of the synagogue and that the gospel is shaped by this forced social dislocation and the founding of the Johannine community separate from the synagogue. Still, the gospel reflects the formative role of Judaism for the Johannine Christians: (1) Jesus is presented as the fulfillment of Israel's Scriptures, (2) John's distinctive "I am" sayings draw on symbolic resources that were well established in ancient Judaism, and (3) while the Pharisees responded to the destruction of the temple in 70 CE by laying the foundation for classical Judaism around torah observance, the Johannine Christians "shifted the significance of the temple as a symbol of God's presence and atonement to Jesus himself and then, subsequently, to their own community" (11). The extent of Judaism's influence on the Gospel of John is readily apparent from these examples, and it is pervasive.

Van der Watt situates John's theological formulations in a fresh perspective by taking up the question of the significance of calling Jesus the Messiah, King of the Jews/Israel, for understanding the Johannine group's perception of their own identity in relation to their Jewish heritage. As is often observed, John frames its narrative by means of a spatial dualism, above and below, heaven and earth:

> The above represents the divine, transcendental space of the unseen God, the Creator and King. John narrates certain events taking place in this transcendental space, forming its own transcendental narrative. In this transcendental narrative the reader learns about what happened in heaven, about the Father having a Son, the preexistent Logos, who is in a communicative and loving relationship in the bosom of the Father, knowing him intimately. (van der Watt, 41)

John may therefore be understood as a "transcendental narrative" that redefines its Jewish heritage. The Johannine claim that Jesus is the Messiah, the Christ, the Son of God, introduces a perspective that leads to conflict with the traditional Jewish transcendental narrative. The hostile language in the gospel should be understood in the light of the role of vilification in ancient rhetoric: "Vilification as rhetorical device aims at stereotyping or labeling people negatively (Malina and Rohrbaugh 1998, 33), thus negotiating identity" (van der Watt, 51). Accordingly, interpreters must be careful about not confusing the rhetoric of vilification with the tenets of Johannine theology. Furthermore, since there are many examples of the genre of vilification in ancient Israel, from the prophets to the Qumran scrolls, John's vilification can likewise be understood as a reflection of intra-Jewish debate rather than as Christian anti-Judaism. On this point, however, other contributors to this volume reach differing conclusions (see below the essays that treat "the parting of the ways").

Typically, New Testament scholars have studied Second Temple Judaism to gain insights into the context in which the Gospel of John was written. Craig R. Koester turns the question around, asking what we can learn about Judaism in the first century from John. His essay makes four exploratory probes. First, in relation to temple practice and the observance of the festivals, John gives us a valuable account of pre-70 Sukkot rituals in the temple. Second, regarding the use of the title *rabbi*, one finds in the gospel that the title functioned in groups other than those whose sages later produced the Mishnah. Third, John suggests that ancient synagogue sermons combined biblical exposition by the main speaker with interaction among the listeners, as one sees in John 6. Fourth, John sheds light on the עם הארץ ("people of the land") and Jewish folk belief as it reveals that "aspects of Greco-Roman belief and quasi-magical ideas circulated in some Jewish circles around questions of healing" (Koester, 76).

Both John's manner of handling scriptural texts and the ethical dilemma posed by Caiaphas's pronouncement regarding the ethical justification of Jesus's death would also have been recognized by the gospel's readers, as the next two essays show.

Catrin H. Williams finds clues to John's relationship to Judaism through close study of its use and interpretation of the Hebrew Scriptures. Study of the interpretation of Scripture in John reveals "its preference for certain scriptural texts and its use of well-documented Jewish exegetical methods and devices, as well as the author's close familiarity with the ways in which the original biblical texts were being received and interpreted in Jewish circles many centuries after their composition" (Williams, 77). John displays both inherited and innovative interpretive techniques. By focusing on associative exegesis through the use of link-words and compilations of quotations in John and contemporaneous sources, Williams is able to show that while the christological content of the gospel's exegesis is distinctive, its exegetical techniques would have been widely recognized. John therefore provides valuable documentation of the similarities and differences between early Jewish hermeneutical trends and later rabbinic practices.

Harold W. Attridge turns to another basis for assessing John's relationship to its Jewish context, namely, that of debate over the place of reason and political expediency in ethical decision making. In John 11 Caiaphas famously declares that it is better that one man should die than that the nation should perish. Attridge shows that the dilemma of one for many was widely debated in rabbinic literature, and most of the rabbinic sages reject political expediency as a worthy basis on which to make ethical decisions. Nevertheless, the question of the weight of reason in such quandaries was well recognized. John invites its readers into an ongoing debate among Jewish sages as well as Stoic philosophers.

Discussion of the relationship between John and Judaism has often focused on the hostile references to the Jews in the gospel and the references to being "put out of the synagogue" in John 9:22; 12:42; and 16:2. Here J. Louis Martyn's monograph, *History and Theology in the Fourth Gospel*, has shaped the understanding of the historical setting of the gospel since its publication in 1968, at least in the United States. Contributors to this volume represent a spectrum of responses to Martyn's influential hypothesis.

Adele Reinhartz perceptively examines not only Martyn's thesis but also its remarkable influence, which she attributes to its clarity, dramatic form, and historical imagination. It allowed us to "to take up temporary residence in the Johannine community" and to "see with the eyes and hear with the ears of that community" (Martyn 2003, 29). Although Reinhartz questions basic tenets of Martyn's hypothesis, including the date and function of the Birkat Haminim and Martyn's two-level reading of the gospel, she does not abandon the historical quest. She maintains that "the focus on affiliation and disaffiliation ... is key to understanding the Gospel of John" (Reinhartz, 126), but she locates the disaffiliation not in the gospel's past but rather in its future; the evangelist is not reflecting on something that has happened but rather framing the narrative rhetorically in order to push its readers to disaffiliate from the synagogue. As she puts it, "the rhetorical thrust of the gospel suggests another possibility: that the gospel was pushing its hearers to separate themselves from the Ἰουδαῖοι. In other words, the gospel was not reacting to a forcible parting but rather attempting to produce one" (Reinhartz, 125).

Jonathan Bernier also rejects Marytn's hypothesis, but his critique moves in the opposite direction. Instead of pushing disaffiliation into the gospel's future, he argues that expulsion from the synagogue was not anachronistic, as Martyn contended, but could have occurred in Judean synagogues during Jesus's ministry. Bernier bases his argument on what he describes as the "New Perspective on the Second Temple Synagogue" that has arisen over the past quarter of a century in the work of Donald Binder (1999), Lee Levine (2005; 2014), Anders Runesson (2001), and Runesson, Binder, and Birger Olsson (2008), which suggests that "the synagogue constituted an institutional space central to Second Temple Jewish life, both in the land and in the diaspora" (Bernier, 131). Bernier further contends that Martyn's claim that the references to expulsion from the synagogue are anachronistic is a weak argument from silence. In response to Martyn, rabbinic scholars have argued that the Birkat Haminim is later than the gospel, it was not directed against Christians, and it was not used to expel anyone from the synagogue. Moreover, the statement in John 9:22 that the Ἰουδαῖοι had agreed (συνετέθειντο) that anyone who confessed Jesus as the Messiah would be made ἀποσυνάγωγος does not require a formal mechanism of expulsion. The reference to killing in John 16:2 suggests "something closer to lynching than to formal proceeding" (Bernier, 131), like the references to the reaction against Jesus in Luke 4:28–30 and the stoning of Stephen in Acts 6:8–7:60. Bernier concludes, therefore, that "the cases for relating the ἀποσυνάγωγος passages to the Birkat Haminim or treating them as little more than fiction begin to look quite weak compared to the case for relating them to events of Jesus's life and the lives of his followers" (Bernier, 133).

Craig A. Evans responds to the question of John's setting by observing that, whether one agrees with Martyn or Bernier, "significant evidence remains for understanding the entire Johannine corpus (i.e., the gospel, the epistles, and the Apocalypse) against the backdrop of conflict with or within the synagogue at the end of the first century or, perhaps, in the first decades of the second century" (Evans, 135). In the course of surveying this evidence Evans uses the authors of the commentaries on the Johannine writings in the *Jewish Annotated New Testament* as dialogue partners.

Evans finds himself "still drawn to aspects of Martyn's hypothesis" and suggests that in passages such as John 3:16 and Rev 3:5 we see "a counterthrust of some sort directed against synagogue practice somewhere, a practice that in time came to expression in the revised twelfth benediction" (Evans, 139). He also agrees with Daniel Streett "that the secessionists [in 1 John] are best understood as Jews who have left the Johannine community and have returned to the synagogue" rather than as docetists (Evans, 143). A detailed review of the seven letters in Revelation confirms this view for Evans: "I am convinced that we need to take a fresh look at the references to the opponents and false teaching in the Johannine epistles. These opponents are not gnostics or Hellenizers; they are Jewish skeptics and members of synagogues who reject the claims that Christian Jews make about Jesus" (Evans, 151). The Gospel of John, Evans concludes, reflects an intramural conflict that arose in Jewish communities after the destruction of the temple, in which those who confess Jesus are threatened with expulsion from the synagogue. This conflict is also reflected in the epistles of John and in the Revelation of John.

Joel Marcus accepts Martyn's theory—"there is no going back from Martyn's insights" (Marcus, 155)—and moves on to the question of the place of the followers of John the Baptist in the gospel's setting. After marshaling the evidence for the gospel's polemic against the followers of John the Baptist, he asks why interest in this polemic has faded in recent scholarship. Marcus suggests that it is "partly because Bultmann overplayed his hand and thereby discredited the hypothesis, and partly because of Martyn's move toward seeing the background of the gospel in the conflict with Pharisaic/rabbinic Judaism" (Marcus, 160). Nevertheless, the two hypotheses are not mutually exclusive, and Marcus turns to the question of how they might be integrated. First, he observes that "in the eyes of the Fourth Evangelist, Baptists are not enemies in the same way that Pharisees are" (Marcus, 160). A plausible explanation for this dynamic is that the Pharisees were the dominant group in the Johannine context, and suspicion and hostility from the Pharisees may have brought the two messianic groups together "on the principle that the enemy of my enemy is my friend" (Marcus, 162). The two groups were, of course, also linked by the memory that Jesus had begun his ministry within the Baptist movement. In this context the evangelist may have held out hope that the followers of the Baptist might be persuaded to join the Johannine community.

Lori Baron also envisions the Johannine context as one of continuing tension between the Johannine believers and the synagogue. Given this context, and the allusions to the Shema, which is not explicitly quoted in the Gospel of John, as it is in the Synoptics, she explores the Johannine echoes of the Shema in the shepherd discourse in John 10 and in Jesus's prayer in John 17. The shepherd discourse echoes the promise that the people will be unified under one shepherd in Ezek 34 and 37. John further asserts that Jesus died to bring together in one the scattered children of God (11:52). John 17 echoes the hope of prophetic restoration, "that they may be one." Against the prophetic background, the unity of the people has a missional purpose: When the people are gathered, "*the nations shall know* (γνώσονται τὰ ἔθνη) that I am Adonai, says the Lord God, when through you I display my holiness before their eyes" (Ezek 36:23). In John "the purpose of the 'oneness' is *in order that* the world may know and believe in Jesus's unique relationship with the Father" (Baron, 171). John's appropriation of the prophetic hope, according to which the believers who have been dispersed gather as the community of God under the one shepherd, comes with a twist: "The good news for the disenfranchised has itself become a rhetorical weapon of exclusion, a weapon that has proven deadly in a later context, in the hands of a powerful church against a Jewish minority" (Baron, 172). Hence the dilemma for interpreters of the gospel: how to take a word of hope for a struggling first-century Christian community, namely, that the vision of the prophets was being fulfilled in them, and interpret it in contemporary contexts so that it continues to be a word of assurance and hope for all people.

Another facet of the issue of John and Judaism concerns the historical and theological relationships between John and other trajectories of early Christianity that were closely related to Judaism, especially Matthew and Paul. William R. G. Loader and R. Alan Culpepper explore aspects of John's similarities and dissimilarities with Matthew, while Jörg Frey traces the Pauline and Johannine interactions in Ephesus.

Loader addresses the impasse among both Matthean and Johannine scholars regarding the soteriology of each gospel. Is their soteriology based on Jesus's death, or is salvation proclaimed in his ministry, through his words and deeds, apart from his death? With each gospel a strong case can be made on each side of this argument. Hence the impasse. Some scholars have chosen one view over the other, while others have simply ignored the problem. Loader suggests an alternative: "a resolution of this tension lies not in playing one side of the argument off against the other, nor in pressing the logic of some statements to the exclusion of others" but by taking into account

> the strongly Jewish background of both documents: Matthew, whose author still wants to hold a place within the Jewish community despite the pain of conflict and failure, and John, having made its own way with pain and conflict because of its extreme christological claims but, with all that behind it, still needing to justify itself in largely Jewish terms. (Loader, 186)

There is no indication that affirming that salvation lay in Jesus's death meant that other bases for forgiveness, salvation, or eternal life were thereby disqualified. In both communities believers could see Jesus's death "as for the forgiveness of sins without having to deny other means of forgiveness" (Loader, 187). Behind both gospels, Loader suggests, we see "a transposing and return to what is the structure of Jewish spirituality of the time: relationship, faithfulness, obedience to the Word is central, but now not as torah but as Jesus" (Loader, 188). This soteriology, or spirituality, is not focused exclusively on the cross but "on ongoing life in relationship through Christ with God and in community with fellow believers. In John, this is apart from torah. In Matthew, it is on behalf of torah" (Loader, 188).

In my essay I note that both Matthew and John address an early Christian community or communities near the point of their separation from the synagogue. Both articulate the Christian gospel in relation to the heritage of Judaism. As a way of mapping the place of Matthew and John in their relationship to Judaism and enabling us to make comparisons between them, I survey seven issues in each gospel: (1) Jesus as a new Moses, (2) fulfillment of the Scriptures, (3) the law, (4) the Sabbath, (5) purity issues, (6) the Pharisees, and (7) the synagogue.

Both the early Christian communities and their Jewish counterparts were diverse and evolving rapidly in the late first century. Current scholarship is divided over the question of whether the Matthean and Johannine communities were still involved in an intra-Jewish debate or had already separated from the Jewish community. These alternatives are sometimes reduced to the metaphorical terms *intra muros* or *extra muros*, but this dichotomy may be too unambiguous.

If the data I collected adds anything to the discussions regarding these issues, it suggests that Matthew is still engaged in interpreting his Jewish heritage so that Jewish believers could continue "to live as practicing Jews while worshipping with believers in the *ekklēsia*, whereas the separation of Johannine believers from the synagogue now lies in the past, and the Fourth Evangelist and his community are engaged in a polemical hermeneutic that justifies this break and claims the spoils of Judaism for the Johannine community/ies" (Culpepper, 219).

Frey reconstructs how this process unfolded in Ephesus. Frey argues that the processes of separation occurred locally, driven by different factors in various group constellations and regions. The situation in Ephesus is particularly illuminating because of the number of literary sources related to the development of the Christian community or communities there: (1) Paul's epistles, (2) Acts 18–20, (3) the Johannine gospel and epistles, (4) Revelation, and finally (5) Ignatius's Letter to the Ephesians. These sources suggest that by the end of the first century there were "a variety of Christian communities" in Ephesus, "including post-Pauline communities, Johannine communities, and perhaps also a circle of prophets around the author of Revelation" (Frey, 223). There was also a large Jewish community in Ephesus.

As Frey reconstructs it, the story begins with the mission activity of Apollos in a synagogue community, where he apparently meets with some success. We know little of Paul's early activities in Ephesus and his discussions with those who had responded to Apollos's preaching, but it is significant that he was not the founder of the church in Ephesus. Later, Paul's influence grew, and his work may have spread to surrounding towns and attracted gentiles as well. One tantalizing detail is suggestive for how the "parting of the ways" began in Ephesus. Acts 19:9–10 reports that Paul withdrew to "the school of Tyrannus," apparently voluntarily and perhaps so that he could work with gentiles without opposition from the Jews. Others may have remained in the synagogue. From the post-Pauline writings we see that after Paul's death, there were still communities in Ephesus linked with Paul. Ephesians suggests there was a mixed community of Jewish and gentile believers. In view of the size of Ephesus it is plausible that there were various groups of Jesus followers, some of whom may have remained within the synagogue communities.

At roughly the same time, late in the first century, the Gospel and Letters of John may have been composed in Ephesus. Revelation, which may be the earliest of the Johannine writings, addresses the problem of the Nicolaitans and the "synagogue of Satan" (Rev 2:9; 3:9). The Jewish War and the imposition of the so-called *fiscus Iudaicus* "triggered the processes of separation between Jewish Jesus followers and the local synagogues" (Frey, 231). This new tax, which only Jews had to pay, may have led gentile believers to disassociate from the Jews. For the first time, membership in a Jewish community became a matter of public record. On the other hand, those who disassociated themselves from the synagogues may have been in a precarious legal situation. Because expulsion from the synagogue is mentioned in the New Testament only in John (9:22; 12:42; 16:2), it may have been a local phenomenon, and one that lay in the past by the time the gospel was completed.

Questions remain regarding the relationship between the Pauline and Johannine groups in Ephesus, but it is clear that Paul's followers separated from the synagogue earlier than the Johannine believers, for whom the issues were more christological. Still, this case study indicates that "the separation between synagogal Judaism and Jesus followers was a rather incoherent process, one that happened not at one particular moment, was influenced by various practical, theological, and sociopolitical reasons, and that differed from group to group and from place to place" (Frey, 238). It also discourages us from adopting "all-too generalizing hypotheses about 'the' expulsion" of believers from the synagogue (Frey, 239).

The third section of this volume addresses the continuing hostility that has been perpetuated by the Gospel of John and its interpreters. Fortunately, both recent scholarship and the church have recognized this challenge and taken decisive steps to address it. Still, it is only a beginning; this task remains for each generation.

In 2000 Reimund Bieringer and his colleagues in Leuven hosted an international, interdisciplinary colloquium on "Anti-Judaism and the Fourth Gospel." Fifteen years later, he reports on the continuing research at Louvain, the impact of the colloquium, and the status of work on anti-Judaism and the Gospel of John in the intervening years. His analysis is a lucid reflection of the issues and the challenges they still pose. Bieringer notes that to his knowledge "no one who holds that those who consider the Gospel of John to have revelatory authority need to be anti-Jewish or supersessionist" (Bieringer, 249). Instead, those who accept that the gospel has revelatory authority choose one of three possibilities: "(1) John is anti-Jewish (supersessionist), and this is authoritative for believers; (2) John is not anti-Jewish (supersessionist), and this is authoritative for believers, and (3) John is anti-Jewish (supersessionist), and this is not authoritative for believers" (Bieringer, 248). Bieringer and his coauthors of the introductory essay in the volume of papers from the colloquium conclude that while many scholars resist the conclusion that John is anti-Jewish, "there is a dangerous potential in the theology of the Gospel of John that goes beyond the first-century conflict and inner-Jewish dispute, a dangerous potential that continues to be an issue in the world before the text and that can only be addressed adequately in a hermeneutical approach" (Bieringer, 249). In an article published in the Festschrift for Johannes Beutler in 2004, Didier Pollefeyt and Bieringer offer a constructively precise interpretation of οἱ Ἰουδαῖοι in the Gospel of John, arguing that the term "has a very specific, unprecedented meaning" in John:

> It is clear that the polemic that is expressed by means of this term does not go against οἱ Ιουδαῖοι as an ethnic designation or against Judaism as a faith. Rather, the evangelist frequently refers to οἱ Ἰουδαῖοι as people who share the same ἔθνος and faith tradition as he but who fundamentally differ from him by not becoming disciples of Jesus as the Christ and the Son of God.... The most important implication of this is that it would be more precise to speak of "anti-unbelievers-in-Jesus-ism" instead of anti-Judaism. (Bieringer, 251–52)

Nevertheless, rather than resolving the problem, Bieringer and Pollefeyt warn that this polemic is not less dangerous than what has been called anti-Judaism.

In a tour de force Paul N. Anderson challenges widely held understandings of the gospel and proposes a reassessment of its relationship to its Jewish setting. His thesis is "that while John has played a role in anti-Semitism and religious violence, such influences represent the distortion of this thoroughly Jewish piece of writing.... The Fourth Gospel represents an intra-Jewish perspective" that offers an inclusive "universalist appeal to all seekers of truth" (Anderson, 267).

In a nuanced review of the uses of οἱ Ἰουδαῖοι in the gospel, Anderson finds that when the term references the Jewish religion in general, it is used in positive and neutral ways, but never in negative or ambivalent ways. When it refers to Jewish leaders in Jerusalem and Judea, it is highly dialectical, occurring in positive, neutral, negative, and ambivalent ways. From this analysis Anderson concludes that "there is no negative presentation of Judaism in itself. Nor are individuals or groups maligned simply for being Jewish" (Anderson, 294).

Affirming Jonathan Bernier's argument that exclusion from the synagogue was practiced early in the first century for political reasons, so the ἀποσυνάγωγος references are not anachronistic references to the exclusion of Johannine believers at the time of the writing of the gospel, Anderson critiques Martyn for failing to recognize the importance of John for understanding its *einmalig* level of meaning—namely, its portrayal of the opposition to Jesus during his ministry. Moreover, the separation from the synagogue late in the first century should still be understood as an intra-Jewish phenomenon. Seen in this light, the Gospel of John is "the most Jewish piece of writing in the entire New Testament"; it gives us a glimpse of "*an intra-faith set of tensions, not an interfaith set of dialogues*" (Anderson, 295). Therefore, "When read correctly, the Fourth Gospel not only ceases to be a source of religious acrimony; it points the way forward for all seekers of truth to sojourn together, across the boundaries of religious movements, time, and space" (Anderson, 265).

Ruth Sheridan perceptively shows how the interpretation of John's hostile references to the Jews developed into a trope that was reproduced in commentaries, thereby extending and exaggerating anti-Jewish sentiment among Christian readers. She focuses on "how commentators have interpreted John 8:32–33 to pejoratively characterize the Jews, effectively exacerbating their already negative portrait in much of the gospel" (Sheridan, 315). This trend, which has its roots in anti-Semitism in early modern Europe, became entrenched in the commentary genre, as commentators label the Jews' response to Jesus as "a perverse embodiment of Jewish nationalism, pride, privilege, and prejudice" (Sheridan, 315). This perpetuation of the text's anti-Judaism is all the more troubling because commentaries have been widely accepted as exegetical tools and resources—reliable guides to the meaning of the gospel. The pervasiveness of this interpretation and variations of it across a century or more of commentary writing is sobering, but the exceptions are noteworthy also. On the basis of her analysis of the pattern, Sheridan suggests that "the absence of anti-Jewish interpretation was nevertheless *most* evident in the commentaries that employed a form of historical-critical methodology that we might call *comparative criticism*," in which multiple "parallel" texts from the ancient sources were assembled, giving the interpreter a critical distance from the text (Sheridan, 326). Several recent German commentaries resist this pattern to the point of reinforcing the legitimacy of the Jews' voice. By contrast, sadly, pastorally oriented commentaries often demonstrate a stronger inclination to reproduce anti-Jewish readings.

Sheridan then cites the exhaustive study of German biblical interpretation from 1738 to 1952 by Anders Gerdmar as documentation that "pejorative ideas about Jews and Judaism formed 'part of the warp that runs through the European and German cultural fabric' " (Sheridan, 330, citing Gerdmar 2009, 609). During that era interpreters regarded the Jews as embodying "national pride," a view that became part of the general theological and cultural stance toward contemporary Jews, which "paved the way for the tropes of 'Jewish pride' and 'false freedom' to merge with John's hostile portrayal of the Jews in John 8:31–34 within the modern exegetical commentary, which was newly developing as a genre" (Sheridan, 330). In response to this potential for abuse through the commentary genre, Sheridan urges readers to maintain a heightened sensitivity to the perpetuation of anti-Judaism through such tropes and to seek alternatives to them.

Noam E. Marans concludes this section with an assessment of "The Place of John in Christian-Jewish Relations Fifty Years after *Nostra Aetate*." Strikingly, Marans, director of Interreligious and Intergroup Relations for the American Jewish Committee, claims that "for Jews, the 'Declaration on the Relation of the Church to Non-Christian Religions,' the official title of *Nostra Aetate*, [published in 1965] represents an interreligious transformation without parallel in Jewish history, perhaps without parallel in all of religious history" (Marans, 333). *Nostra Aetate* effectively reversed and rejected two millennia of ecclesiastical collusion in anti-Jewish sentiment. At the same time, it "recognizes the essentialness of biblical scholarship to the betterment of interreligious relations" (Marans, 334). Challenges certainly remain. As Marans observes, echoing the language of the document, "maybe the 'spirit of Christ' does not demonize Jews or Judaism, but the 'truth of the Gospel' sometimes does" (Marans, 334). How can one reconcile the church's new teaching regarding Judaism and the Jewish people with "the truth of the Gospel," which labels Jews as "children of the devil"?

Succeeding generations addressed the implementation of *Nostra Aetate*, recognizing that "in many ways John would be ground zero in that travail" (Marans, 334). Simply pointing to the positive reference to the Jews in John 4:22, as "The Jewish People and Their Sacred Scriptures in the Christian Bible," the 2002 publication from the Vatican Pontifical Biblical Commission, does, is not sufficient. Nevertheless, Marans contends, Catholic-Jewish relations have progressed much better than such biblical exegesis might reflect. The role of scholarship therefore continues to be important, as it can clarify that a seemingly anti-Jewish sentiment may have originated as an internecine debate within the Jewish community. Modern scholarship can also reframe ways in which Scripture is interpreted and foster dialogue between biblical interpretation and the new stance in relation to Judaism. As a litmus test of the implementation of *Nostra Aetate*, Marans cites changes in the script of "the infamous Oberammergau passion play, the mother of all dramatizations of Jesus's last days" (Marans, 336). While the three most recent versions of the Oberammergau passion play have removed many of its anti-Jewish stereotypes, its portrayal of Jesus as a Jewish rabbi has powerfully mitigated anti-Jewish elements of the play. At one point, Jesus holds up a facsimile of an unfurled Torah while the Oberammergau townspeople sing the Shema in Hebrew!

Marans therefore leaves us with the stirring challenge to be "foundationalists" who "take up the whole text and discredit that which offends," while "we emphasize the overriding messages of love, hope, and redemption that characterize the foundation of sacred religious texts" (Marans, 338).

The assessments of complicated issues related to John and Judaism in this volume, the proposals, new constructions, keen insights, and challenges these essays provide, will hopefully stimulate still further discussion. There is still much we do not know about the various movements and expressions of Judaism in the first century. Sweeping theories regarding John's setting and relationship to Jews and the synagogue have been called into question. "The parting of the ways" should now perhaps be discussed in the plural—"the variety of partings of the ways"—in recognition that groups of believers separated from Jews and Jewish institutions and communities at different times, in different ways, and for different reasons. For a period of decades many Jesus followers either maintained relations with Jews or established their identity by defining themselves over against Jews.

The Gospel of John was composed during this period by Jesus followers who drew deeply from their Jewish heritage: its Scriptures, ways of interpreting those Scriptures, philosophical and ethical ways of reasoning, the centrality of the temple and therefore the need to replace it metaphorically, Jewish festivals and spirituality, law and covenant, and its sense of destiny in God's merciful providence. The Gospel of John can hardly be read without great sensitivity to its pervasive Jewishness. On the other hand, its hostile language directed toward Jews, whatever the circumstances, context, or original intent of that language, has created a virus of hostility that the canonical authority and use of this gospel has conveyed from generation to generation of Christians. Even many of the foremost Johannine commentators have been influenced by this contagion. Only in the past fifty years has the hostile language of the gospel been recognized as an issue that every teacher, preacher, and student of the gospel must address. Knowledge both empowers and conveys responsibility. These essays are offered, therefore, to the church, the academy, and the public as a contribution to both understanding and corrective action. They can also be a reminder of the power of scholarship, institutional pronouncements, collective witness, and personal activism.

Works Cited

Adams, Sean A., and Seth M. Ehorn, eds. 2016a. "Composite Citations in the Septuagint Apocrypha." Pages 119–39 in *Jewish, Graeco-Roman, and Early Christian Uses*. Vol. 1 of *Composite Citations in Antiquity*. LNTS 525. London: Bloomsbury.

———. 2016b. *Jewish, Graeco-Roman, and Early Christian Uses*. Vol. 1 of *Composite Citations in Antiquity*. LNTS 525. London: Bloomsbury.

———. 2017. *New Testament Uses*. Vol. 2 of *Composite Citations in Antiquity*. London: Bloomsbury.

Aitken, James K. 2015. "Psalms." Pages 320–34 in *The T&T Clark Companion to the Septuagint*. Edited by J. K. Aitken. London: Bloomsbury.

Aland, Barbara, et al., eds. 2001. *The Greek New Testament*. 4th rev. ed. New York: United Bible Societies.

Alexander, Philip S. 1983. "Rabbinic Judaism and the New Testament." *ZNW* 74:237–46.

———. 1984. "The Rabbinic Hermeneutical Rules and the Problem of the Definition of Midrash." *PIBA* 8:97–125.

———. 1990. "*Quid Athenis et Hierosolymis?* Rabbinic Midrash and Hermeneutics in the Graeco-Roman World." Pages 101–24 in *A Tribute to Geza Vermes: Essays on Jewish and Christian Literature and History*. Edited by Philip R. Davies and Richard T. White. JSOTSup 100. Sheffield: Sheffield Academic.

———. 1992. "'The Parting of the Ways' from the Perspective of Rabbinic Judaism." Pages 1–25 in *Jews and Christians: The Parting of the Ways A.D. 70 to 135; The Second Durham-Tübingen Research Symposium on Earliest Christianity and Judaism (Durham, September 1989)*. Edited by J. D. G. Dunn. WUNT 66. Tübingen: Mohr Siebeck.

Allen, Garrick V. 2016. "Composite Citations in Jewish Pseudepigraphic Works: Re-presenting Legal Traditions in the Second Temple Period." Pages 140–57 in *Jewish, Graeco-Roman, and Early Christian Uses*. Vol. 1 of *Composite Citations in Antiquity*. LNTS 525. London: Bloomsbury.

Allison, Dale C., Jr. 1993. *The New Moses: A Matthean Typology*. Eugene, OR: Wipf & Stock.
———. 2005. *Studies in Matthew: Interpretation Past and Present*. Grand Rapids: Baker Academic.
———. Forthcoming. "Reflections on Matthew, John, and Jesus." 2016 Princeton-Prague Symposium Papers. Grand Rapids: Eerdmans.
Ameling, Walter. 1996. "Die jüdischen Gemeinden im antiken Kleinasien." Pages 29–55 in *Jüdische Gemeinden und Organisationsformen von der Antike bis zur Gegenwart*. Edited by R. Jütte and A. P. Kustermann. Vienna: Böhlau.
"Ancient Judaism and the Fourth Gospel." n.d. theo.kuleuven.be. https://theo.kuleuven.be/apps/johnandthejews/.
Anderson, Paul N. 1991. "Was the Fourth Evangelist a Quaker?" *Quaker Religious Thought* 76:27–43.
———. 1994. "Jesus and Peace." Pages 105–30 in *The Church's Peace Witness*. Edited by Marlin Miller and Barbara Nelson Gingerich. Grand Rapids: Eerdmans.
———. 1996. *The Christology of the Fourth Gospel: Its Unity and Disunity in the Light of John 6*. WUNT 2/78. Tübingen: Mohr Siebeck. Third printing, Eugene, OR: Cascade Books, 2010.
———. 1997. "The *Sitz im Leben* of the Johannine Bread of Life Discourse and Its Evolving Context." Pages 1–59 in *Critical Readings of John 6*. Edited by Alan Culpepper. BibInt 22. Leiden: Brill.
———. 1999. "The Having-Sent-Me Father—Aspects of Irony, Agency, and Encounter in the Father-Son Relationship." *Semeia* 85:33–57.
———. 2000. *Navigating the Living Waters of the Gospel of John: On Wading with Children and Swimming with Elephants*. Pendle Hill Pamphlet Series 352. Wallingford, PA: Pendle Hill.
———. 2001. "Mark and John—The *Bi-Optic* Gospels." Pages 175–88 in *Jesus in Johannine Tradition*. Edited by Robert Fortna and Tom Thatcher. Philadelphia: Westminster John Knox.
———. 2002. "Interfluential, Formative, and Dialectical—A Theory of John's Relation to the Synoptics." Pages 19–58 in *Für und Wider die Priorität des Johannesevangeliums*. Edited by Peter Hofrichter. TThSt 9. Hildesheim: Olms.
———. 2004a. "The Cognitive Origins of John's Christological Unity and Disunity." Pages 127–49 in *Psychology and the Bible: A New Way to Read the Scriptures*. Edited by J. Harold Ellens. Vol. 3. Westport, CT: Praeger.

———. 2004b. "Genocide or Jesus: A God of Conquest or Pacifism?" Pages 31–52 in *The Destructive Power of Religion: Violence in Judaism, Christianity, and Islam*. Edited by J. Harold Ellens. Vol. 4. Westport, CT: Praeger.

———. 2004c. "Religion and Violence: From Pawn to Scapegoat." Pages 265–83 in *The Destructive Power of Religion: Violence in Judaism, Christianity, and Islam*. Edited by J. Harold Ellens. Vol. 2. Westport, CT: Praeger.

———. 2005. "Petrine Ministry and Christocracy: A Response to *Ut Unum Sint*." *OiC* 40:3–39.

———. 2006a. "Aspects of Historicity in John: Implications for Archaeological and Jesus Studies." Pages 587–618 in *Jesus and Archaeology*. Edited by James H. Charlesworth. Grand Rapids: Eerdmans.

———. 2006b. *The Fourth Gospel and the Quest for Jesus: Modern Foundations Reconsidered*. LNTS 321. London: T&T Clark.

———. 2007a. "Antichristic Errors—Flawed Interpretations Regarding the Johannine Antichrists." Pages 196–216 in *Text and Community: Essays in Commemoration of Bruce M. Metzger*. Edited by J. Harold Ellens. Vol. 1. Sheffield: Sheffield Phoenix.

———. 2007b. "Bakhtin's Dialogism and the Corrective Rhetoric of the Johannine Misunderstanding Dialogue: Exposing Seven Crises in the Johannine Situation." Pages 133–59 in *Bakhtin and Genre Theory in Biblical Studies*. SemeiaSt 63. Edited by Roland Boer. Atlanta: Society of Biblical Literature.

———. 2007c. "Errors of the Antichrists—Proselytizing Schism and Assimilative Teaching within the Johannine Situation." Pages 217–40 in *Text and Community: Essays in Commemoration of Bruce M. Metzger*. Edited by J. Harold Ellens. Vol. 1. Sheffield: Sheffield Phoenix.

———. 2007d. "On Guessing Points and Naming Stars—The Epistemological Origins of John's Christological Tensions." Pages 311–45 in *The Gospel of St. John and Christian Theology*. Edited by Richard Bauckham and Carl Mosser. Grand Rapids: Eerdmans.

———. 2007e. "'*You* Have the Words of Eternal Life!' Is Peter Presented as *Returning* the Keys of the Kingdom to Jesus in John 6:68?" *Neot* 41:6–41.

———. 2008. "From One Dialogue to Another—Johannine Polyvalence from Origins to Receptions." Pages 93–119 in *Anatomies of Narrative Criticism: The Past, Present, and Future of the Fourth Gospel as Literature*. Edited by Stephen Moore and Tom Thatcher. RBS 55. Atlanta: Society of Biblical Literature.

———. 2011a. "John and Qumran: Discovery and Interpretation over Sixty Years." Pages 15–50 in *John, Qumran and the Dead Sea Scrolls: Sixty Years of Discovery and Debate*. Edited by Mary Coloe, PBVM, and Tom Thatcher. Atlanta: Society of Biblical Literature.

———. 2011b. *The Riddles of the Fourth Gospel: An Introduction to John*. Philadelphia: Fortress.

———. 2013. "Mark, John, and Answerability: Interfluentiality and Dialectic between the Second and Fourth Gospels." *Liber Annuus* 63:197–245.

———. 2014a. "The Community That Raymond Brown Left Behind: Reflections on the Dialectical Johannine Situation." Pages 47–93 in *Communities in Dispute: Current Scholarship on the Johannine Epistles*. Edited by R. Alan Culpepper and Paul N. Anderson. Atlanta: Society of Biblical Literature.

———. 2014b. Foreword to *The Gospel of John: A Commentary*, by Rudolf Bultmann. Johannine Monograph Series 1. Eugene, OR: Wipf & Stock.

———. 2014c. *From Crisis to Christ: A Contextual Introduction to the New Testament*. Nashville: Abingdon.

———. 2015. "On 'Seamless Robes' and 'Leftover Fragments': A Theory of Johannine Composition." Pages 169–218 in *Structure, Composition, and Authorship of John's Gospel*. Edited by Stanley E. Porter and Hughson Ong. Leiden: Brill.

———. 2016. "The Johannine *Logos*-Hymn: A Cross-Cultural Celebration of God's Creative-Redemptive Work." Pages 219–42 in *Creation Stories in Dialogue: The Bible, Science, and Folk Traditions*. Edited by R. Alan Culpepper and Jan van der Watt. Radboud Prestige Lecture Series by R. Alan Culpepper. BibInt 139. Leiden: Brill.

Anderson, Paul N., Felix Just, SJ, and Tom Thatcher, eds. 2007. *Critical Appraisals of Critical Views*. Vol. 1 of *John, Jesus, and History*. SymS 44. Atlanta: Society of Biblical Literature.

———. 2009. *Aspects of Historicity in the Fourth Gospel*. Vol. 2 of *John, Jesus, and History*. SymS 49. ECL 1. Atlanta: Society of Biblical Literature.

———. 2016. *Glimpses of Jesus through the Johannine Lens*. Vol. 3 of *John, Jesus, and History*. ECL 18. Atlanta: SBL Press.

Appold, Mark L. 1976. *The Oneness Motif in the Fourth Gospel*. WUNT 2/1. Tübingen: Mohr Siebeck.

Ashton, John. 1985. "The Identity and Function of the Ἰουδαῖοι in the Fourth Gospel." *NovT* 27:40–75.

———. 1994. *Studying John: Approaches to the Fourth Gospel.* Oxford: Clarendon.

———. 2002. Review of *Anti-Judaism and the Fourth Gospel*, by Reimund Bieringer et al. *BibInt* 10:436–38.

———. 2007. *Understanding the Fourth Gospel.* 2nd ed. Oxford: Oxford University Press.

———. 2013. "Intimations of Apocalyptic: Looking Back and Looking Forward." Pages 3–35 in *John's Gospel and Intimations of Apocalyptic.* Edited by C. H. Williams and C. Rowland. London: T&T Clark.

———. 2014. *The Gospel of John and Christian Origins.* Minneapolis: Fortress.

Asiedu-Peprah, Martin. 2001. *Johannine Sabbath Conflicts as Juridical Controversy.* WUNT 2/132. Tübingen: Mohr Siebeck.

Attridge, Harold W. 2010a. "An Emotional Jesus and Stoic Traditions." Pages 77–92 in *Stoicism in Early Christianity.* Edited by Tuomas Rasimus, Troels Engberg-Pedersen, and Ismo Dunderberg. Peabody, MA: Hendrickson.

———. 2010b. *Essays on John and Hebrews.* Tübingen: Mohr Siebeck.

———. 2014. "Divine Sovereignty and Human Responsibility in the Fourth Gospel." Pages 183–99 in *Revealed Wisdom: Studies in Apocalyptic in Honour of Christopher Rowland.* Edited by John Ashton. AJEC 88. Leiden: Brill.

———. 2016. "Stoic and Platonic Reflections on Naming in Early Christian Circles: Or What's in a Name." Pages 277–95 in *From Stoicism to Platonism: The Development of Philosophy 100 BCE–100 CE.* Edited by Troels Engberg-Pedersen. Cambridge: Cambridge University Press.

Aune, David E. 1997. *Revelation 1–5.* WBC 52a. Nashville: Nelson.

———. 2003. "Dualism in the Fourth Gospel and the Dead Sea Scrolls: A Reassessment of the Problem." Pages 281–303 in *Neotestamentica et Philonica: Studies in Honour of Peder Borgen.* Edited by David E. Aune, Torrey Seland, and Jarl Henning Ulrichsen. NovTSup 106. Leiden: Brill.

———. 2006. *Apocalypticism, Prophecy, and Magic in Early Christianity: Collected Essays.* Grand Rapids: Eerdmans.

Aus, Roger David. 1992. "The Death of One for All in John 11:45–54 in Light of Judaic Traditions." Pages 29–63 in Roger David Aus, *Barabbas and Esther and Other Studies in the Judaic Illumination of Earliest Christianity.* SFSHJ 54. Atlanta: Scholars Press.

Avemarie, Friedrich. 2009. "Interpreting Scripture through Scripture: Exegesis Based on Lexematic Association in the Dead Sea Scrolls and the Pauline Epistles." Pages 83–102 in *Echoes from the Caves: Qumran and the New Testament*. Edited by Florentino García Martínez. STDJ 85. Leiden: Brill.

Avery-Peck, Alan J. 1982. *Terumot*. Vol. 6 of *The Talmud of the Land of Israel: A Preliminary Translation and Explanation*. Edited by Jacob Neusner. CSHJ. Chicago: University of Chicago Press.

———. 2002. "Terumot." Pages 131–202 in *The Tosefta: Translated from the Hebrew with a New Introduction*. Vol. 1. Edited by Jacob Neusner. Peabody, MA: Hendrickson.

Baer, David A. 2001. *When We All Go Home: Translation and Theology in LXX Isaiah 56–66*. JSOTSup 318. Sheffield: Sheffield Academic.

Baldensperger, Wilhelm. 1898. *Der Prolog des vierten Evangeliums: Sein polemisch-apologetischer Zweck*. Freiburg: Mohr Siebeck.

Balz, H. 1972. "τεσσαράκοντα." *TDNT* 8:127–39.

Banki, Judith H. 1984. "The Image of Jews in Christian Teaching." *JES* 21.3: 437–51.

Barclay, John M. G. 1996. *Jews in the Mediterranean Diaspora from Alexander to Trajan (323 BCE–117 CE)*. Edinburgh: T&T Clark.

Barker, James. 2015. *John's Use of Matthew*. Minneapolis: Fortress.

Barrett, C. K. 1947. "The Old Testament in the Fourth Gospel." *JTS* 48:155–69.

———. 1972. "The Dialectical Theology of St John." Pages 49–69 in *New Testament Essays*. London: SCM.

———. 1975. *The Gospel of John and Judaism*. Philadelphia: Fortress.

———. 1978. *The Gospel according to St. John: An Introduction with Commentary and Notes on the Greek Text*. 2nd ed. Philadelphia: Westminster.

———. 1982. "Jews and Judaizers in the Epistles of Ignatius." Pages 133–58 in his *Essays on John*. Louisville: Westminster John Knox.

Barth, Gerhard. 1963. "Matthew's Understanding of the Law." Pages 58–164 in *Tradition and Interpretation in Matthew*. Edited by Günther Bornkamm, Gerhard Barth, and Heinz Joachim Held. Translated by Percy Scott. Philadelphia: Westminster.

Basser, Herbert W. 2009. *The Mind behind the Gospels: A Commentary to Matthew 1–14*. Boston: Academic Studies Press.

Bauckham, Richard. 1998a. *God Crucified: Monotheism and Christology in the New Testament*. Carlisle: Paternoster.

———. 1998b. *The Gospels for All Christians: Rethinking the Gospel Audiences*. Grand Rapids: Eerdmans.

———. 2006. "Messianism according to the Gospel of John." Pages 32–68 in *Challenging Perspectives on the Gospel of John*. Edited by J. Lierman. WUNT 2/219. Tübingen: Mohr Siebeck.

———. 2007. "Historiographical Characteristics in the Gospel of John." *NTS* 53:17–36.

———. 2008. "Bridging the Gap: How Might the Fourth Gospel Help Us Cope with the Legacy of Christianity's Exclusive Claim over against Judaism?" Pages 168–82 in *The Gospel of John and Christian Theology*. Edited by Richard Bauckham and Carl Mosser. Grand Rapids: Eerdmans.

———. 2015. *Gospel of Glory: Major Themes in Johannine Theology*. Grand Rapids: Baker Academic.

Bauer, Walter. 1971. *Orthodoxy and Heresy in Earliest Christianity*. Philadelphia: Fortress.

Baur, F. C. 1847. *Kritische Untersuchungen über die kanonischen Evangelien, ihr Verhältniss zu einander, ihren Charakter und Ursprung*. Tübingen: Fues.

———. 1878–1879. *The Church History of the First Three Centuries*. Translated by Allan Menzies. 2 vols. London: Williams & Norgate.

Beasley-Murray, George R. 1987. *John*. WBC 36. Waco: Word Books. 2nd ed. 1999.

Beasley-Murray, Paul. 2000. "Obituary of George Raymond Beasley-Murray." Church Matters. http://tinyurl.com/SBL0398e

Beck, Norman A. 1994. "Anti-Jewish Polemic in John and in the Johannine Epistles." Pages 285–312 in *Mature Christianity in the Twenty-First Century: The Recognition and Repudiation of the Anti-Jewish Polemic of the New Testament*. New York: Crossroad.

Becker, Jürgen. 1979–1981. *Das Evangelium des Johannes*. ÖTK 4.1.2. Gütersloh: Mohn.

Belle, Gilbert van. 1994. *The Signs Source in the Fourth Gospel: Historical Survey and Critical Evaluation of the Semeia Hypothesis*. BETL 116. Leuven: Peeters.

———. 2013. "Anti-Joodse Jezuswoorden? Jezus en de Joden in het Johannesevangelie." Pages 119–50 in *Ongemakkelijke woorden van Jezus*. Edited by P. Kevers. Leuven: Acco.

Belli, Filippo. 2002. "'I giudei' nel Vangelo secondo Giovanni: Come affrontare il problema." *RivB* 50:63–75.

Benedictus XVI. 2010. *Post-Synodal Apostolic Exhortation Verbum Domini of the Holy Father Benedict XVI to the Bishops, Clergy, Consecrated Per-*

sons and the Lay Faithful on the Word of God in the Life and Mission of the Church. Vatican City: Libreria editrice Vaticana.

Bennema, Cornelis. 2009. "The Identity and Composition of οἱ Ἰουδαῖοι in the Gospel of John." *TynBul* 60:239–63.

———. 2013a. "The Chief Priests: Masterminds of Jesus' Death." Pages 382–87 in *Character Studies in the Fourth Gospel: Literary Approaches to Sixty-Seven Figures in John.* Edited by Steven A. Hunt, D. Francois Tolmie, and Ruben Zimmermann. WUNT 314. Tübingen: Mohr Siebeck.

———. 2013b. "'The Jews': Jesus' Opponents Par Excellence." Pages 87–100 in Cornelis Bennema, *Encountering Jesus: Character Studies in the Gospel of John.* Milton Keynes: Paternoster.

Berger, Michael S. 1998. *Rabbinic Authority.* New York: Oxford University Press.

Bernard, J. H. 1928. *A Critical and Exegetical Commentary on the Gospel according to St. John.* 2 vols. ICC. Edinburgh: T&T Clark.

Bernier, Jonathan. 2013. *Aposynagōgos and the Historical Jesus in John: Rethinking the Historicity of the Johannine Expulsion Passages.* BibInt 122. Leiden: Brill.

Bernstein, Moshe J., with Shlomo A. Koyfman. 2013. "The Interpretation of Biblical Law in the Dead Sea Scrolls: Forms and Methods." Pages 448–75 in *Reading and Re-reading Scripture at Qumran.* Vol. 2. STDJ 107. Leiden: Brill.

Beutler, Johannes. 2001. "The Identity of the 'Jews' for the Readers of John." Pages 229–38 in *Anti-Judaism and the Fourth Gospel: Papers of the Leuven Colloquium, 2000.* Edited by R. Bieringer, Didier Pollefeyt, and F. Vandecasteele-Vanneuville. JCH. Assen: Van Gorcum.

———. 2006. *Judaism and the Jews in the Gospel of John.* SubBi 30. Rome: Pontifical Biblical Institute.

———. 2009. "Der Johannes-Prolog-Ouvertüre des Johannesevangeliums." Pages 77–106 in *Der Johannesprolog.* Darmstadt: Wissenschaftliche Buchgesellschaft.

Bieringer, Reimund. 2005. "'Come, and You Will See' (John 1:39): Dialogical Authority and Normativity of the Future in the Fourth Gospel and in Religious Education." Pages 179–201 in *Hermeneutics and Religious Education.* Edited by Herman Lombaerts and Didier Pollefeyt. Leuven: Peeters.

———. 2007. "Das Lamm Gottes, das die Sünde der Welt hinwegnimmt (Joh 1,29): Eine kontextorientierte und redaktionsgeschichtliche

Untersuchung auf dem Hintergrund der Passatradition als Deutung des Todes Jesu im Johannesevangelium." Pages 199–232 in *The Death of Jesus in the Fourth Gospel*. Edited by G. van Belle. BETL 200. Leuven: Peeters.

———. 2012. "'… Because the Father Is Greater than I' (John 14:28): Johannine Christology in Light of the Relationship between the Father and the Son." Pages 181–204 in *Gospel Images of Jesus Christ in Church Tradition and in Biblical Scholarship: Fifth International East-West Symposium of New Testament Scholars, Minsk, September 2 to 9, 2010*. Edited by Christos Karakolis, Karl-Wilhelm Niebuhr, and Sviatoslav Rogalsky. WUNT 288. Tübingen: Mohr Siebeck.

———. 2014. "Ihr habt weder seine Stimme gehört noch seine Gestalt gesehen" (Joh 5,37): Anti-Judaismus und johanneische Christologie." Pages 165–88 in *Studies in the Gospel of John and Its Christology: Festschrift Gilbert Van Belle*. Edited by Joseph Verheyden, Geert Van Oyen, Michael Labahn, and Reimund Bieringer. BETL 265. Leuven: Peeters.

———. 2016. "'Ραββουνί in John 20,16 and Its Implications for Our Understanding of the Relationship between Mary Magdalene and Jesus." Pages 3–42 in *Noli Me Tangere in Interdisciplinary Perspective: Textual, Iconographic and Contemporary Interpretations*. Edited by Reimund Bieringer, Barbara Baert and Karlijn Demasure. Leuven: Peeters.

———. 2017. "The Passion Narrative in the Gospel of John: A Hotbed of Docetism?" In *The Quest for an Elusive Phenomenon: Docetism in the Early Church*. Edited by J. Verheyden, R. Bieringer, J. Schröter, and I. Luthe. WUNT. Tübingen: Mohr Siebeck.

Bieringer, Reimund, and Mary Elsbernd, eds. 2010. *Normativity of the Future: Reading Biblical and Other Authoritative Texts in an Eschatological Perspective*. Annua Nuntia Lovaniensia 61. Leuven: Peeters.

Bieringer, Reimund, and Didier Pollefeyt. 2004. "Open to Both Ways…? Johannine Perspectives on Judaism in the Light of Jewish-Christian Dialogue." Pages 11–32 in *Israel und seine Heilstraditionen im Johannesevangelium: Festgabe für Johannes Beutler SJ zum 70. Geburtstag*. Edited by Michael Labahn, Klaus Scholtissek, and Angelika Strotmann. Paderborn: Schöningh.

———, eds. 2012a. *Paul and Judaism: Crosscurrents in Pauline Exegesis and the Study of Jewish-Christian Relations*. LNTS 463. London: Continuum.

———. 2012b. "Wrestling with the Jewish Paul." Pages 1–14 in *Paul and Judaism: Crosscurrents in Pauline Exegesis and the Study of Jewish-*

Christian Relations. Edited by Reimund Bieringer and Didier Pollefeyt. LNTS 463. London: Continuum.

Bieringer, Reimund, Didier Pollefeyt, and Frederique Vandecasteele-Vanneuville, eds. 2001a. *Anti-Judaism and the Fourth Gospel*. Louisville: Westminster John Knox.

———. 2001b. *Anti-Judaism and the Fourth Gospel: Papers of the Leuven Colloquium, 2000*. JCH 1. Assen: Van Gorcum; Leiden: Brill.

———. 2001c. "Wrestling with Johannine Anti-Judaism: A Hermeneutical Framework for the Analysis of the Current Debate." Pages 3–44 in *Anti-Judaism and the Fourth Gospel: Papers of the Leuven Colloquium, 2000*. Edited by Reimund Bieringer, Didier Pollefeyt, and Frederique Vandecasteele-Vanneuville. JCH 1. Assen: Van Gorcum.

———. 2001d. "Wrestling with Johannine Anti-Judaism: A Hermeneutical Framework for the Analysis of the Current Debate." Pages 3–37 in *Anti-Judaism and the Fourth Gospel*. Edited by Reimund Bieringer, Didier Pollefeyt, and Frederique Vandecasteele-Vanneuville. Louisville: Westminster John Knox.

Bieringer, Reimund, et al., eds. 2014. *Second Corinthians in the Perspective of Late Second Temple Judaism*. Leiden: Brill.

Binder, Donald D. 1999. *Into the Temple Courts: The Place of the Synagogues in the Second Temple Period*. Atlanta: Society of Biblical Literature.

Black, C. Clifton, II. 1988. "The Rhetorical Form of the Hellenistic Jewish and Early Christian Sermon: A Response to Lawrence Wills." *HTR* 81:1–18.

Blank, J. 1962. *Krisis: Untersuchungen zur johanneischen Christologie und Eschatologie*. Freiburg: Lambertus.

Boer, Martinus C. de. 1996. *Johannine Perspectives on the Death of Jesus*. CBET 17. Kampen: Pharos.

———. 2001. "The Depiction of 'the Jews' in John's Gospel: Matters of Behaviour and Identity." Pages 260–80 in *Anti-Judaism and the Fourth Gospel: Papers of the Leuven Colloquium, 2000*. Edited by R. Bieringer, Dieder Pollefeyt, and F. Vandecasteele-Vanneuville. JCH 1. Assen: Van Gorcum.

Bohak, Gideon. 2008. *Ancient Jewish Magic: A History*. Cambridge: Cambridge University Press.

Boismard, Marie-Emile. 1993. *Moses or Jesus: An Essay in Johannine Christology*. Translated by B. T. Viviano. Minneapolis: Fortress.

Bolton, David. 2011. "Justifying Paul among Jews and Christians? A Critical Investigation of the New Perspective on Paul in Light of Jewish-Christian Dialogue." PhD diss., Katholieke Universiteit Leuven.

Borgen, Peder. 1965. *Bread from Heaven: An Exegetical Study of the Concept of Manna in the Gospel of John and the Writings of Philo*. NovTSup 10. Leiden: Brill.

———. 1997. "God's Agent in the Fourth Gospel." Pages 83–96 in *The Interpretation of John*. Edited by John Ashton. 2nd ed. Edinburgh: T&T Clark.

Bornhäuser, Karl. 1928. *Das Johannesevangelium: Eine Missionschrift für Israel*. Gütersloh.

Bornkamm, Günther. 1968. "Zur Interpretation des Johannesevangeliums." Pages 104–21 in *Gesammelte Aufsätze*. Vol. 3.1 of *Geschichte und Glaube*. Munich: Kaiser.

Bousset, Wilhelm. 1913, 1967. *Kyrios Christos: Geschichte des Christusglaubens von den Anfängen des Christentums bis Irenäus*. Göttingen: Vandenhoeck & Ruprecht.

Boyarin, Daniel. 2000. "A Tale of Two Synods: Nicaea, Yavneh, and Rabbinic Ecclesiology." *Exemplaria* 12:21–62.

———. 2002. "The *Ioudaioi* in John and the Prehistory of 'Judaism.'" Pages 224–50 in *Pauline Conversations in Context: Essays in Honor of Calvin J. Roetzel*. Edited by Janice Capel Anderson et. al. Sheffield: Sheffield Academic.

———. 2004. *Border Lines: The Partition of Judaeo-Christianity in Divinations; Rereading Late Ancient Religion*. Philadelphia: University of Pennsylvania Press.

———. 2014. "Der Menschensohn in 1. Henoch und 4. Esra." *BTZ* 31:41–63.

Brant, Jo-Ann. 2011. *John*. Paideia Commentaries on the New Testament. Grand Rapids: Baker Academic.

Bratcher, Robert G. 1974. "'The Jews' in the Gospel of John." *BT* 26.4: 401–9.

Broadhead, Edwin K. 2010. *Jewish Ways of Following Jesus: Redrawing the Religious Map of Antiquity*. WUNT 266. Tübingen: Mohr Siebeck.

Brodie, Thomas L. 1993. *The Gospel according to John: A Literary and Theological Commentary*. Oxford: Oxford University Press.

Broer, I. 1991. "Antijudaismus im Neuen Testament?" Pages 321–55 in *Salz der Erde—Licht der Welt*. Edited by I. Oberlinner and P. Fiedler. Stuttgart: Katholisches Bibelwerk.

Brooke, George J. 1985. *Exegesis at Qumran: 4QFlorilegium in Its Jewish Context*. JSOTSup 29. Sheffield: JSOT Press.

———. 2005a. "Biblical Interpretation in the Qumran Scrolls and the New Testament." Pages 52–69 in *The Dead Sea Scrolls and the New Testament: Essays in Mutual Illumination*. London: SPCK.

———. 2005b. *The Dead Sea Scrolls and the New Testament: Essays in Mutual Illumination*. London: SPCK.

———. 2010. "Shared Exegetical Traditions between the Scrolls and the New Testament." Pages 565–91 in *The Oxford Handbook of the Dead Sea Scrolls*. Edited by Timothy H. Lim and John J. Collins. Oxford: Oxford University Press.

Brown, Raymond E. 1966. *The Gospel according to John, i–xii*. AB 29. New York: Doubleday.

———. 1970. *The Gospel according to John, xiii–xxi*. AB 29A. New York: Doubleday.

———. 1979. *The Community of the Beloved Disciple*. New York: Paulist.

———. 1983. *The Birth of the Messiah*. Garden City, NY: Doubleday.

———. 2003. *An Introduction to the Gospel of John*. Edited by Francis J. Moloney. ABRL. New York: Doubleday.

Brown, Sherri. 2010. *Gift upon Gift: Covenant through Word in the Gospel of John*. PTMS 144. Eugene, OR: Pickwick.

Brumberg-Kraus, J. 2011. "The Third Letter of John." Pages 458–59 in *The Jewish Annotated New Testament*. Edited by A.-J. Levine and M. Z. Brettler. Oxford: Oxford University Press.

Bruner, Frederick Dale. 2012. *The Gospel of John: A Commentary*. Grand Rapids: Eerdmans.

Brunson, Andrew C. 2003. *Psalm 118 in the Gospel of John: An Intertextual Study on the New Exodus Pattern in the Theology of John*. WUNT 2/158. Tübingen: Mohr Siebeck.

Buell, Denise Kimber. 2005. *Why This New Race: Ethnic Reasoning in Early Christianity*. New York: Columbia University Press.

———. 2010. "God's Own People: Specters of Race, Ethnicity, and Gender in Early Christian Studies." Pages 159–90 in *Prejudice and Christian Beginnings: Investigating Race, Gender, and Ethnicity in Early Christianity*. Edited by Laura Salah Nasrallah and Elisabeth Schüssler Fiorenza. Minneapolis: Fortress.

Bultmann, Rudolf. 1923. "Der religionsgeschichtliche Hintergrund des Prologs zum Johannes-Evangelium." Pages 1–26 in *Zur Religion und Literatur des Neuen Testaments*. Part 2 of *Eucharistērion: Studien zur Religion und Literatur des Alten und Neuen Testaments; Hermann Gunkel zum 60. Geburtstage, dem 23. Mai 1922 dargebracht von seinen Schülern und Freunden.* FRLANT 36.2. Göttingen: Vandenhoeck & Ruprecht.

———. 1925. "Die Bedeutung der Neuerschlossenen Mandäischen und Manichäischen Quellen für das Verständnis des Johannesevangeliums." *ZNW* 24:100–146.

———. 1941. *Das Evangelium des Johannes.* KEK. Göttingen: Vandenhoeck & Ruprecht.

———. 1953, 1977. *Theologie des Neuen Testaments.* Tübingen: Mohr Siebeck.

———. 1955. *Theology of the New Testament.* Vol. 2. Translated by Kendrick Grobel. Waco: Baylor University Press.

———. 1963. *History of the Synoptic Tradition.* New York: Harper & Row.

———. 1971. *The Gospel of John: A Commentary.* Translated by George Beasley-Murray et al. Philadelphia: Westminster.

———. 1973. *The Johannine Epistles.* Hermeneia. Philadelphia: Fortress.

———. 1985. "Is Exegesis without Presuppositions Possible?" Pages 145–53 in *New Testament Mythology and Other Basic Writings.* Edited and translated by Schubert M. Ogden. London: SCM, 1985.

Burge, Gary M. 1987. *The Anointed Community: The Holy Spirit in the Johannine Tradition.* Grand Rapids: Eerdmans.

Burnett, Fred W. 2002. Review of *Anti-Judaism and the Fourth Gospel*, by Reimund Bieringer et al. *RelSRev* 28:77.

Busse, Ulrich. 2006. "Metaphorik und Rethorik im Johannesevangelium: Das Bildfeld vom König." Pages 279–317 in *Imagery in the Gospel of John.* Edited by J. Frey, J. G. van der Watt, and R. Zimmermann. Tübingen: Mohr Siebeck.

———. 2014. "Theologie oder Christologie im Johannesprolog?" Pages 1–36 in *Studies in the Gospel of John and Its Christology: Festschrift Gilbert Van Belle.* BETL 265. Edited by J. Verheyden, G. van Oyen, M. Labahn, and R. Bieringer. Leuven: Peeters.

Bynum, William Randolph. 2015. "Quotations of Zechariah in the Fourth Gospel." Pages 47–74 in *Abiding Words: The Use of Scripture in the Gospel of John.* Edited by Alicia D. Myers and Bruce G. Schuchard. RBS 81. Atlanta: SBL Press, 2015.

Campbell, Jonathan G. 1995. *The Use of Scripture in the Damascus Document 1–8, 19–20.* BZAW 228. Berlin: de Gruyter.

Cargas, Harry James. 1981. *A Christian Response to the Holocaust.* Denver: Stonehenge Books.

Carson, Donald A. 1991. *The Gospel according to John.* Grand Rapids: Eerdmans.

———. 2007. “The Challenge of the Balkanization of Johannine Studies.” Pages 133–59 in *John, Jesus, and History*. Vol. 1. Edited by P. N. Anderson, F. Just, and T. Thatcher. Atlanta: Society of Biblical Literature.

Carter, Warren. 2000. *Matthew and the Margins: A Socio-political and Religious Reading.* BLS. Maryknoll, NY: Orbis Books.

———. 2004. *Matthew: Storyteller, Interpreter, Evangelist.* Rev. ed. Peabody, MA: Hendrickson.

———. 2007. “Matthew’s Gospel: Jewish Christianity, Christian Judaism, or Neither?” Pages 155–79 in *Jewish Christianity Reconsidered: Rethinking Ancient Groups and Texts.* Edited by M. Jackson-McCabe. Minneapolis: Fortress.

———. 2008. *John and Empire: Initial Explorations.* New York: T&T Clark.

Casey, Maurice. 1996. *Is John’s Gospel True?* London: Routledge.

———. 2010. *Jesus of Nazareth: An Independent Historian’s Account of His Life and Teaching.* London: T&T Clark.

Cassidy, Richard. 1992. *John’s Gospel in New Perspective: Christology and the Realities of Roman Power.* Maryknoll, NY: Orbis Books.

Chanikuzhy, Jacob. 2012. *Jesus, the Eschatological Temple: An Exegetical Study of Jn 2,13–22 in the Light of the Pre-70 C.E.: Eschatological Temple Hopes and the Synoptic Temple Action.* CBET 58. Leuven: Peeters.

Charles, R. H. 1920. *A Critical and Exegetical Commentary on the Book of Revelation.* 2 vols. ICC. Edinburgh: T&T Clark.

Charlesworth, James H., ed. 1983–1985. *The Old Testament Pseudepigrapha.* 2 vols. Garden City, NY: Doubleday.

———. 2009. “From Old to New: Paradigm Shift concerning Judaism, the Gospel of John, Jesus, and the Advent of ‘Christianity.’” Pages 56–72 in *Jesus Research: An International Perspective.* Edited by J. H. Charlesworth and P. Pokorný. Princeton-Prague Symposia Series on the Historical Jesus. Grand Rapids: Eerdmans.

———. 2010. “The Historical Jesus in the Fourth Gospel: A Paradigm Shift?” *JSHJ* 8:3–46.

———. 2013. “Did They Ever Part?” Pages 281–300 in *How Judaism and Christianity Became Two.* Edited by Hershel Shanks. Washington, DC: Biblical Archaeological Society.

Chernick, Michael. 1990. “Internal Restraints on *Gezerah Shawah’s* Application.” *JQR* 80:253–82.

Chibici-Revneanu, Nicole. 2007. *Die Herrlichkeit des Verherrlichten: Das Verständnis der δόξα im Johannesevangelium.* WUNT 2/231. Tübingen: Mohr Siebeck.

Chilton, Bruce. 2004. Review of *Anti-Judaism and the Fourth Gospel*, by Reimund Bieringer et al. *Shofar* 22.3: 150–52.

Claußen, Carsten. 2003. "Meeting, Community, Synagogue—Different Frameworks of Ancient Jewish Congregations in the Diaspora." Pages 144–67 in *The Ancient Synagogue: From Its Origins until 200 C.E.* Edited by Birger Olsson and Magnus Zetterholm. Stockholm: Almqvist & Wiksell.

Cohen, Shaye J. D. 1981. "Epigraphical Rabbis." *JQR* 72:1–17.

———. 1984. "The Significance of Yavneh: Pharisees, Rabbis, and the End of Jewish Sectarianism." *HUCA* 55:27–53.

———. 1993. "'Those Who Say They Are Jews and Are Not': How Do You Know a Jew in Antiquity When You See One?" Pages 1–45 in *Diasporas in Antiquity.* Edited by Shane J. D. Cohen and Ernest S. Frerichs. BJS 288. Atlanta: Scholars Press.

———. 1999a. "*Ioudaios, Iudaeus,* Judaean, Jew." Pages 69–106 in *The Beginnings of Jewishness: Boundaries, Varieties, Uncertainties.* Berkeley: University of California Press.

———. 1999b. "Were Pharisees and Rabbis the Leaders of Communal Prayer and Torah Study in Antiquity? The Evidence of the New Testament, Josephus, and the Early Church Fathers." Pages 89–105 in *Evolution of the Synagogue: Problems and Progress.* Edited by Howard Clark Kee and Lynn H. Cohick. Harrisburg, PA: Trinity Press International.

Collingwood, R. G. 1946. *The Idea of History.* Oxford: Clarendon.

Collins, John J. 2014. "The Messiah in Ancient Judaism." *BTZ* 31:17–40.

Collins, Nina L. 2014. *Jesus, the Sabbath and the Jewish Debate: Healing on the Sabbath in the 1st and 2nd Centuries CE.* LNTS 474. London: Bloomsbury.

Coloe, Mary L. 2001. *God Dwells with Us: Temple Symbolism in the Fourth Gospel.* Collegeville, MN: Liturgical Press.

———. 2006. "Sources in the Shadows: John 13 and the Johannine Community." Pages 69–82 in *New Currents through John: A Global Perspective.* Edited by Francisco Lozada Jr. and Tom Thatcher. RBS. Atlanta: Society of Biblical Literature.

———. 2007. *Dwelling in the Household of God: Johannine Ecclesiology and Spirituality.* Collegeville, MN: Liturgical Press.

Coman, Viorel. 2016. "Dumitru Stăniloae's Trinitarian Ecclesiology in the Context of the Debates on the Filioque: The Synthesis between Christology and Pneumatology in Ecclesiology." PhD diss., Katholieke Universiteit Leuven.

Commission for the Religious Relation with the Jews. 1985. "Notes on the Correct Way to Present the Jews and Judaism." Vatican.va. http://tinyurl.com/SBL0398i.

Cook, Michael J. 1987a. "The New Testament and Judaism: An Historical Perspective on the Theme." *RevExp* 84:183–99.

———. 1987b. "Rabbinic Judaism and Early Christianity: From the Pharisees to the Rabbis." *RevExp* 84:201–20.

Cooke, Richard. 2009. *New Testament*. SCM Core Text. London: SCM.

Counet, Patrick Chatelion. 2005. "No Anti-Judaism in the Fourth Gospel: A Deconstruction of Reading of John 8." Pages 197–225 in *One Text, a Thousand Methods: Studies in Memory of Sjef van Tilborg*. Edited by U. Berges and P. Chatelion Counet. BibInt 71. Boston: Brill.

Cullmann, Oscar. 1956. "Ὁ ὀπίσω μου ἐρχόμενος." Pages 177–82 in *The Early Church: Studies in Early Christian History and Theology*. Edited by A. J. B. Higgins. Philadelphia: Westminster.

———. 1966. "Die literarischen und historischen Probleme des pseudoklementinischen Romans." Pages 225–31 in *Vorträge und Aufsätze 1925–1962*. Edited by Karlfried Fröhlich. Tübingen: Mohr Siebeck, 1966.

———. 1975. *Der johanneische Kreis: Zum Ursprung des Johannesevangeliums*. Tübingen: Mohr Siebeck.

———. 1976. *The Johannine Circle*. Philadelphia: Fortress; London: SPCK, 1976.

Culpepper, R. Alan. 1975. *The Johannine School*. SBLDS 26. Missoula, MT: Scholars Press.

———. 1980. "The Pivot of John's Prologue." *NTS* 27:1–31.

———. 1983. *Anatomy of the Fourth Gospel*. Philadelphia: Fortress.

———. 1987. "The Gospel of John and the Jews." *RevExp* 84:273–88.

———. 1991. "The Johannine *Hypodeigma*: A Reading of John 13." *Semeia* 53:133–52.

———. 1992. "The Gospel of John as a Threat to Jewish–Christian Relations." Pages 21–43 in *Overcoming Fears between Jews and Christians*. Edited by James H. Charlesworth, F. X. Blisard, and J. L. Gorham. New York: Crossroad.

———. 2001a. "Anti-Judaism in the Fourth Gospel as a Theological Problem for Christian Interpreters." Pages 68–91 in *Anti-Judaism and the*

Fourth Gospel: Papers of the Leuven Colloquium, 2000. Edited by Riemund Bieringer, Didier Pollefeyt, and Frederique Vandecasteele-Vanneuville. JCH. Assen: Van Gorcum.

———. 2001b. "Anti-Judaism in the Fourth Gospel as a Theological Problem for Christian Interpreters." Pages 61–82 in *Anti-Judaism and the Fourth Gospel*. Edited by Reimund Bieringer, Didier Pollefeyt, and Frederique Vandecasteele-Vanneuville. Louisville: Westminster John Knox.

———. 2002. "Inclusivism and Exclusivism in the Fourth Gospel." Pages 85–108 in *Word, Theology and Community in John*. Edited by John Painter, R. Alan Culpepper, and Fernando F. Segovia. St. Louis: Chalice.

———. 2008. "Realized Eschatology in the Experience of the Johannine Community." Pages 253–76 in *The Resurrection of Jesus in the Gospel of John*. Edited by Craig R. Koester and Reimund Bieringer. WUNT 222. Tübingen: Mohr Siebeck.

———. 2015a. "'Children of God': Evolution, Cosmology, and Johannine Thought." Pages 3–31 in *Creation Stories in Dialogue: The Bible, Science, and Folk Traditions*. Edited by R. Alan Culpepper and Jan G. van der Watt. BibInt 139. Leiden: Brill, 2015.

———. 2015b. "Fulfillment of Scripture and Jesus' Teachings in Matthew." *In die Skriflig/In Luce Verbi* 49.2. doi:10.4102/ids.v49i2.1986.

———. 2016. "The Prologue as Theological Prolegomenon to the Gospel of John." Pages 3–26 in *The Prologue of the Gospel of John*. Edited by Jan G. van der Watt, R. Alan Culpepper, and Udo Schnelle. WUNT 359. Tübingen: Mohr Siebeck.

Culpepper, R. Alan, and Paul N. Anderson, eds. 2014. *Communities in Dispute: Current Scholarship on the Johannine Epistles*. ECL 13. Atlanta: SBL Press.

Cuvillier, Élian. 2009. "Torah Observance and Radicalization in the First Gospel. Matthew and First-Century Judaism: A Contribution to the Debate." *NTS* 55:144–59.

Dahl, Nils Alstrup. 1997. "The Johannine Church and History." Pages 147–68 in *The Interpretation of John*. 2nd. ed. Edited by John Ashton. Edinburgh: T&T Clark.

Daise, Michael A. 2007. *Feasts in John: Jewish Festivals and Jesus' "Hour" in the Fourth Gospel*. WUNT 2/229. Tübingen: Mohr Siebeck.

Daly-Denton, Margaret. 2000. *David in the Fourth Gospel: The Johannine Reception of the Psalms*. AGJU 47. Leiden: Brill.

Danby, Herbert. 1933. *The Mishnah: Translated from the Hebrew with Introduction and Brief Explanatory Notes*. Oxford: Oxford University Press.

Daniel, Jerry L. 1979. "Anti-Semitism in the Hellenistic-Roman Period." *JBL* 98:45–65.

Danker, Frederick W. 2002. Review of *Anti-Judaism and the Fourth Gospel*, by Reimund Bieringer et al. *CBQ* 64:796–99.

Daube, David. 1949. "Rabbinic Methods of Interpretation and Hellenistic Rhetoric." *HUCA* 22:239–64.

Davies, W. D. 1966. *The Setting of the Sermon on the Mount*. Cambridge: Cambridge University Press.

———. 1996. "Reflections on Aspects of the Jewish Background of the Gospel of John." Pages 43–64 in *Exploring the Gospel of John. In Honor of D. Moody Smith*. Edited by R. Alan Culpepper and C. Clifton Black. Louisville: Westminster John Knox.

Davies, William D., and Dale C. Allison. 1988–1997. *A Critical and Exegetical Commentary on the Gospel according to Saint Matthew*. 3 vols. ICC. Edinburgh: T&T Clark.

Dennis, John A. 2006a. *Jesus' Death and the Gathering of True Israel: The Johannine Appropriation of Restoration Theology in the Light of John 11.47–52*. WUNT 2/217. Tübingen: Mohr Siebeck.

———. 2006b. "Jesus' Death in John's Gospel: A Survey of Research from Bultmann to the Present with Special Reference to the Johannine Hyper-texts." *CurBR* 4:331–63.

———. 2007. "The 'Lifting Up of the Son of Man' and the Dethroning of the 'Ruler of this World': Jesus' Death as the Defeat of the Devil in John 12, 31–32." Pages 677–92 in *The Death of Jesus in the Fourth Gospel*. BETL 200. Edited by G. van Belle. Leuven: Peeters.

deSilva, David A. 2006. *4 Maccabees: Introduction and Commentary on the Greek Text in Codex Sinaiticus*. Septuagint Commentary Series. Leiden: Brill.

Devillers, Luc. 2004. Review of *Anti-Judaism and the Fourth Gospel*, by Reimund Bieringer et al. *RB* 111:454–60.

Dibelius, Martin. 1911. *Die urchristliche Überlieferung von Johannes der Täufer*. FRLANT 15. Göttingen: Vandenhoeck & Ruprecht.

Diefenbach, Manfred. 2002. *Der Konflikt Jesu mit den "Juden": Ein Versuch zur Lösung der johanneischen Antijudaismus-Diskussion mit Hilfe des antiken Handlungsverständnisses*. NTAbh, NF 41. Münster: Aschendorff.

Dietzfelbinger, Christian. 2001. *Das Evangelium nach Johannes*. 2 vols. ZBK. Zurich: Theologischer Verlag. 2nd ed. 2004.

Dimant, Devorah. 2014. “Sectarian and Nonsectarian Texts from Qumran: The Pertinence and Use of a Taxonomy.” Pages 101–11 in *History, Ideology and Bible Interpretation in the Dead Sea Scrolls: Collected Studies.* FAT 90. Tübingen: Mohr Siebeck.

Dobbeler, Stephanie von. 1988. *Das Gericht und das Erbarmen Gottes. Die Botschaft Johannes des Täufers und ihre Rezeption bei den Johannesjüngern im Rahmen der Theologiegeschichte des Frühjudentums.* BBB 70. Frankfurt: Athenäum.

Dodd, C. H. 1953. *Interpretation of the Fourth Gospel.* Cambridge: Cambridge University Press.

Doering, Lutz. 2006. “Parallels without ‘Parallelomania’: Methodological Reflections on Comparative Analysis of Halakhah in the Dead Sea Scrolls.” Pages 13–42 in *Rabbinic Perspectives: Rabbinic Literature and the Dead Sea Scrolls; Proceedings of the Eighth International Symposium of the Orion Center for the Study of the Dead Sea Scrolls and Associated Literature.* Edited by Steven D. Fraade, Aharon Shemesh, and Ruth A. Clements. STDJ 62. Leiden: Brill.

Donahue, John R., ed. 2005. *Life in Abundance: Studies in John's Gospel in Tribute to Raymond E. Brown.* Collegeville, MN: Liturgical Press.

Donaldson, T. L. 2010. *Jews and Anti-Judaism in the New Testament: Decision Points and Divergent Interpretations.* Waco: Baylor University Press; London: SPCK.

Dray, William H. 1995. *History as Re-Enactment: R. G. Collingwood’s Idea of History.* Oxford: Clarendon; New York: Oxford University Press.

Duff, Paul. 2004. “Glory in the Ministry of Death: Gentile Condemnation and Letters of Recommendation in 2 Cor 3:6–18.” *NovT* 46:313–37.

Dunn, James D. G. 1991, 2006. *The Parting of the Ways between Christianity and Judaism and Their Significance for the Character of Christianity.* London: SCM.

———. 1991, 1998. “Let John Be John: A Gospel for Its Time.” Pages 293–322 in *The Gospel and the Gospels.* Edited by Peter Stuhlmacher. Grand Rapids: Eerdmans. Repr. as pages 345–75 in Dunn, *Christology.* Vol. 1 of The *Christ and the Spirit.* Grand Rapids: Eerdmans.

———, ed. 1992. *Jews and Christians. The Parting of the Ways A.D. 70 to 135.* WUNT 66. Tübingen: Mohr Siebeck.

———. 1999. “The Question of Anti-Semitism in the New Testament Writings of the Period.” Pages 177–211 in *Jews and Christians: The Parting of the Ways, A.D. 70–135.* Edited by James D. G. Dunn. Grand Rapids: Eerdmans.

———. 2001. "The Embarrassment of History: Reflections on the Problem of 'Anti-Judaism' in the Fourth Gospel." Pages 47–67 in *Anti-Judaism and the Fourth Gospel: Papers of the Leuven Colloquium, 2000*. Edited by Reimund Bieringer, Didier Pollefeyt, and Frederique Vandecasteele-Vanneuville. JCH. Assen: Van Gorcum.

Duprez, A. 1970. *Jésus et les dieux guérisseurs a propos de Jean V*. Paris: Gabalda.

Edwards, Mark. 2004. *John through the Centuries*. Blackwell Bible Commentaries. Oxford: Blackwell.

Edwards, Ruth. 2002. Review of *Anti-Judaism and the Fourth Gospel*, by Reimund Bieringer et al. *ExpTim* 113:233–35.

Ehrman, Bart D. 2004. *The New Testament: A Historical Introduction to the Early Christian Writings*. New York: Oxford University Press.

Eichenberg, Fritz. 1983. *Dance of Death*. New York: Abbeville, 1983.

Ekblad, Eugene Robert. 1999. *Isaiah's Servant Poems according to the Septuagint: An Exegetical and Theological Study*. Biblical Exegesis and Theology 23. Leuven: Peeters.

Ellis, Peter F. 1984. *The Genius of John: A Composition-Critical Commentary on the Fourth Gospel*. Collegeville, MN: Liturgical Press.

Ellsberg, Robert, ed. 2004. *Fritz Eichenberg: Works of Mercy*. Maryknoll, NY: Orbis Books.

Engberg-Pedersen, Troels. 2000. *Paul and the Stoics*. Louisville: Westminster John Knox.

Epstein, Isidore, trans. 1935. *The Babylonian Talmud*. 2 vols. London: Soncino.

Eriksen, R. P. 1985. *Theologians under Hitler: Gerhard Kittel, Paul Althaus and Emanuel Hirsch*. New Haven: Yale University Press.

Evans, Craig A. 1987. "Obduracy and the Lord's Servant: Some Observations on the Use of the Old Testament in the Fourth Gospel." Pages 221–36 in *Early Jewish and Christian Exegesis: Studies in Memory of William Hugh Brownlee*. Edited by Craig A. Evans and William F. Stinespring. Atlanta: Scholars Press.

———. 1993. *Word and Glory: On the Exegetical and Theological Background of John's Prologue*. JSNTSup 89. Sheffield: JSOT Press.

Falk, Harvey. 1985. *Jesus the Pharisee: A New Look at the Jewishness of Jesus*. New York: Paulist.

Finkel, Stephen Asher. 1981. "Yavneh's Liturgy and Early Christianity." *JES* 18:231–50.

Fishbane, Michael. 1985. *Biblical Interpretation in Ancient Israel.* Oxford: Clarendon.

Forestell, J. Terence. 1974. *The Word of the Cross.* AnBib 57. Rome: BibInst.

Förster, Hans. 2016. "Der Begriff σημεῖον im Johannesevangelium." *NovT* 58:47–70.

Fortes, Rex. 2016–2019. "A Historical-Critical, Postcolonial and Hermeneutical Reading of Ethnicity in the Gospel of John and the Underlying Assumption in the Recent So-Called Refugee/Migration Crises with Special Attention to the Philippine Context." Leuven doctoral project, Katholieke Universiteit Leuven.

Fortna, Robert T. 1970. *The Gospel of Signs: A Reconstruction of the Narrative Source Underlying the Fourth Gospel.* SNTSMS 11. Cambridge: Cambridge University Press.

France, Richard T. 1989. *Matthew: Evangelist and Teacher.* Downers Grove, IL: InterVarsity.

———. 2007. *The Gospel of Matthew.* NIGTC. Grand Rapids: Eerdmans.

Frankfurter, David. 2011. "The Revelation to John." Pages 463–98 in *The Jewish Annotated New Testament.* Edited by A.-J. Levine and M. Z. Brettler. Oxford: Oxford University Press.

Freedman, H., and Maurice Simon. 1983. *Midrash Rabbah: Translated into English with Notes, Glossary and Indices.* London: Soncino.

Frey, Jörg. 1993. "Erwägungen zum Verhältnis der Johannesapokalypse zu den übrigen Schriften des Corpus Johanneum." Pages 326–429 in *Die johanneische Frage: Ein Lösungsversuch, mit einem Beitrag von Jörg Frey*, by Martin Hengel. WUNT 67. Tübingen: Mohr Siebeck.

———. 1997–2000. *Die johanneische Eschatologie I–III.* WUNT 96, 110, 117. Tübingen: Mohr Siebeck.

———. 2004. "Licht aus den Höhlen? Der 'johanneische Dualismus' und die Texte von Qumran." Pages 117–203 in *Kontexte des Johannesevangeliums: Das vierte Evangelium in religions- und traditionsgeschichtlicher Perspektive*, by Jörg Frey and Udo Schnelle. WUNT 1/175. Tübingen: Mohr Siebeck.

———. 2004. "Das Bild 'der Juden' im Johannesevangelium und die Geschichte der johanneischen Gemeinde." Pages 33–53 in *Israel und seine Heilstraditionen im Johannesevangelium. Festgabe für Johannes Beutler SJ zum 70. Geburtstag.* Edited by Michael Labahn, Klaus Scholtissek, and Angelika Strotmann. Paderborn: Schöningh.

———. 2008. "'… dass sie meine Herrlichkeit schauen" (Joh 17.24): Zu Hintergrund, Sinn und Funktion der johanneischen Rede von der δόξα Jesu." *NTS* 54:375–97.

———. 2009a. "Heil und Geschichte im Johannesevangelium: Zum Problem der 'Heilsgeschichte' und zum fundamentalen Geschichtsbezug des Heilsgeschehens im vierten Evangelium." Pages 459–510 in *Heil und Geschichte: Die Geschichtsbezogenheit des Heils und das Problem der Heilsgeschichte in der biblischen Tradition und in der theologischen Deutung*. Edited by Jörg Frey, Stefan Krauter, and Hermann Lichtenberger. WUNT 248. Tübingen: Mohr Siebeck.

———. 2009b. "Recent Perspectives on Johannine Dualism and its Background." Pages 127–57 in *Text, Thought, and Practice in Qumran and Early Christianity: Proceedings of the Ninth International Symposium of the Orion Center for the Study of the Dead Sea Scrolls and Associated Literature*. Edited by Ruth A. Clements and Daniel R. Schwartz. STDJ 84. Leiden: Brill.

———. 2010. "Critical Issues in the Investigation of the Scrolls and the New Testament." Pages 517–45 in *The Oxford Handbook of the Dead Sea Scrolls*. Edited by Timothy H. Lim and John J. Collins. Oxford: Oxford University Press.

———. 2012a. "The Diaspora-Jewish Background of the Fourth Gospel." *SEÅ* 77:169–96.

———. 2012b. "The Jewishness of Paul." Pages 57–95 in *Paul: Life, Setting, Work, Letters*. Edited by Oda Wischmeyer. Translated by Helen S. Heron with revisions by Dieter T. Roth. London: T&T Clark.

———. 2012c. "Temple and Identity in Early Christianity and in the Johannine Community: Reflections on the 'Parting of the Ways.'" Pages 447–507 in *Was 70 CE a Watershed in Jewish History? On Jews and Judaism before and after the Destruction of the Second Temple*. Edited by D. R. Schwartz and Z. Weiss in collaboration with R. A. Clements. AJEC 78. Leiden: Brill.

———. 2013a. "Das vierte Evangelium auf dem Hintergrund der älteren Evangelientradition. Zum Problem Johannes und die Synoptiker." Pages 239–94 in *Die Herrlichkeit des Gekreuzigten. Studien zu den Johanneischen Schriften I*. WUNT 307. Edited by J. Schlegel. Tübingen: Mohr Siebeck.

———. 2013b. "'Dass sie meine Herrlichkeit schauen' (Joh 17,24): Zu Hintergrund, Sinn und Funktion der johanneischen Rede von der δόξα Jesu." Pages 639–62 in *Die Herrlichkeit des Gekreuzigten: Studien*

zu den Johanneischen Schriften I. WUNT 307. Edited by J. Schlegel. Tübingen: Mohr Siebeck.
———. 2013c. "'Die Juden' im Johannesevangelium und die Frage nach der 'Trennung der Wege' zwischen der johanneischen Gemeinde und der Synagoge." Pages 339–77 in *Die Herrlichkeit des Gekreuzigten: Studien zu den Johanneischen Schriften I*. Edited by J. Schlegel. WUNT 307. Tübingen: Mohr Siebeck.
———. 2013d. "Die 'theologia crucifixi' des Johannevangeliums." Pages 485–554 in *Die Herrlichkeit des Gekreuzigten. Studien zu den Johanneischen Schriften I*. WUNT 307. Edited by J. Schlegel. Tübingen: Mohr Siebeck.
———. 2013e. "Edler Tod—wirksamer Tod—stellvertretender Tod—heilschaffender Tod: Zur narrativen und theologischen Deutung des Todes Jesu im Johannesevangelium." Pages 555–84 in *Die Herrlichkeit des Gekreuzigten: Studien zu den Johanneischen Schriften I*. WUNT 307. Edited by J. Schlegel. Tübingen: Mohr Siebeck.
———. 2013f. "'Ethical' Traditions, Family Ethos, and Love in the Johannine Literature." Pages 167–204 in *Early Christian Ethics in Interaction with Jewish and Greco-Roman Contexts*. Edited by Jan Willem van Henten and Joseph Verheyden. STR 17. Leiden: Brill.
———. 2013g. "Von Paulus zu Johannes. Die Diversität 'christlicher' Gemeindekreise und die 'Trennungsprozesse' zwischen der Synagoge und den Gemeinden der Jesusnachfolger in Ephesus im ersten Jahrhundert." Pages 235–78 in *The Rise and Expansion of Christianity in the First Three Centuries of the Common Era*. Edited by C. K. Rothschild and J. Schröter. WUNT 301. Tübingen: Mohr Siebeck.
———. 2015a. "Das Corpus Johanneum und die Apokalypse des Johannes. Die Johanneslegende, die Probleme der johanneischen Verfasserschaft und die Frage der Pseudonymität der Apokalypse." Pages 71–133 in *Poetik und Intertextualität der Apokalypse*. Edited by St. Alkier, Th. Hieke, and T. Nicklas. WUNT 346. Tübingen: Mohr Siebeck.
———. 2015b. "Der Philipperbrief im Rahmen der Paulusforschung." Pages 1–31 in *Der Philipperbrief in der hellenistisch-römischen Welt*. Edited by J. Frey and J. Schliesser. WUNT 353. Tübingen: Mohr Siebeck.
———. 2015c. "Paul the Apostle: A Life between Mission and Captivity." Pages 553–77 in *The Last Years of Paul: Essays from the Tarragona Conference, June 2013*. Edited by A. Puig I. Tàrrech, J. Barclay, and J. Frey. WUNT 352. Tübingen: Mohr Siebeck.

Freyne, Sean. 1985. "Villifying the Other and Defining the Self: Matthew's and John's Anti-Jewish Polemic in Focus." Pages 117–44 in *"To See Ourselves as Others See Us": Christians, Jews, "Others" in Late Antiquity*. Edited by Jacob Neusner and Ernest S. Frerichs. Chico, CA: Scholars Press.

Fuchs, A. 2003. Review of *Anti-Judaism and the Fourth Gospel*, by Reimund Bieringer et al. *SNTSU* 28:245–46.

Fugsleth, Kåre Sigvald. 2005. *Johannine Sectarianism in Perspective: A Sociological, Historical and Comparative Analysis of Temple and Social Relationships in the Gospel of John, Philo, and Qumran*. NovTSup 119. Leiden: Brill.

Gager, John. 1983. *The Origin of Anti-Semitism: Attitudes toward Judaism in Pagan and Christian Antiquity*. Oxford: Oxford University Press.

Galambush, Julie. 2011. "The Second Letter of John." Pages 456–57 in *The Jewish Annotated New Testament*. Edited by A.-J. Levine and M. Z. Brettler. Oxford: Oxford University Press.

García Martínez, Florentino. 1994. *The Dead Sea Scrolls Translated: The Qumran Texts in English*. Translated by Wilfred G. E. Watson. Leiden: Brill.

Gardner, Daniel K. 1998. "Confucian Commentary and Chinese Intellectual History." *The Journal of Asian Studies* 57:397–422.

Garland, David E. 1979. *The Intention of Matthew 23*. Leiden: Brill.

Garribba, Dario, and Annalisa Guida, eds. 2010. *Giovanni e il giudaismo: Luoghi, tempi, Protagonist*. Oi Christianoi 11. Trapani: Il pozzo di Giacobbe.

Genette, Gérard. 1997. *Palimpsests: Literature in the Second Degree*. Translated by Channa Newmann and Claude Doubinsky. Lincoln: University of Nebraska Press.

Gerdmar, Anders. 2009. *Roots of Theological Anti-Semitism: German Biblical Interpretation and the Jews, from Herder and Semler to Kittel and Bultmann*. SJHC 20. Leiden: Brill.

Gerhardsson, Birger. 1974. "Sacrificial Service and Atonement in the Gospel of Matthew." Pages 25–35 in *Reconciliation and Hope: New Testament Essays on Atonement and Eschatology*. Edited by Robert Banks. Grand Rapids: Eerdmans.

Ginzberg, Louis. 1909–1938. *The Legends of the Jews*. 7 vols. Philadelphia: Jewish Publication Society of America.

Gladwell, Malcolm. 2000. *The Tipping Point: How Little Things Can Make a Big Difference*. Boston: Little, Brown.

Good, Deirdre. 2003. Review of *Anti-Judaism and the Fourth Gospel*, by Reimund Bieringer et al. *AThR* 85.2: 377.

Goodenough, Edwin R. 1945. "John: A Primitive Gospel." *JBL* 64:145–82.

Gosse, Bernard. 1991. "Isaïe 52, 13–53, 12 et Isaïe 6." *RB* 98:537–43.

Gottwald, Norman K. 2001. *The Politics of Ancient Israel*. Louisville: Westminster John Knox.

Goulder, Michael D. 1999. "Ignatius' 'Docetists.'" *VC* 53:16–30.

Gourgues, Michel. 2005. Review of *Anti-Judaism and the Fourth Gospel*, by Reimund Bieringer et al. *ScEs* 57:71–98.

Greenberg, Moshe. 1983–1997. *Ezekiel: A New Translation with Introduction and Commentary*. 2 vols. AB 22–22A. New York: Doubleday.

Griffith, Terry. 2008. "'The Jews Who Had Believed in Him' (John 8:31) and the Motif of Apostasy in the Gospel of John." Pages 183–92 in *The Gospel of John and Christian Theology*. Edited by Richard Bauckham and Carl Mosser. Grand Rapids: Eerdmans.

Gundry, Robert H. 1991. "A Responsive Evaluation of the Social History of the Matthean Community in Roman Syria." Pages 62–127 in *Social History of the Matthean Community: Cross-Disciplinary Approaches*. Edited by David Balch. Minneapolis: Fortress.

———. 1994. *Matthew: A Commentary on His Handbook for a Mixed Church under Persecution*. 2nd ed. Grand Rapids: Eerdmans.

———. 2005. *The Old Is Better: New Testament Essays in Support of Traditional Interpretations*. WUNT 178. Tübingen: Mohr Siebeck.

Günther, Matthias. 1995. *Die Frühgeschichte des Christentums in Ephesus*. Arbeiten zur Religion und Geschichte des Urchristentums 1. Frankfurt: Lang.

Gurtner, Daniel M. 2007. *The Torn Veil: Matthew's Exposition of the Death of Jesus*. SNTSMS 139. Cambridge: Cambridge University Press.

———. 2011. "The Gospel of Matthew from Stanton to Present: A Survey of Some Recent Developments." Pages 23-38 in *Jesus, Matthew's Gospel and Early Christianity: Studies in Memory of Graham N. Stanton*. Edited by Daniel M. Gurtner, Joel Willits, and Richard A. Burridge. LNTS 435. London: T&T Clark.

———. 2012. "'Fasting' and 'Forty Nights': The Matthean Temptation Narrative (4:1–11) and Moses Typology." Pages 1–11 in *'What Does the Scripture Say?' Studies in the Function of Scripture in Early Judaism and Christianity*. Vol. 1 of *The Synoptic Gospels*. Edited by Craig A. Evans and H. Daniel Zacharias. LNTS 469. London: T&T Clark.

Gurtner, Daniel M., Joel Willits, and Richard A. Burridge, eds. 2011. *Jesus, Matthew's Gospel and Early Christianity: Studies in Memory of Graham N. Stanton*. LNTS 435. London: T&T Clark.

Gutbrod, W. 1967. "νόμος." *TDNT* 4:1036–85.

Gutiérrez, J. 2002. Review of *Anti-Judaism and the Fourth Gospel*, by Reimund Bieringer et al. *La Ciudad de Dios* 215.3: 1050–52.

Güting, Eberhard. 2000. "Kritik an den Judäern in Jerusalem. Literarkritische Beitrage zu einem unabgeschlossenen Gesprach iiber den Evangelisten Johannes." Pages 158–201 in *Israel als Gegenüber: Vom Alten Orient bis in die Gegenwart: Studien zur Geschichte eines wechselvollen Zusammenlebens Hrsg. von Folker Siegert*. Edited by Folker Siegert. Göttingen: Vandenhoeck & Ruprecht.

Haenchen, Ernst. 1980. *Johannesevangelium. Ein Kommentar*. Edited by U. Busse. Tübingen: Mohr Siebeck.

———. 1984. *John 1–2*. Translated by Robert W. Funk. Hermeneia. 2 vols. Philadelphia: Fortress.

Hägerland, Tobias. 2003. "John's Gospel: A Two-Level Drama?" *JSNT* 25:309–22.

Hagner, Donald A. 1993–1995. *Matthew*. 2 vols. WBC 33A–33B. Dallas: Word.

Hahn, Ferdinand. 2002. *Theologie des Neuen Testaments*. 2 Bände. Tübingen: Mohr Siebeck.

Hakola, Raimo. 2005a. "The Counsel of Caiaphas and the Social Identity of the Johannine Community (John 11:46–53)." Pages 140–63 in *Lux Humana, Lux Aeterna: Essays on Biblical and Related Themes in Honour of Lars Aejmelaeus*. Edited by A. Mustakallio in collaboration with H. Leppä and H. Räisänen. Publications of the Finnish Exegetical Society 89. Helsinki, Finnish Exegetical Society; Göttingen: Vandenhoeck & Ruprecht.

———. 2005b. *Identity Matters: John, the Jews, and Jewishness*. NovTSup 118. Leiden: Brill.

Hall, Jonathan. 2002. *Hellenicity: Between Ethnicity and Culture*. Chicago: University of Chicago Press.

Hamerton-Kelly, Robert G. 1976. "Some Techniques of Composition in Philo's Allegorical Commentary with Special Reference to *De Agricultura:* A Study in the Hellenistic Midrash." Pages 45–56 in *Jews, Greeks and Christians: Religious Cultures in Late Antiquity; Essays in Honor of William David Davies*. Edited by Robert Hamerton-Kelly and Robin Scroggs. Leiden: Brill.

Hamm, Dennis. 2000. Introduction to *The Historical Jesus through Catholic and Jewish Eyes*, edited by Leonard J. Greenspoon, Dennis Hamm, and Bryan F. LeBeau. Harrisburg, PA: Trinity Press International.

Hammond, Terry. 2000. "Fritz Eichenberg: Witness to the Twentieth Century." *Types & Shadows* 18, Summer. http://fqa.quaker.org/types/t18-hammond.html.

Harrington, Daniel J. 1980. *God's People in Christ: New Testament Perspectives on the Church and Judaism*. OBT. Philadelphia: Fortress.

———. 1991. *The Gospel of Matthew*. SP 1. Collegeville, MN: Liturgical Press.

———. 1992. "The Rich Young Man in Mt 19, 16–22: Another Way to God for Jews?" Pages 1425–32 in *Four Gospels: Festschrift Frans Neirynck*. Edited by Frans van Segbroeck et al. Leuven: Peeters.

Harris, Elizabeth. 1994. *Prologue and Gospel: The Theology of the Fourth Evangelist*. JSNTSup 107. Sheffield: Sheffield Academic.

Harrison, Carol. 2013. *The Art of Listening in the Early Church*. Oxford: Oxford University Press.

Harstine, Stan. 2002. *Moses as a Character in the Fourth Gospel: A Study of Ancient Reading Techniques*. JSNTSup 229. London: Sheffield Academic.

Hartman, Lars. 2009. "A Commentary: A Communication about a Communication." *NovT* 51:389–400.

Hasitschka, Martin. 2005. "Joh 8,44 im Kontext des Gesprächsverlaufes von Joh 8,12–59." Pages 109–16 in *Theology and Christology in the Fourth Gospel*. Edited by G. van Belle, J. G. van der Watt, and P. Maritz. BETL 184. Leuven: Peeters.

———. 2008. "Matthew and Hebrews." Pages 87–103 in *Matthew and His Christian Contemporaries*. Edited by David C. Sim and Boris Repschinski. LNTS 333. London: T&T Clark.

Hays, Richard B. 2005. "The Gospel of Matthew: Reconfigured Torah." *HvTSt* 61:165–90. doi: 10.4102/hts.v61i1/2.447.

Heckel, Ulrich. 2004. "Die Einheit der Kirche im Johannesevangelium und im Epheserbrief: Ein Vergleich der ekklesiologischen Strukturen." Pages 613–40 in *Kontexte des Johannesevangeliums*. Edited by J. Frey and U. Schnelle with J. Schlegel. WUNT 175. Tübingen: Mohr Siebeck.

Heemstra, Marius. 2010. *The Fiscus Judaicus and the Parting of the Ways*. WUNT 2/277. Tübingen: Mohr Siebeck.

Heinemann, Joseph. 2007. "Preaching: In the Talmudic Period." *EncJud* 16:467–70.

Hemer, Colin J. 1986. *Letters to the Seven Churches of Asia in their Local Setting*. JSNTSup 11. Sheffield: JSOT Press.

Hengel, Martin. 1993. *Die johanneische Frage: Ein Lösungsversuch, mit einem Beitrag von Jörg Frey*. WUNT 67. Tübingen: Mohr Siebeck.

———. 1999. "Das Johannesevangelium als Quelle für die Geschichte des antiken Judentums." Pages 41–73 in *Jüdische Geschichte in hellenistisch-römischer Zeit: Wege der Forschung; Vom alten zum neuen Schürer*. Edited by Aharon Oppenheimer. Schriften des Historischen Kollegs Kolloquien 44. Münich: Oldenbourg Verlag.

Hengstenberg, Ernst W. 1859. *Über den Eingang des Evangeliums St. Johannis*. Berlin: Schlawitz.

———. 1865. *Commentary on the Gospel of St. John*. Vol. 1. Edinburgh: T&T Clark.

Heschel, Susannah. 2008. *The Aryan Jesus: Christian Theologians and the Bible in Nazi Germany*. Princeton: Princeton University Press.

Hiemstra, M. 2009. *How Rome's Administration of the Fiscus Judaicus Accelerated the Parting of the Ways between Judaism and Christianity*. Veenendaal: Universal Press.

Hirschberg, Peter. 1999. *Das eschatologische Israel: Untersuchungen zum Gottesvolkverständnis der Johannesoffenbarung*. WMANT 84. Neukirchen-Vluyn: Neukirchener.

Hoegen-Rohls, Christina. 2004. "Johanneische Theologie im Kontext paulinischen Denkens? Eine forschungsgeschichtliche Skizze." Pages 593–612 in: *Kontexte des Johannesevangeliums*. Edited by J. Frey and U. Schnelle with J. Schlegel. WUNT 175. Tübingen: Mohr Siebeck.

Holtz, Gudrun. 2009. "Rabbinische Literatur und Neues Testament: Alte Schwierigkeiten und neue Möglichkeiten." *ZNW* 100:173–98.

Horbury, William. 1998. "The Benediction of the Minim and Early Jewish-Christian Controversy." Pages 67–110 in *Jews and Christians in Contact and Controversy*. Edinburgh: T&T Clark.

Horrell, Davil G. 2016. "Ethnicisation, Marriage and Early Christian Identity: Critical Reflections on 1 Corinthians 7, 1 Peter 3 and Modern New Testament Scholarship." *NTS* 62:439–60.

Horsley, Richard A. 1987. *Jesus and the Spiral of Violence: Popular Jewish Resistance in Roman Palestine*. San Francisco: Harper & Row.

———. 1996. *Archaeology, History, and Society in Galilee: The Social Context of Jesus and the Rabbis*. Valley Forge, PA: Trinity Press International.

Horsley, Richard, and Tom Thatcher. 2013. *John, Jesus and the Renewal of Israel.* Grand Rapids: Eerdmans.

Hoskyns, Sir Edwyn Clement. 1947. *The Fourth Gospel.* 2nd ed. Edited by Francis Noel Davey. London: Faber & Faber.

Hübner, Reinhard M. 1997. "Thesen zur Echtheit und Datierung der sieben Briefe des Ignatius von Antiochien." *ZAC* 1:44–72.

Hughes, Aaron. 2003. "Presenting the Past: The Genre of Commentary in Theoretical Perspective." *MTSR* 15:148–68.

Hughes, Julie A. 2006. *Scriptural Allusions and Exegesis in the Hodayot.* STDJ 59. Leiden: Brill.

Hummel, Reinhard. 1966. *Die Auseinandersetzung zwischen Kirche und Judentum im Matthäusevangelium.* BEvT 33. Munich: Kaiser.

Hunt, Steven A. 2009. "Nicodemus, Lazarus, and the Fear of 'the Jews' in the Fourth Gospel." Pages 199–212 in *Repetitions and Variations in the Fourth Gospel: Style, Text, Interpretation.* Edited by G. van Belle, M. Labahn, and P. Maritz. BETL 223. Leuven: Peeters.

Hurtado, Larry W. 2003. *Lord Jesus Christ: Devotion to Jesus in Earliest Christianity.* Grand Rapids: Eerdmans.

———. 2007. "Remembering and Revelation: The Historic and Glorified Jesus in the Gospel of John." Pages 195–214 in *Israel's God and Rebecca's Children: Christology and Community in Early Judaism and Christianity; Essays in Honor of Larry W. Hurtado and Alan F. Segal.* Edited by D. B. Capes, A. D. DeConick, H. K. Bond, and T. A. Miller. Waco: Baylor University Press.

Ibita, Ma. Marilou S., 2014. "'No One Comes to the Father Except through Me' (Jn 14:6b): Revisiting an Alternative Hermeneutics for Exclusive Texts in the Fourth Gospel." Paper presented at Society of Biblical Literature International Meeting. Vienna, Austria, July 6–10.

———. 2015a. "From Symposium to Symposium: A Hermeneutical Journey with New Testament Food and Meal Scenes, Material Culture, and Anti-Judaism. Significant Changes and Transitions in the Study of the New Testament and in Our Own Development as Interpreters." Paper presented at International Conference. Leuven, May 24–26.

———. 2015b. "The 'I Am' Sayings at the Johannine Farewell Meal: Exploring the Possible Influence of Segregative Association Meals and the Implications for Jewish-Christian Dialogue." Paper presented at the Joint Conference of the SNTS Asia-Pacific and the Catholic Biblical Association of the Philippines (CBAP). Quezon City, Philippines, February 28–March 1.

———. 2017. "Identity Construction in Rev 2,8–11 and 3,7–13: A Normativity of the Future Reading and Its Implications for Jewish-Christian Dialogue." Pages 489–509 in *New Perspectives on the Book of Revelation*. Edited by Adela Yarbro Collins. BETL 291. Leuven: Peeters.

Infante, Joan Brigida Corazon. 2017. "A World beyond the Divide: A Cognitive-Linguistic and Historical-Critical Analysis of the Construal of Select Texts of ΚΟΣΜΟΣ in the Fourth Gospel." Unpublished doctoral dissertation, Katholieke Universiteit Leuven, Faculty of Theology and Religious Studies.

Instone-Brewer, David. 1992. *Techniques and Assumptions in Jewish Exegesis before 70 CE.* TSAJ 30. Tübingen: Mohr Siebeck.

Janzen, J. Gerald. 1987. "On the Most Important Word in the Shema (Deuteronomy VI 4–5)." *VT* 37:280–300.

Jenkins, Richard. 2008. *Social Identity.* London: Routledge.

Jensen, Matthew David. 2014. "Jesus 'Coming' in the Flesh: 2 John 7 and Verbal Aspect." *NovT* 56:310–22.

Jeremias, Joachim. 1968. "παῖς θεοῦ." *TDNT* 5:654–717.

Johnson, Luke Timothy. 1989. "The New Testament's Anti-Jewish Slander and the Conventions of Ancient Polemic." *JBL* 108:419–41.

Johnson, William A. 1989. "Anti-Semitism in Saint John's Gospel." Pages 149–70 in *From Ancient Israel to Modern Judaism; Intellect in Quest of Understanding (Essays in Honor of Marvin Fox)*. Vol. 1. Edited by Jacob Neusner, Ernest S. Frerichs, and Nahum M. Sarna. BJS 159. Atlanta: Scholars Press.

Jones, F. Stanley. 1995. *An Ancient Jewish Christian Source on the History of Christianity: Pseudo-Clementine Recognitions 1.27–71*. SBLTT 37. Atlanta: Scholars Press.

Jonge, Henk Jan de. 2001. "The 'Jews' in the Gospel of John." Pages 239–59 in *Anti-Judaism and the Fourth Gospel: Papers of the Leuven Colloquium, 2000*. Edited by R. Bieringer, D. Pollefeyt, and F. Vandecasteele-Vanneuville. JCH. Assen: Van Gorcum.

Jonge, Marinus de. 1978. "The Son of God and the Children of God in the Fourth Gospel." Pages 44–63 in *Saved by Hope: Essays in Honor of Richard C. Oudersluys*. Edited by James I. Cook. Grand Rapids: Eerdmans.

Joosten, Jan. 2003. 'L'Ondée et les moutons: La Septante de Michée 5,6 et l'exégèse juive traditionnelle." *REJ* 162:357–63.

———. 2012. "The Impact of the Septuagint Pentateuch on the Greek Psalms." Pages 147–55 in *Collected Studies on the Septuagint: From*

Language to Interpretation and Beyond. FAT 83. Tübingen: Mohr Siebeck.

Josephus. 1926. *The Life* and *Against Apion*. Vol. 1 of *Josephus*. Translated by H. St. J. Thackeray. LCL. Cambridge: Harvard University Press.

———. 1927–1928. *The Jewish War*. Vols. 2–3 of *Josephus*. Translated by H. St. J. Thackeray. LCL. Cambridge: Harvard University Press.

———. 1930–1965. *Jewish Antiquities*. Vols. 4–9 of *Josephus*. Translated by H. St. J. Thackeray et al. LCL. Cambridge: Harvard University Press.

Just, Felix, SJ. 1999. Review of *Is John's Gospel True?*, by Maurice Casey. *RBL*: http://tinyurl.com/SBL0398a1.

Kaiser, Otto. 2014. "Der Messias nach dem Alten und Neuen Testaments." *BTZ* 31:64–107.

Kanagaraj, J. J. 2001. "The Implied Ethics of the Fourth Gospel: A Reinterpretation of the Decalogue." *TynBul* 52:33–60.

Käsemann, Ernst. 1964. "The Disciples of John the Baptist in Ephesus." Pages 136–48 in *Essays on New Testament Themes*. Philadelphia: Fortress.

———. 1968. *The Testament of Jesus: A Study of the Gospel of John in the Light of Chapter 17*. Translated by G. Krodel. Philadelphia: Fortress.

———. 1971. *Jesu letzter Wille nach Johannes 17*. 3rd ed. Tübingen: Mohr Siebeck.

Katz, Stephen T. 1984. "Issues in the Separation of Judaism and Christianity after 70 C.E.: A Reconsideration." *JBL* 103:43–76.

Kee, Howard Clark. 1999. "Defining the First century C.E. Synagogue: Problems and Progress." Pages 7–26 in *Evolution of the Synagogue*. Edited by Howard Clark Kee and Lynn H. Cohick. Harrisburg, PA: Trinity Press International.

Keener, Craig S. 2003. *The Gospel of John: A Commentary*. 2 vols. Peabody, MA: Hendrickson.

Kennedy, George A. 1984. *New Testament Interpretation through Rhetorical Criticism*. Chapel Hill: University of North Carolina Press.

Kerr, Alan R. 2002. *The Temple of Jesus' Body: The Temple Theme in the Gospel of John*. JSNTSup. New York: Sheffield Academic.

Kierspel, Lars. 2006. *The Jews and the World in the Fourth Gospel: Parallelism, Function, and Content*. WUNT 2/220. Tübingen: Mohr Siebeck.

Kimelman, Reuven. 1981. "*Birkat Ha-Minim* and the Lack of Evidence for an Anti-Christian Jewish Prayer in Late Antiquity." Pages 226–44 in *Aspects of Judaism in the Graeco-Roman Period*. Vol. 2 of *Jewish and Christian Self-Definition*. Edited by E. P. Sanders, A. I. Baumgarten, and Alan Mendelssohn. London: SCM.

Kingsbury, Jack D. 1976. *Matthew: Structure, Christology, Kingdom.* London: SPCK.

Kittel, Gerhard. 1946. "Meine Verteidigung" (November–December 1946). Unpublished. Cited in R. P. Eriksen, *Theologians under Hitler: Gerhard Kittel, Paul Althaus and Emanuel Hirsch.* New Haven: Yale University Press, 1985.

———. 1964. "ἔρημος." *TDNT* 2:657–60.

———. 1967. "λέγω." *TDNT* 4:91–136.

Kittredge, Cynthia Briggs. 2007. *Conversations with Scripture: The Gospel of John.* Harrisburg, PA: Morehouse.

Klink, Edward W., III. 2009. "Overrealized Expulsion in the Gospel of John." Pages 175–84 in *Aspects of Historicity in the Fourth Gospel.* Vol. 2 of *John, Jesus, and History.* Edited by Paul N. Anderson, Felix Just, SJ, and Tom Thatcher. SymS 49; ECL 1. Atlanta: Society of Biblical Literature.

Kloppenborg, John S. 2011. "Disaffiliation in Associations and the ἀποσυναγωγός of John." *HvTSt* 67:159–74.

———. 2015. "The Farrer/Mark without Q Hypothesis: A Response." Pages 226–44 in *Marcan Priority without Q: Explorations in the Farrer Hypothesis.* Edited by John C. Poirier and Jeffrey Peterson. LNTS 455. London: Bloomsbury.

Knight, G. A. F. 1968. "Antisemitism in the Fourth Gospel." *The Reformed Theological Journal* 27.3: 81–88.

Knöppler, Thomas. 1994. *Die theologia crucis des Johannesevangeliums: Das Verständnis des Todes Jesu im Rahmen der johanneischen Inkarnations- und Erhöhungschristologie.* WMANT 69. Neukirchen-Vluyn: Neukirchener Verlag.

Knust, Jennifer Wright. 2006. *Abandoned to Lust: Sexual Slander and Ancient Christianity; Gender, Theory and Religion.* New York: Columbia University Press.

Koenig, Jean. 1982. *L'Herméneutique analogique du Judaïsme antique d'apres les témoins textuels d'Isaïe.* VTSup 33. Leiden: Brill.

Koester, Craig R. 2001. *Hebrews: A New Translation with Introduction and Commentary.* AB 36. New York: Random House.

———. 2003. *Symbolism in the Fourth Gospel: Meaning, Mystery, Community.* 2nd ed. Minneapolis: Fortress.

———. 2014. *Revelation: A New Translation with Introduction and Commentary.* AB 38A. New Haven: Yale University Press.

Kok, Kobus. 2010. "As the Father Has Sent me, I Sent You: Towards a

Missional-Incarnational Ethos in John 4." Pages 168–93 in *Moral Language in the New Testament*. Edited by Ruben Zimmermann and Jan G. van der Watt. WUNT 296. Tübingen: Mohr Siebeck.

Konradt, Matthias. 2014. *Israel, Church, and the Gentiles in the Gospel of Matthew*. Translated by Kathleen Ess. Waco: Baylor University Press.

Köstenberger, Andreas J. 2003. Review of *Anti-Judaism and the Fourth Gospel*, by Reimund Bieringer et al. *Them* 28.2: 71–73.

———. 2004. *John*. Grand Rapids: Baker Academic.

Kovacs, Judith. 1995. "'Now Shall the Ruler of This World Be Driven Out': Jesus' Death as Cosmic Battle in John 12:20–26." *JBL* 114:227–47.

Kraemer, David. 2016. *Rabbinic Judaism: Space and Place*. New York: Routledge.

Kruijf, Theo de. 2001. Review of *Anti-Judaism and the Fourth Gospel*, by Reimund Bieringer et al. *Bijdr* 62:471–72.

Kümmel, Werner Georg. 1975. *Introduction to the New Testament*. Translated by Paul Feine. Nashville: Abingdon.

Kysar, Robert. 1986. *John*. ACNT. Minneapolis: Augsburg.

———. 1993. "Anti-Semitism and the Gospel of John." Pages 113–27 in *Anti-Semitism and Early Christianity: Issues of Polemic and Faith*. Edited by C. A. Evans and D. A. Hagner. Minneapolis: Fortress.

———. 2002. Review of *Anti-Judaism and the Fourth Gospel*, by Reimund Bieringer et al. *RBL*: http://tinyurl.com/SBL0398b1.

———. 2006. *Voyages with John: Charting the Fourth Gospel*. Waco: Baylor University Press.

Labahn, Michael. 2003. Review of *Anti-Judaism and the Fourth Gospel*, by Reimund Bieringer et al. *TLZ* 128: col. 515–17.

Lamb, David A. 2014. *Text, Context and the Johannine Community*. LNTS 477. London: Bloomsbury.

Langbrandtner, W. 1977. *Weltferner Gott oder Gott der Liebe*. BEvT 6. Frankfurt: Lang.

Lange, Tineke de. 2008. *Abraham in John 8,31–59: His Significance in the Conflict between Johannine Christianity and Its Jewish Environment / Abraham in Johannes 8,31–59, zijn betekenis in het conflict tussen Johannëisch christendom & Joodse omgeving*. Amsterdam: Amphora Books.

Langer, Ruth. 2011. *Cursing the Christians? A History of the Birkat HaMinim*. Oxford: Oxford University Press.

Lattke, Michael. 1975. *Einheit im Wort*. SANT 41. Munich: Kösel.

Le Déaut, R. 1963. *La nuit pascale*. AnBib 22. Rome: BibInst.

Lechner, Thomas. 1999. *Ignatius adversus Valentinianos? Chronologische und theologiegeschichtliche Studien zu den Briefen des Ignatius von Antiochien*. VCSup 47. Leiden: Brill.

Lee, Dorothy A. 2011. "Paschal Imagery in the Gospel of John: A Narrative and Symbolic Reading." *Pacifica* 24:13–28.

Leibig, Janis E. 1983. "John and 'the Jews': Theological Anti-Semitism in the Fourth Gospel." *Christian Jewish Relations* 16:27–38.

Lett, Jonathan. 2016. "The Divine Identity of Jesus as the Reason for Israel's Unbelief in John 12:36–43." *JBL* 135:159–73.

Leung, Mavis M. 2011. *The Kingship-Cross Interplay in the Gospel of John: Jesus' Death as Corroboration of His Royal Messiahship*. Eugene, OR: Wipf & Stock.

Levine, Amy-Jill. 2002. "Is the New Testament Anti-Jewish?" *Trinity Seminary Review* 23:131–41.

Levine, Amy-Jill, and M. Z. Brettler, eds. 2011. *The Jewish Annotated New Testament*. Oxford: Oxford University Press.

Levine, Lee I. 1990. *The Rabbinic Class of Roman Palestine in Late Antiquity*. 2nd ed. New York: Jewish Theological Seminary of America.

———. 2005. *The Ancient Synagogue: The First Thousand Years*. 2nd ed. New Haven: Yale University Press.

———. 2014. "The Synagogues of Galilee." Pages 129–50 in *Life, Society, and Culture*. Vol. 1 of *Galilee in the Late Second Temple and Mishnaic Periods*. Edited by David A. Fiensy and James Riley Strange. Minneapolis: Fortress.

Lieberman, Saul. 1950. *Hellenism in Jewish Palestine: Studies in the Literary Transmission, Beliefs and Manners of Palestine in the I Century B.C.E.–IV Century C.E.* New York: Jewish Theological Seminary of America.

Lietzmann, Hans. 1958. "Ein Beitrag zur Mandäerfrage." Pages 124–40 in *Kleine Schriften I: Studien zur spätantiken Religionsgeschichte*. TU 67. Berlin: Akademie-Verlag.

Lieu, Judith M. 2001. "Anti-Judaism and the Fourth Gospel: Explanation and Hermeneutics." Pages 126–43 in *Anti-Judaism and the Fourth Gospel: Papers of the Leuven Colloquium, 2000*. Edited by Riemund Bieringer, Didier Pollefeyt, and Frederique Vandecasteele-Vanneuville. JCH. Assen: Van Gorcum.

———. 2002. "'The Parting of the Ways': Theological Construct or Historical Reality?" Pages 11–29 in *Neither Jew nor Greek: Constructing Early Christianity*. London: T&T Clark.

———. 2008. "Anti-Judaism, 'the Jews' and the Worlds of the Fourth Gospel." Pages 168–82 in *The Gospel of John and Christian Theology*. Edited by Richard Bauckham and Carl Mosser. Grand Rapids: Eerdmans.

Lightfoot, J. B. 2015. *The Gospel of St John: A Newly Discovered Commentary*. Edited by Ben Witherington III and Todd D. Stills. Lightfoot Legacy Series 2. Downers Grove, IL: InterVarsity.

Lincoln, Andrew T. 2002. Review of *Anti-Judaism and the Fourth Gospel*, by Reimund Bieringer et al. *JTS* 53:652–57.

———. 2005. *The Gospel according to St John*. BNTC 4. London: Continuum.

Lindars, Barnabas. 1972. *The Gospel of John*. NCB. London: Oliphants.

———. 1990. *John*. NTG. Sheffield: JSOT Press.

Ling, Timothy J. M. 2006. *The Judean Poor and the Fourth Gospel*. SNTSMS. Cambridge: Cambridge University Press.

Loader, William R. G. 2012. "The Law and Ethics in John." Pages 143–58 in *Rethinking the Ethics of John. "Implicit Ethics" in the Johannine Writings: Kontexte und Normen neutestamentlicher Ethik / Contexts and Norms of New Testament Ethics*. Vol. 3. Edited by Jan G. van der Watt and Ruben Zimmermann. Tübingen: Mohr Siebeck.

———. 2016. "The Significance of the Prologue for Understanding John's Soteriology." Pages 45–55 in *The Prologue of the Gospel of John: Its Literary and Philosophical Context*. Edited by Jan G. van der Watt, R. Alan Culpepper, and Udo Schnelle. WUNT 359. Tübingen: Mohr Siebeck.

———. 2017. *Jesus in John's Gospel: Structure and Issues in Johannine Christology*. Grand Rapids: Eerdmans.

Lohfink, N., and J. Bergman. 1974. "אחד." *TDOT* 1:194–95.

Long, A. A., and D. N. Sedley. *The Hellenistic Philosophers*. Vol. 1 of *Translations of the Principal Sources with Philosophical Commentary*. Cambridge: Cambridge University Press, 1987.

Lowe, Malcolm. 1976. "Who Are the Ἰουδαῖοι?" *NovT* 18:101–30.

Lundbom, Jack. 2004. *Jeremiah 21–36: A New Translation with Introduction and Commentary*. AB 21B. New York: Doubleday.

Luomanen, Petri. 1998. *Entering the Kingdom of Heaven: A Study on the Structure of Matthew's View of Salvation*. WUNT 2/101. Tübingen: Mohr Siebeck.

Lupieri, Edmondo. 1988. *Giovanni Battista fra storia e leggenda*. BCR. Brescia: Paideia.

———. 2002. *The Mandaeans: The Last Gnostics*. Italian Texts and Studies on Religion and Society. Grand Rapids: Eerdmans.

Luthe, Ines. 2013–2017. "In Search for Docetism: A Critical Study of the History of Research, with Special Attention to Ignatius of Antioch and the Johannine Literature." Doctoral dissertation in progress, Katholieke Universiteit Leuven and Humboldt Universität zu Berlin.

Luz, Ulrich. 1995. *The Theology of the Gospel of Matthew*. Translated by J. Bradford Robinson. New Testament Theology. Cambridge: Cambridge University Press.

———. 2002a. *Das Evangelium nach Matthäus*. Vol. 1. EKKNT 1. Düsseldorf: Benziger; Neukirchen: Neukirchener.

———. 2002b. *Das Evangelium nach Matthäus*. Vol. 2. EKKNT 1. Düsseldorf: Benziger; Neukirchen: Neukirchener.

———. 2007a. *Das Evangelium nach Matthäus*. Vol. 3. EKKNT 1. Düsseldorf: Benziger; Neukirchen: Neukirchener.

———. 2007b. *Matthew 1–7*. Translated by James E. Crouch. Hermeneia. Minneapolis: Fortress.

———. 2012. *Das Evangelium nach Matthäus*. Vol. 4. EKKNT 1. Düsseldorf: Benziger; Neukirchen: Neukirchener.

MacDonald, Margaret Y. 2007. "The Art of Commentary Writing: Reflections from Experience." *JSNT* 29:313–21.

Mackie, Timothy P. 2015. *Expanding Ezekiel: The Hermeneutics of Scribal Addition in the Ancient Text Witnesses of the Book of Ezekiel*. FRLANT 257. Göttingen: Vandenhoeck & Ruprecht.

Maier, Gerhard. 2009–2012. *Die Offenbarung des Johannes: Historisch-Theologische Auslegung*. 2 vols. Witten: Brockhaus.

Malina, Bruce J., and Jerome H. Neyrey. 1996. *Portraits of Paul: An Archaeology of Ancient Personality*. Louisville: Westminster John Knox.

Malina, Bruce J., and Richard L. Rohrbaugh. 1998. *A Social Science Commentary on the Gospel of John*. Minneapolis: Fortress.

Manning, Gary T., Jr. 2004. *Echoes of a Prophet: The Use of Ezekiel in the Gospel of John and in Literature of the Second Temple Period*. JSNTSup 270. London: T&T Clark.

Manns, Frédéric. 1988. *John and Jamnia: How the Break Occurred between the Jews and Christians c. 80–100 A.D.* Jerusalem: Franciscan Printing.

———. 1991. "Exégese rabbinique et exégese johannique." Pages 307–19 in *L'Évangile de Jean à la lumière du Judaïsme*. Studium Biblicum Franciscanum 33. Jerusalem: Franciscan Printing.

Marans, Noam, and Dave Rosen. 2015. Foreword to "In Our Time," by American Jewish Committee. http://tinyurl.com/SBL0398g.

Marcheselli, Maurizio. 2009. "Antigiudaismo nel Quarto Vangelo? Presentazione e bilancio degli orientamenti recenti nella ricerca esegetica." *RivB* 57:399–478.

Marcus, Joel. 2009. "Birkat Ha-Minim Revisited." *NTS* 55:523–51.

Marshall, David. 2001. "Christianity in the Qurʾān." Pages 3–29 in *Islamic Interpretations of Christianity*. Edited by Lloyd Ridgeon. New York: St. Martin's.

Martyn, J. Louis. 1968. *History and Theology in the Fourth Gospel*. Nashville: Abingdon.

———. 1977. "Glimpses into the History of the Johannine Community." Pages 149–76 in *L'Evangile de Jean: Sources, rédaction, théologie*. Edited by M. de Jonge. BETL 44. Leuven: Leuven University Press.

———. 1978. *The Gospel of John in Christian History*. New York: Paulist.

———. 1979. *History and Theology in the Fourth Gospel*. 2nd ed. Nashville: Abingdon.

———. 1996. "A Gentile Mission That Replaced an Earlier Mission?" Pages 124–44 in *Exploring the Gospel of John. In Honor of D. Moody Smith*. Edited by R. Alan Culpepper and C. Clifton Black. Louisville: Westminster John Knox.

———. 2003. *History and Theology in the Fourth Gospel*. 3rd ed. Nashville: Abingdon.

———. 2007. "The Johannine Community among Jewish and Other Early Christian Communities." Pages 183–90 in *What We Have Heard from the Beginning: The Past, Present, and Future of Johannine Studies*. Edited by Tom Thatcher. Waco: Baylor University Press.

Meeks, Wayne A. 1967. *The Prophet-King: Moses Traditions and the Johannine Christology*. NovTSup 14. Leuven: Brill.

———. 1972. "Man from Heaven in Johannine Sectarianism." *JBL* 91:44–72.

———. 1975. "'Am I a Jew?' Johannine Christianity and Judaism." Pages 163–86 in *Christianity, Judaism and Other Greco-Roman Cults*. Edited by Jacob Neusner. SJLA 12. Leiden: Brill.

———. 1976. "The Divine Agent and His Counterfeit in Philo and the Fourth Gospel." Pages 43–67 in *Aspects of Religious Propaganda in Judaism and Early Christianity*. Edited by Elisabeth Schüssler Fiorenza. Notre Dame: University of Notre Dame Press.

———. 1985. "Breaking Away: Three New Testament Pictures of Christianity's Separation from Jewish Communities." Pages 93–115 in *"To See Ourselves as Others See Us": Christians, Jews, "Others" in Late Antiquity*. Edited by Jacob Neusner and Ernest S. Frerichs. Chico, CA: Scholars Press.

———. 1990. "Equal to God." Pages 309–21 in *The Conversation Continues: Studies in Paul and John, in Honor of J. Louis Martyn*. Edited by Robert T. Fortna and Beverly R. Gaventa. Nashville: Abingdon.

Meier, John P. 1979. *The Vision of Matthew: Christ, Church and Morality in the First Gospel*. New York: Paulist.

———. 1983. *Matthew*. Wilmington, DE: Glazier.

Menken, Maarten J. J. 1996. *Old Testament Quotations in the Fourth Gospel: Studies in Textual Form*. Biblical Exegesis & Theology 15. Kampen: Pharos.

Merwe, Dirk G. van der. 2006. "'A Matter of Having Fellowship': Ethics in the Johannine Epistles." Pages 535–63 in *Identity, Ethics, and Ethos in the New Testament*. Edited by Jan G. van der Watt. BZNW 141. Berlin: de Gruyter.

Metzner, Rainer. 2000. *Das Verständnis der Sünde im Johannesevangelium*. WUNT 122. Tübingen: Mohr Siebeck.

Mielziner, M. 1925. *Introduction to the Talmud: Historical and Literary Introduction: Legal Hermeneutics of the Talmud, Talmudical Terminology and Methodology, Outlines of Talmudical Ethics*. 3rd ed. New York: Bloch.

Miller, Ron. 2004. *The Hidden Gospel of Matthew*. Woodstock, VT: Skylight Paths.

Moloney, Francis J. 1998. *The Gospel of John*. SP 4. Collegeville, MN: Liturgical Press.

———. 2002. "'The Jews' in the Fourth Gospel: Another Perspective." *Pacifica* 15:16–36.

———. 2005. "The Gospel of John as Sacred Scripture." *CBQ* 67:456–66.

Moses, A. D. A. 1996. *Matthew's Transfiguration Story and Jewish-Christian Controversy*. JSNTSup 122. Sheffield: Sheffield Academic.

Motyer, Stephen. 1997. *Your Father the Devil? A New Approach to John and 'the Jews.'* Paternoster Biblical Monographs. London: Paternoster, 1997.

———. 2008. "Bridging the Gap: How Might the Fourth Gospel Help Us Cope with the Legacy of Christianity's Exclusive Claim over against Judaism?" Pages 143–67 in *The Gospel of John and Christian Theology*.

Edited by Richard Bauckham and Carl Mosser. Grand Rapids: Eerdmans.

Müller, T. E. 1966. *Das Heilsgeschehen im Johannesevangelium*. Zurich: Gotthelf.

Müller, Ulrich B. 1975. "Die Bedeutung des Kreuzestodes im Johannesevangelium." *KD* 21:49–71.

———. 1990. *Die Menschwerdung des Gottessohnes. Frühchristliche Inkarnations—vorstellungen und die Anfänge des Doketismus*. SBS 140. Stuttgart: KBW.

Murray, M. 2011. "The First Letter of John." Pages 448–55 in *The Jewish Annotated New Testament*. Edited by A.-J. Levine and M. Z. Brettler. Oxford: Oxford University Press.

Myers, Alicia D. 2012a. *Characterizing Jesus: A Rhetorical Analysis on the Fourth Gospel's Use of Scripture in Its Presentation of Jesus*. LNTS 458. London: T&T Clark.

———. 2012b. "'The One of Whom Moses Wrote': The Characterization of Jesus through Old Testament Moses Traditions in the Gospel of John." Pages 1–20 in *The Letter and Liturgical Traditions*. Vol. 2 of '*What Does the Scripture Say?' Studies in the Function of Scripture in Early Judaism and Christianity*. Edited by Craig A. Evans and H. Daniel Zacharias. LNTS 470. London: T&T Clark.

———. 2015. "Abiding Words: An Introduction to Perspectives on John's Use of Scripture." Pages 1–20 in *Abiding Words: The Use of Scripture in the Gospel of John*. Edited by Alicia D. Myers and Bruce G. Schuchard. RBS 81. Atlanta: SBL Press.

Nagel, Joane. 1994. "Constructing Ethnicity: Creating and Recreating Ethnic Identity and Culture." *Social Problems* 41:152–76.

Nasrallah, Laura Salah, and Elisabeth Schüssler Fiorenza, eds. 2010. *Prejudice and Christian Beginnings: Investigating Race, Gender, and Ethnicity in Early Christianity*. Minneapolis: Fortress.

Nathan, Emmanuel. 2010. "New Perspectives on Paul and the New Covenant in 2 Cor 3:6.7–18: Hermeneutical and Heuristic Considerations on Continuity and Discontinuity." PhD diss., Katholieke Universiteit Leuven.

Nathan, Emmanuel, and Reimund Bieringer. 2011. "Paul, Moses, and the Veil: Paul's Perspective on Judaism in Light of 2 Corinthians 3l; Part 1 (Nathan): On Paul's Use of καταργέω and τέλος in 2 Cor 3:7, 11, 13 and 14; Part 2 (Bieringer): The Glory and the Veil." Pages 201–28 in *Paul's Jewish Matrix: With an Introductory Essay by Karl P. Donfried*. Edited by Thomas G. Casey and Justin Taylor. Bible in Dialogue 2. Rome: Gregorian and Biblical Press.

Neill, Stephen C. 1988. *The Interpretation of the New Testament, 1861–1986*. 2nd ed. New York: Oxford University Press.

Neubrand, Maria. 2009. "Das Johannesevangelium und 'die Juden': Antijudaismus im vierten Evangelium?" *TGl* 99:205–17.

Neusner, Jacob. 1973. *From Politics to Piety: The Emergence of Rabbinic Judaism*. Englewood Cliffs, NY: Prentice Hall.

———. 1980. "'Judaism' after Moore: A Programmatic Statement." *JJS* 31:141–56.

———. 2002. *Judaism When Christianity Began: A Survey of Belief and Practice*. Louisville: Westminster John Knox.

Newport, Kenneth G. C. 1995. *The Sources and Sitz im Leben of Matthew 23*. JSNTSup 313. Sheffield: Sheffield Academic.

Nicklas, Tobias. 2014. *Jews and Christians? Second Century 'Christian' Perspectives on the 'Parting of the Ways.'* Tübingen: Mohr Siebeck.

Nielsen, Jesper Tang. 2006. "The Lamb of God: The Cognitive Structure of a Johannine Metaphor." Pages 217–56 in *Imagery in the Gospel of John*. Edited by Jörg Frey, Jan G. van der Watt, and Ruben Zimmermann. WUNT 1/200. Tübingen: Mohr Siebeck.

Nissen, Johannes. 1999. "Community and Ethics in the Gospel of John." Pages 194–212 in *New Readings in John: Literary and Theological Perspectives; Essays from the Scandinavian Conference on the Fourth Gospel, Arhus, 1997*. Edited by Johannes Nissen and C. Pedersen. JSNTSup 182. Sheffield: Sheffield Academic.

Nolland, John. 2005. *The Gospel of Matthew: A Commentary on the Greek Text*. NIGTC. Grand Rapids: Eerdmans.

Nongbri, B. 2005. "The Use and Abuse of 𝔓52: Papyrological Pitfalls in the Dating of the Fourth Gospel." *HTR* 98:23–48.

North, Wendy E. S. 2010. "'The Jews' in John's Gospel: Observations and Inferences." Pages 207–26 in *Judaism, Jewish Identities and the Gospel Tradition: Essays in Honour of Maurice Casey*. Edited by James G. Crossley. London: Equinox.

Norton, Jonathan D. H. 2016. "Composite Quotations in the Damascus Document." Pages 92–118 in *Jewish, Graeco-Roman, and Early Christian Uses*. Vol. 1 of *Composite Citations in Antiquity*. Edited by Sean A. Adams and Seth M. Ehorn. LNTS 525. London: Bloomsbury.

Obermann, Andreas. 1996. *Die christologische Erfüllung der Schrift im Johannesevangelium*. WUNT 2/83. Tübingen: Mohr Siebeck.

O'Day, Gail R. 1995. "John." Pages 493–865 in *Luke and John*. Vol. 9 of *New Interpreter's Bible Commentary*. Edited by Leander E. Keck. Nashville: Abingdon.

O'Leary, Anne M. 2006. *Matthew's Judaization of Mark: Examined in the Context of the Use of Sources in Graeco-Roman Antiquity*. LNTS 323. London: T&T Clark.

Omerzu, Heike. 2009. "Spurensuche: Apostelgeschichte und Paulusbriefe als Zeugnisse einer ephesinischen Gefangenschaft." Pages 295–326 in *Die Apostelgeschichte im Kontext antiker und frühchristlicher Historiographie*. Edited by J. Frey, C. K. Rothschild, and J. Schröter. BZNW 129. Berlin: de Gruyter.

Onuki, T. 1984. *Gemeinde und Welt im Johannesevangelium*. WMANT 56. Neukirchen: Neukirchener Verlag.

Oppenheimer, Aharon. 1977. *The ʿAm Ha-aretz: A Study in the Social History of the Jewish People in the Hellenistic-Roman Period*. ALGHJ 8. Leiden: Brill.

Orsini, Pasquale, and Willy Clarysse. 2012. "Early New Testament Manuscripts and Their Dates: A Critique of Theological Palaeography." *ETL* 88:443–74.

Overman, J. Andrew. 1990. *Matthew's Gospel and Formative Judaism: The Social World of the Matthean Community*. Minneapolis: Fortress.

Painter, John. 1974. "Eschatological Faith in the Gospel of John." Pages 36–52 in *Reconciliation and Hope: Festschrift for L. Morris*. Edited by R. Banks. Exeter: Paternoster.

———. 1978. "The Church and Israel in the Gospel of John: A Response." *NTS* 25:103–12.

———. 1989. "Quest and Rejection Stories in John." *JSNT* 36:17–46.

———. 2004. "Sacrifice and Atonement in the Gospel of John." Pages 287–313 in *Israel und seine Heilstraditionen im Johannesevangelium: Festgabe für Johannes Beutler SJ zum 70. Geburtstag*. Edited by M. Labahn, K. Scholtissek, and A. Strotmann. Paderborn: Schöningh.

———. 2008. "Matthew and John." Pages 66–86 in *Matthew and His Christian Contemporaries*. Edited by David C. Sim and Boris Repschinski. LNTS 333. London: T&T Clark.

Pancaro, Severino. 1970. "'People of God' in St John's Gospel." *NTS* 16:114–29.

———. 1975. *The Law in the Fourth Gospel*. NovTSup 42. Leiden: Brill.

Paul VI. 1965. "Declaration on the Relation of the Church to Non-Christian Religions, *Nostra Aetate*." Speech. Second Vatican Council. October 28. Vatican.va. http://tinyurl.com/SBL0398f.

Pedersen, Sigfred. 1999. "Anti-Judaism in John's Gospel: John 8." Pages 172–93 in *New Readings in John: Literary and Theological Perspectives; Essays from the Scandinavian Conference on the Fourth Gospel, Aarhus 1997*. Edited by Johannes Nissen and Sigfred Pedersen. JSNTSup 182. Sheffield: Sheffield Academic.

Pesch, Rudolf. 2005. *Antisemitismus in der Bibel? Das Johannesevangelium auf dem Prüfstand*. Augsburg: Sankt Ulrich Verlag.

Petersen, S. 2008. *Brot, Licht und Weinstock: Intertextuelle Analysen johanneischer Ich-bin-Worte*. Tübingen: Mohr Siebeck.

Phillips, Peter M. 2006. *The Prologue of the Fourth Gospel: A Sequential Reading*. LNTS 294. London: T&T Clark.

Philo. 1854–1890. *The Works of Philo Judaeus, the Contemporary of Josephus, Translated from the Greek*. Translated by Charles Duke Yonge. 4 vols. London: Bohn.

———. 1929. *On the Creation: Allegorical Interpretation of Genesis 2 and 3*. Vol. 1 of *Philo*. Translated by F. H. Colson. Edited by G. H. Whitaker. LCL 226. Cambridge: Harvard University Press.

———. 1954. *Hypothetica*. In vol. 9 of *Philo*. Translated by F. H. Colson. LCL. Cambridge: Harvard University Press.

Pippin, Tina. 1996. "'For Fear of the Jews': Lying and Truth-Telling in Translating the Gospel of John." Pages 81–97 in *Race, Class, and the Politics of Bible Translation*. Edited by R. C. Bailey and T. Pippin. SemeiaSt 76. Atlanta: Society of Biblical Literature.

Pollefeyt, Didier. 2001. "Christology after the Holocaust." Pages 229–47 in *Jesus Then and Now: Images of Jesus in History and Christology*. Edited by Marvin Meyer and Charles Hughes. Harrisburg, PA: Trinity Press International.

———. 2002. "Christology after Auschwitz: A Catholic Perspective." http://tinyurl.com/SBL0398d

Pollefeyt, Didier, and Reimund Bieringer. 2005. "*Hoi Ioudaioi*." Pages 188–89 in *A Dictionary of Jewish Christian Relations*. Edited by Edward Kessler and Neil Wenborn. Cambridge: Cambridge University Press.

Pontifical Biblical Commission. 2002. "The Jewish People and Their Sacred Scriptures in the Christian Bible." Vatican.va. Section 76, http://tinyurl.com/SBL0398h.

———. 2014. *The Inspiration and Truth of Sacred Scripture: The Word That Comes from God and Speaks of God for the Salvation of the World*.

Translated by Thomas Esposito and Stephen Gregg. Collegeville, MN: Liturgical Press.

Poplutz, Uta. 2013. "The Pharisees: A House Divided." Pages 116–26 in *Character Studies in the Fourth Gospel*. Edited by Steven A. Hunt, D. Francois Tolmie, and Ruben Zimmermann. WUNT 314. Tübingen: Mohr Siebeck.

Porsch, Felix. 1974. *Pneuma und Wort*. Frankfurter Theologische Studien 16. Frankfurt: Knecht.

Porter, Stanley. 2002. Review of *Anti-Judaism and the Fourth Gospel*, by Reimund Bieringer et al. *JSNT* 25.2: 263–64.

———. 2013. "Recent Efforts to Reconstruct Early Christianity on the Basis of Its Papyrological Evidence." Pages 71–84 in *Christian Origins and Greco-Roman Culture: Social and Literary Contexts for the New Testament*. Edited by Stanley E. Porter and Andrew W. Pitts. TENTS 9. Leiden: Brill.

———. 2015. *John, His Gospel and Jesus: In Pursuit of the Johannine Voice*. Grand Rapids: Eerdmans.

———. 2016. "The Date of John's Gospel and Its Origins." Pages 11–29 in *The Origins of John's Gospel*. Edited by Stanley E. Porter and Hughson T. Ong. Johannine Studies 2. Leiden: Brill.

Porton, Gary G. 2004. "Exegetical Techniques in Rabbinic Literature." *Review of Rabbinic Judaism* 7:27–51.

Potterie, Ignace de la. 1977. *La Vérité dans Saint Jean*. 2 vols. AnBib 73–74. Rome: BibInst.

———. 2007. "The Truth in Saint John." Pages 67–82 in *The Interpretation of John*. 2nd ed. Edited by John Ashton. Edinburgh: T&T Clark.

Probst, Christopher J. 2012. *Demonizing the Jews: Luther and the Protestant Church in Nazi Germany*. Bloomington: Indiana University Press.

Puech, Émile. 2005. "Le diable, homicide, menteur et père du mensonge en Jean 8,44." *RB* 112:215–52.

Radford Reuther, Rosemary. 1979. "The Faith and Fratricide Discussion: Old Problems and New Dimensions." Pages 230–56 in *Anti-Semitism and the Foundations of Christianity*. Edited by Alan Davies. New York: Paulist.

Reed, Annette Yoshiko. 2003. "'Jewish Christianity' after the 'Parting of the Ways': Approaches to Historiography and Self-Definition in the Pseudo-Clementines." Pages 189–231 in *The Ways That Never Parted: Jews and Christians in Late Antiquity and the Early Middle Ages*. Edited by A. H. Becker and A. Y. Reed. TSAJ 95. Tübingen: Mohr Siebeck.

Reed, Annette Yoshiko, and Adam H. Becker, eds. 2003. *The Ways That Never Parted: Jews and Christians in Late Antiquity and the Early Middle Ages*. TSAJ 95. Tübingen: Mohr Siebeck.

Reicke, B. 1984. "Judaeo-Christianity and the Jewish Establishment, A.D. 33–66." Pages 145–52 in *Jesus and the Politics of His Day*. Edited by Ernst Bammel and C. F. D. Moule. Cambridge: Cambridge University Press.

Reinbold, W. 2006. "Das Mattäusevangelium, die Pharisäer und die Tora." *BZ* 50:51–73.

Reinhartz, Adele. 1992. *The Word in the World: The Cosmological Tale in the Fourth Gospel*. Atlanta: Scholars Press.

———. 1998. "The Johannine Community and Its Jewish Neighbors: A Reappraisal." Pages 111–38 in *Literary and Social Readings of the Fourth Gospel*. Vol. 2 of "*What Is John?*" SymS. Edited by Fernando Segovia. Atlanta: Scholars Press.

———. 2001a. *Befriending the Beloved Disciple: A Jewish Reading of the Gospel of John*. London: T&T Clark; New York: Continuum.

———. 2001b. "'Jews' and Jews in the Fourth Gospel." Pages 341–56 in *Anti-Judaism and the Fourth Gospel: Papers of the Leuven Colloquium, 2000*. Edited by Riemund Bieringer, Didier Pollefeyt, and Frederique Vandecasteele-Vanneuville. JCH. Assen: Van Gorcum.

———. 2001c. "'Jews' and Jews in the Fourth Gospel." Pages 213–29 in *Anti-Judaism and the Fourth Gospel*. Edited by Reimund Bieringer, Didier Pollefeyt, and Frederique Vandecasteele-Vanneuville. Louisville: Westminster John Knox.

———. 2004. "The Grammar of Hate in the Gospel of John: Reading John in the Twenty-First-Century." Pages 416–27 in *Israel und seine Heilstraditionen im Johannesevangelium: Festgabe für Johannes Beutler SJ zum 70. Geburtstage*. Edited by M. Labahn, K. Scholtissek, and A. Strotmann. Paderborn: Schöningh.

———. 2005a. "John and Judaism: A Response to Burton Visotzky." Pages 108–16 in *Life in Abundance: Studies in John's Gospel in Tribute to Raymond E. Brown*. Edited by John R. Donahue. Collegeville, MN: Liturgical Press.

———. 2005b. "John, Gender and Judaism: A Feminist Dilemma." Pages 182–95 in *Kontexte der Schrift*, Bd. 1. *Text—Ethik—Judentum und Christentum—Gesellschaft. Festschrift für Ekkehard W. Stegemann zum 60. Geburtstag*. Edited by Gabriella Gelardini et al. Stuttgart: Kohlhammer.

———. 2007. "Reading History in the Fourth Gospel." Pages 191–94 in *What We Have Heard from the Beginning: The Past, Present, and Future of Johannine Studies*. Edited by Tom Thatcher. Waco: Baylor University Press.

———. 2008. "'Juden' und Juden im vierten Evangelium." *Kirche und Israel* 23:127–42.

———. 2009a. *Jesus of Hollywood*. New York: Oxford University Press.

———. 2009b. "Judaism in the Gospel of John." *Int* 63:382–93.

———. 2011a. *Caiaphas the High Priest*. Columbia: University of South Carolina Press.

———. 2011b. "The Gospel according to John." Pages 152–96 in *The Jewish Annotated New Testament*. Edited by A.-J. Levine and M. Z. Brettler. Oxford: Oxford University Press.

Rensberger, David. 1988. *Johannine Faith and Liberating Community*. Philadelphia: Westminster.

———. 1999. "Anti-Judaism and the Gospel of John." Pages 120–57 in *Anti-Judaism and the Gospels*. Edited by W. R. Farmer. Harrisburg, PA: Trinity Press International.

———. 2001. "The Messiah Who Has Come into the World: The Message of the Gospel of John." Pages 15–24 in *Jesus in Johannine Tradition*. Edited by R. Fortna and T. Thatcher. Louisville: Westminster John Knox.

Repschinski, Boris. 2006. "'For He Will Save His People from Their Sins' (Matthew 1:21): A Christology for Christian Jews." *CBQ* 68:248–67.

———. 2009. *Nicht aufzulösen sondern zu erfüllen. Das jüdische Gesetz in den synoptischen Jesus Erzählungen*. FB 120. Würzburg: Echter.

Riches, John K. 1982. *Jesus and the Transformation of Judaism*. New York: Seabury.

Ridderbos, Herman. 1997. *The Gospel of John: A Theological Commentary*. Grand Rapids: Eerdmans.

Ripley, Jason J. 2015. "Killing as Piety? Exploring Ideological Contexts Shaping the Gospel of John." *JBL* 134:605–35.

Robinson, John A. T. 1960–1961. "The Destination and Purpose of the Johannine Epistles." Pages 191–209 in *New Testament Issues*. Edited by R. A. Batey. SBT 34. London: SCM.

Rogers, T. 2012. "The Great Commission as the Climax of Matthew's Mountain Scenes." *BBR* 22:383–98.

Royse, James R. 2016. "Composite Quotations in Philo of Alexandria." Pages 74–91 in *Jewish, Graeco-Roman, and Early Christian Uses*. Vol. 1

of *Composite Citations in Antiquity*. Edited by Sean A. Adams and Seth M. Ehorn. LNTS 525. London: Bloomsbury.

Rudolph, Kurt. 1960–1961. *Die Mandäer*. 2 vols. FRLANT 74, NF 56. Göttingen: Vandenhoeck & Ruprecht.

Runesson, Anders. 2001. *The Origins of the Synagogue: A Socio-historical Study*. Stockholm: Almqvist & Wiksell.

Runesson, Anders, Donald D. Binder, and Birger Olsson, eds. 2008. *The Ancient Synagogue from Its Origins to 200 C.E.: A Source Book*. Leiden: Brill.

Runia, David T. 1984. "The Structure of Philo's Allegorical Treatises: A Review of Two Recent Studies and Some Additional Comments." *VC* 38:209–56.

———. 1987. "Further Observations on the Structure of Philo's Allegorical Treatises." *VC* 41:105–38.

———. 2010. "The Structure of Philo's Allegorical Treatise *De Agricultura*." *SPhiloA* 22:87–109.

Rusam, D. 2005. "Das 'Lamm Gottes' (Joh 1, 29.36) und die Deutung des Todes Jesu im Johannesevangelium." *BZ* 49:60–80.

Ruyter, B. W. J. de. 1998. *De gemeente van de evangelist Johannes: Haar polemiek en haar geschiedenis*. Delft: Eburon.

———. 2003. Review of *Anti-Judaism and the Fourth Gospel*, by Reimund Bieringer et al. *NedTT* 56.4: 343–44.

Ruzer, Serge. 2007. *Mapping the New Testament: Early Christian Writings as a Witness for Jewish Biblical Exegesis*. JCP 13. Leiden: Brill.

Saldarini, Anthony J. 1994. *Matthew's Christian-Jewish Community*. Chicago: University of Chicago Press.

Samely, Alexander. 2002. *Rabbinic Interpretation of Scripture in the Mishnah*. Oxford: Oxford University Press.

Sanders, E. P. 1977. *Paul and Palestinian Judaism: A Comparison of Patterns of Religion*. Minneapolis: Augsburg Fortress.

———. 1985. *Jesus and Judaism*. Philadelphia: Fortress.

Sandmel, Samuel. 1978. *Antisemitism in the New Testament?* Philadelphia: Fortress.

Schäfer, Peter. 1986. "Research into Rabbinic Literature: An Attempt to Define the Status Quaestionis." *JJS* 37:139–52.

Schaper, Joachim. 1995. *Eschatology in the Greek Psalter*. WUNT 2/76. Tübingen: Mohr Siebeck.

Schillebeeckx, E. 1980. *Christ: The Christian Experience in the Modern World*. London: SCM.

Schmidt, Andreas. 1989. "Zwei Anmerkungen zu P. Ryl. III 457." *APF* 35:11–12.

Schnackenburg, Rudolf. 1967. "Johannesevangelium als hermeneutische Frage." *NTS* 13:197–210.

———. 1968. *The Gospel according to St. John*. Vol. 1. New York: Herder.

———. 1977. *Kommentar zu Kap. 5–12*. Part 2 of *Das Johannesevangelium*. 2nd ed. HThKNT 4.2. Freiburg: Herder.

———. 1980. *The Gospel according to St. John*. Vol. 2. Translated by Cecily Hastings et al. HThKNT. New York: Seabury.

———. 1991. "Ephesus. Entwicklung einer Gemeinde von Paulus zu Johannes." *BZ* 35:41–64.

———. 1993. *Die Person Jesu Christi im Spiegel der vier Evangelien*. Herders theologische Kommentar Supplements 4. Freiburg: Herder.

Schnelle, Udo. 1987. "Paulus und Johannes." *EvT* 47:212–28.

———. 1992. *Antidocetic Christology in the Gospel of John: An Investigation of the Place of the Fourth Gospel in the Johannine School*. Translated by Linda A. Maloney. Minneapolis: Fortress.

———. 1998. *Das Evangelium nach Johannes*. THKNT 4. Berlin: Evangelische Verlagsanstalt.

———. 1999. "Die Juden im Johannesevangelium." Pages 217–30 in *Gedenkt das Wort*. Edited by C. Kähler, M. Böhm, and C. Böttrich. Leipzig: Evangelische Verlagsanstalt.

———. 2007. "Markinische und johanneische Kreuzestheologie." Pages 233–58 in *The Death of Jesus in the Fourth Gospel*. Edited by G. van Belle. BETL 200. Leuven: Peeters.

Scholtissek, Klaus. 2002. "Johannes auslegen III. Ein Forschungsbericht." *SNTU* 27:133–35.

———. 2003. Review of *Anti-Judaism and the Fourth Gospel*, by Reimund Bieringer et al. *Freiburger Rundbrief* NF 10:51–53.

———. 2004. Review of *Anti-Judaism and the Fourth Gospel*, by Reimund Bieringer et al. *TRev* 100.2: 155–58.

———. 2004. "'Eine grössere Liebe als diese hat niemand, als wenn einer sein Leben hingibt für seine Freunde' (Joh 15,13): Die hellenistische Freundschaftsethik und das Johannesevangelium." Pages 413–39 in *Kontexte des Johannesevangeliums: Das vierte Evangelium in religions- und traditionsgeschichtlicher Perspektive*. Edited by J. Frey and U. Schnelle. WUNT 175. Tübingen: Mohr Siebeck.

Schoon, Simon. 2001. "Escape Routes as Dead Ends: On Hatred towards Jews and the New Testament, Especially in the Gospel of John." Pages

144–58 in *Anti-Judaism and the Fourth Gospel: Papers of the Leuven Colloquium, 2000*. Edited by Reimund Bieringer, Didier Pollefeyt, and Frederique Vandecasteele-Vanneuville. JCH 1. Assen: Van Gorcum.

Schuchard, Bruce G. 1992. *Scripture within Scripture: The Interrelationship of Form and Function in the Explicit Old Testament Citations in the Gospel of John*. SBLDS 133. Atlanta: Scholars Press.

Schürer, Emil, et al. 1979. *The History of the Jewish People in the Age of Jesus Christ*. Rev. ed. Vol. 2. Edinburgh: T&T Clark.

Schüssler Fiorenza, Elisabeth. 1977. "The Quest for the Johannine School: The Apocalypse and the Fourth Gospel." *NTS* 23:402–27.

Schwartz, Joshua, and Yehoshua Peleg. 2007. "Are the 'Halachic Temple Mount' and the 'Outer Courts' of Josephus One and the Same?" Pages 207–22 in *Studies in Josephus and the Varieties of Ancient Judaism*. Edited by Shaye J. D. Cohen and Joshua J. Schwartz. AJEC 67. Leiden: Brill.

Scott, E. F. 1908. *The Fourth Gospel: Its Purpose and Theology*. Edinburgh: T&T Clark.

Segal, Alan F. 1994. "Universalism in Judaism and Christianity." Pages 1–29 in *Paul in His Hellenistic Context*. Edited by Troels Engberg-Pedersen. Edinburgh: T&T Clark.

Senior, Donald. 1997. *The Gospel of Matthew*. Interpreting Biblical Texts. Nashville: Abingdon.

———. 1999. "Between Two Worlds: Gentiles and Jewish Christians in Matthew's Gospel." *CBQ* 61:1–23.

———. 2002. Review of *Anti-Judaism and the Fourth Gospel*, by Reimund Bieringer et al. *The Bible Today* 40:132.

———, ed. 2011. *The Gospel of Matthew at the Crossroads of Early Christianity*. BETL 243. Leuven: Peeters.

Shanks, Hershel. 1963. "Is the Term Rabbi Anachronistic in the Gospels?" *JQR* 53:337–45.

———. 1968. "Origins of the Title 'Rabbi.'" *JQR* 59:152–57.

———. 2013. *Partings: How Judaism and Christianity Became Two*. Washington, DC: Biblical Archaeological Society.

Sheridan, Ruth. 2012. *Retelling Scripture: "The Jews" and the Scriptural Citations in John 1:19–12:15*. BibInt 110. Leiden: Brill.

———. 2013. "Issues in the Translation of *Hoi Ioudaioi* in the Fourth Gospel." *JBL* 132:671–95.

Shinan, Avigdor. 1987. "Sermons, Targums, and the Reading from Scriptures in the Ancient Synagogue." Pages 97–110 in *The Synagogue in Late Antiquity*. Edited by Lee I. Levine. Philadelphia: American Schools of Oriental Research.

Shirbroun, G. Franklin. 1985. "The Giving of the Name of God to Jesus in John 17:11, 12." PhD diss., Princeton Theological Seminary.

Siegert, Folker. 2003. "Vermeintlicher Antijudaismus und Polemik gegen Judenchristen im Neuen Testament." Pages 74–105 in *The Image of Judaeo-Christians in Ancient Jewish and Christian Literature*. Edited by Peter J. Tomson and Doris Lambers-Petry. WUNT 158. Tübingen: Mohr Siebeck.

Sim, David C. 1998. *The Gospel of Matthew and Christian Judaism: The History and Setting of the Matthean Community*. SNTW. Edinburgh: T&T Clark.

Simoens, Yves. 2007. "L'évangile selon Jean et les juif: Un paradigme d'interprétation en dialogue." Pages 63–116 in *Les versets douloureux: Bible, Évangile et Coran entre conflit et dialogue*. Edited by D. Meyer et al. L'Autre et les autres 9. Brussels: Lessius.

Slomovic, Elieser. 1969. "Towards an Understanding of the Exegesis in the Dead Sea Scrolls." *RevQ* 7:3–15.

Smalley, Stephen. 2002. Review of *Anti-Judaism and the Fourth Gospel*, by Reimund Bieringer et al. *Theology* 105:139–40.

Smith, D. Moody. 1965. *The Composition and Order of the Fourth Gospel*. New Haven: Yale University Press.

———. 1984. *Johannine Christianity: Essays on Its Setting, Sources, and Theology*. Columbia: University of South Carolina Press.

———. 1990. "The Contribution of J. Louis Martyn to the Understanding of the Gospel of John." Pages 275–94 in *The Conversation Continues: Studies in Paul and John, In Honor of J. Louis Martyn*. Edited by Robert T. Fortna and Beverly R. Gaventa. Nashville: Abingdon.

———. 1996. "What Have I Learned from the Gospel of John?" Pages 217–35 in "*What Is John?": Readers and Readings of the Fourth Gospel*. Edited by Fernando F. Segovia. SymS 3. Atlanta: Scholars Press.

———. 1997. *The Theology of the Gospel of John*. Cambridge: Cambridge University Press.

———. 1999. *John*. ANTC. Nashville: Abingdon.

———. 2008. *The Fourth Gospel in Four Dimensions: Judaism and Jesus, the Gospels and Scripture*. Columbia: University of South Carolina Press.

Smith, Jonathan Z. 1990. "On Comparison." Pages 36–53 in *Drudgery Divine: On the Comparison of Early Christianities and the Religions of Late Antiquity*. Chicago: University of Chicago Press.

Smith, Mark S. 2008. *God in Translation: Deities in Cross-Cultural Discourse in the Biblical World*. Tübingen: Mohr Siebeck.

Smith, Morton. 1965. "The Account of Simon Magus in Acts 8." Pages 735–49 in *Harry Austryn Wolfson Jubilee Volume: On the Occasion of His Seventy-Fifth Birthday; English Section*. Vol. 2. Jerusalem: American Academy for Jewish Research.

Söding, Thomas. 2000. "'Was kann aus Nazareth schon Gutes kommen?' (Joh 1.46): Die Bedeutung des Judenseins Jesu im Johannesevangelium." *NTS* 46:21–41.

———. 2001. "Die Wahrheit des Evangeliums: Anmerkungen zur johanneischer Hermeneutik." *ETL* 77:318–55.

Sommer, Benjamin D. 1998. *A Prophet Reads Scripture: Allusion in Isaiah 40–66*. Stanford: Stanford University Press.

Spencer, F. Scott. 2010. "Scripture, Hermeneutics, and Matthew's Jesus." *Int* 64:368–78.

Stanley, Christopher D. 1992. *Paul and the Language of Scripture: Citation Technique in the Pauline Epistles and Contemporary Literature*. SNTSMS 69. Cambridge: Cambridge University Press.

———. 2016. "Composite Citations: Retrospect and Prospect." Pages 203–9 in *Jewish, Graeco-Roman, and Early Christian Uses*. Vol. 1 of *Composite Citations in Antiquity*. Edited by Sean A. Adams and Seth M. Ehorn. LNTS 525. London: Bloomsbury.

Stanton, Graham N. 1982. "Salvation Proclaimed: X. Matthew 11:28–30: Comfortable Words?" *ExpTim* 94:3–8.

———. 1992. *A Gospel for a New People: Studies in Matthew*. Edinburgh: T&T Clark.

———. 1995. *The Interpretation of Matthew*. 2nd ed. Edinburgh: T&T Clark.

———. 1997. "The Communities of Matthew." Pages 49–62 in *Gospel Interpretation: Narrative-Critical and Social-Scientific Approaches*. Edited by Jack Dean Kingsbury. Harrisburg, PA: Trinity Press International.

Stark, Rodney. 1997. *The Rise of Christianity: How the Obscure, Marginal Jesus Movement Became the Dominant Religious Force in the Western World*. San Francisco: HarperSanFrancisco.

Stegner, William Richard. 1988. "The Ancient Jewish Synagogue Homily." Pages 51–69 in *Greco-Roman Literature and the New Testament: Selected Forms and Genres*. Edited by David E. Aune. SBLSBS 21. Atlanta: Scholars Press.

Stendahl, Krister. 1964. "*Quis et Unde?* An Analysis of Mt 1–2." Pages 94–105 in *Judentum, Urchristentum, Kirche: Festschrift für Joachim Jeremias*. Edited by W. Eltester. BZNW 26. Berlin: Töpelmann.

———. 1976. *Paul among the Jews and the Gentiles*. Philadelphia: Fortress.

Stevens, G. B. 1889. *The Theology of the New Testament*. Edinburgh: T&T Clark.

Stibbe, Mark W. G. 1993. *John*. Readings: A New Bible Commentary. Sheffield: JSOT Press.

Strack, Hermann L., and Paul Billerbeck. 1922–1961. *Kommentar zum Neuen Testament aus Talmud und Midrasch*. 6 vols. Munich: Beck'sche.

Strack, Hermann L., and Gunther Stemberger. 1992. *Introduction to Talmud and Midrash*. Minneapolis: Fortress.

Strecker, Georg. 1981. *Das Judenchristentum in den Pseudoklementinen*. TU 70. Berlin: Akademie-Verlag.

Streett, Daniel R. 2011. *They Went Out from Us: The Identity of the Opponents in First John*. BZNW 177. Berlin: de Gruyter.

Strelan, Rick. 1996. *Paul, Artemis and the Jews in Ephesus*. BZNW 80. Berlin: de Gruyter.

Suggs, M. Jack. 1970. *Wisdom, Christology, and Law in Matthew's Gospel*. Cambridge: Harvard University Press.

Tack, Laura. 2015. "Weg van de waarheid. Een historisch-kritisch en hermeneutisch onderzoek van Joh. 14,6 in het licht van de joods-christelijke dialog." PhD diss., Katholieke Universiteit Leuven.

Talbert, Charles H. 2011. "The Fourth Gospel's Soteriology between New Birth and Resurrection." Pages 176–91 in *Getting "Saved": The Whole Story of Salvation in the New Testament*. Edited by Charles H. Talbert and Jason A. Whitlark. Grand Rapids: Eerdmans.

Tellbe, Michael. 2009. *Christ-Believers in Ephesus: A Textual Analysis of Early Christian Identity Formation in a Local Perspective*. WUNT 242. Tübingen: Mohr Siebeck.

Thatcher, Tom. 2006. *Why John Wrote a Gospel: Jesus—Memory—History*. Louisville: Westminster John Knox.

———. 2008. *Greater than Caesar: Christology and Empire in the Fourth Gospel*. Minneapolis: Fortress.

Theißen, Gerd. 2007. *Die Entstehung des Neuen Testaments als literaturgeschichtliches Problem*. Heidelberg: Winter.

Theobald, Michael. 1983. *Im Anfang war das Wort: Textlinguistische Studie zum Johannesprolog*. Stuttgart: Katholisches Bibelwerk.

———. 1988. *Die Fleischwerdung des Logos: Studien zum Verhältnis des Johannesprologs zum Corpus des Evangeliums und zu 1 Joh.* NTAbh, NF 20. Münster.

———. 2009. *Das Evangelium nach Johannes. Kapitel 1–12.* RNT. Regensburg: Pustet.

———. 2010. "Abraham—(Isaak)—Jakob. Israels Väter im Johannesevangelium." Pages 282–302 in *Studien zum Corpus Johanneum*. Edited by Michael Theobald. WUNT 267. Tübingen: Mohr Siebeck.

———. 2010. "Das Johannesevangelium—Zeugnis eines synagogalen Judenchristentums." Pages 204–55 in *Studien zum Corpus Johanneum*. Edited by Michael Theobald. WUNT 267. Tübingen: Mohr Siebeck.

Theocharous, Myrto. 2012. *Lexical Dependence and Intertextual Allusion in the Septuagint of the Twelve Prophets: Studies in Hosea, Amos and Micah.* LHBOTS 570. London: Bloomsbury.

Thissen, Werner. 1995. *Christen in Ephesus: Die historische und theologische Situation in vorpaulinischer und paulinischer Zeit und zur Zeit der Apostelgeschichte und der Pastoralbriefe.* Text und Arbeiten zum neutestamentlichen Zeitalter 12. Tübingen: Francke.

Thomas, Joseph. 1935. *Le mouvement baptiste en Palestine et Syrie (150 av. J.-C.–300 ap. J.-C.).* Universitas catholica lovaniensis. Dissertationes ad gradum magistri in Facultate theologica vel in Facultate iuris canonici consequendum conscriptae 2/58. Gembloux: Duculot.

Thompson, Marianne Meye. 2001. *The God of the Gospel of John.* Grand Rapids: Eerdmans.

———. 2017. "Baptism with Water and with Holy Spirit: Purification in the Gospel of John." Pages 59–78 in *The Opening of John's Narrative (John 1:19–2:22): Historical, Literary, and Theological Readings from the Colloquium Ioanneum 2015 in Ephesus.* Edited by R. Alan Culpepper and Jörg Frey. WUNT 385. Tübingen: Mohr Siebeck.

Thüsing, Wilhelm. 1979. *Die Erhöhung und Verherrlichung Jesu im Johannesevangelium.* 3rd ed. NTAbh 21. Münster: Aschendorff.

Thyen, Hartwig. 1988. "Johannesbriefe." *TRE* 17:186–200.

———. 2005. *Das Johannesevangelium.* HNT 6. Tübingen: Mohr Siebeck.

Tilborg, Sjef van. 2002. Review of *Anti-Judaism and the Fourth Gospel*, by Reimund Bieringer et al. *TvT* 42:207.

Toit, A. B. du. 1994. "Vilification as Pragmatic Device in Early Christian Epistolography." *Bib* 75:403–12.

Toit, Philip du. 2015. “The Hermeneutical Dilemma behind ‘Anti-Judaism’ in the New Testament: An Evangelical Perspective.” *Conspectus* 20:43–88.

Töllner, Axel. 2007. *Eine Frage der Rasse? Die evangelisch-lutherische Kirche in Bayern, der Arierparagraph und die bayrischen Pfarrfamilien mit jüdischen Vorfahren im “Dritten Reich.”* Stuttgart: Kohlhammer.

Tomson, Peter J. 2001. “ ‘Jews’ in the Gospel of John as Compared with the Palestinian Talmud, the Synoptics and Some New Testament Apocrypha.” Pages 301–40 in *Anti-Judaism and the Fourth Gospel: Papers of the Leuven Colloquium, 2000*. Edited by R. Bieringer, D. Pollefeyt, and F. Vandecasteele-Vanneuville. Assen: Van Gorcum.

Trachtenberg, Joshua. 2002. *The Devil and the Jews: The Medieval Conception of the Jew and Its Relation to Modern Anti-Semitism*. 2nd ed. Philadelphia: Jewish Publication Society of America.

Trebilco, Paul. 1991. *Jewish Communities in Asia Minor*. SNTSMS 69. Cambridge: Cambridge University Press.

———. 2004. *The Early Christians in Ephesus from Paul to Ignatius*. WUNT 166. Tübingen: Mohr Siebeck.

Turner, M. 1990. “Atonement and the Death of Jesus in John—Some Questions to Bultmann and Forestell.” *EvQ* 62:99–122.

Ueberschaer, Nadine. 2017. *Theologie des Lebens*. WUNT. Tübingen: Mohr Siebeck.

Ulmer, Rivkin. 2013. “Pesiqta Rabbati: A Text-Linguistic and Form-Critical Analysis of the Rabbinic Homily.” *JJS* 64:64–97.

Urbach, Ephraim E. 1981. “Self-Isolation or Self-Affirmation in Judaism in the First Three Centuries: Theory and Practice.” Pages 269–98 in *Aspects of Judaism in the Graeco-Roman Period*. Vol. 2 of *Jewish and Christian Self-Definition*. Edited by E. P. Sanders, A. I. Baumgarten, and Alan Mendelssohn. London: SCM.

Van Voorst, Robert E. 1989. *The Ascents of James: History and Theology of a Jewish-Christian Community*. SBLDS 112. Atlanta: Scholars Press.

Vanneuville, Frederique. 2001. “Jesus and ‘the Jews’ in John 8:31–59: An Interdisciplinary Investigation into the Problem of Anti-Judaism in the Gospel of John.” PhD diss., Katholieke Universiteit Leuven.

Verheyden, Jospeh, et al., eds. 2017. *The Quest for an Elusive Phenomenon: Docetism in the Early Church*. WUNT 1. Tübingen: Mohr Siebeck.

Vermes, Geza. 1961. *Scripture and Tradition in Judaism*. Leiden: Brill.

———. 1973. “The Story of Balaam.” Pages 127–77 in *Scripture and Tradition in Judaism: Haggadic Studies*. Leiden: Brill.

———. 1980. "Jewish Studies and New Testament Interpretation." *JJS* 31:1–17.

———. 1982. "Jewish Literature and New Testament Exegesis: Reflections on Methodology." *JJS* 33:361–76.

———. 1985. "Methodology in the Study of Jewish Literature in the Graeco-Roman Period." *JJS* 36:143–58.

Vielhauer, Philipp. 1965. "Das Benedictus des Zacharias (Luk 1, 68–79)." Pages 28–46 in *Aufsätze zum Neuen Testament*. TB 31. München: Kaiser Verlag.

Viljoen, François P. 2007. "Fulfilment in Matthew." *Verbum et ecclesia* 28:301–24.

———. 2014a. "Hosea 6:6 and Identity Formation in Matthew." *AcT* 34:214–37.

———. 2014b. "Jesus Healing a Leper and the Purity Law in Matthew." *In die Skriflig* 48.2: doi:10.4102/ids.48i2.1751.

———. 2014c. "The Law and Purity in Matthew; Jesus Touching a Bleeding Woman and Dead Girl (Matt. 9:18–26)." *NGTT* 55.1–2: doi:10.5952/55-1-2-535.

———. 2015. "Matthew and the *Torah* in Jewish Society." *In die Skriflig* 49.2. doi:10.4102/ids.v49i2.1946.

Visotzsky, Burton L. 1995. *Fathers of the World: Essay in Rabbinic and Patristic Literatures*. WUNT 80. Tübingen: Mohr Siebeck.

———. 2005. "Methodological Considerations in the Study of John's Interaction with First-Century Judaism." Pages 91–107 in *Life in Abundance: Studies of John's Gospel in Tribute to Raymond E. Brown*. Edited by John R. Donahue. Collegeville, MN: Liturgical Press.

———. 2009. "Rabbi, Rabbouni." *NIDB* 4:718.

Vogel, Manuel. 2015. "Jesusgemeinden und Täufergruppen zwischen Abgrenzung und Wertschätzung—Eine Skizze." Pages 74–84 in *Juden und Christen unter römischer Herrschaft. Selbstwahrnehmung und Fremdwahrnehmung in den ersten beiden Jahrhunderten n. Chr.* Edited by Niclas Förster and Jacobus Cornelis de Vos. Göttingen: Vandenhoeck & Ruprecht.

Volf, Miroslav. 1996. *Exclusion and Embrace: A Theological Exploration of Identity, Otherness, and Reconciliation*. Nashville: Abingdon.

Vouga, François. 1993. "Antijudaismus im Johannesevangelium." *TGl* 83:81–89.

Wahlde, Urban C. von. 1979. "The Terms for Religious Authorities in the Fourth Gospel: A Key to Literary Strata." *JBL* 98:233–42.

———. 1982. “The Johannine ‘Jews’: A Critical Survey.” *NTS* 28:33–60.
———. 1989. *The Earliest Version of John's Gospel: Recovering the Gospel of Signs*. Wilmington, DE: Glazier.
———. 1996. “The Relationship between Pharisees and Chief Priests: Some Observations on the Texts in Matthew, John and Josephus.” *NTS* 42:506–22.
———. 2000. “The Jews in the Gospel of John: Fifteen Years of Research (1983–1998).” *ETL* 76:30–55.
———. 2006. “Archaeology and John's Gospel.” Pages 523–86 in *Jesus and Archaeology*. Edited by James H. Charlesworth. Grand Rapids: Eerdmans.
———. 2007. “The Road Ahead: Three Aspects of Johannine Scholarship.” Pages 343–53 in *What We Have Heard from the Beginning: The Past, Present, and Future of Johannine Studies*. Edited by Tom Thatcher. Waco: Baylor University Press.
———. 2009. “The Pool(s) of Bethesda and the Healing in John 5: A Reappraisal of Research and of the Johannine Text.” *RB* 116:111–36.
———. 2010a. *The Gospel and Letters of John*. 3 vols. ECC. Grand Rapids: Eerdmans.
———. 2010b. “The Johannine Literature and Gnosticism: New Light on Their Relationship?” Pages 221–54 in *From Judaism to Christianity: Tradition and Transition; A Festschrift for Thomas H. Tobin, S.J., on the Occasion of His Sixty-Fifth Birthday*. Edited by P. Walters. NovTSup 136. Leiden: Brill.
———. 2011. “The Puzzling Pool of Bethesda: Where Jesus Cured the Crippled Man.” *BAR* (September–October): 40–47.
———. 2015. *Gnosticism, Docetism, and the Judaisms of the First Century: The Search for the Wider Context of the Johannine Literature and Why It Matters*. LNTS 517. London: Bloomsbury.
Walter, N. 2002. “Nikolaos, Proselyt aus Antiochien, und die Nikolaiten in Ephesus.” *ZNW* 93:200–26.
Wan, Sze-Kar. 2010. “To the Jew First and also to the Greek”: Reading Romans as Ethnic Construction.” Pages 129–58 in *Prejudice and Christian Beginnings: Investigating Race, Gender, and Ethnicity in Early Christianity*. Edited by Laura Salah Nasrallah and Elisabeth Schüssler Fiorenza. Minneapolis: Fortress.
Wander, Bernd. 1999. *Trennungsprozesse zwischen frühem Christentum und Judentum im 1. Jh. n. Chr.* Text und Arbeiten zum neutestamentlichen Zeitalter 16. Tübingen: Francke.

Watt, Jan G. van der. 1995. "The Composition of the Prologue of John's Gospel: The Historical Jesus Introducing Divine Grace." *WTJ* 57:311–32.

———. 2000. *Family of the King: Dynamics of Metaphor in the Gospel according to John*. BibInt 47. Leiden: Brill.

———. 2004. Review of *Anti-Judaism and the Fourth Gospel*, by Reimund Bieringer et al. *RBL*: http://tinyurl.com/SBL0398b1.

———. 2005. "Salvation in the Gospel According to John." Pages 101–31 in *Salvation in the New Testament: Perspectives on Soteriology*. Edited by J. G. van der Watt. NovTSup 121. Leiden: Brill.

———. 2006a. "Ethics and Ethos in the Gospel according to John." *ZNW* 97:147–76.

———. 2006b. Preface to *Identity, Ethics, and Ethos in the New Testament*. Edited by Jan G. van der Watt. BZNW 141. Berlin: de Gruyter.

———. 2016. "Are John's Ethics Apolitical?" *NTS* 62:484–97.

Watt, Jan G. van der, and J. Kok. 2012. "Violence in a Gospel of Love." Pages 151–84 in *Coping with Violence in the New Testament*. Edited by P. G. R. de Villiers and J. W. van Henten. Leiden: Brill.

Watt, Jan G. van der, and Ruben Zimmermann, eds. 2012. *Rethinking the Ethics of John: "Implicit Ethics" in the Johannine Writings: Kontexte und Normen neutestamentlicher Ethik*. Contexts and Norms of New Testament Ethics 3. WUNT 291. Tübingen: Mohr Siebeck.

Wehnert, Jürgen. 2011. "Taufvorstellungen in den Pseudoklementinen." Pages 1071–1114 in *Ablution, Initiation, and Baptism*. Edited by David Hellholm et al. BZNW 176. Berlin: de Gruyter.

Weidemann, H.-U. 2004. *Der Tod Jesu im Johannesevangelium. Die erste Abschiedsrede als Schlüsseltext für den Passions- und Osterbericht*. BZNW 122. Berlin: de Gruyter.

Weinfeld, Moshe. 1991. *Deuteronomy 1–11: A New Translation with Introduction and Commentary*. AB 5. New York: Doubleday.

Weiss, Herold. 1991. "The Sabbath in the Fourth Gospel." *CBQ* 110:311–21.

Welch, David. 1983. *Propaganda and the German Cinema, 1933–1945*. Oxford: Clarendon.

Wengst, Klaus. 2000. *Das Johannesevangelium*. 1 Teilband: Kapitel 1–10. THKNT. Stuttgart: Kohlhammer.

Westcott, B. F. 1892. *The Gospel according to St. John*. London: Murray.

Wheaton, Gerry. 2015. *The Role of Jewish Feasts in John's Gospel*. SNTSMS 162. Cambridge: Cambridge University Press.

Whitehouse, Harvey. 1995. *Inside the Cult: Religious Innovation and Transmission in Papua New Guinea*. Oxford: Clarendon.

———. 2000. *Arguments and Icons: Divergent Modes of Religiosity*. Oxford: Oxford University Press.

———. 2004. *Modes of Religiosity: A Cognitive Theory of Religious Transmission*. Walnut Creek, CA: Altamira.

Wild, Robert A., SJ. 1985. "The Encounter between Pharisaic and Christian Judaism: Some Early Gospel Evidence." *NovT* 27:105–24.

Williams, Catrin H. 2000. *I Am He: The Interpretation of 'Anî Hû' in Jewish and Early Christian Literature*. WUNT 2/113. Tübingen: Mohr Siebeck.

———. 2011. "First-Century Media Culture and Abraham as a Figure of Memory in John 8:31–59." Pages 205–22 in *The Fourth Gospel and First-Century Media Culture*. Edited by Anthony Le Donne and Tom Thatcher. LNTS 296. London: T&T Clark; New York: Continuum.

———. 2013. "John and the Rabbis Revisited." Pages 107–25 in *The Gospel of John and Jesus of History: Engaging with C. H. Dodd on the Fourth Gospel*. Edited by Tom Thatcher and Catrin H. Williams. Cambridge: Cambridge University Press.

———. Forthcoming. "Composite Citations in John's Gospel." In *The New Testament*. Vol. 2 of *Composite Citations in Antiquity*. Edited by Sean A. Adams and Seth M. Ehorn. LNTS. London: Bloomsbury.

Wills, Lawrence. 1984. "The Form of the Sermon in Hellenistic Judaism and Early Christianity." *HTR* 77:277–99.

Wilson, Stephen G. 1995. *Related Strangers: Jews and Christians, 70—170 CE*. Minneapolis: Fortress.

Wink, Walter. 1968. *John the Baptist in the Gospel Tradition*. SNTSMS 7. Cambridge: Cambridge University Press.

———. 1992. *Engaging the Powers: Discernment and Resistance in an Age of Domination*. Minneapolis: Fortress.

Winter, Sean F. 2009. "The Rhetorical Function of John's Portrayal of the Jewish Law." Pages 82–95 in *Torah in the New Testament: Papers Delivered at the Manchester-Lausanne Seminar of June 2008*. Edited by Michael Tait and Peter Oakes. LNTS 401. London: T&T Clark.

Witetschek, Stefan. 2008. *Ephesische Enthüllungen 1: Frühe Christen in einer antiken Großstadt. Zugleich ein Beitrag zur Frage nach den Kontexten der Johannesapokalypse*. BTS 6. Leuven: Peeters.

Witherington, Ben, III. 1995. *John's Wisdom: A Commentary on the Fourth Gospel*. Louisville: Westminster John Knox.

Witmer, Stephen E. 2006. "Approaches to Scripture in the Fourth Gospel and the Qumran Pesharim." *NovT* 48:313–28.

Yang, Yong-Eui. 1997. *Jesus and the Sabbath in Matthew's Gospel*. JSNTSup 139. Sheffield: Sheffield Academic.

Yee, Gale. 1988. *Jewish Feasts and the Gospel of John*. Zacchaeus Studies. Wilmington, DE: Glazier.

Zeitlin, Solomon. 1963. "Is the Title 'Rabbi' Anachronistic in the Gospels? A Reply." *JQR* 53:345–49.

———. 1968. "The Title Rabbi in the Gospels Is Anachronistic." *JQR* 59:158–60.

Zeller, Dieter. 1987. "Paulus und Johannes. Methodischer Vergleich im Interesse neutestamentlicher Theologie." *BZ* 27:167–82.

Zimmerli, Walther. 1979. *Ezekiel 1: A Commentary on the Book of the Prophet Ezekiel, Chapters 1–24*. Translated by R. E. Clement. Hermeneia. Minneapolis: Fortress.

Zimmermann, Ruben. 2004. *Christologie der Bilder im Johannesevangelium: Die Christopoetik des vierten Evangeliums unter besonderer Berücksichtigung von Joh 10*. WUNT 171. Tübingen: Mohr Siebeck.

———. 2013. "'The Jews': Unreliable Figures or Unreliable Narration?" Pages 71–109 in *Character Studies in the Fourth Gospel: Narrative Approaches to Seventy Figures in John*. WUNT 314. Edited by Steven A. Hunt, D. Francois Tolmie, and Ruben Zimmermann. Tübingen: Mohr Siebeck.

Zumstein, Jean. 2014. *L'évangile selon Saint Jean (1–12)*. CNT 4a. Geneva: Labor et Fides.

Contributors

Paul N. Anderson, Professor of Biblical and Quaker Studies
George Fox University, Newberg, Oregon
Extraordinary Professor of Religion
North-West University, Potchefstroom, South Africa
Visiting Griset Chair of Bible and Christian Tradition
Chapman University, Orange, California

Harold W. Attridge, Sterling Professor of Divinity
Yale Divinity School, New Haven, Connecticut

Lori Baron, Postdoctoral Fellow in Theology/New Testament
St. Louis University, St. Louis, Missouri

Jonathan Bernier, Assistant Professor, Religious Studies
Saint Francis Xavier University, Antigonish Nova Scotia, Canada

Reimund Bieringer, Professor of New Testament Exegesis
Faculty of Theology and Religious Studies, Katholieke Universiteit Leuven, Belgium

R. Alan Culpepper, Dean Emeritus and Professor of New Testament Emeritus
James and Carolyn McAfee School of Theology, Mercer University, Atlanta, Georgia
Research Fellow, Department of Old and New Testament
University of the Free State, Bloemfontein, South Africa

Craig A. Evans, John Bisagno Distinguished Professor of Christian Origins
Houston Baptist University, Houston, Texas

Jörg Frey, Professor of New Testament
Theological Faculty, University of Zurich, Switzerland
Research Fellow, Department of Old and New Testament
University of the Free State, Bloemfontein, South Africa

Craig R. Koester, Academic Dean and Asher O. and Carrie Nasby Professor of New Testament
Luther Theological Seminary, Saint Paul, Minnesota
Research Fellow, Department of Old and New Testament
University of the Free State, Bloemfontein, South Africa

William R. G. Loader, Emeritus Professor
Murdoch University, Perth, Western Australia
Research Fellow, Department of Old and New Testament
University of the Free State, Bloemfontein, South Africa

Noam E. Marans, Director of Interreligious and Intergroup Relations
American Jewish Committee, New York, New York

Joel Marcus, Professor of New Testament and Christian Origins
Duke Divinity School, Durham, North Carolina

Adele Reinhartz, Professor
Department of Classics and Religious Studies/Département des études anciennes et des sciences de religion, Université d'Ottawa / University of Ottawa, Ottawa, Ontario, Canada
Research Fellow, Department of Old and New Testament
University of the Free State, Bloemfontein, South Africa

Ruth Sheridan, Postdoctoral Fellow, Faculty of Arts
Charles Sturt University, Sydney, Australia

Tom Thatcher, Professor of Biblical Studies
Cincinnati Christian University, Cincinnati, Ohio

Jan G. van der Watt, Professor in New Testament
Radboud University Nijmegen, Netherlands
Research Fellow, Department of Old and New Testament
University of the Free State, Bloemfontein, South Africa

Catrin H. Williams, Reader in New Testament Studies
University of Wales Trinity Saint David, Lampeter, Wales, U.K.
Research Fellow, Department of Old and New Testament
University of the Free State, Bloemfontein, South Africa

Ancient Sources Index

New Testament

Rabbinic Works

Qur'an

Modern Authors Index

CPSIA information can be obtained
at www.ICGtesting.com
Printed in the USA
FFOW03n1133051217
43928416-42994FF